*American Furniture*

# AMERICAN FURNITURE 2000

*Edited by Luke Beckerdite*

Published by the CHIPSTONE FOUNDATION

Distributed by University Press of New England

Hanover and London

CHIPSTONE FOUNDATION BOARD OF DIRECTORS
Dudley Godfrey, Jr.
Charles Hummel
Brock Jobe
W. David Knox, II.   *President*
Jere D. McGaffey
John S. McGregor
Jonathan Prown   *Executive Director*
Philip L. Stone
Allen M. Taylor   *Chairman*

EDITOR
Luke Beckerdite

BOOK AND EXHIBITION REVIEW EDITOR
Gerald W. R. Ward

EDITORIAL ADVISORY BOARD
Luke Beckerdite, *Editor*
John Bivins, Jr., *Conservator and Decorative Arts Consultant*
Edward S. Cooke, Jr., *Associate Professor, Department of the History of Art, Yale University*
Wallace Gusler, *Master of the Shop–Gunsmith, Colonial Williamsburg Foundation*
Morrison H. Heckscher, *Curator of American Decorative Arts, Metropolitan Museum of Art*
Brock Jobe, *Professor of American Decorative Arts, Winterthur Museum*
Robert F. Trent, *Conservator and Decorative Arts Consultant*
Gerald W. R. Ward, *Katharine Lane Weems Curator, Museum of Fine Arts, Boston*
Gregory R. Weidman, *Museum and Decorative Arts Consultant*
Philip D. Zimmerman, *Museum and Decorative Arts Consultant*

*Cover Illustration:* Detail of a mummy head on a pier table attributed to Baltimore cabinetmaker Edward Priestley. (Private collection.)

*Design:* Wynne Patterson, Pittsfield, Vermont
*Photography:* Gavin Ashworth, New York, New York

Published by the Chipstone Foundation, 7820 North Club Circle, Milwaukee, WI 53217
Distributed by University Press of New England, Hanover, NH 03755
© 2000 by the Chipstone Foundation
All rights reserved
Printed in the United States of America   5 4 3 2 1
ISSN 1069–4188
ISBN 1–58465–055–9

# Contents

| | |
|---|---|
| Editorial Statement<br>*Luke Beckerdite* | VII |
| Preface<br>*Allen M. Taylor* | IX |
| Introduction<br>*Luke Beckerdite* | XI |
| The Early Furniture of Christopher and Job Townsend<br>*Luke Beckerdite* | 1 |
| "The True Antiques of Tomorrow": Furniture by the Potthast Brothers of Baltimore, 1892–1975<br>*Catherine Rogers Arthur* | 31 |
| The Genesis of Neoclassical Style in Baltimore Furniture<br>*Sumpter Priddy III, J. Michael Flanigan, and Gregory R. Weidman* | 59 |
| A New Suspect: Baltimore Cabinetmaker Edward Priestley<br>*Alexandra Alevizatos Kirtley* | 100 |
| New Insights on John Cadwalader's Commode-Seat Side Chairs<br>*Leroy Graves and Luke Beckerdite* | 152 |
| Patronage in Early Salem: The Symonds Shops and Their Customers<br>*Martha H. Willoughby* | 169 |
| Cultural Negotiations: A Study of the New Mexican *Caja*<br>*Elizabeth A. Fleming* | 185 |
| Book Reviews | 205 |

*The Book on the Bookshelf*, Henry Petroski; review by
Neville Thompson

*Art & Enterprise: American Decorative Art, 1825–1917,
The Virginia Carroll Crawford Collection*, Donald C. Peirce;
review by Anna Tobin D'Ambrosio

*Worldly Goods: The Arts of Early Pennsylvania, 1680–1758,* Jack Lindsey, with essays by Richard S. Dunn, Edward C. Carter II, and Richard Saunders; review by Philip D. Zimmerman

*The History of Furniture: Twenty-Five Centuries of Style and Design in the Western Tradition,* John Morley; review by Gerald W. R. Ward

Recent Writing on American Furniture: A Bibliography     219
Gerald W. R. Ward

Index     229

# Editorial Statement

*American Furniture* is an interdisciplinary journal dedicated to advancing knowledge of furniture made or used in the Americas from the seventeenth century to the present. Authors are encouraged to submit articles on any aspect of furniture history, essays on conservation and historic technology, reproductions or transcripts of documents, annotated photographs of new furniture discoveries, and book and exhibition reviews. References for compiling an annual bibliography also are welcome.

Manuscripts must be typed, double-spaced, illustrated with black-and-white prints or transparencies, and prepared in accordance with the *Chicago Manual of Style*. Computer disk copy is requested but not required. The Chipstone Foundation will offer significant honoraria for manuscripts accepted for publication and reimburse authors for all photography approved in writing by the editor.

*Luke Beckerdite*

# Preface

The Chipstone Foundation was organized in 1965 by Stanley Stone and Polly Mariner Stone of Fox Point, Wisconsin. Representing the culmination of their shared experiences in collecting American furniture, American historical prints, and early English pottery, the foundation was created with the dual purpose of preserving and interpreting their collection and stimulating research and education in the decorative arts.

The Stones began collecting American decorative arts in 1946, and by 1964 it became apparent to them that provisions should be made to deal with their collection. With the counsel of their friend Charles Montgomery, the Stones decided that their collection should be published and exhibited.

Following Stanley Stone's death in 1987, the foundation was activated by an initial endowment provided by Mrs. Stone. This generous donation allowed the foundation to institute its research and grant programs, begin work on three collection catalogues, and launch an important new journal, *American Furniture*.

*Allen M. Taylor*

# Introduction

## *Luke Beckerdite*

This volume of American Furniture presents new information on a variety of subjects, ranging from southwestern joined chests, or *cajas,* to colonial revival furniture made by members of the Potthast family of Baltimore, Maryland. Although the articles are quite diverse, all underscore the importance of patronage in the design, construction, marketing, and use of American furniture.

Martha Willoughby's essay on the products of the Symonds shops of Salem, Massachusetts, and Luke Beckerdite's article on the furniture of Job and Christopher Townsend of Newport, Rhode Island, suggest that Quaker communities functioned as conduits for the movement of people, ideas, and styles during the seventeenth and eighteenth centuries. Both groups of joiners clearly profited from the patronage of fellow Quakers as well as from trade associations with other Friends. In Newport, these connections facilitated the formation of cabinetmaking dynasties that challenged Boston's dominance of the furniture export trade.

The *cajas* discussed in Elizabeth Fleming's article reflect the convergence of Hispanic and Pueblo culture in New Mexico. During the seventeenth and eighteenth centuries, marriage and material culture were both vehicles whereby Hispanic patrons sought to preserve their heritage. Some of the chests from this region have carved motifs derived from Spanish heraldry, whereas others have designs rooted in Pueblo cosmology. As Fleming demonstrates, these objects are neither purely Spanish nor purely Native American. They are composite forms produced by a creolized culture.

Leroy Graves and Luke Beckerdite's essay, "New Insights on John Cadwalader's Commode-Seat Side Chairs," examines the carving and upholstery on a renowned set of seating furniture commissioned by that Philadelphia merchant and his wife Elizabeth Lloyd, one of the wealthiest women in colonial America. Soon after their wedding, the couple commissioned the city's leading artisans to renovate and furnish their townhouse—converting it into what one observer called "a grand and elegant" residence. The extensive documentation surrounding this work illuminates the patterns of interaction between patrons and artisans at the highest level, since many of the tradesmen involved in furnishing Cadwalader's house were London-trained immigrants.

Few early urban centers benefited from the arrival of European immigrants more than Baltimore—the fastest growing city in America during the last decades of the eighteenth century. In "The Genesis of Neoclassicism in Baltimore Furniture," Sumpter Priddy, Michael Flanigan, and Gregory

Weidman present a convincing argument that the earliest, largest, and most sophisticated group of Baltimore neoclassical furniture can be attributed to Richard Lawson, a London-trained cabinetmaker, and his partner John Bankson. As the authors note, immigrant tradesmen like Lawson "helped shape material culture in the new republic at precisely the point when Americans perceived themselves to be increasingly free of British influence."

Alexandra Alevizatos Kirtley's article on Baltimore cabinetmaker Edward Priestley is a compelling study of the career, patrons, and furniture of one of that city's most important cabinetmakers. Many of his clients were wealthy, well-educated, cosmopolitan individuals with a taste for the latest European fashions. Priestley's success, as Ms. Kirtley demonstrates, "lay in his ability to accommodate . . . his patrons and respond to diverse styles and changing economic trends."

Baltimore's most prolific furniture-making firm was in business from 1892 to 1975. Established by four German immigrants, Potthast Brothers received national acclaim for their "authentic replicas" as well as for the historic forms they adapted for modern use. As Catherine Arthur's article reveals, the firm played an important role in the development and longevity of the colonial revival—a style that "satisfied the needs of native-born Americans who wished to maintain and assert their heritage and of immigrants who endeavored to be more like them."

The field of American furniture is greatly indebted to immigrants like the Potthasts who sought to identify with their new home. Many early dealers—the people largely responsible for popularizing American antiques—were Jewish emigrés such as Israel Sack. The death of his son Harold in July 2000 was a tremendous loss to the furniture world. Under the direction of Harold and his brothers Albert and Robert, the Sack firm became a leader in furniture research and scholarship. They showed us that furniture was an art form that demands the same level of appreciation and study as paintings, sculpture, and architecture. For that we are immensely grateful.

Another scholar whose keen mind and kind heart will be sorely missed is Zeke Liverant, who passed away in October. Building on his father Nathan's legacy, Zeke and his son Arthur established one of the country's most respected antiques firms. Always willing to share his knowledge, Zeke made immeasurable contributions to the field of American furniture.

*American Furniture*

*Luke Beckerdite*

# The Early Furniture of Christopher and Job Townsend

▼ THE DISTINCTIVE and cohesive style of colonial Newport furniture had much more to do with mass-producing a marketable commodity than with the refinement and perfection of furniture forms. From the outset, Rhode Island differed from the other New England colonies. During the 1650s and 1660s, it became a center for Quakerism as members of the Society of Friends sought to escape religious persecution in England and in Massachusetts. This attitude of religious tolerance subsequently extended to other sects. In 1729, Anglican minister George Berkely wrote:

> The inhabitants [of Newport] are of a mixed kind. . . . Here are four sorts of Anabaptists, besides Presbyterians, Quakers, Independents, and many of no profession at all. Notwithstanding so many differences, here are fewer quarrels about religion than elsewhere. The people living peaceably with their neighbors of whatever persuasions. They all agree on one point, that the Church of England is second best.

Historian William G. McLoughlin has asserted that "the privatization of religion led to a new emphasis on economic self-interest as a motivating force in the colony."[1]

Like most other New England cities, Newport had an economy based on processing, manufacturing, and shipping rather than the production of staples such as tobacco, rice, or indigo. The three principal sources of Rhode Island's wealth were the sugar trade, the slave trade, and fisheries. Ships left the colony with livestock, cheese, barrel staves, lumber, fish, and manufactured goods that could be bartered for tobacco, sugar, or bills of exchange in southern ports and the West Indies. Many of these vessels continued on to Africa, where part of their cargo was exchanged for slaves. Most of the slaves were bartered or sold in the West Indies and southern colonies on the return voyage.[2]

Several subsidiary industries developed as a result of the triangular trade. Rum, which was distilled from West Indian molasses, became Rhode Island's most important export commodity. In 1741, Governor Richard Ward noted that "the neighboring governments have been in great measure supplied with rum, sugar, molasses, and other West Indian goods by us. . . . Nay, Boston, itself, the metropolis of Massachusetts, is not a little obliged to us." By 1750, the colony had thirty-three distilleries, twenty-two of which were in Newport. Rhode Island's shipping industry also grew to meet the demands of increased trade. In 1708, the colony had only 30 ships, which were primarily sloops engaged in the North American coastal trade. The fleet grew to 80 vessels in 1731, to 120 in 1740, to more than 500 in 1763. Arti-

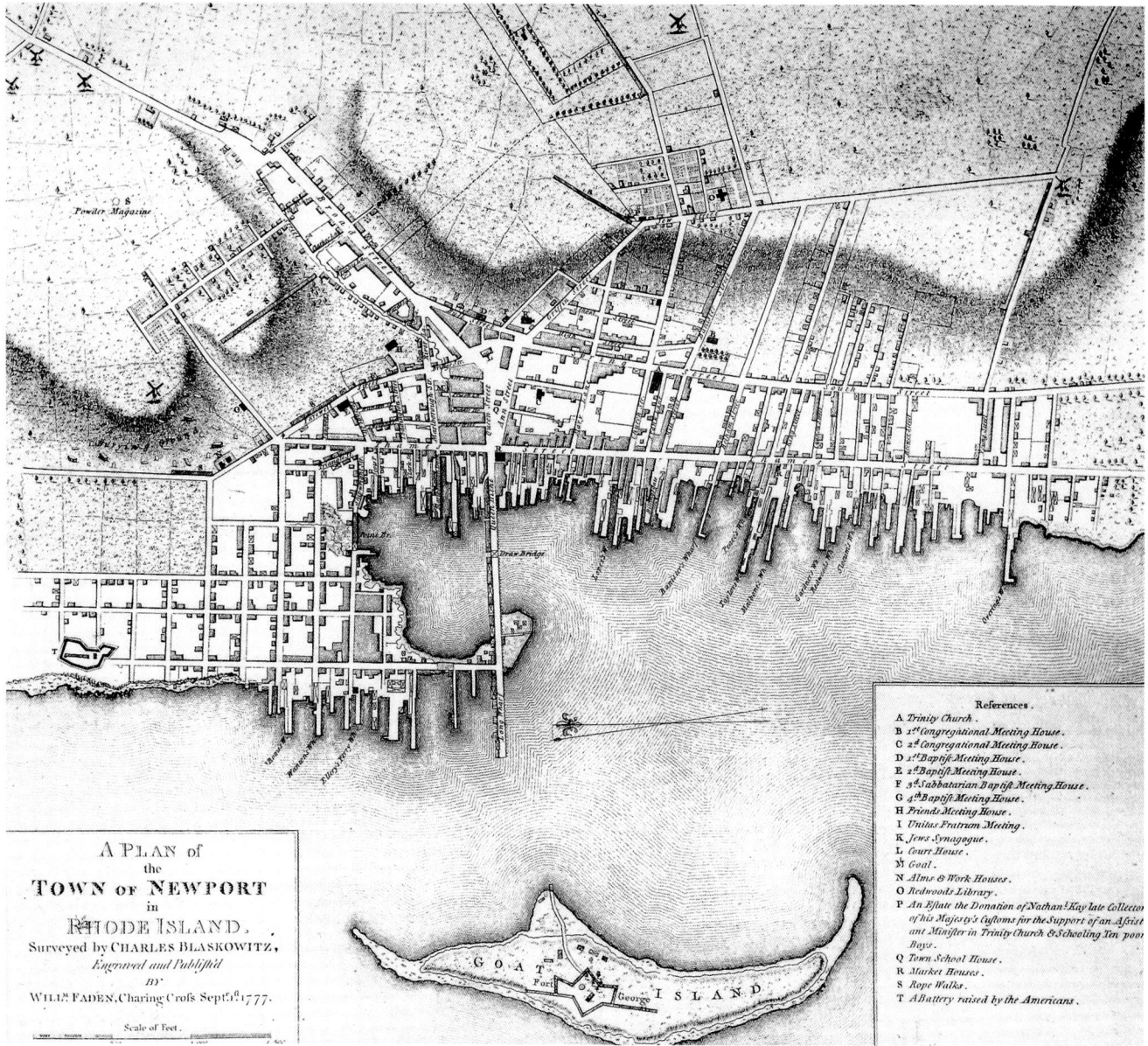

*Figure 1   A Plan of the Town of Newport in Rhode Island*, surveyed by Charles Blaskowitz for the British Admiralty, 1777. Engraving on paper. (Courtesy, Newport Historical Society.) Easton's Point is shown above and to the left of Goat Island.

sans, merchants, and entrepreneurs were quick to capitalize on the expansion of the carrying trade. Cabinetmakers, for example, began producing furniture for export as well as for local consumption. At least fifty-six cabinetmakers were active in Rhode Island between 1745 and 1774. By comparison, Boston had approximately sixty-four, although its population, fleet, and manufacturing base were much larger.[3]

As Rhode Island's economy developed, its dependence on Boston as a source for British manufactured goods decreased. Newport merchant John Banister was among the first to establish direct trade with London. In a 1739 letter to John Thomlinson of London, Banister wrote that the residents of Newport desired "to make themselves independent of the Bay Government to whom they have a mortal aversion." Like Banister, many Rhode Island merchants and tradesmen resented Boston's dominance of the coastal trade in manufactured goods. Since the late seventeenth century, the "metropolis of Massachusetts" had led all New England ports in the export of such items as British textiles and locally made furniture, particularly chairs. Although Newport merchants and tradesmen did not ship significant quantities of furniture before mid-century, the social, economic, and cultural forces that allowed them to compete with Boston emerged decades earlier. During the 1720s, artisans such as Job and Christopher Townsend began developing efficient methods of production and securing the patronage of local merchants and ship captains who would become allies in the furniture export trade.[4]

Members of the Townsend family of Oyster Bay began immigrating to Newport during the seventeenth century. Widower Thomas Townsend, whose mother and aunts had grown up in Newport, arrived about 1686 and married Mary Almy. His son John and nephew Solomon married into the same family, consolidating their positions among the Quaker communities in Newport and Oyster Bay. John and his wife Rebecca moved from Newport to Long Island about 1694, and Solomon, his wife Catherine, and children Job (1699–1765), Christopher (1701–1787), Solomon, and Hannah moved from Long Island to Newport in 1707.[5]

The earliest documented Newport furniture is associated with Job and Christopher Townsend. Although their training remains a mystery, they probably served their apprenticeships between 1713 and 1721. Similarities in the construction of their furniture suggest that both brothers had the same master. Job married Rebecca Casey in 1722, and referred to himself as a carpenter the following year. The earliest reference to him making furniture, however, is a 1733 letter in which Christopher describes a desk-and-bookcase that Job sold for £59.[6]

Christopher married Patience Easton (1703–1789) in 1723. Her grandfather, Nicholas, was an English-born tanner who arrived with the first Quaker settlers in the region. Her step-grandmother, Ann Bull Easton, left the Quakers a tract of land called Easton's Point, which became one of the town's leading residential and manufacturing centers (fig. 1). Christopher undoubtedly profited from his association with the Eastons. Patience's brothers were in the house-joinery, shipbuilding, and furniture-making trades, and several other members of her family were ship captains.[7]

Christopher and Job both settled at Easton's Point. Job purchased lot 86 and Christopher purchased lots 49 and 51. Job's house was demolished during the mid–twentieth century, but Christopher's still stands with his shop attached to one side (fig. 2). The shop, which measures 12' × 24', is comparable in size to those managed by contemporaries such as Constant Bailey. As historian Margaretta Lovell has noted, the small size of these shops suggests that they were not the sole place of production. Like other urban artisans, Newport cabinetmakers undoubtedly purchased components and commissioned services such as carving and gilding from other tradesmen.[8]

During the 1720s and 1730s, Job and Christopher may have spent much of their time working as house joiners. Evidence suggests that each built his own house (see figs. 2, 3) and received commissions for public and private buildings. Accounts pertaining to the construction of the Colony House

*Figure 2* Christopher Townsend house and shop, 74 Bridge Street, Newport, Rhode Island, 1725–1735. (Courtesy, Newport Historical Society.)

Figure 3  Detail of the interior of Christopher Townsend's house. (Courtesy, Newport Historical Society.)

(fig. 4) reveal that Christopher Townsend was the principal joiner and that Thomas Melvil and Israel Champan were hired as carpenters. Townsend probably furnished many of the interior components including the paneling in the senate chamber (figs. 5, 6) and the stair balusters and newel posts (figs. 7–9). He may also have constructed two turned and joined tables (see figs. 10, 11) that were among the original furnishings. These tables, which have turning sequences identical to those on the stair, probably stood in either the senate chamber or courtroom below.[9]

Many eighteenth-century cabinetmakers supplemented their income by doing house joinery. Their work often entailed fabricating architectural components such as chimneypieces, paneling, and "bowfats" as well as more mundane fixtures like the cupboard illustrated in fig. 12. The cupboard probably dates from the mid-1740s, when Christopher Townsend and the carpenters working on the Colony House were completing their work. It has finely wrought dovetail hinges and remnants of dry pigment that appear to match the blue paint on the joined tables.

Architectural historians Antoinette F. Downing and Vincent J. Sculley, Jr., were the first to note that elements of the frame and panel moldings in the senate chamber of the Colony House (fig. 6) match those in Trinity

*Figure 4* Colony House, Newport, Rhode Island, 1739–1749. (Courtesy, State of Rhode Island and Providence Plantations; photo, Gavin Ashworth.)

*Figure 5* Detail of the senate chamber of the Colony House. (Photo, Gavin Ashworth.)

*Figure 6* Detail of the paneling in the senate chamber of the Colony House. (Photo, Gavin Ashworth.)

*Figure 7* Detail of a newel post in the Colony House. (Photo, Gavin Ashworth.)

*Figure 8* Detail of two newel posts in the Colony House. (Photo, Gavin Ashworth.)

*Figure 9* Detail of a turned pendant on a newel post in the Colony House. (Photo, Gavin Ashworth.)

*Figure 10*  Joined table, Newport, Rhode Island, 1739–1749. Maple and white pine; blue paint. H. 28 1/2", W. 42", D. 35 3/4". (Courtesy, State of Rhode Island and Providence Plantations; photo, Gavin Ashworth.)

*Figure 11*  Detail of a leg on the table illustrated in fig. 10. (Photo, Gavin Ashworth.)

*Figure 12*  Cupboard, Newport, Rhode Island, 1739–1749. White pine; blue paint. Dimensions not recorded. (Courtesy, State of Rhode Island and Providence Plantations; photo, Gavin Ashworth.)

Church (figs. 13, 14) and the Seventh Day Baptist Meeting House (figs. 15, 16). Although it is possible that other Newport joiners owned sets of planes similar to those of Christopher Townsend, his involvement with these buildings and several contemporary houses is quite plausible. The newel posts on the gallery stair in Trinity Church have distinctive, acorn-shaped pendants or "drops" (fig. 17) that appear to be precursors to those in the Colony House (fig. 9), and the "barley-twist" balusters in the Seventh Day Baptist Meeting House (fig. 18) are similar to those shown in figure 8. A furniture joiner like Christopher Townsend undoubtedly worked on the interior of the meeting house. The balusters on the gallery stair (fig. 19) have

*Figure 13* Detail of the interior of Trinity Church, Newport, Rhode Island, 1725–1730. (Photo, Gavin Ashworth.)

*Figure 14* Detail of the paneling in Trinity Church. (Photo, Gavin Ashworth.)

*Figure 15* Detail of the interior of the Seventh Day Baptist Meeting House, Newport, Rhode Island, 1725–1730. (Photo, Gavin Ashworth.)

*Figure 16* Detail of the paneling in the Seventh Day Baptist Meeting House. (Photo, Gavin Ashworth.)

*Figure 17* Detail of a turned pendant on a newel post in Trinity Church. (Photo, Gavin Ashworth.)

*Figure 18*  Detail of a newel post and balusters on the stair leading to the pulpit in the Seventh Day Baptist Meeting House. (Photo, Gavin Ashworth.)

*Figure 19*  Detail of balusters on the stair leading to the gallery in the Seventh Day Baptist Meeting House. (Photo, Gavin Ashworth.)

turnings that match those on a group of Newport gateleg tables from the 1720s and 1730. Oral tradition credits Newport master builder Richard Mundy, the "architect" of the Colony House with the design of the Seventh Day Baptist Meeting House and Trinity Church.[10]

The earliest reference to Christopher's working in the furniture-making trades is his purchase of hardware, nails, and other materials in 1732. On February 4, 1738, Christopher wrote Newport merchant Abraham Redwood:

> According to thy Request . . . I indevoured to finish a Desk and Book Case Agreeable to thy directions to send thee by Brother Pope but could not quite finish . . . and understanding it was not for thee but a friend of thine, I concluded it would be Equal to thee, If I send it by another opertunity. And having an opertunity to send it by Brother Solomon, I . . . ordered him to Deliver it to thee or thy order, thou paying him one Moyodore freight, the Desk and Bookcase amounts to Sixty Pounds this currency; including the two Ruf cases which is equal to fourteen heavy Pistole at £4.5.8 or fourty-four ounces and a half of Silver. . . . I may let thee know that I sold such a Desk and Book Case without any Ruf cases, for £58 in hand this winter. Brother Job, also sold one to our Collector for £59. I mention this, that thou may know that I have not imposed on thee.

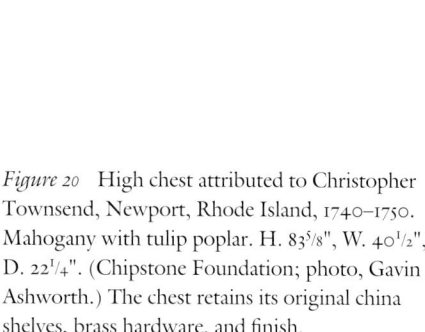

*Figure 20*  High chest attributed to Christopher Townsend, Newport, Rhode Island, 1740–1750. Mahogany with tulip poplar. H. 83⁵⁄₈", W. 40¹⁄₂", D. 22¹⁄₄". (Chipstone Foundation; photo, Gavin Ashworth.) The chest retains its original china shelves, brass hardware, and finish.

Christopher had several important patrons in addition to Redwood. In 1742, he sold Newport merchant Isaac Stelle a desk-and-bookcase for £65. Christopher may also have worked for Samuel Ward, who served as Governor of Rhode Island twice during the 1760s. The high chest illustrated in figure 20

II CHRISTOPHER AND JOB TOWNSEND

*Figure 21*  Dressing table attributed to Job Townsend, Newport, Rhode Island, 1746. Mahogany with white pine. H. 30 1/2", W. 34 1/2", D. 22 1/2". (Chipstone Foundation; photo, Gavin Ashworth.)

*Figure 22*  High chest, probably Long Island, New York, 1730–1740. Apple with tulip poplar. H. 70", W. 40", depth not recorded. (Courtesy, Florene Maine and Society for the Preservation of Long Island Antiquities.)

descended in his family, and Ward is known to have purchased at least eight pieces of furniture from Job Townsend.[11]

The dressing table illustrated in figure 21 is the earliest piece of furniture that can be associated with Job. It is thought to be the one valued at £13.10 in his 1746 bill to Quaker merchant Samuel Ward:

Bot of Job Townsend

| | | |
|---|---|---|
| a mahogany High Chest of Drawers | | £30.0.0 |
| a mahogany Dressing Table | | 13.10.0 |
| a mahogany Dining Table | 5 foot 6 in at 65/ | 17.7.6 |
| 1 ditto | 4 foot 8 in at 65/ | 15.3.4 |
| a mahogany tea table | | 8.10.0 |
| 1 Square Kitchen table | | 5.0.0 |
| a maple tea table | | 2.10.0 |
| a maple stool | | 2.0.0 |
| | | £94.10.10 |

The slipper feet and cyma reversa curves of the front rail are repeated, with minor variation, on Long Island high chests and dressing tables made during the late 1720s and 1730s. With a history of descent in the Cox family of Oyster Bay, the high chest shown in figure 22 is one of the earliest New York examples. Its bold ogee cornice, pulvinated frieze, and broad waist molding have parallels in baroque case furniture made in New York City, Flushing, and Oyster Bay. At least five high chests and two dressing tables appear to be from the same shop as the Cox example, the most elaborate of which have knees with carved strapwork and thick line inlay on the drawer fronts (fig. 23). One high chest reputedly belonged to Oyster Bay merchant Samuel Townsend, who was a relative of Job and Christopher. Samuel married Sarah Stoddard, whose father William was a cabinetmaker. William probably moved from Rhode Island to Oyster Bay during the mid-1720s.[12]

Like many Rhode Island Quakers, Job and Christopher Townsend maintained ties with family members and business associates in New York City and Long Island. Christopher attended the New York Men's Monthly Meeting at least twice during the early 1740s and consigned furniture to Quaker cabinetmaker Joshua Delaplaine in 1744. In exchange, Delaplaine shipped Townsend flour, bread, butter, and milk. Delaplaine had been selling foodstuffs to Quaker merchants in Newport since the early 1730s. One of his patrons, Samuel Holmes, was an acquaintance of Christopher Townsend. Like the case pieces mentioned above, these commercial and familial connections strongly suggest that Quaker communities functioned as conduits for the movement of people, ideas, and styles during the seventeenth and eighteenth centuries.[13]

Although the high chests and dressing tables attributed to Christopher and Job Townsend share details with early New York examples, their construction is entirely different. The New York pieces have cabriole legs that are joined to the back, sides, and front rails with mortise-and-tenon joints (see figs. 22, 23), whereas the Newport ones have dovetailed cases and legs that are attached to the inside corners with glue and glue blocks (see figs.

*Figure 23*  High chest, probably Long Island, New York, 1730–1740. Red gum with pine. H. 70", W. 43", D. 22". (Private collection; photo, Society for the Preservation of Long Island Antiquities.)

*Figure 24*  Detail of the dovetailed case construction of the dressing table illustrated in fig. 21. (Photo, Gavin Ashworth.)

*Figure 25*  Detail of the case and leg construction of the dressing table illustrated in fig. 21.

*Figure 26*  Dressing table, Rappahannock River Basin of eastern Virginia, 1755–1770. Walnut with yellow pine. H. 28<sup>1</sup>/<sub>2</sub>", W. 38", D. 20<sup>1</sup>/<sub>4</sub>". (Courtesy, Sumpter Priddy, Inc.)

24, 25, 30). The dovetails on the front corners of Newport high chests and dressing tables are typically concealed by thick, vertical strips of veneer. Considering the fact that Christopher and Job apprenticed during the 1710s and early 1720s, it is logical to assume that some of their construction techniques developed from earlier practices. Baroque high chests and dressing tables almost invariably have dovetailed cases and turned legs that are tenoned into blocks glued (or glued and nailed) to the inside corners.

Further research may reveal Irish antecedents for these distinctive Newport construction features. An unusual dressing table from the Rappahannock River Basin of eastern Virginia has a dovetailed case and angular cabriole legs that are attached with glue and glue blocks like those on most Newport high chests and dressing tables (figs. 26, 27). As furniture historian Ronald L. Hurst has observed, Irish influences account for many of the stylistic and structural features found on mid–eighteenth-century tables and chairs from Virginia's Northern Neck.[14]

Scholars have long contended that Newport cabinetmakers used glued-on legs to facilitate transport, but evidence suggests otherwise. If cases and legs were shipped disassembled, why do none of the examples with southern histories have glue blocks made of indigenous woods such as yellow pine or cypress? A more logical explanation for the persistence of this structure and its use by virtually every cabinetmaker in colonial Newport is that it saved time and materials. A tradesman could cut and fit the dovetails for

*Figure 27* Detail of the case and leg construction of the dressing table illustrated in fig. 26.

*Figure 28* High chest signed by Christopher Townsend, Newport, Rhode Island, 1748. Walnut with pine. H. 70", W. 38½", D. 20½". (Private collection; photo, Gavin Ashworth.)

the lower case of a high chest or the carcass of a dressing table (see fig. 24) faster than chopping and fitting the fourteen or more mortise-and-tenon joints required to construct a comparable form. Because the cabriole legs of Newport case pieces have much shorter stiles than those attached with mortise-and-tenon joints, they required less wood. A Newport cabinetmaker could conceivably produce five legs with the same amount of stock required to make four legs using mortise-and-tenon joinery. Evidence also indicates

*Figure 29*  Detail of the case construction of the high chest illustrated in fig. 28. (Photo, Gavin Ashworth.)

*Figure 30*  Detail of a rabbeted rear leg on the high chest illustrated in fig. 20. (Photo, Gavin Ashworth.)

that Newport cabinetmakers and carvers produced legs as piecework and sold them to other tradesmen in town. In 1759, William Barker charged fellow cabinetmaker Benjamin Hunt £1.5 for "1 set legs" and on numerous occasions in 1774 Joseph Martin paid £1.2 for sets of legs. With four saw cuts, virtually any Newport leg could be adapted to fit a given case.[15]

The patterns and construction techniques used by Christopher Townsend differed slightly from those of his brother. The high chest illustrated in figure 28 is the earliest documented example of his work. Its delicate slipper feet, angular cabriole legs, and lower case construction (fig. 29) are similar to those of the Ward family dressing table, but the skirt has cyma curves interrupted with fillets and arches rather than a carved shell.

Judging from the Ward dressing table and the high chests illustrated in figures 20 and 28, Christopher Townsend's construction was superior to that of his brother. His dovetailing tends to be more precise, and the interior surfaces of his stock are better finished. The high chest shown in figure 20 and a slipper-foot dressing table (in the Metropolitan Museum of Art) display additional features that occasionally occur on work attributed to Christopher's shop. On both examples, the rear legs are glued into shallow rabbets planed in the backboard (see fig. 30). These rabbets increased the glue surface and made the joints stronger.

From the standpoint of form, the high chest illustrated in figure 20 is the most elaborate example attributed to Christopher Townsend and the only Newport piece with stepped shelves for displaying valuables. The shelves are made in three sections and attached to the upper case with glue blocks and nails driven through the scalloped backboard into the upper edge of the top. Typical of Christopher Townsend's work, the front corners of the shelves have finely cut dovetails that are smaller versions of those on the case drawers. Although "china shelves" are rare in New England furniture, the feet of the high chest (fig. 31) are equally noteworthy features. With their ovoid balls and competently carved toes, these feet are much less mannered than those of other Newport tradesmen. The toes are also more "professional" in being finished with gouges and chisels rather than with abrasives as was most Newport carving.

The dining table illustrated in figure 32 and a high chest discussed in Michael Moses' *Master Craftsmen of Newport* are the only other Rhode Island objects with related feet. All of these feet have flattened ovoid balls and no webbing between the toes (see fig. 31). The toes of the dining table have larger knuckles and shorter claws than those on the high chest; however, the feet on these pieces have more in common with each other than with other Newport work. Other features of the dining table have parallels in furniture documented and attributed to Christopher Townsend and his son John (1732/33–1809). The frame has tightly interlocking dovetails cut at approximately the same angle as those on the high chest, three cross-braces dovetailed to the upper edge, and two cross-braces dovetailed and nailed to the bottom edge. Separating the work of these two tradesmen is extremely difficult because John Townsend trained with his father. Many pieces attributed to him may be by Christopher, who worked for nearly sixty years and amassed an estate greater than any other cabinetmaker in his extended family.[16]

*Figure 31* Detail of a foot on the high chest illustrated in fig. 20. (Photo, Gavin Ashworth.)

*Figure 32* Dining table probably by Christopher or John Townsend, Newport, Rhode Island, 1745–1755. Mahogany with maple and pine. H. 30 5/8", W. 68 1/2", D. 68 3/4" (open). (Courtesy, Colonial Williamsburg Foundation.)

*Figure 33* Desk-and-bookcase by Christopher Townsend, Newport, Rhode Island, 1745–1755. Mahogany throughout. Dimensions not recorded. (Private collection; photo, Gavin Ashworth.)

*Figure 34*  Detail of the silver mount on the right fallboard support of the desk-and-bookcase illustrated in fig. 33. (Courtesy, Sotheby's.)

The pinnacle of Christopher Townsend's known work is a desk-and-bookcase (fig. 33) that reputedly belonged to Reverend Nathaniel Appleton (1693–1784) and his wife Margaret (Gibbs) (1699–1771). Appleton graduated from Harvard College and served as minister of the First Church in Cambridge, Massachusetts, from 1717 until his death in 1784. Three of his children also attended Harvard, including his son Nathaniel (junior) (1731–1798) who reputedly inherited the desk-and-bookcase. The piece subsequently passed to the younger Nathaniel's son John (1758–1829), to his son John-James (1792–1864), to his son Charles-Louis (1846–1935), to his son Henri.[17]

Although the façade of the desk section is relatively plain, it is fitted with ornate silver pulls, escutcheon plates, and bird-shaped mounts (fig. 34) by Samuel Casey (ca. 1724–1779). Casey apprenticed with Boston silversmith Jacob Hurd and established his own shop in Exeter, Rhode Island, by 1745. Five years later he moved to Kingston, about seventeen miles west of Newport across the Naragansett Bay. Casey evidently cast the bird-shaped mounts from patterns carved by Christopher Townsend or one of his associates. Two Newport desks have fallboard supports with similarly carved wooden birds, and another has cast brass mounts of the same basic pattern. The silver mounts on the desk-and-bookcase differ from the brass ones primarily in having inlaid agate eyes.[18]

The interior of the desk section features a central prospect compartment with a shell-carved door flanked by blocked drawers surmounted by pigeonholes with turned and carved valances and tiers of three drawers. The two lower drawers in each tier are blocked and the upper ones have carved shells. This interior design is very similar to that of a desk-and-bookcase made by Job Townsend (fig. 35) and another example attributed to Christopher (fig. 36). As Christopher's letter to Abraham Redwood suggests, he and Job were familiar with each other's designs, prices, and patrons. They may have collaborated on important projects and farmed out work to each other and to other family members.[19]

The upper section of the desk-and-bookcase has only one parallel in Newport furniture (see fig. 36). It features an enclosed domed pediment, which may have been inspired by imported British examples, and doors with complex panel moldings and shells carved in relief. In typical Newport fashion, the lobes of the shells were originally finished with an abrasive. Although the cornice molding is an enlarged version of that on the high chests documented and attributed to Christopher Townsend, its attachment is different. The pieces on the sides of the bookcase are rabbeted in addition to being glued and nailed (fig. 37). The molded plaques on the tympanum of the desk-and-bookcase are one of the most conventional features. The finials also relate to Newport work, but they are more attenuated than those on other regional case forms (fig. 38).[20]

The interior of the bookcase is fitted with shelves, pigeonholes with elaborately shaped dividers, blocked drawers, and a prospect compartment flanked by document drawers with Doric column appliqués. The document drawers are unusual in having sides that are glued as opposed to being

*Figure 35* Desk-and-bookcase bearing the label of Job Townsend, Newport, Rhode Island, 1750–1765. Mahogany with chestnut and tulip poplar. H. 82 1/2", W. 40", D. 24 1/2". (Courtesy, Rhode Island School of Design; photo, Gavin Ashworth.) The pediment is missing.

nailed or dovetailed. Like some of his contemporaries, Christopher Townsend often used nothing more than glue to secure drawer components, moldings, and other elements. The small drawers of the desk-and-bookcase, for example, have bottom boards that are glued into rabbets in the front, sides, and back (fig. 39).[21]

The stock preparation, dovetailing, and blocking on the desk-and-bookcase are meticulous, but other aspects of its construction are relatively coarse

*Figure 36* Desk-and-bookcase attributed to Christopher Townsend, Newport, Rhode Island, 1735–1755. Mahogany with unrecorded secondary woods. H. 108", W. 36", depth not recorded. (Parke-Bernet Galleries, Inc., *Important American Furniture from the Estate of the late Cornelius C. Moore, Newport, Rhode Island*, New York, October 30, 1971, lot 154.) The door panels are missing, and the feet are incorrect replacements.

*Figure 37* Detail showing the attachment of the cornice molding on the desk-and-bookcase illustrated in fig. 33. (Photo, Gavin Ashworth.)

*Figure 38*  Detail of a finial and section of cornice molding on the desk-and-bookcase illustrated in fig. 33. (Photo, Gavin Ashworth.)

*Figure 39*  Detail of a glued-in drawer bottom on the desk-and-bookcase illustrated in fig. 33. (Photo, Gavin Ashworth.)

by contemporary urban standards. Like the upper cases of the high chests illustrated in figures 20 and 28, the desk section has drawer blades with exposed dovetails and drawer supports that are nailed to the sides of the case. Nailed supports prevent the sides from expanding and contracting with seasonal changes in temperature and humidity. As a result, they can force the drawer blades and backboards out of their joints and cause the sides to split. Nailed supports are, however, faster and cheaper to install than dustboards.

As furniture historian Wallace Gusler has noted, styles and construction techniques were profoundly influenced by the "economic and commercial conditions prevailing at the time and place . . . [of manufacture] as well as by the professional and ethnic background of the maker." From the outset, cabinetmakers like Christopher and Job Townsend understood the potential of the middle-class market in Rhode Island and abroad. They had witnessed the success of Boston artisans, merchants, and entrepreneurs who shipped vast quantities of furniture to nearly every colonial port. To compete for a segment of this market, Newport tradesmen had to develop construction methods that saved time and materials and form partnerships with other tradesmen, ship captains, and merchants.[22]

Collaborative arrangements helped small shops increase production and cut costs. Job and Christopher Townsend's extended family included at least twelve joiners. Artisans within this circle probably purchased materials together; sold each other lumber, prepared stock and piecework; and formed partnerships to produce and ship venture cargo. Job and Christopher, for example, purchased brasses, locks, screws, and nails from their brother Solomon, who also shipped furniture for them. Their brass purchases suggest that Christopher made at least two major case pieces each month, whereas Job made approximately four. The latter's son Job Townsend, Jr., purchased mahogany and at least one set of maple legs from his brother-in-law John Goddard and helped his brother Edmund Townsend make a "Large Mahogany Desk" for Nicholas Anderese in 1767.[23]

A desk-and-bookcase formerly in the collection of Cornelius C. Moore (fig. 36) also appears to be from Christopher Townsend's shop. Like the preceding example (fig. 33), it has a tall bookcase section with an enclosed ogee head and applied panels on the tympanum. The tympanum openings, panel shapes, and cornice moldings differ, however. On the Moore piece, the tympanum and panel arcs are larger and the cornice molding has a bold cyma reversa element rather than a cove. The desk sections differ primarily in the width of the drawers on either side of the prospect door and the number of pigeonhole brackets above them. Not surprisingly, the Moore desk, which has one less pigeonhole, is slightly narrower than Appleton's.[24]

An imported case piece may have inspired the design of the Moore and Appleton desk-and-bookcases. Domed pediments were popular on British desk-and-bookcases, chest-on-chests, and tall clock cases from the late 1600s to the 1720s. Architectural books represent another possible source for Townsend's designs. Prototypes for his domed pediments can be found in numerous volumes including William Salmon's *Palladio Londonensis* (1734),

James Gibb's *Book of Architecture* (1728), and Batty Langley's *The City and Country Builder's and Workman's Treasury of Designs* (1740).

Although external styles clearly influenced Rhode Island furniture, evidence suggests that Newport cabinetmakers intentionally developed forms that were very different from those made in Boston, New York, and Britain. In effect, they created a "brand name," a style recognizable both to local consumers and those in distant ports. In *The London Tradesman* (1747), Robert Campbell observed: "He who first hits upon any New Whim is sure to make by the Invention before it becomes common in the Trade; but he that must always wait for a new Fashion till it comes from *Paris*, or is hit upon by his neighbor, is never likely to grow rich or eminent in his Way." The "new whim" that contributed to the success of Newport artisans was not really new at all. Instead, it involved the distillation, modification, and, often, exaggeration of stylistic details from Boston, New York, Britain, continental Europe, and the Orient. During the late 1730s, Newport cabinetmakers began codifying these details, and by 1750 they had refined them to the point that stylistic changes from shop to shop remained almost imperceptible for the next half century.[25]

Two factors reinforced this stylistic hegemony. Most Newport shops were connected either through marriage or trade associations. Christopher Townsend, for example, trained his sons Job, Edmund, Thomas, and John Townsend, who in turn passed their knowledge on to the next generation. Similarly, John Goddard apprenticed with Job Townsend, married his daughter Hannah, and trained three of their sons. Because of the importance of the venture cargo trade, artisans within these family networks appear to have focused their efforts on competing with Boston tradesmen and merchants rather than with each other.

Newport's large Quaker population also had a profound influence on local styles. Like Pennsylvania Quaker William Penn, some members of the sect endeavored to "avoid the vain arts and inventions of a luxurious world." Newport cabinetmakers and their patrons typically eschewed such superficial forms of decoration as gilding and veneer in favor of solid figured woods and restrained carving. The high chest illustrated in figure 40 is the only veneered case piece attributed to an eighteenth-century Newport shop. Its drawer construction, cornice molding, and skirt shape are consistent with work attributed to Job and Christopher Townsend, but the unusually thick leg stock and composite core of the lower case suggest that the maker was unaccustomed to producing veneered forms. By contrast, the structure of conventional Newport high chests varies little from piece to piece.[26]

The standardization of style and construction clearly occurred at all levels of production. The bureau tables shown in figures 41 and 42 probably date from the late 1740s or early 1750s and are the earliest Newport examples known. Their wood selection, case construction, dovetailing, and shell carving have close parallels in furniture attributed to Job Townsend and John Goddard. The concave shells (see fig. 43), for example, are similar to those on the waist doors of a circa 1755 tall clock case that furniture historian Michael Moses associates with Goddard and an earlier example (in the

*Figure 40* High chest, probably Job or Christopher Townsend, Newport, Rhode Island, 1730–1750. Walnut, maple and walnut veneer, and lightwood inlay with white pine and maple. H. 70 3/8", W. 38", D. 20 1/4". (Chipstone Foundation; photo, Gavin Ashworth.) The mid-molding is replaced.

*Figure 41* Bureau table, probably Job or Christopher Townsend, Newport, Rhode Island, 1740–1750. Mahogany with white pine. H. 34 1/4", W. 37 1/2", D. 21". (Joseph and June Hennage collection; photo, Hans Lorenz.)

Winterthur Museum) with a movement by James Wady. Unlike most Newport bureau tables from the 1760–1780 period, which vary primarily in the number and detail of their carved shells, these examples have an experimental quality to their construction and design. The cyma-shaped drawers above the recesses on the early examples represent a departure from conventional Newport work. These drawers appear to have been inspired by those on Boston bureau tables, which were undoubtedly imported into Rhode Island during the second quarter of the eighteenth century.[27]

Later bureau tables attributed to John Townsend (see fig. 44) and his cousin Edmund (see fig. 45) demonstrate how Newport cabinetmakers "perfected a narrow range of designs and motifs" for this form. Both pieces are made of dense figured mahogany, and both have blocked façades, an upper drawer with a concave relief-carved shell flanked by two convex applied shells, a recess with a paneled door and a concave shell, cyma-and-fillet base moldings, and similar ogee feet. Aside from minor differences in construction and carving, these pieces are visually the same even though their makers trained in different shops. The same can be said about other case forms and tables produced by the Townsends and Goddards as well as by their non-Quaker contemporaries.[28]

*Figure 42* Bureau table, probably Job or Christopher Townsend, Newport, Rhode Island, 1740–1750. Mahogany with white pine. H. 34 1/2", W. 39 1/4", D. 21". (Private collection; photo, Gavin Ashworth.)

*Figure 43* Detail of the concave shell on the upper drawer of the bureau table illustrated in fig. 42. (Photo, Gavin Ashworth.)

*Figure 44* Bureau table attributed to John Townsend, Newport, Rhode Island, 1765–1770. Mahogany with white pine, chestnut, and tulip poplar. H. 34 3/8", W. 36 1/2", D. 20 1/2". (Courtesy, Metropolitan Museum of Art, gift of Mrs. Russell Sage.)

*Figure 45* Bureau table attributed to Edmund Townsend, Newport, Rhode Island, 1760–1780. Mahogany with chestnut and white pine. H. 33", W. 36 1/4", D. 20 1/2". (Private collection; photo, Sotheby's.)

*Figure 46* Desk by John Goddard, Newport, Rhode Island, 1745. Mahogany with white pine. H. 42", W. 35 1/2", D. 19". (Chipstone Foundation; photo, Gavin Ashworth.)

*Figure 47* Desk, Newport, Rhode Island, 1760–1770. Maple with chestnut and tulip poplar. H. 40⁷/₈", W. 38³/₈", D. 20⁷/₁₆". (Private collection; photo, Museum of Early Southern Decorative Arts.)

In the venture cargo arena, Newport cabinetmakers were so successful that they had little need to develop new forms. John Goddard made the desk illustrated in figure 46 in 1745, shortly after he completed his apprenticeship with Job Townsend. Aside from its mahogany primary wood, it differs little from a circa 1765 desk (fig. 47) that descended in a family from Edenton, North Carolina—undoubtedly a relic of the coastal furniture trade. Most Newport cabinetmakers produced desks of this type. Christopher Townsend, the most successful of the town's cabinetmakers, left his son John a one-third interest in all of the unfinished desks in his shop, except for one large mahogany example made by his son Jonathan. Maple desks like the one shown in figure 47 probably accounted for a much higher percentage of Christopher's income than elaborate table and case forms.[29]

Although plain maple desks and simple pad-foot tables may be visually less appealing than the great shell-carved, blockfront case pieces and serpentine tables attributed to the Townsends and Goddards, they are, nevertheless, critical to understanding the origin and development of Newport furniture styles. Early cabinetmakers like Job and Christopher Townsend understood that mass-producing furniture for the middle-class market and export trade could be more profitable than commissioned work. Judging from the small body of furniture that can be documented and attributed to their shops, they developed many of the procedures for quickly and efficiently manufacturing furniture that are manifest in even the most costly Newport pieces. They also established much of the stylistic vocabulary that gave and continues to give the town's furniture its "brand appeal."

ACKNOWLEDGMENTS   For assistance with this article, the author thanks Gavin Ashworth, Ralph Carpenter, Dean Failey, John Hays, Leigh Keno, Leslie Keno, Deanne Levison, Jack Lindsey, John Nye, Nancy Sazama, Robert Trent, Joan Youngkin, and the museums and collectors who shared their knowledge and objects. I am especially grateful to Joan Barzilay Freund for her research on Newport Quakers and to Jeanne Vibert Sloane and Margaretta M. Lovell for their insightful publications on the cabinetmaking business there.

1. William G. McLoughlin, *Rhode Island* (New York: W. W. Norton, 1978), pp. 46, 71 (for the Berkely quote), and passim.

2. Ibid, pp. 63–65.

3. Ibid., p. 64. As quoted in Elaine Forman Crane, *A Dependent People: Newport, Rhode Island in the Revolutionary Era* (New York: Fordham University Press, 1985), p. 11. McLoughlin, *Rhode Island*, p. 58. Jeanne Vibert Sloane, "John Cahoone and the Newport Furniture Industry," in *New England Furniture: Essays in Memory of Benno Forman*, edited by Brock Jobe (Boston: Society for the Preservation of New England Antiquities, 1987), p. 91.

4. As quoted in Leigh Keno, Joan Barzilay Freund, and Alan Miller, "The Very Pink of the Mode: Boston Georgian Chairs, Their Export and Their Influence," in *American Furniture*, edited by Luke Beckerdite (Hanover, N.H.: University Press of New England, 1996), p. 298. For more on the export of Rhode Island furniture, see Sloane, "John Cahoone." Margaretta M. Lovell, "'Such Furniture as Will Be Most Profitable': The Business of Cabinetmaking in Eighteenth-Century Newport," *Winterthur Portfolio* 26, no. 1 (Spring 1991): 52–56.

5. Ralph E. Carpenter, Jr., *The Arts and Crafts of Newport, Rhode Island, 1640–1820* (Newport, R.I.: Preservation Society of Newport County, 1954), pp. 10–13. Lovell, "'Such Furniture as Will Be Most Profitable,'" p. 53.

6. Mabel M. Swan, "The Goddard and Townsend Joiners, Part I," *Antiques* 49, no. 4 (April 1946): 228–31. In 1718, Christopher was serving on the *Elizabeth* when a pirate sloop robbed the ship and took two sailors. Carpenter, *The Arts and Crafts of Newport*, pp. 10–13.

7. Lovell, "'Such Furniture as Will Be Most Profitable,'" pp. 53, 56.

8. Carpenter, *The Arts and Crafts of Newport*, pp. 11, 12. Antoinette F. Downing and Vincent J. Scully, Jr., *The Architectural Heritage of Newport, Rhode Island, 1640–1915* (1952; 2d rev. ed., New York: American Legacy Press, 1967), pp. 75–76. Lovell, "'Such Furniture as Will Be Most Profitable,'" pp. 50–52.

9. Downing and Scully, *The Architectural Heritage of Newport*, p. 63.

10. Ibid.

11. Abraham Redwood Letterbook, 1723–1740, as quoted in Ethel Hall Bjerkoe, *The Cabinet-makers of America* (New York: Doubleday, 1957), pp. 213-14. Carpenter, *The Arts and Crafts of Newport*, pp. 11–12. Public commissions, which required the support and involvement of prominent individuals, were important avenues of patronage for colonial tradesmen. Christopher Townsend worked as a house joiner on the Redwood Library in 1743 and may have been involved with several other public projects during the period. Like many cabinetmakers in coastal communities, he also did ship joinery (Downing and Scully, *The Architectural Heritage of Newport*, pp. 63, 75–76). The author thanks Michael Flanigan for information on the history of the high chest. For more on Samuel Ward's purchases from Job Townsend, see Carpenter, *The Arts and Crafts of Newport*, pp. 11, 12.

12. Carpenter, *The Arts and Crafts of Newport*, p. 11. For more on this New York group, see Dean Failey, *Long Island Is My Nation: The Decorative Arts and Craftsmen, 1640–1830*, 2d rev. ed. (Cold Harbor, N.Y.: Society for the Preservation of Long Island Antiquities, 1998), pp. 9–29, 116, 117. For more on Stoddard, see ibid., pp. 9–27, 258, 287. Benjamin F. Thomas, *The History of Long Island From Its Discovery and Settlement to the Present Time*, 2d rev. ed. (New York: Gould, Banks Co., 1843), p. 347.

13. In 1745 Joshua Delaplaine recorded a debit entry to Christopher Townsend for "selling fitting & delivering acording to agreement desks" and credited him "By ye produce of ye mahogany desk £6.5" and "by ditto of ye maple ditto." On the bottom of his bill to Townsend, Delaplaine wrote: "Respected frd . . . Pursuant to thy request have sold and bought ye above mentioned. Hope it may be to satisfaction. I have been offered but 30/ for ye tea table and thought it too little" (Joshua Delaplaine Account with Christopher Townsend, 1744–1745, Delaplaine Papers, New York Historical Society). For more on Delaplaine and Quaker cabinetmakers in New York, see J. Stewart Johnson, "New York Cabinetmaking Prior to the Revolution" (M.A. thesis, University of Delaware, 1964). On March 20, 1746, Townsend acknowledged payment of a commission administered by Delaplaine: "Rec'd of John Freebody the sum of Sixty one pounds in ful for One Case of Draws & one tea table of Mahogany Made for Mr. Thos. Moone of New York, March" (Lois Olcott Price, "Furniture Craftsmen and the Queen Anne Style in Eighteenth-Century New York" [M.A. thesis, University of Delaware, 1977], p. 79). In 1740, Delaplaine wrote Newport Quaker Samuel Holmes "hoping this [letter] may find thee in better health than Christopher Townsend informed us thou wast in when he left those parts." The author thanks Joan Barzilay Freund for her research on Quakers in New York and Rhode Island.

14. The author thanks Sumpter Priddy for the information on the Virginia dressing table. Ronald L. Hurst, "Irish Influences on Cabinetmaking in Virginia's Rappahannock River Basin," in *American Furniture*, edited by Luke Beckerdite (Hanover, N.H.: University of New England Press for the Chipstone Foundation, 1997), pp. 170–96. A dressing table with Massachusetts features and Newport case and leg construction is in the files of the Decorative Arts Photographic Collection, Winterthur Museum, no. 75.875.

15. The author is grateful to Mack Headley for his opinions on both methods of case construction. Mabel Munson Swan, "The Goddard and Townsend Joiners: Part I," *Antiques* 49, no. 2 (April 1946): 228–31; Mabel Munson Swan, "The Goddard and Townsend Joiners: Part II," *Antiques* 49, no. 5 (May 1946): 292–95; Mabel Munson Swan, "John Goddard's Sons," *Antiques* 57, no. 6 (June 1950): 448–49.

16. Ralph Carpenter has suggested that John worked in Christopher's shop until 1773 (Carpenter, *The Arts and Crafts of Newport*, pp. 16, 17).

17. Sotheby's, *Important Americana, Furniture, and Folk Art*, New York, January 16–17, 1998, lot 704, pp. 201–8. Although the history of the desk-and-bookcase was provided by Appleton descendants, it is possible that the piece entered the family through a different line. During the first half of the eighteenth century, Newport patrons purchased large quantities of Boston furniture; however, trade between the two cities almost never flowed in the opposite direction. The urban British design of the pediment and use of figured mahogany as a secondary wood suggest that the original owner may have resided in the Carribean, Surinam, or another trop-

ical colony before moving to Newport. Case pieces from these regions often have mahogany secondary wood. Newport merchants such as Abraham Redwood occasionally traveled to the Carribean and South America. Redwood, for example, resided in Antigua from 1737 to at least 1740 (Nancy E. Richards and Nancy Goyne Evans, *New England Furniture at Winterthur: Queen Anne and Chippendale Periods* [Hanover, N.H.: University Press of New England for the Winterthur Museum, 1997], p. 171).

18. Ibid., p. 208. Carpenter, *The Arts and Crafts of Newport,* pp. 74, 206.

19. Job Townsend, Jr., occasionally worked for his brother Edward. In 1767 they collaborated on a "Large Mahogany Desk" for Nicholas Anderese.

20. A china table and a basin stand that descended in the Bullock family of Rhode Island have tops with rabbets around the perimeter of the underside. The rabbets helped "trap" the glue blocks used to attach the tops to the frame. For the china table, see Richards and Evans, *New England Furniture at Winterthur,* pp. 244–45. Baltimore antique dealer J. Michael Flanigan exhibited the basin stand at the Philadelphia Antique Show in April 1999. The attachment of the cornice molding on the signed Christopher Townsend desk-and-bookcase is very unusual. The side moldings, which are comprised of two vertically laminated pieces, are attached to the sides with a modified mortise-and-tenon joint. The tenons are cut on the sides and have a single shoulder on the inside edge. The tenons extend the full depth of the case and appear to have been cut with a rabbet plane.

21. A chest of drawers attributed to Job Townsend, Jr., had moldings beneath the top that were originally secured with glue alone (see Martha Willoughby, "The Accounts of Job Townsend, Jr.," in *American Furniture,* edited by Luke Beckerdite [Hanover, N.H.: University Press of New England for the Chipstone Foundation, 1999], p. 110, fig. 1). The side pieces probably fell off due to cross-grain shrinkage and expansion of the case. The large drawers on the signed Christopher Townsend desk-and-bookcase match those of the high chests documented and attributed to his shop.

22. Wallace B. Gusler, "Variations in 18th-Century Casework," *Fine Woodworking,* July/August 1980, no. 23, pp. 50–53. Most Boston case pieces, for example, have nailed runners and drawer blades with exposed dovetails. For more on Boston furniture exports, see Neil D. Kamil, "Hidden in Plain Sight: Disappearance and Material Life in Colonial New York," in *American Furniture,* edited by Luke Beckerdite (Hanover, N.H.: University Press of New England for the Chipstone Foundation, 1995), pp. 192–96; Keno, Freund, and Miller, "The Very Pink of the Mode"; and Joan Barzilay Freund and Leigh Keno, "The Making and Marketing of Boston Seating Furniture in the Late Baroque Style," in *American Furniture,* edited by Luke Beckerdite (Hanover, N.H.: University Press of New England for the Chipstone Foundation, 1998), pp. 1–40.

23. Carpenter, *The Arts and Crafts of Rhode Island*, pp. 10–13. Lovell, "'Such Furniture as Will Be Most Profitable.'"

24. Parke-Bernet Galleries, *Important American Furniture from the Estate of the Late Cornelius C. Moore, Newport, Rhode Island*, New York, October 30, 1971, p. 58, lot 154. The author is grateful to Robert Trent for calling this piece to his attention.

25. Margaretta Lovell was the first scholar to suggest that Newport cabinetmakers endeavored to create a "predictable commodity." (Lovell, "'Such Furniture as Will Be Most Profitable,'" p. 33.) Robert Campbell, *The London Tradesman* (1747).

26. William Penn as quoted in Jack L. Lindsey, *Worldly Goods: The Arts of Early Pennsylvania, 1680–1758* (Philadelphia: Philadelphia Museum of Art, 1999), p. 21.

27. Michael Moses, *Master Craftsmen of Newport: The Townsends and Goddards* (Tenafly, N.J.: MMI Americana Press, 1984), p. 235, fig. 5.23.

28. Lovell, "'Such Furniture as Will Be Most Profitable,'" p. 33.

29. Sloane, "John Cahoone", pp. 106–6.

Catherine Rogers Arthur

"The True Antiques of Tomorrow": Furniture by the Potthast Brothers of Baltimore, 1892-1975

▼ THE SECRET OF MAKING HOMES *look beautifully furnished with unending charm . . . is not only cost, as many sometimes are inclined to believe. . . . It is a knowledge of furniture history, furniture making, and "where" to buy.*

Potthast Brothers, Inc., "Interesting Facts: Inside Secrets of Selecting Furniture Correctly," 1935

In 1892, four German immigrants—William, Vincent, John, and Theodore Potthast (fig. 1)—founded Potthast Brothers, Inc. (1892–1975), the most prolific cabinetmaking shop in late-nineteenth- and twentieth-century Baltimore. The firm's copyrighted slogan, "The True Antiques of Tomorrow," was not only prophetic but reflected the philosophy behind the Potthasts' handmade reproduction furniture. Their desire to create furniture with intrinsic value affected the way the brothers and their workmen designed, manufactured, and marketed their products. Throughout its existence, Potthast Brothers was influenced by and has contributed to the popularity of the colonial revival style. The history and products of this firm shed light on twentieth-century interest in American antiques and the continuing popularity of reproductions.[1]

*Figure 1* Photograph showing the interior of the Potthast shop with (left to right) William, Vincent, Theodore, and John Potthast and their accountant (standing), Baltimore, Maryland, ca. 1903. (Courtesy, Potthast family collection.)

*Potthast Brothers and Its Colonial Revival Context*

Although the Potthasts' high regard for handwork echoed ideals expressed in the arts and crafts movement, one of their early sales brochures noted that "the utter simplicity of the so-called 'modern' style does not call for . . . rare, artistic ability like that of the Old Masters whose art will last forever." The brothers' criticism of the arts and crafts movement probably had as much to do with self-image as with salesmanship. Just as neoclassical furniture embodied and embraced a wide vocabulary of symbols and motifs from classical antiquity, colonial revival furniture offered consumers a connection with America's past. This was especially appealing to the Potthasts and other immigrants who sought to identify themselves with their new home. As historian Kenneth L. Ames has observed:

> While an ethnically heterogeneous citizenry fostered America's image as a land of prosperity open to all, it created significant social tensions, both among the older stock, which felt threatened on many levels by the newcomers themselves, the "uprooted," who sometimes found social and cultural change excruciatingly difficult. Here the role of the colonial revival was to expedite acculturation and socialization.[2]

The colonial revival and its material culture satisfied the needs of native-born Americans who wished to maintain and assert their heritage and of immigrants who endeavored to be more like them. As Ames notes, both groups understood "the necessity of preserving relics in order to keep ideas and ideals alive." Like Earnest F. Hagen, who restored and reproduced furniture made by New York cabinetmaker Duncan Phyfe and his contemporaries during the late nineteenth and early twentieth centuries, the Potthasts created a variety of "relics" with historical associations and connotations. With its conservative amalgam of established families and newcomers, Baltimore was the perfect location for their business. Like the Potthasts' furniture, the colonial revival taste remained popular in the city throughout the twentieth century.[3]

Hundreds of pieces of Potthast furniture are known, most of which reside in private collections and museums in the Baltimore-Washington area. The work is usually branded or labeled because the Potthasts considered their name synonymous with quality and "authenticity." A tremendous amount of documentary material relating to the firm also survives. The Maryland Historical Society has fifty glass plate negatives taken by John Potthast, five books containing correspondence with customers and suppliers, and approximately four hundred shop drawings. Additional papers and photographs are in the possession of Potthast descendants. A large group of images, most taken by Harry B. Leopold (1891–1977) of Baltimore, includes views of window displays, retail salesrooms, and individual pieces of furniture produced by the firm. These photographs were assembled as a sample book to show prospective clients examples of work done by the firm.[4]

Sales literature published by the Potthasts documents many of the sources they consulted and provides information on the firm's marketing strategies. Their brochures typically cite early-twentieth-century furniture histories in conjunction with eighteenth- and early-nineteenth-century design books, but make no distinction between primary and secondary sources. Although their ultimate goal was to boost sales, the Potthasts understood the importance of teaching potential patrons about period styles, design, and craftsmanship. They believed that educated consumers would be more likely to consider handmade reproductions superior to mass-produced furniture. By assuming the role of "mentor," the Potthasts positioned themselves as arbiters of taste to their well-established, predominately upper-class clientele.[5]

The ability to recognize period styles was important to collectors who sought to formulate and express their own notions of good taste. During the 1930s, the Potthasts published several individual brochures devoted to different furniture styles, most of which were associated with English monarchs and British and American cabinetmakers and designers. The terms used to describe these styles parallel those found in early-twentieth-century periodicals and furniture anthologies: "Queen Anne," "Chippendale," "Sheraton," "Hepplewhite," "Robert and J. Adam," and "Duncan Phyfe." The dates assigned to these styles correspond to monarchial reigns ("Queen Anne, 1702–1714") and the life dates of designers and furniture makers ("Chippendale, 1705–1779") rather than to their original period of popularity. Like many of their contemporaries, the Potthasts used the term "colonial" (see fig. 2) in the broadest possible sense. In *The Quest of the Colonial* (1906), Robert and Elizabeth Shackleton noted that "'colonial' is attached to all the furniture of the early times and the early shapes. It has come to be so generally employed, and is a term in itself so suggestive . . . that it would be invidious . . . to limit its use with chilly literalness." During the early twentieth century, the term "colonial" was most often used to describe what modern scholars call "empire revival," the latest of the revival styles, rather than the earliest as one might expect.[6]

Fortunately for the Potthasts, a national interest in American antique furniture spurred demand for reproductions. Such books as Irving Whitehall Lyon's *The Colonial Furniture of New England* (1891), Esther Singleton's *The Furniture of Our Forefathers* (1901), and Wallace Nutting's *Furniture Treasury* (1928) guided both collectors and individuals interested in decorating their homes. Women's magazines frequently included articles on antiques and decorating, and a variety of books and periodicals advocated the purchase of reproductions for those unable to afford period furniture. The magazine *Antiques* (1922 to the present), which was one of the most important vehicles for the dissemination of the "colonial" taste, regularly featured advertisements by colonial revival furniture manufacturers.

In 1915, the nation's "first interior decorator," Elsie de Wolfe (1865–1950) published *The House in Good Taste*, which remained influential for decades. She devoted an entire chapter to reproductions of antique furniture and objects of art, and asserted that unless one was a collector of rare antiques, reproductions were preferable for everyday comfort and use:

> No one can swear to a piece of furniture having been made in the workshops of the Chippendales. Even the pieces in the Metropolitan Museum are marked "Chippendale Style" or "In the Sheraton Manner". . . . If the furniture is in the style of these makers, and if it is really old, you will pay a small fortune for it. . . . Why then lend yourself to possible deception?

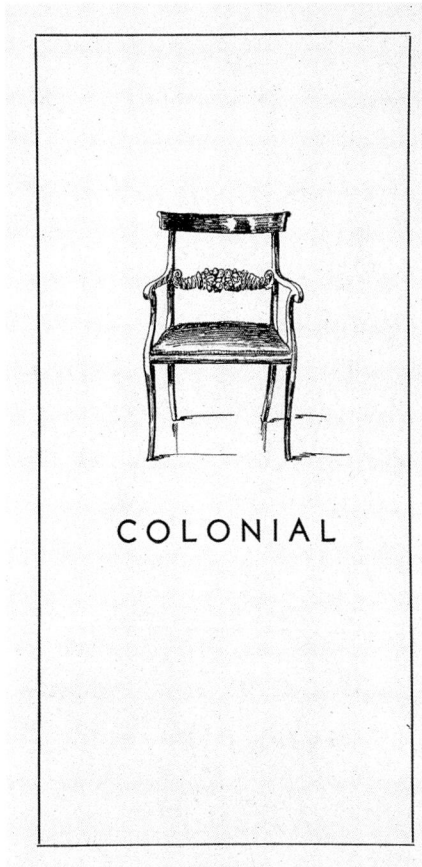

*Figure 2*  Potthast Bros., Inc., brochure titled "Colonial," Baltimore, Maryland, ca. 1930. (Private collection.)

Why pay for names when museums are unable to buy them? If your object is to furnish your home suitably, what need have you of antiques? The serious amateur will fight shy of miracles. If he admires the beauty of line of a fine old Hepplewhite bed or Sheraton sideboard, he will have reproductions made by an expert cabinetmaker. The new piece will not have the soft darkness of the old, but the owner will be planning that soft darkness for his grandchildren, and in the meantime he will have a beautiful thing to live with.

Letterbooks and account books maintained by the Potthasts reveal that Elsie de Wolfe was a regular client of their firm. It is quite possible that Potthast Brothers, Inc., was the "expert cabinetmaker" she alluded to in her book.[7]

A sketch of an "Adam style" chair in the firm's 1907 letterbook (fig. 3) is inscribed "Miss de Wolfe." Although it is impossible to determine if examples were made for her or for one of her clients, the sketch may have been

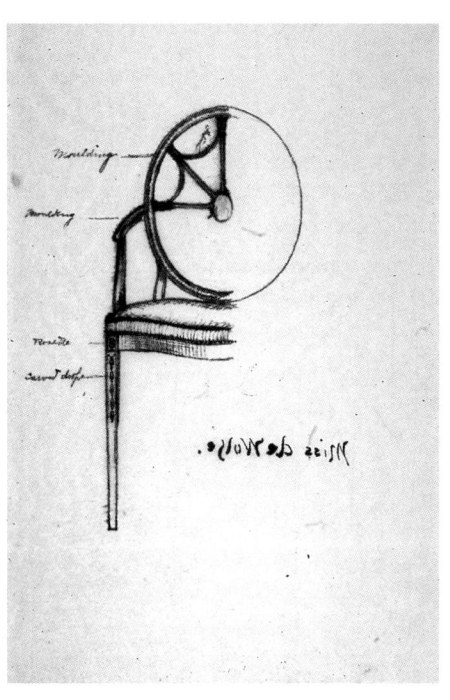

*Figure 3*  Potthast Bros., Inc., sketch for a chair inscribed "Miss de Wolfe," Potthast letterbook, 1907, p. 305. (Courtesy, Potthast family collection.)

*Figure 4*  Potthast Bros., Inc., "Huntmaster's chair," Baltimore, Maryland, ca. 1917. Mahogany and lightwood inlay with oak. H. 51½", W. 27½", D. 23". (Private collection; photo, Gavin Ashworth.)

*Figure 5* Detail of the back of the "Huntmaster's chair" illustrated in fig. 4.

the basis for a dining-room suite subsequently made for Pleasant Hill (built in 1917), the home of C. Wilbur and Edith (Davison) Miller of Baltimore. This suite consists of a dining table with five leaves, a large sideboard with a pair of matching knife urns, a huntboard, two breakfront silver cabinets, twenty-two side chairs, two armchairs, and an oversize "huntmaster's chair" (see figs. 4, 5). Baltimore architect James Edmunds designed Pleasant Hill. The original plans survive along with a series of photographs of the completed interiors, two of which show the Potthast suite in situ (fig. 6).[8]

*Figure 6* Photograph showing the suite of Potthast furniture commissioned for Pleasant Hill, Baltimore, Maryland, ca. 1920. (Private collection.)

### The Origins and Development of the Potthast Firm

In 1891, two of six Potthast brothers left their home and family cabinetmaking business in Borgholtz, Germany, to immigrate to America. William Potthast (1862–1935) (fig. 7) and his younger brother Vincent (1866–1911) (fig. 8) arrived in Baltimore and found employment as cabinetmakers for the William Knabe and Company Piano Forte factory at the corner of Eutaw and West Streets. While working for Knabe and Company, William and Vincent spent evenings and weekends buying and restoring antique furniture. By 1892 they had acquired enough furniture to open an antique shop at 321 North Howard Street. Shortly thereafter, John (1870–1962) and Theodore Potthast (1875–1966) arrived in Baltimore to join their brothers' business. Several antique dealers were already located in the vicinity. The *Baltimore City Directory* listed one furniture dealer specializing in antiques in 1886 and eighteen antique dealers in 1900. Twelve of the eighteen dealers maintained shops on North Howard Street, the current site of Baltimore's "Antiques Row."[9]

*Figure 7*   Photograph of William Potthast, Baltimore, Maryland, ca. 1900. (Courtesy, Potthast family collection.)

*Figure 8*   Photograph of Vincent Potthast, Baltimore, Maryland, ca. 1900. (Courtesy, Potthast family collection.)

*Figure 9*   Lithograph showing Potthast Bros., Inc.'s shop at 507 North Howard Street and factory at 506–508 Tyson Street. The photograph of this image is taken from *Das Neue Baltimore* (1905).

The Potthasts moved to larger quarters at 507 North Howard Street in 1899 (fig. 9). Four years later they relocated their restoration business to 506–508 Tyson Street and began using the Howard Street building as a showroom. In 1905, the German-language newspaper *Das Neue Baltimore* reported that Potthast Brothers was where "high society meets, when it is seeking original art furniture or truly antique wares." The earliest labels used by the firm give both addresses and read "POTTHAST BROS./ DEALERS IN/ ANTIQUE FURNITURE/ and/ ARTISTIC FURNITURE MFRS." As their label suggests, the Potthasts began by selling and restoring antiques, but quickly moved into designing and manufacturing furniture.[10]

A chest of drawers (fig. 10) attributed to Baltimore cabinetmaker William Camp (fl. 1801–1822) is one of several locally made antiques repaired by the Potthasts. Evidence of their work can be found in the thick varnish that covers the case, drawer sides, and drawer interiors. In typical fashion, the brothers placed labels on the chest (see fig. 11), one on the back of the case, and one on each of two drawer bottoms. A sketch of a similar chest (fig. 12) is included in a 1907 letter from the Potthasts to a customer in Massachusetts:

> We are sending herewith a rough sketch of an old chest of drawers which we have on hand in the rough & which we can put in order for thirty-five . . . dollars including crating. If this sketch should not be satisfactory, we could send others of pieces we have on hand for forty or forty-five dollars.[11]

One of the Potthasts' most important patrons was Baltimore physician William H. Crim (1845–1902). His antique collection, which was one of the earliest assembled in America, sold at auction in Baltimore in April 1903 (see fig. 13). The sale featured 2,841 lots and realized over seventy thousand dollars. This event was extremely important to the Potthasts because they had restored many of the pieces for Crim. As a result of their work, the craftsmen had become familiar with the design and construction of his furniture. They had also measured and drawn several pieces in his collection in order to make reproductions. This proved to be advantageous for the Potthasts, since the notoriety of the sale and its record-setting prices created a strong market for copies of Crim's furniture.[12]

*Figure 10* Chest of drawers attributed to William Camp, Baltimore, Maryland, ca. 1820. Mahogany with tulip poplar and yellow pine. H. 41", W. 40½", D. 21¼". The Potthasts repaired and labeled this chest about 1903. (Private collection.)

*Figure 11* Detail showing the label on the chest illustrated in fig. 10.

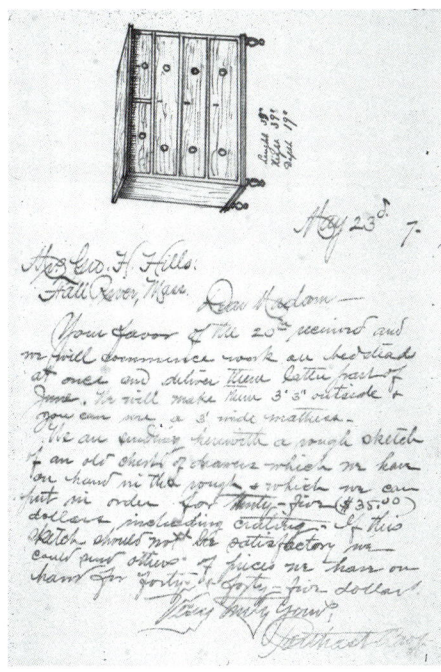

*Figure 12* Potthast Bros., Inc., sketch of a chest submitted to Mrs. Geo. Hills, Fall River, Massachusetts, May 23, 1907. This sketch, which resembles the chest illustrated in fig. 10, is in Potthast letterbook, 1907. (Courtesy, Potthast family collection.)

*Figure 13* Title page from O. A. Kirkland Auctioneer, *Catalogue of the Celebrated Dr. William H. Crim Collection of Genuine Antiques*, Baltimore, Maryland, 1903. (Private collection.)

In response to this demand, or possibly in anticipation of it, the Potthasts made reproductions of several items in the sale catalogue. These reproductions immediately became best-sellers and were frequently illustrated in

*Figure 14*   Potthast Bros., Inc., reproduction "Crim chair," Baltimore, Maryland, ca. 1930. Mahogany with oak. H. 40 1/4", W. 24", D. 17 3/4". (Private collection; photo, Gavin Ashworth.)

*Figure 15*   Philadelphia side chair illustrated as lot 231 in O. A. Kirkland Auctioneer, *Catalogue of the Celebrated Dr. William H. Crim Collection of Genuine Antiques*, Baltimore, Maryland, 1903. (Private collection.)

brochures published by the firm. The Potthast side chair shown in figure 14 is based on a "Magnificent Rare Old Mahogany Ball and Claw Foot Chippendale Chair" described as "one of the finest in the [Crim] collection" (fig. 15). Made in Philadelphia about 1750, the antique sold for three hundred dollars, a remarkable sum in 1903. A brochure published by the Potthasts cites both the sale and the hammer prices, which stood in stark contrast to the price of the reproduction (fig. 16). The "Crim chair," as it was known, continued as the Potthasts' best-selling model and remains desirable today.[13]

Although the Potthasts succeeded in replicating the basic form of the Crim chair, they were unable to duplicate the carving. The acanthus leaves on the knees and back of the reproduction are crude in comparison with those on the original (see figs. 17, 19), which are attributed to an anonymous Philadelphia tradesman referred to today as the "Garvan carver." The claw-

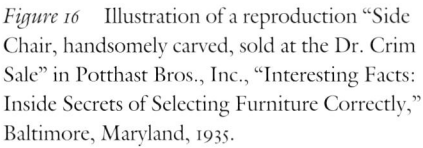

*The illustrated Side Chair, handsomely carved, sold at the Doctor Crim Sale in 1903 for $300. Today it would bring many more times this sum.*

*Figure 16*   Illustration of a reproduction "Side Chair, handsomely carved, sold at the Dr. Crim Sale" in Potthast Bros., Inc., "Interesting Facts: Inside Secrets of Selecting Furniture Correctly," Baltimore, Maryland, 1935.

*Figure 17*   Detail of the carving on the back of the side chair illustrated in fig. 14. (Photo, Gavin Ashworth.)

*Figure 18*   Side chair, Philadelphia, Pennsylvania, ca. 1750. Mahogany with pine. H. 39", W. 24", D. 22½". (Chipstone Foundation; photo, Gavin Ashworth.) This chair sold as lot 231 in O. A. Kirkland Auctioneer, *Catalogue of the Celebrated Dr. William H. Crim Collection of Genuine Antiques,* Baltimore, Maryland, 1903.

*Figure 19*   Detail of the carving on the back of the side chair shown in fig. 18.

and-ball feet on the Potthast chair also have large knuckles and thick webbing like those on many other chairs made in the colonial revival style.

Eight "fine armchairs" that reputedly belonged to Maryland attorney Francis Scott Key (see fig. 20) inspired another Potthast reproduction (fig. 21). The original set, which sold for eight thousand dollars in the Crim sale, was catalogued as "one of the handsomest and most delicately carved [seating forms] . . . ever created by Chippendale." Although the Potthasts may have given some credence to this provenance, they realized that there was no basis for attributing them to Chippendale and refrained from mentioning the designer in advertisements and sales literature for the reproduction chairs. The "Key chairs" were especially popular with local patrons, owing to their association with the lyricist of the "Star-Spangled Banner."[14]

The Jamestown Tercentennial Exposition held in Norfolk, Virginia, in 1907 allowed the Potthasts to display their "artistic furniture" before a national audience. Twenty-one states participated by constructing state buildings to honor their respective histories, modern day industries, and commerce. The General Assembly of Maryland appointed twenty-five commissioners and an auxiliary board of five women and appropriated sixty-five thousand dollars for a Maryland Building. After rejecting a proposal to construct a replica of the state house in Annapolis, the commission selected the plan of architect Douglas H. Thomas, Jr., to build a version of Homewood, the country house of Charles Carroll, Jr. (fig. 22). In this modified replica, Thomas substituted the senate chamber of the Maryland State House (figs. 23, 24) for the principal first story room. The Potthasts lent furniture for the

*Figure 20*  Armchair illustrated as lot 774 in O. A. Kirkland Auctioneer, *Catalogue of the Celebrated Dr. William H. Crim Collection of Genuine Antiques,* Baltimore, Maryland, 1903. (Private collection.) This armchair is one of eight that reputedly belonged to Francis Scott Key.

*Figure 21*  Potthast Bros., Inc., reproduction "Key chair," Baltimore, Maryland, ca. 1910. Mahogany with oak. H. 36 3/4", W. 23 3/4", D. 20 1/4". (Courtesy, Maryland Historical Society.)

building, realizing that it would generate interest in their firm and add prestige to their reproductions. A report published by the commission in Baltimore in 1908 documented every aspect of the project and included photographs of the interiors and comments on the furnishings:

> It was the purpose of the Commission to furnish the Maryland Building so far as it was possible with colonial furniture. . . . The Commission was very fortunate in enlisting the cooperation of the Potthast Brothers of Baltimore who from the very first showed every desire to contribute all they could for the benefit of the State. They loaned . . . free of charge, sixty-two chairs, five tables, four sofas, a mahogany low-boy, two mahogany and gilt mirrors, a mahogany cabinet, a mahogany table, an inlaid side table, a mahogany desk and a mahogany stand, all these pieces being of large size and extremely handsome. They formed the main part of the furnishing . . . and gave the whole interior a dignity and a solid elegance which elicited cordial tributes from thousands of visitors . . . There has been quite a revival of the eighteenth century styles and the extraordinary popularity of such original pieces as are extant has caused this colonial furniture to be

*Figure 22* Photograph of the Maryland Building in the 1907 Tercentennial Exposition in Norfolk, Virginia, illustrated in *Report of the Maryland Commission to the Jamestown Ter-Centennial Exposition* (1908).

*Figure 23* Photograph showing the "Senate Chamber" of the Maryland Building in the 1907 Tercentennial Exposition in Norfolk, Virginia, illustrated in *Report of the Maryland Commission to the Jamestown Ter-Centennial Exposition* (1908).

*Figure 24* Photograph showing the "Senate Chamber" of the Maryland Building in the 1907 Tercentennial Exposition in Norfolk, Virginia, illustrated in *Report of the Maryland Commission to the Jamestown Ter-Centennial Exposition* (1908).

much copied. The furniture of Messrs. Potthast Brothers had therefore an interest far beyond its historical value because of its practical relations to the home furniture of the present day.

The participation of the Potthasts is further documented by interior views of the building; the firm's inventory of loans (fig. 25); correspondence detailing the selection of upholstery fabrics, crating, and shipping; and a letter offering the loaned objects for sale to Tiffany Studios at the close of the exposition.[15]

Several antiques were also exhibited in the Maryland Building. The Potthasts lent a sideboard that descended in the Key family; Mrs. John Ridgely, a member of the women's auxiliary commission, lent a "colonial table" from Hampton; and William Knabe and Company lent a harpsichord formerly owned by Charles Carroll of Carrollton. The table, harpsichord, and a variety of reproductions loaned by the Potthasts are visible in photographs of the "Senate Chamber" (figs. 23, 24). At least thirteen of the firm's chair designs are documented in these images and the loan inventory. Potthast Brothers, Inc., did not provide all the furnishings for the Maryland Building, however. A report by the commission also includes photographs of other rooms, such as the "Reading Room," which show reproductions made by the Potthasts along with Mission-style furniture made by students from the Maryland Manual Training Schools and School for Boys.[16]

Although the Potthasts loaned seventy-nine reproductions to the Tercentennial Exposition, only two sofas (see fig. 26) can be linked definitively with the Maryland exhibit. These objects do not appear in any of the photographs, but they are mentioned in the loan inventory (fig. 25) and both descended in the Potthast family. The upholstery fabrics selected for the sofas and other seating forms loaned by Potthast Brothers are described in an April 1907 letter from the firm to Mrs. Henry Rogers.[17]

The Potthasts' correspondence during the period of the Tercentennial Exposition is replete with references to furniture on display in the Maryland

Building. This exhibit was one of the first to open, and the firm received many inquiries regarding the prices of items they had loaned. As the exposition drew to a close, the Potthasts endeavored to sell the furniture as a single lot, possibly because they lacked the space to display the pieces in their Baltimore showroom. On October 5, 1907, they wrote Tiffany Studios:

> We have in the Maryland Building of the Jamestown Exposition a lot of our hand-made furniture which at retail prices is valued at $3430; it consists of 49 side chairs, 17 arm chairs, 8 tables, 4 sofas, 1 china press, 1 sideboard, and 2 mirrors—They are all first class pieces in every respect. We will sell the entire lot crated, f.o.b. at Norfolk for $2400.00. We could make arrangements with the . . . Commission to put a sign in the Maryland Building stating by whom the furniture was purchased if desired as an ad.

Three days later they sent another letter along with photographs, sketches, and a list of retail prices. "You will see by the photos that this is entirely different from the furniture of similar styles which you find in the market," wrote the Potthasts. "We hope you will give this matter careful consideration and let us hear from you as soon as possible." A final letter sent on October 19, 1907, states, "[W]e are anxious to hear from you regarding the furniture at the Maryland State Bldg. . . . The fair is nearing a close & we would like to have time to dispose of these goods to some other purchaser if you do not require them. If you will figure the prices up on these goods piece by piece, you will find them below cost of their manufacture." There is no evidence that Tiffany Studios purchased any of this furniture, even though they did considerable business with the Potthasts. The financial panic of 1907 may explain Tiffany Studios' lack of interest as well as the Potthasts' desire to liquidate the furnishings in the Maryland Building. Other correspondence in the 1907 letterbook reveals that the firm made a concerted effort to collect debts on outstanding accounts to improve cash flow.[18]

*Figure 25*  Inventory of objects loaned by Potthast Bros., Inc., for the Maryland Building in the 1907 Tercentennial Exposition in Norfolk, Virginia. (Courtesy, Potthast family collection.) The inventory is in Potthast letterbook, 1907.

*Figure 26*  Potthast Bros., Inc., "Jamestown" sofa, Baltimore, Maryland, ca. 1906–1907. Mahogany with oak. H. 35 1/2", W. 79", D. 27 3/4". (Private collection; photo, Gavin Ashworth.)

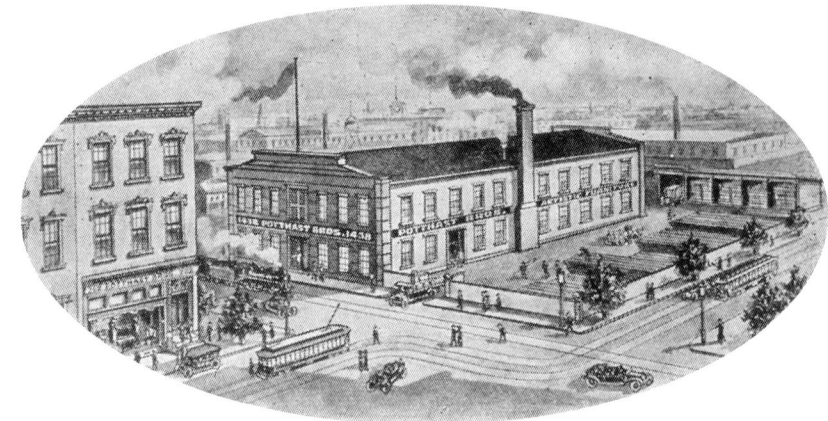

*Figure 27*  Lithograph composite view of the Potthast shop at 702 North Howard Street and the Wicomico Street factory illustrated on the back cover of the firm's brochure titled "The Dining Room Beautiful," Baltimore, Maryland, ca. 1922. Potthast Bros., Inc., began to specialize in dining-room furniture by the mid-1920s. Advertisements and surviving objects suggest that tables, chairs, and sideboards constituted the bulk of the firm's manufacturing work.

*Figure 28*  Photograph showing part of Potthast Bros., Inc.'s Wicomico Street factory with a delivery truck in the foreground, Baltimore, Maryland, ca. 1925. The vehicle is painted with a variety of slogans and catchwords including "Dining Room Furniture Our Specialty" and "Antique Furniture."

In spite of this brief economic downturn, Potthast Brothers flourished. The firm grew, moving into new quarters at 702 North Howard Street in 1914. The next expansion occurred in 1921, after the brothers purchased land in southwest Baltimore and erected a large factory at 1438 Wicomico Street. A composite view from 1921 or 1922 (fig. 27) shows both the 702 North Howard Street store and the 1438 Wicomico Street factory (fig. 28). Visible in the background of the lithograph are the lumberyard and smokestack for the drying kiln. The factory expanded again in 1925, when the Potthasts moved their showroom to its final location at 920 (later renumbered to 924) North Charles Street. In the mid-1930s, Potthast Brothers purchased 926 North Charles Street and had showrooms in the adjoining buildings. The firm sold the 926 North Charles Street location in the mid-1940s, and the building was destroyed.[19]

A second generation of Potthasts entered the family business during the 1920s and 1930s. Six of the founders' sons served apprenticeships in addition to studying architectural drawing at the Maryland Institute College of Art in Baltimore. Although Vincent Potthast had three sons, none appear to have joined the firm. William's sons, Frank J. (1894–1942) and George J. (1895–1988), held important positions by 1938, the former serving as secretary-treasurer and the latter as general manager of the cabinet shops. John Potthast, Sr., was president and his sons, William A. (1902–1971) and Theodore J. (1905–1998), were the assistant secretary-treasurer and manager of the shops, respectively. Theodore Potthast, Sr., was vice-president; his son Michael Potthast (1911–1973) was office manager; and his other son Berthold (b. 1913) was assistant manager in the shops. All of these positions were based on seniority, skill, and interest.[20]

Potthast Brothers manufactured enormous quantities of furniture during the 1940s and 1950s, both for local patrons and for consumers in more distant locales. During World War II, the firm also completed various defense work projects for the U.S. Government. After the war, the Potthasts trained veterans as part of a special government project.[21]

Because of the firm's renown, Potthast Brothers received many important commissions. They made dining room suites for movie producer Cecil B. de Mille and for President Woodrow Wilson upon his departure from the

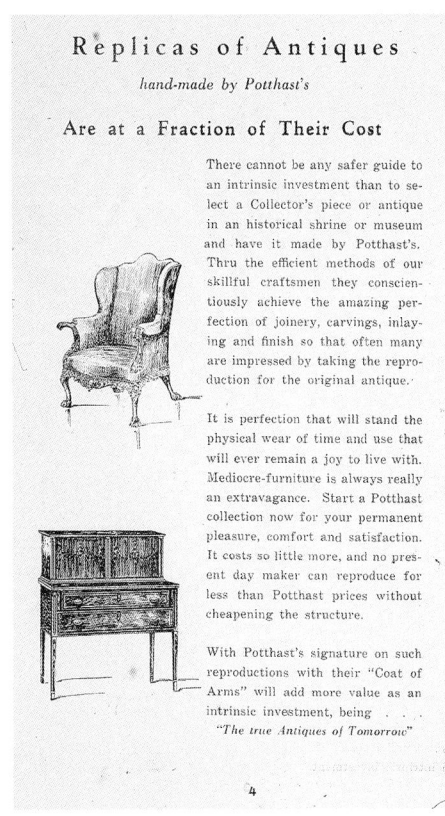

*Figure 29*  Illustration from Potthast Bros., Inc., "Reproductions That Are An Investment," Baltimore, Maryland, ca. 1930.

White House. They also made furniture for the Catholic archbishop's residence in Baltimore and the Governor's Mansion in Annapolis, Maryland.[22]

The second generation of Potthasts reached retirement age in the 1970s. With the death of William Potthast in 1971 and the retirement of George Potthast shortly thereafter, Theodore J. Potthast, Sr., was the sole family member remaining in the business. Although the market for the firm's furniture continued to be strong, the Potthast family dissolved the business in 1975. At that time the firm had thirty-five employees. The inventory sold quickly after the closure was announced. The factory and equipment were auctioned and the building was sold and converted to the Brass Elephant restaurant. The interior remains virtually unchanged from its appearance during Potthast Brothers' occupancy.[23]

*The Influence of Auctions and Private Collections on Potthast Furniture*
Auctions such as the Crim sale were an important influence on the Potthasts and their contemporaries who also produced colonial revival furniture. Auction catalogues were excellent design sources, and sales results helped the Potthasts gauge demand for different furniture styles and forms. Several highly publicized auctions occurred during the early twentieth century, including *Colonial Furniture: The Superb Collection of the Late Howard Reifsnyder* (1929) and *The Philip Flayderman Collection: Historic American Furniture* (1930). Both sales brought record prices owing to the popularity of American antiques and competition among collectors such as Henry Ford, Francis Garvan, and Henry Francis du Pont.[24]

Pieces commanding unusually high prices were a carved Philadelphia easy chair attributed to Benjamin Randolph (now in the Philadelphia Museum of Art) that brought thirty-three thousand dollars in the Reifsnyder sale and a labeled John Seymour tambour desk (now in the Winterthur Museum) that fetched thirty thousand dollars in the Flayderman sale. Potthast Brothers made reproductions of both pieces and used them as illustrations in sales brochures (see fig. 29), including one titled "Reproductions That Are An Investment" (ca. 1930). They also reproduced other forms from the Reifsnyder and Flayderman sales and noted that individuals without the means to collect antiques could achieve the same look for "a fraction of the cost." Another brochure, titled "Replicas from Collectors' Antiques," points out the difficulty in collecting period furniture and offers a predictable solution:

> Often one may search in vain to find the desirable piece or pieces of furniture that they [sic] would like to enjoy in their home. Many likewise . . . have visited museums, historical shrines which offer their contribution for furnishing the home in authentic good taste, but have not found their wishes realized. . . . The thoughtful home furnisher making a choice from these authoritative books—connoisseur's collections, and having them reproduced by Potthast's hand-methods, individually-made, like the original antiques, can never err in good judgment for excellent taste, for beauty, and for enhancing in value with Potthast's signature and Coat of Arms as, "The True Antiques of Tomorrow."[25]

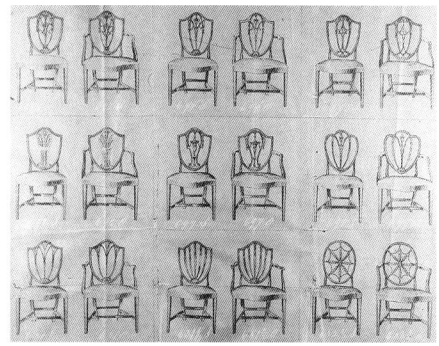

*Figure 30* Potthast Bros., Inc., chair designs with identification numbers, Baltimore, Maryland, ca. 1910. (Courtesy, Potthast family collection.) This page of chair designs was found among a group of photographs and shop drawings. Such materials may have been used as a reference for both patrons and workmen.

*Figure 31* Side chair, Baltimore, Maryland, 1790–1810. Mahogany with tulip poplar. H. 37 1/4", W. 20 1/2", D. 16 3/4". (Private collection; photo, Gavin Ashworth.) This chair is part of a set originally owned by Charles Carroll of Homewood.

Several auction catalogues and furniture anthologies owned by Potthast Brothers are annotated. These notations help document the forms the firm copied or adapted to produce such novelties as "Queen Anne" sideboards, "Chippendale" coffee tables, and "Hepplewhite" telephone stands. The Potthasts were undoubtedly familiar with the works of British designers such as Chippendale and Hepplewhite. A page of chair designs produced by the firm is reminiscent of engravings in eighteenth- and nineteenth-century pattern books (fig. 30).[26]

Furniture in local collections was another source of inspiration for the Potthasts. Their shop copy of Baltimore furniture historian Edgar G. Miller's *American Antique Furniture: A Book for Amateurs* (1937) has notations regarding pieces that the firm either copied or repaired. Most of the individ-

*Figure 32* Potthast Bros., Inc., side chair, Baltimore, Maryland, ca. 1930. Mahogany with oak. H. 38", W. 20", D. 17". (Private collection; photo, Gavin Ashworth.)

uals who allowed Miller to illustrate objects in their collection were from Maryland and many were direct descendants of the original owners.[27]

One of the Potthasts' most successful reproductions was based on a pair of oval-back chairs (see fig. 31) reputedly commissioned by Charles Carroll of Carrollton, one of four Maryland signers of the Declaration of Independence. In 1801 Carroll built and furnished Homewood as a wedding present for his son Charles and daughter-in-law Harriet (Chew) of Philadelphia. Given the date and provenance of the chairs, it is likely that they were part of the original furnishings of the house. No other Carroll family houses were being built or furnished during this period. These chairs probably sat in the dining room and were part of a set of ten or twelve. At least two other examples are owned by other Carroll family descendants.[28]

In the early twentieth century Mrs. Mary-Lee Carroll Muth owned the chair illustrated in figure 31. During the 1930s, she commissioned Potthast Brothers to repair her pair and make additional examples (see fig. 32) for use in her dining room. Shortly thereafter, the firm began selling a virtually identical model described as a "Hepplewhite oval back chair, originally owned by Charles Carroll of Carrollton—Signer of the Declaration." One brochure boasted that "the amazing perfection of joinery, carvings, inlaying and finish" attained by Potthast craftsmen often caused the firm's reproductions to be mistaken for the original antiques. Although the chairs made to expand Mrs. Muth's set are similar to the originals, there are slight differences in the shape of the oval, angle of the back, arrangement and position of the stretchers, and outline of the carved husks (figs. 33, 34). From a distance, however, the Potthast chairs are difficult to spot.[29]

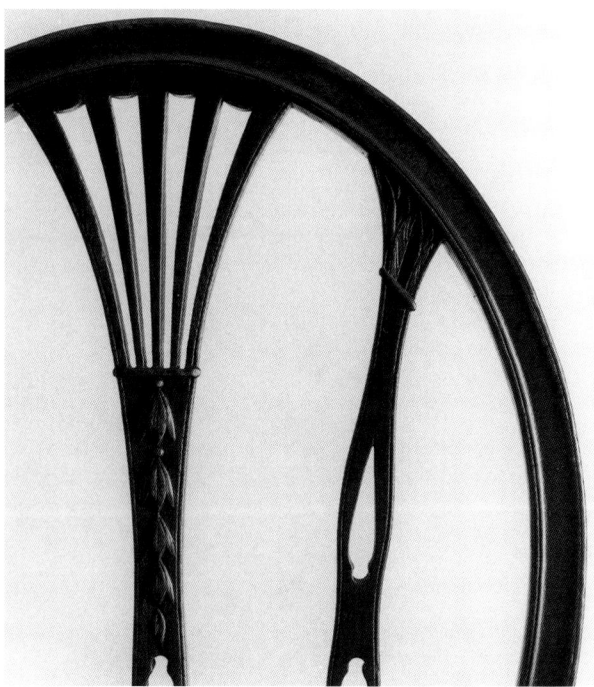 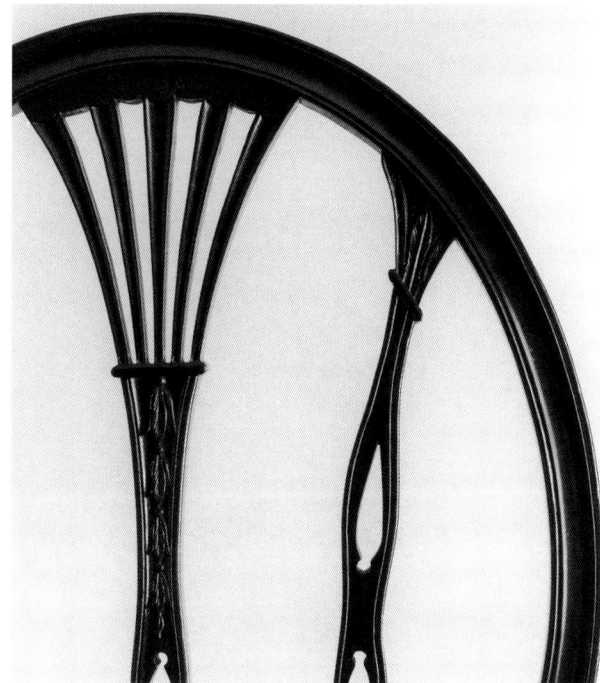

*Figure 33* Detail of the carved husks on the back of the side chair illustrated in fig. 31. (Photo, Gavin Ashworth.)

*Figure 34* Detail of the carved husks on the back of the side chair illustrated in fig. 32. (Photo, Gavin Ashworth.)

Potthast Brothers also made reproductions for several museums and historical organizations that were attempting to create room settings. Their institutional patrons included Continental Memorial Hall, the Museum of the Daughters of the American Revolution, and the Hammond-Harwood House. Many of the reproductions made for these organizations subsequently became part of the Potthasts' line. As in the case of the Carroll chairs, the firm used historical and institutional connections to promote their products.[30]

According to Theodore J. Potthast, a member of the second generation, most museums allowed their members to copy objects in their collection prior to the advent of licensing agreements. The firm's craftsmen would travel to a museum, make sketches, and, when no guards were present, they would take measurements. Theodore noted that he, his brother, and his cousins were adept at technical drawing owing to their training at the Maryland Institute College of Art. In September 1938 the *Baltimore Magazine* reported:

> Once [Potthast Brothers] received [an order] for something . . . not previously made—the initial step is for meticulously correct drawings to be made, together with minute descriptions of the wood and other necessary details. As an aid to securing such information, the company holds memberships in a number of the larger museums in this country.

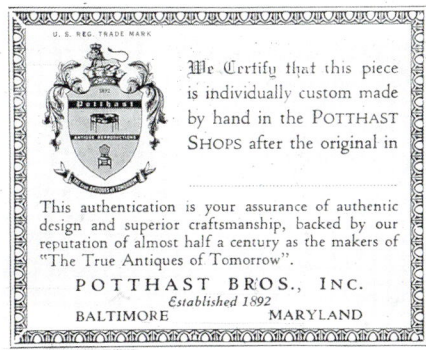

*Figure 35*  Potthast Bros., Inc., label for "Authenticated Replicas."

The Potthasts described their institutional reproductions as "authenticated replicas," and about 1930 they began identifying them with a label (see fig. 35). They also published a series of brochures, printed on an in-house press, devoted to the Metropolitan Museum of Art, Mount Vernon, Greenfield Village, the Philadelphia Museum of Art, and Colonial Williamsburg. Other museums and historic houses mentioned in general sales literature include the Brooklyn Museum; the Museum of Fine Arts, Boston; the Baltimore Museum of Art; the Minneapolis Museum of Art; the Cleveland Museum of Art; Dumbarton House; the Hammond-Harwood House; the Peggy Stewart House; the Brice House; Homewood; Mount Clare; Monticello; and Kenmore.[31]

Based on an example formerly in the Metropolitan Museum of Art (fig. 36), the sideboard illustrated in figure 37 was one of the Potthasts' most ambitious institutional reproductions. This model invariably has beautifully figured mahogany veneer and fine inlay work. A brochure published soon after the firm introduced the reproduction encouraged their customers to visit the museum and noted that "it stands without peerage among the exhibi-

*Figure 36*  Sideboard, New York, 1790–1810. Mahogany with unrecorded secondary woods. H. 41½", W. 72¾", D. 28¾". (Courtesy, Christie's.)

*Figure 37* Potthast Bros., Inc., "Metropolitan" sideboard, Baltimore, Maryland, ca. 1940. Mahogany with oak. H. 40½", W. 72", D. 24". (Private collection; photo, Gavin Ashworth.)

*Figure 38* Photograph showing the "Metropolitan" window display at the Potthast Bros., Inc., store at 924 North Charles Street, Baltimore, Maryland, ca. 1930. (Potthast family collection; photo, Harry B. Leopold.)

tion places of the earth . . . no other American institution . . . affords such charming demonstrations of home styles as shown in the American Wing." A window display at the firm's 924 North Charles Street location (fig. 38) was devoted to reproductions of pieces from the Metropolitan's collection and includes an example of this sideboard.[32]

A similar brochure capitalized on the allure of George Washington's home, Mount Vernon, arguably the most important "shrine" of the colonial revival:

*Figure 39*  Photograph showing the "Mount Vernon" window display at the Potthast Bros., Inc., store at 924 North Charles Street, Baltimore, Maryland, ca. 1930. This display may have been constructed in Febuary 1930 to commemorate Washington's birthday. (Potthast family collection; photo, Harry B. Leopold.)

George Washington, noted for his military qualities and his statesmanship, at Mount Vernon demonstrated his ability as a homemaker. He possessed discriminating taste in both [the] interior and exterior treatment of his home and, no doubt, was greatly assisted by his wife, Martha.

In this clever promotional piece, "discriminating taste" and "statesmanship" are given nearly equal billing. By purchasing reproductions from Potthast Brothers, modern consumers could identify themselves with George and Martha and the patriotic sentiments they and their home invoked. A window display at 924 North Charles Street (fig. 39) featured several reproductions derived from Mount Vernon furniture, the most notable of which was a sideboard like the example shown in figure 40. The "Mount Vernon" sideboard was second only to the "Metropolitan" example in design and popularity.[33]

*Figure 40*  Potthast Bros., Inc., "Mount Vernon" sideboard, Baltimore, Maryland, ca. 1940. Mahogany and mahogany veneer with unidentified secondary woods. (Courtesy, Potthast family collection.)

*Construction Techniques and the Identification of Potthast Furniture*

In addition to associating their work with objects in important auctions, private and public collections, and the homes of historical figures, the Potthasts used craftsmanship as a selling point for their furniture. They referred to their products as "individually hand-made" and used slogans proclaiming "the charm of . . . hand-made furniture." By contrast, most colonial revival furniture was mass-produced by large firms in Chicago, Illinois, Grand Rapids, Michigan, and other modern furniture centers. In these factories, which often employed as many as five hundred workers, mechanization was critical to cutting costs since these firms supplied the mail-order giants Sears Roebuck and Montgomery Ward, as well as smaller department stores across the country. Typical features of mass-produced furniture are doweled joints, machine-cut dovetails with rounded pins and tails, applied spindle or embossed "carving," and inlay decals.

Although the Potthasts used machinery and power tools, they described their firm as a "medium-size hand shop." In a brochure titled "Interesting Facts: Inside Secrets of Selecting Furniture Correctly," they claimed:

> Factory mass-made counterfeits . . . are lacking in distinction, values, and true charm. The reason [they] . . . will never . . . approach the inherent beauties of the great masterpieces is because the former are built in large quantities by machine methods. The genuine reproductions when made after the methods of the Old Masters are . . . INDIVIDUALLY MADE with infinite pains by an artistic craftsman . . . [and] will result in a rich piece that . . . becomes a masterpiece! When made in the Potthast shops, it will live forever as, "The True Antiques of Tomorrow" becoming as famous and its value apt to increase as much as those made by the Old Masters.

The Potthasts' brochures also advised consumers to avoid the work of "small shops," whose owners lacked "real knowledge of furniture designing," were "prone to clumsy proportions," executed "details poorly," and produced "crude carvings and poor workmanship." These remarks were probably designed to ward off competition from two local firms—J. W. Berry & Son (fl. 1899–1987), which specialized in the sale and repair of antique furniture, and Enrico Liberti (fl. 1930–1977), the proprietor of Chimney Corner Antiques. Liberti, who was born and trained in Italy, immigrated to Baltimore in 1920 and worked for Knabe Piano Company

*Figure 41* Drawing showing a chair leg being carved, in Potthast Bros., Inc., "Interesting Facts: Inside Secrets of Selecting Furniture Correctly," Baltimore, Maryland, 1935.

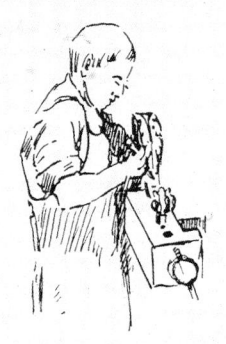

*Wood carvings not made of composition materials—and not made by machines and then "skinned" over—but actually carved out of the solid wood.*

*Figure 42*   Potthast Bros., Inc., carved rail from an unfinished "Duncan Phyfe" chair, Baltimore, Maryland, ca. 1940. Mahogany. Dimensions not recorded. (Potthast family collection.)

*Figure 43*   Potthast Bros., Inc., carved capital from an unfinished "colonial" chest of drawers, Baltimore, Maryland, ca. 1940. Mahogany. Dimensions not recorded. (Potthast family collection.)

before opening his own shop in 1930. Contrary to the Potthasts' claim, the Berry and Liberti shops both produced good reproductions using traditional craft methods and excellent materials.[34]

A "medium-size shop" like the Potthasts' typically employed ten to forty craftsmen who specialized in different aspects of production. The firm's use of the phrase "hand-made" did not exclude the use of power tools; rather it meant that machine-cut components were assembled, carved, and finished by hand. "Interesting Facts" illustrates and describes a variety of construction and carving techniques employed by Potthast Brothers and contrasts them with mass-production methods (fig. 41). The Potthasts noted that their carving was executed "in solid wood" rather than "composition materials 'skinned over' by machines." Details of a reproduction "Duncan Phyfe" chair (fig. 42) and a "colonial" chest of drawers (fig. 43) illustrate the quality of their work.[35]

Although the Potthasts used a variety of traditional construction methods including handcut dovetails, mortise-and-tenon joints, and fully paneled backs, they also employed some modern techniques. The firm's craftsmen cut, planed, and shaped their stock on machines, attached corner blocks with screws (fig. 44), and secured the tops of tables (fig. 45), sideboards, and

*Figure 44*   Detail of a corner block and brands on the side chair illustrated in fig. 14. (Photo, Gavin Ashworth.)

*Figure 45*   Detail of a top fastener used by Potthast Bros., Inc. (Photo, Gavin Ashworth.)

*Figure 46*   Potthast Bros., Inc., dining table, Baltimore, Maryland, ca. 1930. Mahogany with tulip poplar and oak. H. 29 3/4", W. 60" (without extra leaves), D. 44 1/4". (Courtesy, Maryland Historical Society.)

chests of drawers with metal fasteners. Because these fasteners "floated" in grooves, they allowed the top to expand and contract without splitting. Modern improvements of this type were acceptable provided they did not affect the outward appearance or accuracy of "authentic reproductions." As the mahogany "Hepplewhite" dining table illustrated in figure 46 reveals, however, the firm did not limit itself to replicas. This model, which appears in "Interesting Facts," was adapted from "a pair of end tables" and made to accommodate additional leaves.[36]

The woods used by Potthast Brothers were carefully selected for quality and figure and seasoned in a drying kiln at the factory. They purchased pulls, escutcheons, and other brass mounts from Faneuil Hall Hardware in Boston and inlay from Dover Inlay of New York. Many of the inlays were stock items, but some were custom-made. The paterae and husk designs shown in figure 47 are simplified versions of late-eighteenth- and early-nineteenth-century Baltimore inlays. The husks hang from an elliptical dot rather than an open ring and the petals are not shaded as strongly as those on period examples.[37]

During the construction process, Potthast craftsmen worked from full-scale drawings. The earliest drafts are on standard roller-type window shades (see fig. 48), which were more durable than later paper ones. Their drawing for the "Mount Vernon" sideboard is color-coded and shows all of the joinery details. The Potthasts' workmen undoubtedly used such drafts as templates as well as reference points for laying out joints and other details.

Many of the pieces made by Potthast Brothers are marked with labels, brands, or a combination of the two. The firm's printed address or slogan "The True Antiques of Tomorrow" (see fig. 49), which the Potthasts adopted after 1931, provides a rough chronology for their labels. Furniture

*Figure 47*  Detail of the inlay on a card table by Potthast Bros., Inc., Baltimore, Maryland, ca. 1930. (Courtesy, Maryland Historical Society.)

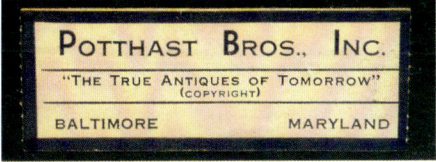

*Figure 49*  Potthast Bros., Inc., label, Baltimore, Maryland, 1930–1940.

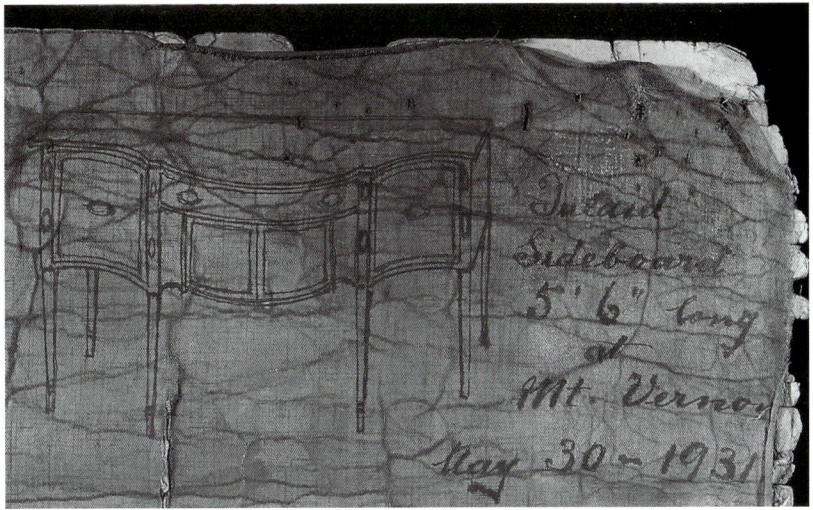

*Figure 48*  Potthast Bros., Inc., working drawings for the "Mount Vernon" sideboard, Baltimore, Maryland, 1931. (Courtesy, Potthast family collection.)

made after 1910 is often branded, although labels continued in use. The firm used two brands, one simply the name "POTTHAST" in block letters, the other a more elaborate oval mark (see figs. 44, 45). Case pieces usually have labels or brands on a backboard or on the interior of a drawer side, whereas tables, chairs, and sofas are frequently marked on the interior of the frame or on the inner surface of a leg. One antique sideboard, probably repaired by the firm, has the inscription "Potthast" penciled on the underside of its center drawer. The Potthasts also marked pieces made for family members. These objects include "authentic reproductions," adaptations, and items that were not part of their product line—jewelry boxes, mantle clocks, wall brackets, floor lamps, picture frames, and crucifixes. The last were typically made as presents for holidays and birthdays or to commemorate anniversaries and other special events.

*"The True Antiques of Tomorrow"*

The presence of Potthast furniture in such notable collections as those of the Maryland Historical Society, the Baltimore Museum of Art, and the Smithsonian Institution attests to the firm's success and its role in the development and promotion of the colonial revival style. When the Maryland Historical Society moved its headquarters into the Pratt-Keyser Building in 1919, the organization hired the Potthasts to make two large library bookcases with glazed doors. The bookcases were installed in the Keyser Building, which was added to the Enoch Pratt House (1846–48) in 1919. Sixty years later the society acquired a large group of Potthast furniture including a sideboard, dining table, card table, and chairs in recognition of the firm's contribution to the colonial revival and the history of cabinetmaking in Baltimore. It is in this and other institutional venues that the Potthasts' slogan "The True Antiques of Tomorrow" is ultimately validated.[38]

ACKNOWLEDGMENTS    The author is deeply grateful to the Potthast family, especially the late Theodore J. Potthast and his widow, Marie Corcoran Potthast, for sharing their documentary materials, personal accounts, and memories. For inspiration and encouragement beyond the scope of this article, the author thanks Gregory R. Weidman.

1. Potthast Bros., Inc., patented the slogan "The True Antiques of Tomorrow" (no. 13082) on March 10, 1931. Potthast Bros., Inc., "Interesting Facts: Inside Secrets of Selecting Furniture Correctly," 1935, p. 21; collection of author.

2. Interest in preindustrial craft methods and indigenous styles was at the core of the arts and crafts movement and of the Potthasts' philosophy. Several prominent craftsmen, including L. & J. G. Stickley, made reproductions of antique furniture before turning to the Mission style. See Wendy Kaplan, *"The Art That Is Life": The Arts & Crafts Movement in America, 1875–1920* (Boston: Museum of Fine Arts, Boston, 1987), for more on the relationship between the arts and crafts movement and the colonial revival. Potthast Bros., Inc., "Interesting Facts," p. 21. Although the Potthast brothers married other German-Americans and maintained social connections within Baltimore's large German-born population, the furniture produced and sold by their firm was thoroughly American in design. William B. Rhoads, "The Colonial Revival and the Americanization of Immigrants," in *The Colonial Revival in America*, edited by Alan Axelrod (New York: W. W. Norton, 1985). Kenneth L. Ames, "Introduction," in ibid., pp. 13–14.

3. Ames, "Introduction," pp. 13–14. For more on Hagen, see Deborah Dependall Waters, "Is It Phyfe?" in *American Furniture*, edited by Luke Beckerdite (Hanover, N.H.: University Press of New England for the Chipstone Foundation, 1996), pp. 63–81.

4. Letterbook 1: 1908–9, letterbook 2: 1914–17, letterbook 3: 1919, letterbook 4: 1920–21, letterbook 5: 1926–32, ms2183, library collection, Maryland Historical Society, Baltimore. Additional correspondence is in ms 2659. Harry B. Leopold (1891–1977) worked as a news photographer for the *Baltimore Sun* and the now defunct *News American*. He also operated a commercial photography business. Leopold's work illustrates many Baltimore buildings and businesses. His obituary was published in the July 22, 1977, issue of the *Baltimore Sun*. Sample book of photographs, Potthast family collection.

5. One brochure titled "Replicas from Collectors' Antiques" (ca. 1930) serves as a virtual bibliography for the firm's sales literature. It cites Thomas Chippendale's *The Gentleman and Cabinet-Maker's Director* (1754), George Hepplewhite's *The Cabinet-Maker and Upholsterer's Guide* (1788), Thomas Sheraton's *The Cabinet-Maker & Upholsterer's Drawing Book* (1793), and the Society of Upholsterer's *The London Cabinet-Maker's Book of Prices* (1788). This brochure also states that "[in addition to museums] there is . . . another genuine source of much reliable information that is available through distinguished authorities—writers of furniture history with many illustrations in their books."

6. Additional references include "Sheraton, 1751–1806," and "Hepplewhite, 1780 A.D." Robert and Elizabeth Shackleton, *The Quest of the Colonial*, 3d ed. (1906; reprint ed., New York: Century Co., 1921).

7. Jane S. Smith, *Elsie de Wolfe: A Life in the High Style* (New York: Atheneum, 1982). Elsie de Wolfe, *The House in Good Taste* (New York: Century Co., 1915), pp. 260–61.

8. Letterbook, 1907, p. 305, Potthast family collection. Mrs. Barbara White interviews with the author, Baltimore, Maryland, spring 1999. Mrs. White was the granddaughter-in-law of C. Wilbur and Edith Miller. No records supporting a business relationship between Edmunds and de Wolfe have surfaced, but it is possible that she was involved in the design of the Millers' chairs. This important suite of furniture represents the zenith of the colonial revival style and some of the finest custom designs of Potthast Bros., Inc.

9. Gregory R. Weidman, *Furniture in Maryland, 1740–1940: The Collection of the Maryland Historical Society* (Baltimore: Maryland Historical Society, 1984), pp. 210, 213.

10. *Das Neue Baltimore*, translated by Sister Benedicta, SSND (Baltimore: German Publishing Company, 1905), p. 174. This publication highlighted German-American businesses in Baltimore after the 1904 fire that destroyed seventy city blocks, more than fifteen hundred buildings, and twenty-five hundred businesses. For details of the fire, see Robert J. Brugger, *Maryland: A Middle Temperament 1634–1980* (Baltimore, Md.: Johns Hopkins University Press, 1988), p. 416.

11. For more on William Camp, see Gregory R. Weidman, "The Furniture of Classical Maryland," in *Classical Maryland, 1815–1845: Fine and Decorative Arts from the Golden Age* (Baltimore:

Maryland Historical Society, 1993). The Camp chest sold at Richard Opfer Auctioneers, Timonium, Maryland, in July 1994. Potthast Bros., Inc., to Mrs. Geo. H. Hills, Fall River, Massachusetts, May 23, 1907, letterbook, 1907.

12. Weidman, *Furniture in Maryland*, p. 235.

13. O. A. Kirkland Auctioneer, *Catalogue of the Celebrated Dr. William H. Crim Collection of Genuine Antiques*, Baltimore, April 22–May 2, 1903. Potthast, Bros., Inc., "Interesting Facts," illustration, p. 21.

14. Kirkland Auctioneer, *Crim Collection*, lot. 774.

15. *Report of the Maryland Commission to the Jamestown Ter-Centennial Exposition* (Baltimore, Md.: Williams & Co., 1908). Built in 1801, Homewood is owned by Johns Hopkins University and has been open to the public as a historic house museum since 1987. The Maryland Building from the 1907 Jamestown Exposition survives along with twelve of the original twenty-one state buildings. All are currently used as admirals' housing on the Norfolk Naval Base. C. F. Meislahn & Co. (w. 1887–1941) of Baltimore produced the interiors of the Maryland Building. The firm had made architectural models and done work for the 1904 restoration of the senate chamber in the Maryland State House in Annapolis in an effort to return the room to its Revolutionary era appearance. *Report of the Maryland Commission*. Loan inventory, letterbook, 1907.

16. *Report of the Maryland Commission*, pp. 38–42.

17. Letterbook, 1907.

18. Potthast Bros., Inc., to Tiffany Studios, New York, October 5, 8, and 19, 1907, letterbook, 1907.

19. *Baltimore City Directories*, 1928 and 1930.

20. Potthast Bros., Inc., "The 'Antiques of Tomorrow' Produced by Potthast Bros. Inc.," *Baltimore Magazine*, September 1938, pp. 21–23. Theodore J. Potthast, Jr., and Marie Corcoran Potthast, "Potthast Bros., Inc.: A Brief History," unpublished manuscript, 1990, n.p. Other Potthast genealogical information was derived from company letterheads, labeled family photographs, and interviews with various family members.

21. Potthast and Potthast, "Potthast Bros., Inc."

22. Fred Judd, "The Wonderful Potthast Past," *Baltimore Evening Sun*, October 3, 1985.

23. Lucien Rhodes, "Handmade Furniture: Potthast Closes after 85 years," *Baltimore Sun*, February 3, 1975. Judd, "The Wonderful Potthast Past."

24. American Art Association, *Colonial Furniture: The Superb Collection of the Late Howard Reifsnyder*, New York, April 24–27, 1929. American Art Association, *Colonial Furniture, Silver, and Decorations: The Collection of the late Philip Flayderman*, New York, January 2–4, 1930.

25. Potthast Bros., Inc., "Replicas from Collectors' Antiques," ca. 1930.

26. Potthast Bros., Inc., "Reproductions That Are An Investment," ca. 1930, p. 4.

27. Edgar G. Miller, Jr., *American Antique Furniture: A Book for Amateurs* (Baltimore, Md.: Lord Baltimore Press, 1937). The Potthasts' shop copy of this book is in a private collection.

28. Susan G. Tripp, "Homewood in Baltimore, Maryland," *Antiques* 133, no. 1 (January 1980): 248–57. Examples of similar chairs, or possibly others from this set, were in the Crim sale. This may have given the Potthast craftsmen additional exposure to this form.

29. Mrs. Muth was a descendent of Charles Carroll of Homewood. Theodore J. Potthast interview with the author, summer 1995, Baltimore, Maryland. Potthast Bros., Inc., "Interesting Facts:," p. 18.

30. Potthast Letterbooks, passim.

31. Theodore J. Potthast interview with the author, summer 1995, Baltimore, Maryland. Potthast Bros., Inc., "The 'Antiques of Tomorrow,'" pp. 2–4.

32. Potthast Bros., Inc., "The Metropolitan Museum," ca. 1930. The Metropolitan Museum of Art deaccessioned their sideboard at Christie's, *Important American Furniture, Silver, Folk Art, and Decorative Art*, New York, June 19, 1996, lot 179. For more on this sale, see *Maine Antique Digest*, August 1996, 20-E. The opening of the American Wing in the Metropolitan Museum of Art stimulated interest in antique furniture and fueled the demand for reproductions. The Potthasts' library includes a copy of R. T. H. Halsey and Charles Over Cornelius's *Handbook of the American Wing* (New York: Metropolitan Museum of Art, 1924). In 1936, the price of the "Metropolitan" sideboard was $415. Potthast Bros., Inc., "44th Anniversary—Expansion Sale."

33. Potthast Bros., Inc., "Mount Vernon," ca. 1930. In 1936 the price of the "Mount Vernon" sideboard was $240. Potthast Bros., Inc., "44th Anniversary—Expansion Sale."

34. Potthast Bros., Inc., "Interesting Facts." Weidman, *Furniture in Maryland*, pp. 14, 213–14, nos. 221, 252.

35. Ibid.

36. Weidman, *Furniture in Maryland*, pp. 259–60. Potthast Bros., Inc., "Interesting Facts," p. 2.

37. Theodore J. Potthast interview with the author, summer 1995, Baltimore, Md.

38. The Maryland Historical Society purchased a Potthast card table (67.57.11) in 1967, probably because it belonged to H. L. Mencken (1880–1956)—a journalist and essayist known as the "Sage of Baltimore." For more on the card table, see Weidman, *Furniture in Maryland*, p. 258. The society's collection of Potthast furniture also includes a "Crim" chair (57.3.6) and a "Key" chair (57.3.4). Both were added to the collection in 1957, while the Potthasts were still in business. Early on, the society recognized the significance of Dr. Crim's collection and sale and the importance of the Potthasts' decision to reproduce objects owned by him. For more on the sideboard, dining table, card table and chairs, see acc. 79.75.1–5, Maryland Historical Society.

Sumpter Priddy III,
J. Michael Flanigan, and
Gregory R. Weidman

The Genesis of
Neoclassical Style in
Baltimore Furniture

▼ ENGLISH TASTE *and workmanship have, of late years, been much sought for by surrounding nations . . . who seek a knowledge . . . in the various articles of household furniture.*

George Hepplewhite, *The Cabinet-Maker and Upholsterer's Guide* (1788)

In the aftermath of the Revolution, America's strong economy provided an opportunity for an unprecedented number of British artisans to escape the depression that had crept over the empire during the 1770s and 1780s. Ironically, these artisans helped to shape material culture in the new republic at precisely the point when Americans perceived themselves to be increasingly free of British influence.[1]

Of all the American cities, few benefited more strongly or more visibly from the influx of British artisans than did Baltimore—the most rapidly growing urban area during the last two decades of the eighteenth century. When John Moale made the original sketch for "Baltimore in 1752" (fig. 1) there were fewer than 30 houses and 250 inhabitants. By 1776 there were 564 houses and over 6,000 inhabitants. The population grew to 13,503 by 1790 and to 26,500 by 1800.[2]

Once a small trading center conveniently located at the juncture of the Patapsco River and the Chesapeake Bay, Baltimore became the leading port for the export of grain in America. Farmers in western Maryland, the Shenandoah Valley, and central Pennsylvania shipped vast quantities of flour and grain to Baltimore, where it was loaded onto ships bound for other American ports, Europe, and the West Indies. This hinterland also became an in-

*Figure 1*  Daniel Bowley, Esq., *Baltimore in 1752, From a Sketch Made by John Moale, Esq.*, Baltimore, Maryland, 1817. Aquatint. 19 1/2" × 29". (Courtesy, Museum of Early Southern Decorative Arts.)

creasingly important market for the products of Baltimore tradesmen as well as for European goods imported by the city's merchants. In 1770, British traveler William Eddis noted that the city was "the most wealthy and populous . . . in the province" and possessed a "well conducted and universal commercial connexion." Trade with the piedmont region was so lucrative that it "became an object of universal attention," attracting people of a "commercial and enterprising spirit . . . to this new and promising scene of industry." In the same year, Virginia diarist Mary Ambler wrote that she had "not heard of a single inhabitant who [did] not carry on a trade or follow some Business."[3]

Approximately thirty cabinetmakers worked as shop masters in Baltimore during the 1780s and early 1790s. At least 80 percent were born or trained in America and the vast majority came from Maryland. Only six cabinetmakers can be confirmed as adult British immigrants, of which three were English (Richard Lawson, Gualter Hornby, and William Singleton), two were Irish (John Dougherty and James McCormick), and one may have been Scottish (Thomas Aiton).[4]

Although small in number, these British artisans had a disproportionately large influence on Baltimore's art and culture. The largest and most clearly identifiable group of Baltimore neoclassical furniture reflects the strong influence of English taste and the skills and imagination of an artisan, or group of artisans, trained in a British metropolitan center. With their progressive forms and ambitious pictorial and naturalistic inlays, the earliest pieces document the flowering of neoclassical taste in urban Maryland during the mid-1780s. During the 1790s, the styles and construction techniques

*Figure 2*  Chest of drawers attributed to Bankson and Lawson, Baltimore, Maryland, 1785–1792. Mahogany and mahogany, maple, and satinwood veneer with tulip poplar and yellow pine. H. 34 3/4", W. 40 1/2", D. 22 1/2". (Private collection; photo, Gavin Ashworth.)

introduced by immigrant artisans filtered into Baltimore's furniture-making trades as their journeymen and apprentices established their own shops or went to work for other masters in the city.

*Urban British Influences in Baltimore Neoclassical Furniture*
The earliest furniture associated with these immigrant artisans appears to be the product of a single, previously unidentified shop. In the mid-Atlantic region, this shop was the first to engage in the large-scale production of British neoclassical forms such as serpentine sideboards and tambour and cylinder "writing tables" and desks. This shop also introduced sophisticated continental forms—albeit interpreted through the filter of British taste. These included blockfront and serpentine chests (see figs. 2, 3) radically different from other American examples and French style *secretaires à abattant* (see fig. 4)—the earliest neoclassical examples produced this side of the Atlantic.[5]

A serpentine chest (fig. 3), two writing tables with bookcases (figs. 5, 6), and several sideboards (see figs. 7, 8) suggest that the artisans in this shop trained abroad and arrived in America fully versed in the latest "antique" taste. Related forms appear in George Hepplewhite's *Cabinet-Maker and Upholsterer's Guide* (1788) (figs. 9–11), the Society of Upholsterer's *Cabinet-Makers' London Book of Prices* (1788) (fig. 12), and Thomas Shearer's *Designs for Household Furniture* (1788). The earliest pieces in the Baltimore group are stylistically rooted in the 1770s, however, and appear to predate these volumes. None of these publications illustrate designs that were new in the late 1780s; rather, they depict forms and decorative details that had been fashionable for over a decade. The accounts of British cabinetmakers working

*Figure 3*  Chest of drawers attributed to Bankson and Lawson, Baltimore, Maryland, 1785–1792. Mahogany and mahogany, maple, and satinwood veneer with tulip poplar, white pine, and yellow pine. H. 36¼", W. 39¼", D. 22⅛". (Courtesy, Colonial Williamsburg Foundation; photo, Hans Lorenz.) The inlay woods used by this shop include mahogany, maple, satinwood, rosewood, tulip poplar, and boxwood.

*Figure 4* *Secretaire à abattant* attributed to Bankson and Lawson, Baltimore, Maryland, 1785–1792. Mahogany and mahogany veneer with tulip poplar and yellow pine. H. 63 1/4", W. 40 3/8", D. 17 1/4". (Courtesy, Chrysler Museum of Art, Moses Myers House; photo, Gavin Ashworth.)

during the 1770s and early 1780s are replete with references to details used by this Baltimore shop.[6]

The advanced neoclassical style that emanated from this shop created a peculiar set of problems for the master to resolve. As the first in the region to use complex inlays, he had the option of importing them from abroad, purchasing them from a local inlay maker, or manufacturing them in his shop. A similar situation developed in Charleston, South Carolina, during the 1770s, but no other American parallels are known. In fact, the special circumstances that confronted these early masters were alleviated in the late 1780s by the growth of shops that specialized in the production of inlay medallions and ornamental banding that could be purchased in quantity and inserted in furniture when and where it was needed.[7]

Inlay making had been a specialty in Europe since the Renaissance, but it did not become widespread in America until the 1790s. The artisan who

*Figure 5* Writing table and bookcase attributed to Bankson and Lawson, Baltimore, Maryland, 1785–1792. Mahogany and mahogany veneer with tulip poplar and yellow pine. H. 83 1/4", W. 40 1/2", D. 24". (Private collection; photo, Gavin Ashworth.) This writing table and bookcase reportedly descended from Nicholas Rodgers of Druid Hill in Baltimore.

*Figure 6*   Writing table and bookcase attributed to Bankson and Lawson, Baltimore, Maryland, 1785–1792. Mahogany and mahogany veneer with tulip poplar and yellow pine. H. 83", W. 41½", D. 24". (Private collection, location unknown.)

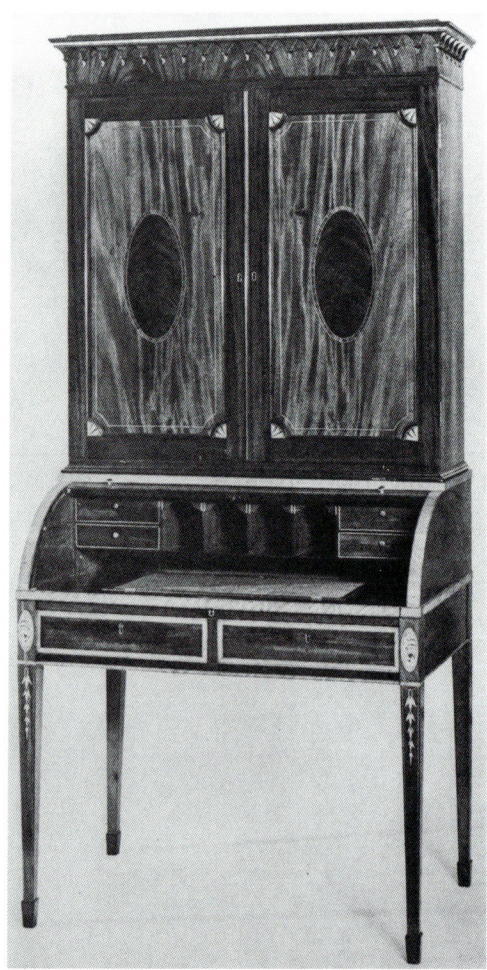

*Figure 7*   Sideboard attributed to Bankson and Lawson, Baltimore, Maryland, 1785–1792. Mahogany and mahogany veneer with tulip poplar and yellow pine. H. 37½", W. 76½", D. 25¾". (Private collection; photo, Gavin Ashworth.)

*Figure 8* Sideboard attributed to Bankson and Lawson, Baltimore, Maryland, 1785–1792. Mahogany and mahogany veneer with tulip poplar and yellow pine. H. 39 1/2", W. 79", D. 26". (Private collection, location unknown.) The shells on the upper leg stiles are exceptionally large.

*Figure 9* Design for a "Commode Dressing Table" illustrated on plate 77 of George Hepplewhite's *Cabinet-Maker and Upholsterer's Guide* (1788). (Courtesy, Winterthur Museum.) The second and third editions of Hepplewhite's design book appeared in 1789 and 1794, respectively.

*Figure 10* Design for a "Tambour Writing Table and Bookcase" illustrated on plate 69 of George Hepplewhite's *Cabinet-Maker and Upholsterer's Guide* (1788). (Courtesy, Winterthur Museum.)

*Figure 11* Design for a "Side Board" illustrated on plate 30 of George Hepplewhite's *Cabinet-Maker and Upholsterer's Guide* (1788). (Courtesy, Winterthur Museum.)

*Figure 12* Design for a "Serpentine Front Celleret Sideboard" illustrated on plate 4 of the Society of Upholsterers' *Cabinet-Makers' London Book of Prices* (1788). (Courtesy, Winterthur Museum.) The second and third editions of this publication appeared in 1793 and 1803, respectively. George Shearer provided the design for this sideboard.

produced the inlays on the earliest furniture attributed to this Baltimore shop was an exception. Working for or in close cooperation with the shop master, he produced inlays that were sophisticated in concept and carefully integrated into the design of each form. These inlays encompass a wide variety of subject matter including ribbons, husks, naturalistic foliage, rustic landscapes, animals, and classical and allegorical figures.

The chest of drawers illustrated in figure 13 has one of the most creative inlay designs found on American neoclassical furniture. The demonic face on

*Figure 13* Chest of drawers attributed to Bankson and Lawson, Baltimore, Maryland, 1785–1792. Mahogany and mahogany veneer with tulip poplar and yellow pine. H. 35 7/8", W. 37 1/8", D. 20 3/4". (Collection of Stiles Tuttle Colwill; photo, Gavin Ashworth.)

*Figure 14* Detail of the inlay on the skirt of the chest illustrated in fig. 13. (Photo, Gavin Ashworth.) Although the grotesque is extremely graphic, it is comprised of a small number of individual pieces. Its visual complexity is the result of careful shading with hot sand. Using this technique, the inlay maker gave the grotesque's forehead, ears, eyes, and cheeks a three-dimensional quality rarely seen in American inlay.

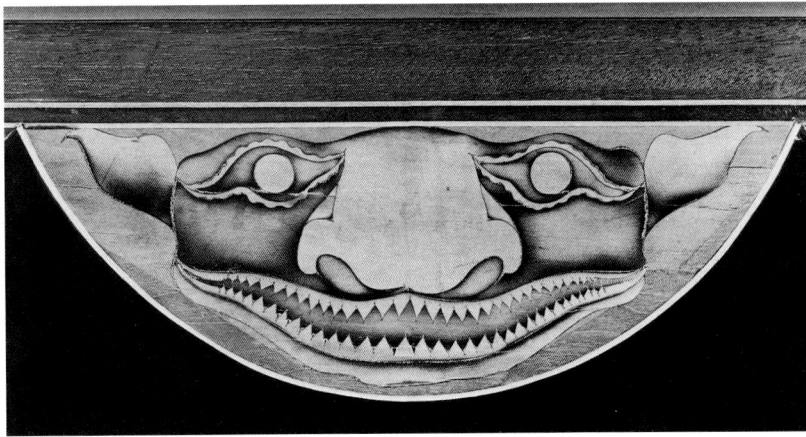

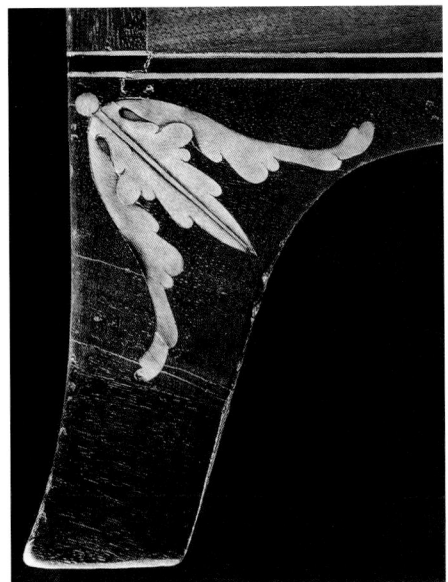

*Figure 15* Detail of the inlaid husk on the left foot of the chest illustrated in fig. 13. (Photo, Gavin Ashworth.) The husks are made in three pieces. The components on either side of the shaded central spine were stacked and then sawn to shape, rather than being cut out individually. The shaded central spine dividing each half is a separate piece. Numerous variations of this design occur on other pieces attributed to Bankson and Lawson.

*Figure 16* Detail of the inlay on the drawers of the chest illustrated in fig. 3.

the skirt (fig. 14) was almost certainly inspired by an early engraving, and may well represent Cerberus, the mythical three-headed dog that guards the gates of hell. Similar grotesques appear in a variety of seventeenth-century publications, including Daniel Rabel's *Cartouches de Différentes Inventions* (1632).

The techniques used by this inlay maker are very distinctive. His work is extremely graphic, but less complex than that of later inlay makers. The most ambitious figural medallions typically have less than twenty pieces, and the individual components are large and have relatively simple outlines (see figs. 14, 15). Their principal definition was accomplished with heated sand, which scorched the edges of selected pieces, and blue-green (copper) and red dyes.

Many of the inlays were made for specific locations on specific pieces. The leafy meanders on the drawer fronts of the chest illustrated in figure 3 are similar to those on the friezes of several bookcases in the group, but their scrolled ends were designed to wrap around and accentuate the neoclassical backplates (fig. 16). Even the most elaborate pictorial compositions ap-

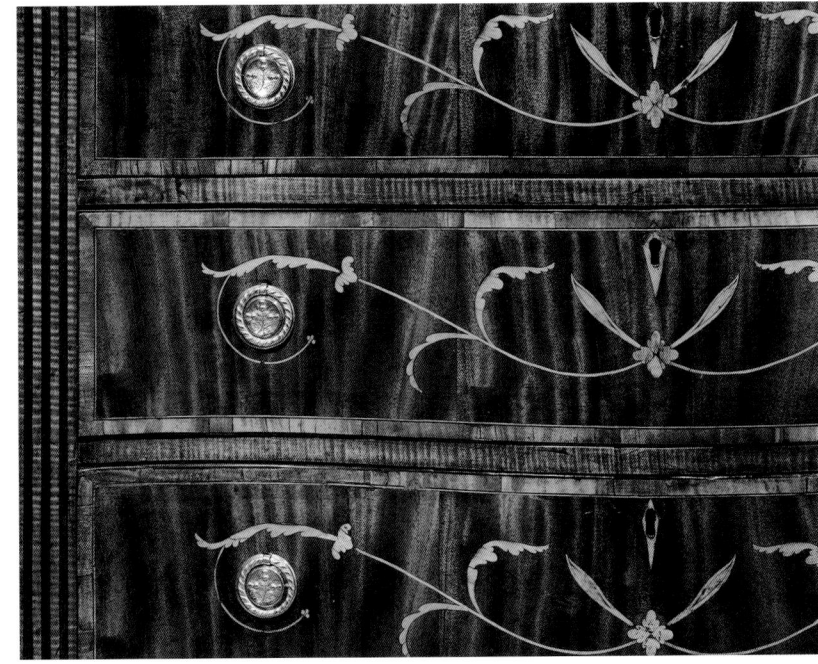

*Figure 17* Detail of the case construction of the chest illustrated in fig. 2. (Photo, Gavin Ashworth.)

*Figure 18* Detail of the base and foot construction of the chest illustrated in fig. 2. (Photo, Gavin Ashworth.)

pear to have been produced one at a time. Few of the subjects occur in multiples, and when they do, the images usually differ in size or detail.

Although the inlays on furniture in this Baltimore group are idiosyncratic, the construction of the earliest case pieces has parallels in contemporary London work. All of the desks, bookcases, and chests have dovetailed cases, and many of the bookcases have paneled backs. Drawer dividers are approximately three inches deep, and the dustboards behind them extend to the back of the case. Each dustboard is set into a groove on the back edge of the drawer divider and into dadoes in the sides of the case. To conserve materials and reduce the weight of the case, the cabinetmakers in this shop used thin dustboards with laminated strips that extend into the dadoes at each side (see fig. 17). They oriented the grain of the strips parallel to that of the dustboards so they would shrink and expand sympathetically, which helped prevent the sides from cracking. Even the base of one chest (fig. 2) is constructed in a similar manner (fig. 18). Strips glued at either end provided extra thickness and strength around the dovetails and allowed the maker to use a thinner and lighter board for the bottom. None of these structural features is unique, but in combination and in an American context they are exclusive to this shop.[8]

Four basic foot designs appear on pieces in the group. The ogee (see fig. 19) and French (see figs. 13, 14) forms are typically supported from behind by a single vertical block with smaller horizontal flankers. Cabriole feet (see fig. 4) are invariably cut from extensions of the front and rear stiles, just as they are on the Louis XV furniture that inspired them. The construction techniques for spade feet vary slightly according to the form of the case. On the serpentine chest illustrated in figure 3, the front feet are composed of two facings with a block behind. On the blockfront chest illustrated in figure 2, the front feet have three faces (fig. 18).

The finest serpentine and blockfront pieces (see figs. 2, 3) have drawers veneered with vertically grained crotch mahogany. Drawer "fronts veneered with upright birchings" were an option offered by the Gillow firm of London and Lancaster in 1789. Another stylish alternative was the use of oval or lozenge-shaped veneer panels, a more expensive option than the horizontally figured veneers found on most of the chests and desks in the early Baltimore group. On many of these pieces, the drawers are decorated with satinwood or mahogany banding and edged with light-and-dark stringing.[9]

The earliest hardware on furniture in the Baltimore group consists of two types—bail and rosette brasses and ring pulls with a single post. The ring pulls typically have cast or stamped backplates emblazoned with urns, husks, or floral designs. Stamped oval brasses with two posts do not appear on any pieces attributed to this shop, but they are common on later Baltimore work. The earliest known illustration of such brasses is in the appendix of the third edition of Sheraton's *Cabinet-Maker and Upholsterer's Drawing Book* (1802).[10]

The design, construction, and ornament of the furniture in the early Baltimore group suggest that the shop master was a British-trained immigrant conversant with the latest cabinetmaking techniques and neoclassical styles. His production of technically demanding forms, such as cylinder-front

*Figure 19* Desk-and-bookcase attributed to Bankson and Lawson, Baltimore, Maryland, 1785–1792. Mahogany and mahogany veneer with tulip poplar and yellow pine. H. 86", W. 41 1/2", D. 21 1/4". (Private collection; photo, Gavin Ashworth.)

desks, and careful integration of visually complex inlays indicate that he had worked in a large shop with a high degree of specialization. The only Baltimore cabinetmaker whose training and subsequent career fits all these criteria and dovetails with the dates assigned to the early Baltimore group is Richard Lawson (1749–1803).

*Authorship: The Case for Bankson and Lawson*

A strong case can be made for attributing all of the furniture in the early group to Lawson and his partner John Bankson (1754–1814). Lawson (fig. 20) was born at Keighley in Yorkshire, England, in 1749. He arrived in Baltimore by June 18, 1785, when he billed Richard Tilghman for a counting-house desk valued at £3.15, a bookcase valued at £12, and locks, hinges, and other hardware valued at £1.5. Two weeks later Lawson announced his partnership with Bankson:

> The subscribers, having formed a connection in the [cabinetmaking] . . . business, inform their friends, and the public, that they have removed to their large and convenient ware-house, next door to Mr. M'Candless's tavern and nearly opposite Messrs. Samuel and John Smith, merchants, in Gay-Street. As their joint stock in trade consists of a large and general assortment of mahogany, &c. they enabled to have on hand a variety of cabinet and chair work, of the most new and approved patterns, where their former customers in Town, on the Eastern Shore of Maryland, and elsewhere may be supplied at the shortest notice.

In a subsequent advertisement Lawson reported that he had "experience of 13 years, in Mr. Seddon's cabinet warehouse, in London . . . [where] he . . . acquired such knowledge in the business, as to give general satisfaction." His career provides one of the most significant connections to a prominent London cabinetmaker recorded in eighteenth-century America. No other Baltimore cabinetmaker boasted such credentials.[11]

Seddon and Sons was the largest furniture-making business in London in the last quarter of the eighteenth century. Founded by George Seddon (ca. 1727–1801) during the 1750s, the firm first appears in city directories in 1763. Newspaper accounts in 1768 reveal that the company employed eighty cabinetmakers and was "one of the most eminent . . . in London." Seddon and Sons expanded their operation during the 1760s and 1770s, hiring both local and provincial joiners. A disastrous fire that swept through their establishment in 1783 may have prompted Lawson to immigrate. By the time Lawson left, the company employed nearly three hundred workers. When German traveler Sophie von La Roche visited the reconstructed shop in 1786, she observed joiners, carvers, gilders, painters, upholsterers, drapers, glass grinders, and bronze casters—a workforce capable of manufacturing virtually anything Seddon's patrons demanded. This was the environment in which Lawson trained and worked.[12]

Seddon and Sons was one of the few British cabinetmaking firms that produced furniture for American patrons during the neoclassical period. Among the company's clients were Philadelphia financier William Bingham and his wife, Ann Willing. During a trip to Europe after the Revolution, they commissioned plans for a neoclassical townhouse from London archi-

*Figure 20*  Charles Peale Polk, *Richard Lawson*, Baltimore, Maryland, 1794. Oil on canvas. 37 1/2" × 33 1/2". (Courtesy, Maryland Historical Society.) The painting is signed and dated on the reverse: "Chas. P. Polk pinxt Baltimore, Maryland, November, 1794. Richard Lawson, son of Stephen and Agnes Lawson, born 25 December 1749 at Keigby, Yorkshire, England."

tect John Plaw. Subsequently built in Philadelphia, their home had carved reliefs on the façade, a formal garden furnished with classical statuary, and the earliest marble staircase recorded in America. When Englishman Henry Wansey visited in 1794, he wrote:

> [The Binghams have a] magnificent house and gardens in the best English style, with elegant and even superb furniture: the chairs of the drawing room were from Seddon's of London, of the newest taste; the back in the form of a lyre, adorned with festoons of crimson and yellow silk, the curtains of the room a festoon of the same.

Three years later, Baltimore merchant Hugh Thompson purchased a "Mahogany Writing Screen banded with sattin wood" and a "Sattin wood Oval Purse Table fine wood, rich Jappan'd center & highly varnished" from the firm, which had changed its name to Seddon Sons and Shackleton. These references document the demand for sophisticated neoclassical furniture similar to that produced by Bankson and Lawson.[13]

Bankson's early career differed significantly from Lawson's, but was equally important in the development of their business. The former was born on July 1, 1754, the son of Andrew and Sarah (Allen) Bankson of Philadelphia. If he was trained as a cabinetmaker, he probably completed his term by October 27, 1775, when he enlisted as an ensign in the Pennsylvania militia.

*Figure 21* Desk-and-bookcase, probably coastal South Carolina, ca. 1790. Mahogany and mahogany veneer with cypress. H. 96¼", W. 41¼", D. 21⅛". (Private collection; photo, Gavin Ashworth.)

Bankson was promoted to captain the following year and subsequently served as paymaster with various Pennsylvania regiments.[14]

Bankson's military career suggests that he had little exposure to the neoclassical style before moving to Baltimore in 1784, and that Richard Lawson was primarily responsible for the design of the firm's furniture. Evidence of the shop's work in the new taste is found in a series of advertisements in newspapers from both Baltimore and Charleston, South Carolina. On July 29, 1785, the *Maryland Journal and Baltimore Advertiser* reported that Bankson and Lawson had "a variety of cabinet and chair work, of the most new and approved patterns," and that "former customers in town, on the eastern shore of Maryland, and elsewere . . . [could] be supplied at the shortest notice." The following May, Bowen and Markland, the printers of the *Columbia Herald* in Charleston, stated that they would transmit orders for furniture to Bankson and Lawson. Among the forms the cabinetmakers advertised were mahogany desks priced at thirty-eight to forty-five dollars, bureau or dressing tables priced at twenty-four dollars, and fashionable "wardrobe[s] . . . with large drawers and sliding doors within, and large drawers below." Their use of the term "wardrobe" is significant, since it does not occur in British design books published before 1788. Bankson and Lawson's venture must have met with some success, for just over a year later Bowen and Markland advertised furniture made by Bankson and Lawson for a "gentleman lately deceased." Included were a wardrobe, sideboard, a set of "Northumberland" dining tables, a dozen vase-back chairs, and a pair of circular card tables—furniture unquestionably made in the neoclassical style.[15]

The frieze inlay on the desk-and-bookcase illustrated in figure 21 may have been inspired by one of the firm's low-country exports. Although the composition of the meander (fig. 22) has parallels in work associated with

*Figure 22*  Detail of the inlay on the pediment of the desk-and-bookcase illustrated in fig. 21. (Photo, Gavin Ashworth.)

Bankson and Lawson (see figs. 3, 7, 19), the design of the pediment, inlaid star, and cypress secondary woods suggest that the desk-and-bookcase is the product of a South Carolina shop (see fig. 23). None of the Baltimore meanders are engraved like those on the desk-and-bookcase (fig. 24); however, similar shading occurs on Charleston furniture from the mid-1770s to the late 1790s.[16]

Bankson and Lawson's advertisements also reveal that they operated a "Ware-house" and maintained stock-in-trade consisting of "a variety of ele-

*Figure 23*  Secretary-and-bookcase, Charleston, South Carolina, c. 1790. Mahogany and mahogany veneer with pine. Dimensions not recorded. (Private collection; photo, Gavin Ashworth.)

*Figure 24*  Detail of the inlay on the frieze of the desk-and-bookcase illustrated in fig. 21. (Photo, Gavin Ashworth.)

gant and useful furniture." They specified eighteen different furniture forms, most of which were available in "ornamented and plain" versions. Although most American cabinetmakers maintained a small inventory, few had the capital, credit, or workforce to support a warehouse. The federal census of 1790 reveals that the firm employed eight males over sixteen years of age and one younger male, making it the largest shop in eighteenth-century Baltimore—one of sufficient size to employ specialized tradesmen. No other furniture warehouse was recorded in Baltimore at that date.[17]

Lawson's background in one of the most accomplished circles of London's cabinetmaking trade and Bankson's strong regional connections all but guaranteed the success of their partnership. Within four years of establishing their business, they had attained an eminent position within Baltimore's cabinetmaking community. In 1788, they led the cabinetmakers in a procession celebrating the ratification of the Constitution, displaying an "ensign" representing a cabinet and emblazoned with the motto "May our cabinet be enriched by a union of the states."[18]

The firm's prominence is also suggested by its clients, who included members of Baltimore's wealthiest and most influential families. General Otho Holland Williams bought expensive settees from the partnership in 1789, and Charles Carnan Ridgely purchased at least £195 worth of unspecified furniture for his new country house, Hampton, in 1792. Located approximately twelve miles north of Baltimore, Hampton was built between 1783 and 1790 and was one of the largest houses in America. Throughout the 1790s, Ridgely furnished his home with expensive goods purchased from London, New York, and Baltimore.[19]

Like many of their contemporaries, Bankson and Lawson augmented their business by selling mahogany logs and planks and imported goods such as tea caddies, looking glasses, and upholstery fabrics. In the October 25, 1791, issue of the *Maryland Journal and Baltimore Advertiser*, they advertised "an assortment of hardware suitable for Cabinet-Makers." This implies that they had direct access to London, Birmingham, and Liverpool suppliers or their British agents and a broad range of options for the brasses they used. Bankson and Lawson must have been enjoying a brisk business at the time, since they also advertised for "a few good journeymen cabinet and chair-makers."[20]

On December 13, 1792, the *Maryland Journal and Baltimore Advertiser* reported that "the partnership of Bankson and Lawson will be dissolved on the 31st Instant, by mutual consent" and that Bankson proposed "to carry on the cabinet and chair manufactory in the same extensive line as heretofore." Six weeks later, Bankson advertised that he had formed a partnership with Robert Wilkinson (fl. 1793–1799), a former apprentice of Baltimore cabinetmaker William Askew (fl. 1780–1786). Bankson evidently retained all the tools, materials, cabinetwork, and imported goods from his former partnership. The dissolution of Bankson and Lawson and the subsequent formation of new businesses by the principals and their workmen contributed significantly to the dissemination of London neoclassical style in the Baltimore school.[21]

## Furniture Attributed to Bankson and Lawson

Richard Lawson's London training and his partnership with John Bankson provide strong circumstantial evidence for attributing all of the pieces in the early Baltimore group to their shop. The sophisticated construction, distinctive inlays, and chronology of forms—some of which combine late rococo and nascent neoclassical details—represent the work of a large, multifaceted cabinetmaking enterprise that flourished from the mid-1780s to

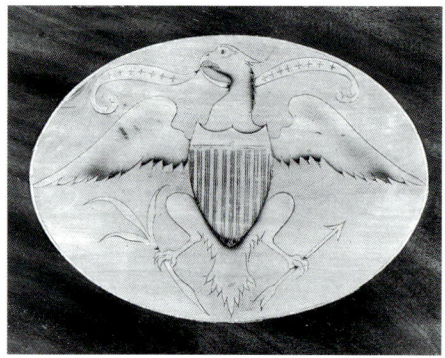

*Figure 25*  Detail of the eagle inlay on the fallboard of the desk-and-bookcase illustrated in fig. 19. (Photo, Gavin Ashworth.)

*Figure 26*  Desk-and-bookcase attributed to Bankson and Lawson, Baltimore, Maryland, 1785–1792. Mahogany and mahogany veneer with tulip poplar and yellow pine. H. 89", W. 42½", D. 20½". (Private collection; photo, Joel Breger.) The mullion arrangement on the bookcase appears related to that of a "Secretary and Bookcase" illustrated on plate 43 of George Hepplewhite's *Cabinet-Maker and Upholsterer's Guide* (1788).

the early 1790s. No other British furniture makers who immigrated to Baltimore established shops of this size or complexity during the period, and no larger group of contemporaneous furniture is known.[22]

From a stylistic standpoint, the desk-and-bookcase illustrated in figure 19 is one of the earliest pieces in the Baltimore group. Its slanted fall front, ogee feet, "Chinese" mullions, and bail-and-rosette brasses reflect conservative rococo tastes that fell from favor in Baltimore soon after the Revolutionary War. The construction of the case, and the design and execution of the eagle inlay on the fallboard (fig. 25) and meander on the frieze, however, clearly link it with the most advanced neoclassical pieces (see fig. 3) attributed to Bankson and Lawson. A smaller version of this eagle also appears on an inlaid oval on the prospect door of the writing compartment.[23]

The tambour writing tables and bookcases (figs. 5, 6) attributed to Bankson and Lawson are among the earliest American examples and may predate the firm's cylinder-front forms. In 1788, Hepplewhite noted that writing tables were "very convenient . . . answering all the uses of a desk, with a much lighter appearance." The legs on the example illustrated in the *Cabinet-Maker and Upholsterer's Guide* are relatively plain, whereas those on the Baltimore writing tables are decorated with ovals and graduated pendant husks.[24]

Cylinder-front forms were particularly well suited for the display of elaborate pictorial inlays. The desk-and-bookcase shown in figure 26 has an oval panel inlaid with a stag and hound (fig. 27) derived from an allegorical illustration similar to those depicting Aesop's fables. British carver Thomas Johnson used allegorical imagery in his publications for furniture and architectural details, and his apprentice Hercules Courtenay introduced many of his master's designs when he immigrated to Philadelphia in 1765. The continued popularity of these designs in the mid-Atlantic region is demonstrated by an advertisement for Thomas Johnson's *One Hundred and Fifty New Designs* (1758) in the November 18, 1783, issue of the *Maryland Journal and Baltimore Advertiser*.[25]

*Figure 27* Detail of the stag and hound inlay on the cylinder of the desk-and-bookcase illustrated in fig. 26.

*Figure 28* Desk attributed to Bankson and Lawson, Baltimore, Maryland, 1785–1792. Mahogany and mahogany veneer with tulip poplar and yellow pine. H. 44 1/2", W. 42 1/2", D. 20 1/2". (Courtesy, Israel Sack, Inc.)

Three cylinder-front desks (see fig. 28) attributed to Bankson and Lawson are known, the most elaborate of which have large eagle inlays and shaped skirts veneered with satinwood. Identical inlays appear on several pieces in the group, including the *secretaire à abattant* illustrated in figure 4 and the clothespress shown in figure 29. The cylinders and writing slides on furniture attributed to Bankson and Lawson are not connected and require the user to raise the former before pulling out the latter. Later cabinetmakers improved this design by constructing a cylinder that retracts when the slide is pulled out, a mechanism described in Thomas Sheraton's *Cabinet-Maker and Upholsterer's Drawing Book* (1793).[26]

A clothespress with a secretary drawer (fig. 29) is one of the most elaborate case pieces attributed to Bankson and Lawson. The pediment, prospect door, and skirt have exceptional pictorial inlays, and the upper doors have large ovals set in mitered fields similar to those on the cylinders of several desks and desk-and-bookcases (see figs. 26, 28). Like most Maryland clothespresses, this example has doors below the writing compartment and, presumably, linen drawers behind the doors. The grotesque inlay on the skirt is virtually identical to that on the early straight-front chest (figs. 13, 14).[27]

*Secretaires à abattant* are the most distinctive writing forms associated with Bankson and Lawson's partnership. The earliest example (fig. 4) is tripartite in design, with a tambour upper section, writing compartment concealed by a large inlaid fall front, and three drawers below. As this piece sug-

*Figure 29* Clothespress with secretary drawer attributed to Bankson and Lawson, Baltimore, Maryland, 1785–1792. The current location of this piece is not known. It was illustrated in Parke-Bernet Galleries, *The William Randolph Hearst Collection,* New York, November 17, 1938, lot 385.

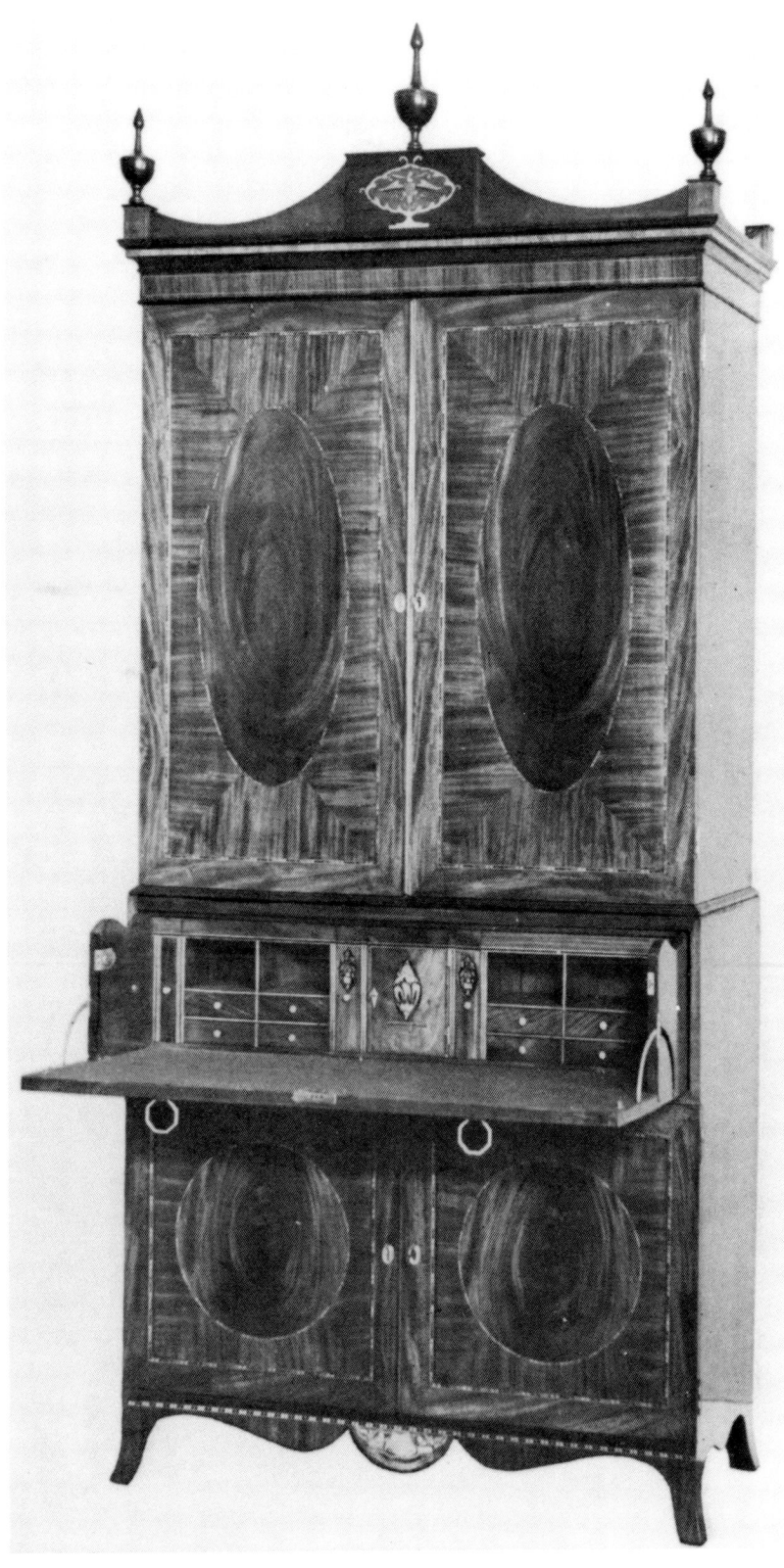

gests, French styles had a strong influence on British neoclassical design. The cabriole feet, flush-joined case sides, and vertical tambour have parallels in *secretaires à abattant* and armoires from France and areas of transplanted French culture. The tambour segments are relatively thick, ovoid in

cross section, and decorated with the same multicolored, segmented block inlay found on the edges of the drawers, doors, and cases of several other pieces in the group. The stiles have inlaid pilasters with capitals composed of stylized leaves (fig. 30)—a detail that occurs on several related tall clock cases—similar to those on the skirt below (fig. 31).

*Figure 30* Detail of the right inlaid capital of the *secretaire à abattant* illustrated in fig. 4. (Photo, Gavin Ashworth.)

*Figure 31* Detail of the inlay on the skirt on the *secretaire à abattant* illustrated in fig. 4. (Photo, Gavin Ashworth.)

The original owner of the *secretaire à abattant* (fig. 4) was Norfolk, Virginia, merchant Moses Myer. He may have purchased the piece shortly after the completion of his stylish neoclassical house in 1792, the final year of Bankson and Lawson's partnership. Many merchants and planters in eastern Virginia owned Baltimore furniture after 1790.[28]

Sideboards with deep drawers and storage compartments were relatively new forms during the period when Lawson worked in Seddon's shop and they appear to have been one of the mainstays of his and Bankson's business. Commode examples (see figs. 7, 8, 32, 33) were available in a variety of forms, the most architectural of which have arched spandrels and keystones below the center drawer. The husks on the sideboard illustrated in

*Figure 32* Sideboard attributed to Bankson and Lawson, Baltimore, Maryland, 1785–1792. Mahogany and mahogany veneer with tulip poplar and yellow pine. H. 39¼", W. 58⅞", D. 25¼". (Courtesy, Baltimore Museum of Art; purchased as the gift of Mr. and Mrs. Kenneth S. Battye.) The brasses are replaced.

*Figure 33* Sideboard attributed to Bankson and Lawson, Baltimore, Maryland, 1785–1792. Mahogany and mahogany veneer with tulip poplar and yellow pine. H. 40 1/4", W. 69 1/2", D. 26". (Private collection; photo, Sotheby's.)

figure 7 and birds on the example shown in figure 8 appear on other pieces in the group (see figs. 15, 40), although few equal them in scale. With their geometric veneers and striking inlays, these sideboards undoubtedly occupied a prominent position in the households of their owners. George Hepplewhite noted that "the great utility of this piece of furniture has procured it a very general reception, and the conveniences it affords renders a dining room incomplete without a sideboard."[29]

Some of the commode sideboards attributed to Bankson and Lawson have central cabinets or drawers rather than an arched skirt with spandrels.

*Figure 34* Sideboard attributed to Bankson and Lawson, Baltimore, Maryland, 1785–1792. Mahogany and mahogany veneer with tulip poplar and yellow pine. H. 37 1/2", W. 69 1/2", D. 27 1/2". (Courtesy, Israel Sack, Inc.)

*Figure 35* Sideboard attributed to Bankson and Lawson, Baltimore, Maryland, 1785–1792. Mahogany and mahogany veneer with tulip poplar and yellow pine. H. 40 1/2", W. 72 3/8", D. 27 7/8". (Courtesy, Diplomatic Reception Rooms, United States Department of State; gift of Mr. and Mrs. Mitchell Taradash.)

An example that reputedly descended in a family from Sandy Spring, Maryland (fig. 32), was clearly made for a niche, and its small size suggests that it may have been one of a pair. A larger, more elaborate sideboard (fig. 33) has leafy meanders on the upper leg stiles and satinwood banding on the lower cabinets and drawers. The husk pendants on the legs of these examples are miniature versions of those on the feet (fig. 15) of the straight-front chest (fig. 13) and spandrels of the sideboard shown in figure 7.[30]

Bowfront sideboards similar to those attributed to Bankson and Lawson became popular in England during the 1770s. In 1778, George Seddon invoiced one of his patrons for a "sweep front sideboard with . . . wine keeper in each end." The bowfront sideboards in the early Baltimore group (see figs. 34, 35) are similar in form. All have long central drawers surmounting an arched skirt and a deep door or drawer on either side. One has no inlays, but the others display a variety of decorative options including shells, fans, husks, and vase-and-flower inlay. The sideboard shown in figure 35 was undoubtedly more expensive than the one illustrated in figure 34. The former has stiles with elaborate vase-and-flower inlays and spandrels with three-petal leaf motifs.[31]

*Continuing the Shop Tradition: Artisans Associated with Bankson and Lawson*
In the absence of signed or labeled furniture by Bankson and Lawson, the most direct link between their shop and the early Baltimore group is a tall clock case (fig. 36) bearing the label (fig. 37) of their former apprentice William Patterson (1774–1816). By the time Patterson completed his term in

*Figure 36*  Tall clock case by William Patterson, Baltimore, Maryland, ca. 1797. Mahogany and mahogany veneer with tulip poplar and yellow pine. H. 90", W. 21 1/8", D. 9 1/2". (Private collection; photo, Gavin Ashworth.) The case has an eight-day movement by Baltimore clockmakers Mountjoy and Welsh (w. 1797).

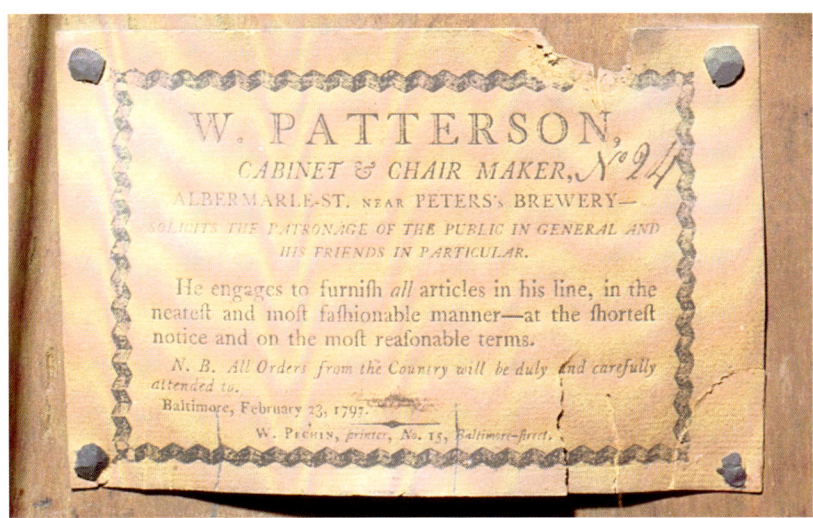

*Figure 37*  Detail of the label on the tall clock case illustrated in fig. 36. (Photo, Gavin Ashworth.)

1795, he had incorporated the unusual combination of London structure and design and the idiosyncratic inlays characteristic of his masters' shop.[32]

Patterson's clock case has a broken-scroll pediment with a pierced tympanum and naturalistic inlays that are clearly derived from case pieces made a decade before he established his shop. The folded leaves on the waist door (fig. 38) have distinctive rounded lobes identical to those on numerous pieces in the group, including the drawers of the serpentine chest (figs. 3, 16) and friezes of several bookcases (see figs. 5, 19, 21, 26). The finished edges of these leaves appear to have been cut with carving tools—the same type of gouges used to clean up the sawn outline of tympana piercings on this and other related tall clock cases. Similarly, the shell on the plinth of the Patterson clock (fig. 39) is one of several closely related variants found on earlier pieces, including the fallboard of a desk and skirt of the serpentine chest (fig. 3).[33]

On November 20, 1800, Patterson purchased 238 "shells" from the estate of Thomas Barrett, the earliest professional "ebonist" documented in Baltimore. Two days later, the *Baltimore American* reported that Patterson had begun the "Manufacturing of Stringing, Banding and Shells of every description at No. 24 Albemarle Street, Old Town." The timing of Patterson's advertisement suggests that he was attempting to attract Barrett's clientele. The former remained in business until 1817.[34]

*Figure 38* Detail of the inlay on the waist door of the tall clock case illustrated in fig. 36. (Photo, Gavin Ashworth.)

*Figure 39* Detail of the shell on the plinth of the tall clock case illustrated in fig. 36. (Photo, Gavin Ashworth.)

Barrett is first recorded as an independent artisan on February 18, 1795, barely six weeks after Bankson and Wilkinson dissolved their partnership. The fact that Patterson acquired inlays from Barrett's estate that were compatible with those on earlier pieces attributed to his master, suggest that Barrett may have worked for Bankson and Lawson, Bankson and Wilkinson, or both.[35]

In Baltimore, the trade of an ebonist involved two allied skills—inlay making and cabinetmaking. This duality is implied in John Lennox's apprenticeship agreement with Barrett, wherein the latter agreed to provide instruction in the "cabinetmaking" and "inlaying" trades. This indenture also suggests that Barrett was well established, and that he had previously worked in a shop where those trades had coexisted.[36]

Cabinetmaker William Singleton (1757–1803) may also have been associated with Bankson and Lawson. Described as a "native of England," he first appears in Baltimore records in a petition supporting local manufactures submitted to the United States House of Representatives in March 1789. On May 18, 1790, Singleton reported that he and William McFadon had formed a partnership in the cabinetmaking business and that one of the principals had "experience in Europe" and "different parts of this continent." The partners also boasted that "their Manufactures will be found equal to any imported, or made on the Continent." Newspaper advertisements suggest that McFadon was in the lumber business with Richard Lawson at this time. Singleton may also have worked with Lawson when he first moved to town. If so, that would explain how he came to know his future partner McFadon.[37]

Singleton's later connections to Lawson are easily verified. The former's father-in-law, William Slater, was an immigrant hardware merchant whose second wife, Hannah (James), was Lawson's sister-in-law. Both men were actively involved in St. Paul's Church and had businesses that were, at the

*Figure 40*  Tall clock case with eight-day movement by William Thompson, Baltimore, Maryland, ca. 1794. Mahogany and mahogany veneer with tulip poplar and yellow pine. H. 98 1/4", W. 22 1/2", D. 11 1/2". (Private collection; photo, Jeff Goldman.) The tympanum, scroll moldings, and feet are replaced. The original feet were almost certainly ogee in form.

very least, indirectly connected. Goods for Slater's hardware store occasionally arrived on Lawson's ship, the *Diana*.[38]

By July 30, 1793, Singleton and McFadon had moved their shop to Water Street, in the heart of the business district. Their partnership ended three years later, and Singleton moved back to 11 North Gay Street. By this time, he must have been a prominent member of Baltimore's cabinetmaking trade. Merchant Hugh Thompson purchased over £230 worth of mahogany furniture from him in the late 1790s.[39]

*Furniture Attributed to the Bankson and Lawson School*
A large group of Baltimore furniture made between 1795 and 1805 shares details with work attributed to Bankson and Lawson. Variations in the construction and design of the objects in this later group suggest that the pieces represent the work of several different tradesmen, which should come as no surprise given the size and complexity of Bankson and Lawson's shop. Although cataloging all of these objects is outside the scope of this article, a survey of several different forms suggests the influence that the partnership had on Baltimore neoclassical furniture.

Many Baltimore tall clock cases have inlays similar to those used by Bankson and Lawson; however, most have movements that postdate the partnership and cases that probably represent the work of journeymen. Among the earliest examples are a case with a movement by William Thompson (w. 1796–1822) (fig. 40), a case with a movement by William Elvins (w. 1795–1816) (figs. 41, 42), and a case with an unsigned movement (fig. 43). The Thompson and Elvins clocks have ogee feet, square plinths, minimal stringing, and inlays that are both technically and stylistically related to those on furniture attributed to Bankson and Lawson. The Thompson clock also has inlaid birds that are virtually identical to those on the sideboard illustrated in figure 8, and the Elvins clock has spandrel inlays that are comprised of large segments (fig. 42) assembled in the same manner as many of the husks and floral designs in the early group. The tall clock case with the unsigned movement (fig. 43) is one of the most ornate Baltimore examples from the last decade of the eighteenth century. Its advanced neoclassical style—evident in the satinwood fields and crossbanding of the door and plinth and lavish inlay—places it squarely in the Bankson and Lawson shop tradition. Similarly, the oriole on the pediment (fig. 44) displays the same workmanlike techniques and creative design found on pictorial inlays in the early group.[40]

*Figure 41*  Tall clock case with eight-day movement by William Elvins, Baltimore, Maryland, 1795–1800. Mahogany and mahogany veneer with tulip poplar and yellow pine. H. 96 1/2", W. 19 1/2", D. 10 3/8". (Private collection; photo, Gavin Ashworth.)

*Figure 42*  Detail of the hood of the tall clock case illustrated in fig. 41. (Photo, Gavin Ashworth.)

86   PRIDDY / FLANIGAN / WEIDMAN

*Figure 43*  Tall clock case, Baltimore, Maryland, 1795–1800. Mahogany and mahogany veneer with tulip poplar and yellow pine. H. 102½", W. 20", D. 10". (Private collection; courtesy, Israel Sack, Inc.)

*Figure 44*  Detail of the oriole inlay on the pediment of the tall clock case illustrated in fig. 43.

*Figure 45* Tall clock case, possibly Baltimore, Maryland, 1795–1805. Mahogany and mahogany veneer with tulip poplar and yellow pine. H. 104 1/2", W. 21 1/2", D. 10". (Private collection; photo, Gavin Ashworth.)

*Figure 46* Detail of the hood of the tall clock case illustrated in fig. 45. (Private collection; photo, Gavin Ashworth.)

The inlays on a slightly later tall clock case (fig. 45) indicate that it belonged to a mason. Emblems of the craft include the compass, square, and plumb rules on the pediment (fig. 46), and Corinthian capital on the plinth (fig. 47). The most conspicuous symbol, however, is the figure on the waist door, which may depict the new republic's most renowned leader and mason, George Washington (1732–1799), with his left elbow resting on a column and his right hand holding a square (fig. 48). Figural inlays by the same maker appear on pieces attributed to Bankson and Lawson's shop.[41]

*Figure 47*  Detail of the inlay on the plinth of the tall clock case illustrated in fig. 45. (Private collection; photo, Gavin Ashworth.)

*Figure 48*  Detail of the inlay on waist door of the tall clock case illustrated in fig. 45. (Private collection; photo, Gavin Ashworth.)

*Figure 49* Secretaire à abattant attributed to Bankson and Lawson, Baltimore, Maryland, ca. 1792. Mahogany and mahogany veneer with tulip poplar. H. 82", W. 37", D. 17¼". (Private collection; photo, Jeff Goldman.)

*Figure 50* Detail of the figural inlay on a front stile of the *secretaire à abattant* illustrated in fig. 49. The maker of this inlay was occasionally indifferent to anatomy. The feet of the flutist are brought to a point like the toes of the bird and animal inlays shown in figs. 25, 27, and 44.

A *secretaire à abattant* (fig. 49) from the early 1790s helps bridge the gap between their firm's work and that of their journeymen and apprentices. Like the Moses Myers example, this *secretaire à abattant* has a framed case, tripartite facade, and simple board top. Although most of the distinctive structural details and continental designs introduced by Bankson and Law-

*Figure 51* Card table (one of a pair), Baltimore, Maryland, 1795–1800. Mahogany and mahogany veneer with tulip poplar, yellow pine, and oak. Dimensions not recorded. (Private collection; photo, Gavin Ashworth.) The undersides of the tops are inscribed "P Lightfoot/ Port Royal."

*Figure 52* Detail of the lily inlay on the card table illustrated in fig. 50. (Photo, Gavin Ashworth.)

son were subsequently abandoned by the artisans who had worked for them, inlays associated with their shop appear on later pieces made in Baltimore and its hinterland. The classical flutists capping the pilasters (fig. 50), for example, appear to be by the same inlay maker responsible for the figure on the preceding clock case (fig. 48).

No tables or chairs can be definitively attributed to Bankson and Lawson, but a pair of card tables (see fig. 51) that originally belonged to Philip Lightfoot of Port Royal, Virginia, are clearly part of their shop tradition. The lily inlays at the top of each front leg (fig. 52) have outlines that are remarkably similar to those of the feet on the eagle and oriole inlays shown in figures 25 and 44 and the classical flutists (fig. 50) on the *secretaire á abattant*. Like the serpentine and blockfront chests attributed to Bankson and Lawson, the Lightfoot tables are exceptionally bold forms. Possible sources for the shape of their frames and tops are a pier table illustrated on plate 64 of Hepplewhite's *Cabinet-Maker and Upholsterer's Guide* and a card table illustrated on plate 11 in the appendix of Sheraton's *Cabinet-Maker and Upholsterer's Drawing Book*.

The side chairs illustrated in figures 53, 56, and 57 may also be part of the Bankson and Lawson shop tradition. An example reputedly found on the eastern shore of Maryland has vine inlay and ebonized cuffs (figs. 53, 54) related to those on the Lightfoot card tables (figs. 51, 55). Another shield-back chair of a different pattern (fig. 56) has vertical slats with leaf inlays whose edge profiles and central spine appear to have been derived from earlier work associated with Bankson and Lawson's shop.[43]

The vase-back side chair illustrated in figure 57 also has related inlay. Although its back design is unconventional, it has parallels in published engravings, including plate 4 of Hepplewhite's *Cabinet-Maker and Upholsterer's Guide*. Bankson and Lawson made vase-back chairs as early as 1788, when the printers of the *Columbia Herald* advertised "one dozen Vanzebank chairs with two Elbow ditto to suit" made by the firm for a "gentleman lately deceased."[44]

These later objects only begin to suggest the influence that Bankson and Lawson had on Baltimore furniture in the neoclassical style. Although their

*Figure 53*  Side chair, Baltimore, Maryland, 1795–1800. Mahogany with maple and tulip poplar. H. 38", W. 19 7/8", D. 18 1/2". (Courtesy, Colonial Williamsburg Foundation.)

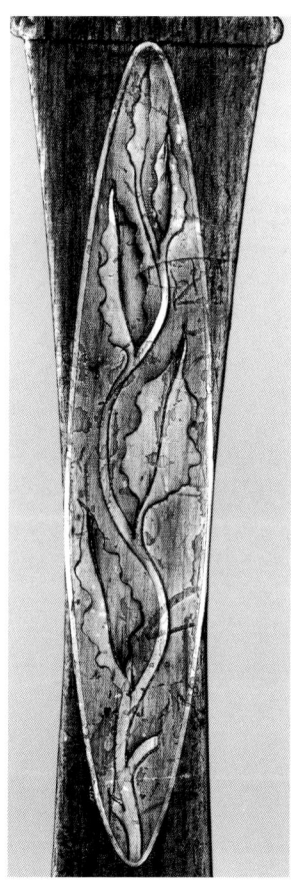

*Figure 54*  Detail of the vine inlay on the back of the side chair illustrated in fig. 53.

*Figure 55*  Detail of the vine inlay on the card table illustrated in fig. 51. (Photo, Gavin Ashworth.)

*Figure 56*  Side chair, Baltimore, Maryland, 1795–1805. Mahogany with tulip poplar. H. 37 3/4", W. 20 1/4", D. 17 1/2". (Courtesy, Winterthur Museum.)

*Figure 57*  Side chair, Baltimore, Maryland, 1795–1805. H. 37 1/4". Mahogany; secondary woods not recorded. (Courtesy, Museum of Early Southern Decorative Arts.)

partnership lasted only seven years, they assembled a large workforce capable of producing London-style furniture as well as pieces that accommodated more conservative Baltimore tastes. With the dissolution of their partnership and subsequent establishment of new businesses by their journeymen and apprentices, their shop tradition extended into the early years of the nineteenth century. Much of the stylistic vocabulary they introduced has become synonymous with Baltimore's neoclassical school.

ACKNOWLEDGMENTS  For assistance with this article, the authors thank Gavin Ashworth, Wendy Battaglino, Frank Horton, Deanne Levison, Martha Rowe, Jane Webb Smith, and all of the institutions and individuals who allowed them to inspect and illustrate their furniture. Special thanks are due to Ronald L. Hurst for his substantial intellectual contributions and Ann Rodgers Haley, Joan Quinn, Page Talbott, and Michael Hall for their genealogical research.

1. George Hepplewhite, *The Cabinet-Maker and Upholsterer's Guide* (1788), preface.

2. Wilbur H. Hunter, "Baltimore in the Revolutionary Generation," in *Maryland Heritage: Five Baltimore Institutions Celebrate the American Bicentennial*, edited by John B. Boles (Baltimore: Maryland Historical Society, 1976), p. 189.

3. From a letter by William Eddis in *Letters from America*, edited by Aubrey C. Land (Cambridge, Mass.: Belknap Press, 1969), p. 13. Gary B. Nash, *The Urban Crucible: Social Change, Political Consciousness, and the Origins of the American Revolution* (Cambridge: Harvard University Press, 1979), p. 408.

4. Richard Lawson's birthplace is recorded on the painting illustrated in fig. 20. Gualter Hornby's name appears in the Baltimore County Naturalization Docket (Robert Barnes, *Baltimore Naturalizations, 1796–1803*, a supplement to the *Baltimore Town and Fell's Point Directory of 1796* [1796; reprint ed., Silver Spring, Md.: Family Line Publications, 1983], p. 61). William Singleton is described as a "native of England" in the records of St. Paul's Parish (Bill and Martha Reamy, *Records of St. Paul's Parish,* 2 vols. [Westminster, Md.: Family Line Publications, 1989], 2:23). John Dougherty and James McCormick were described as being from Great Britain in the Baltimore County Naturalization Docket (Barnes, *Baltimore Naturalizations*, p. 59). For more on McCormick, who was born in County Tyrone, Ireland, see Dr. J. Hall Pleasants Files in Early American Portraiture, file no. 513, Gallery Office, Maryland Historical Society, Baltimore (hereafter cited MHS). In the February 21, 1786, issue of the *Maryland Journal and Baltimore Advertiser*, McCormick reported that he had "for some years past worked in the first shops in Dublin. Aiton reported that he was "from Europe" in an advertisement in the April 22, 1783, *Maryland Journal and Baltimore Advertiser*.

5. For more on the production of *secretaires à abattant,* see Peter M. Kenny, Francis Bretter, and Ulrich Leben, *Honoré Lannuier: Cabinetmaker from Paris* (New York: Harry Abrams for the Metropolitan Museum of Art, 1998), pp. 16–18, 71, 79; and Charles L. Venable, "Germanic Craftsmen and Furniture Design in Philadelphia, 1820–1850," in *American Furniture*, edited by Luke Beckerdite (Hanover, N.H.: University Press of New England for the Chipstone Foundation, 1998), passim. The earliest *secretaires à abattant* in the Baltimore group (see fig. 4) appear to predate those associated with Lannuier by more than a decade.

6. The terms "antique" and "palmyrian" were often used to describe the neoclassical taste. For more on these design sources, see Elizabeth White, comp., *Pictorial Dictionary of British Eighteenth-Century Furniture Design: The Printed Sources* (Woodbridge, Suffolk, England: Antique Collector's Club, 1990), passim.

7. J. Thomas Savage, "The Holmes-Edwards Library Bookcase and the Origins of the German School in Pre-Revolutionary Charleston," in *American Furniture*, edited by Luke Beckerdite (Hanover, N.H.: University Press of New England for the Chipstone Foundation, 1997), pp. 106–27; John Bivins, "The Convergence and Divergence of Three Stylistic Traditions in Charleston Neoclassical Case Furniture, 1785–1800," in ibid., pp. 47–106; research files of the Museum of Early Southern Decorative Arts (hereafter cited MESDA), Winston-Salem, North Carolina.

8. The backs of standard chests typically have vertically grained boards with tongue-and-groove joints. Many of these construction practices evolved in London during the 1730s and continued in use for high-end British furniture throughout the eighteenth century.

9. Lindsay Boynton, ed., *Gillow Furniture Designs* (Royston, England: Bloomfield Press, 1995), p. 168, entry for March 11, 1789. Cock-beading is rarely found in the early Baltimore group. The bottoms of large drawers are set in a groove in the front, dadoed to the sides, nailed at the back, and reinforced along the sides and front with tightly clustered glue blocks. In contrast, the bottoms of the small drawers are glued into rabbets in the front and sides. The rear edges of all the drawers are secured with wrought sprigs. Some furniture scholars consider this structure less sophisticated than the rabbeted drawer construction typical of mid-eighteenth-century London casework; however, many cabinetmakers abandoned such early construction

practices during the last quarter of the century in favor of the simpler work found here, particularly for large case drawers. The bottom boards of all large drawers in the early Baltimore group run side to side. Most are nailed up into the drawer backs with four or five wrought finish nails, although forged T- and L-shaped heads occur sporadically. The bottom boards on interior drawers run front to back. The boards are rabbeted to the sides and front and secured with tiny wrought finish nails at the rear. The dovetails of the large and small drawers have tight, narrow pins and precisely sawn tails. No kerfs are visible on the interior surfaces, indicating that the cabinetmakers finished their work with chisels like many of their British contemporaries. The large drawer fronts typically have mahogany cores and mahogany veneer. On some examples (see figs. 2, 3) the cores are laminated.

10. Marston and Bellamy of Birminghan patented the process for die-stamping brasses in 1779 (Ralph Edwards, *The Shorter Dictionary of English Furniture* [London: Country Life, 1954], p. 306).

11. The earliest information on Lawson comes from the inscription on his portrait by Maryland artist Charles Peale Polk (fig. 20). Polk charged Lawson £17.10 for this portrait and another of Lawson's wife (Charles Peale Polk to Richard Lawson, November 27, 1794, Library Manuscripts Collection, MHS). Richard Lawson's father, Stephen, was a carpenter who married Agnes Simpson in 1743. Richard was baptized in 1750. His father subsequently worked as a baker in Keighley. Tench Tilghman Papers, ms. 1445, MHS. *Maryland Journal and Baltimore Advertiser*, July 29, 1785. Although dated July 1, this advertisement did not run until four weeks later. Several Baltimore cabinetmakers had shops on Gay Street. Bankson and Lawson's shop was on the east side in the first block south of Market, the city's main commercial thoroughfare. In 1786, the firm moved approximately three blocks west, to the southwest corner of Light Lane and Bank Street, a location closer to the city's wharves.

12. For more on the Seddon firm, see Sir Ambrose Heal, *The London Furniture Makers from the Restoration to the Victorian Era, 1660–1840's* (1933; reprint ed., New York: Dover, 1972), pp. 161–62; and Geoffrey Beard and Christopher Gilbert, eds., *Dictionary of English Furniture Makers, 1660–1840* (Leeds, England: W. S. Maney and Son for the Furniture History Society, 1986), pp. 793–99. Like many of his contemporaries, George Seddon produced architectural woodwork in addition to furniture. Between 1781 and 1789, his firm furnished interior components for the Greenwich Hospital Chapel, where he assisted cabinetmaker James Arrow (Geoffrey Beard, *Craftsmen and Interior Decoration in England, 1660–1820* [New York: Holmes and Meier, 1981], p. 242). No record identifying Seddon's early apprentices is known, nor are there daybooks or objects surviving from the period when Lawson reputedly worked for the firm. George Seddon II (1765–1815) and his brother Thomas (1761–1804) joined the firm in 1785 and subsequently took Thomas's brother-in-law Thomas Shackleton as a partner. During the 1790s, the firm received the first of many documented royal commissions and became the largest cabinet shop in London. By 1827, when the elder George Seddon's grandson and namesake took Nicholas Morel as a partner, most of the company's clients were members of the royal family. Sophie von La Roche's visit is described in ibid.

13. Henry Wansey, *Journal of an Excursion to the United States of North America in the Summer of 1794*, 2d ed., as quoted in David Barquist, "'The Honours of a Court' or 'the Severity of Virtue,'" in *Shaping a National Culture: The Philadelphia Experience, 1750–1800*, edited by Catherine Hutchins (Winterthur, Del.: Winterthur Museum, 1994), p. 324. The author thanks Ron Fuchs for this reference. Invoice from William Murdoch to Hugh Thompson for "sundries shipped from Seddon Sons & Shackleton," May 2, 1797, ms. 990, MHS.

14. John D. Kilbourne, *Vitruvius Praemium: The Men Who Founded the State Society of the Cincinnati of Pennsylvania* (Rockport, Maine: Picton Press, n.d.), pp. 6, 255, 1100. From May 1784 to June 12, 1785, Bankson was in partnership with Baltimore cabinetmaker William Gordon (d. 1798) (*Maryland Journal and Baltimore Advertiser*, May 18, 1784, and June 10, 1785).

15. *Maryland Journal and Baltimore Advertiser*, May 18, 1784. The *Oxford English Dictionary* cites the third edition of Hepplewhite's *Cabinet-Maker and Upholsterer's Guide* (1794) as having the first use of the term "wardrobe"; however, it also appears in the first edition (1788). *Columbia Herald* (Charleston), May 1, 1786, and June 14, 1787.

16. *Columbia Herald* (Charleston), May 1, 1786. Savage, "The Holmes-Edwards Library Bookcase," pp. 106–27.

17. *Maryland Journal and Baltimore Advertiser*, June 17, 1788.

18. The procession is described in the *Gazette of the State of Georgia* (Savannah), June 12, 1788.

19. Gregory R. Weidman, "Baltimore Federal Furniture: In the English Tradition," in *The American Craftsman and the European Tradition*, edited by Francis J. Puig and Michael Con-

forti (Minneapolis, Minn.: Minneapolis Institute of Arts, 1989), p. 258. Charles Carnan Ridgley, Ledger L, January 19, 1792, folio 62, G. Howard White Collection, Maryland State Archives, Annapolis.

20. *Maryland Journal and Baltimore Advertiser*, October 25, 1791; April 17, 1792, and February 11, 1793. Bankson took Englehart Reams as an apprentice in the cabinetmaking trade on October 10, 1792 (Baltimore County Orphans Court Proceedings, No. 3, 1792–1798, p. 13).

21. *Baltimore Daily Repository*, February 11, 1793. For more on Askew's brief career, see Gergory R. Weidman, *Furniture in Maryland, 1740–1940: The Collection of the Maryland Historical Society* (Baltimore: By the society, 1984), p. 73. *Baltimore Daily Repository*, February 11, 1793, and August 23, 1793. Bankson and Wilkinson's partnership lasted through 1795. Robert Wilkinson (1769–1853) was in business with William Smith at 16 Light Street by the time the first Baltimore city directory was published in 1796 (*Baltimore Town and Fell's Point Directory of 1796*). On December 5, 1796, the *Federal Gazette and Baltimore Advertiser* reported that "a fire broke out in a frame building on the West side of Light Street. . . . The flames immediately caught Messrs. Wilkinson and Smith's cabinet manufactory." Two days later, Wilkinson and Smith thanked the public "for their particular attention and exertions at the late fire" and reported that they would "soon . . . establish and carry on their business as heretofore" (*Federal Gazette and Baltimore Advertiser*, December 7, 1796). Six months later, they dissolved their partnership (*Federal Gazette and Baltimore Advertiser*, June 6, 1797). Wilkinson continued in business on his own through 1799 (*Baltimore Directory for 1799*). The following year, the cabinet and chair manufactory of Combs and Jenkins moved from Water Street into the building formerly occupied by Wilkinson, Bankson and Wilkinson, and Bankson and Lawson (*Federal Gazette and Baltimore Daily Advertiser*, April 1, 1800). This marked the end of a business carried on by a succession of accomplished artisans for nearly two decades. By 1801, Bankson had established a lumber and import business on McElderry's Wharf. This business prospered until Bankson's death on June 5, 1814 (*Baltimore Directory for 1801*). Lawson had established a separate business as a lumber merchant at Bowly's Wharf in 1789 (*Maryland Gazette and Baltimore Advertiser*, September 25, 1789). In January 1792, he sold his company to John McFadon (*Maryland Gazette and Baltimore Advertiser*, January 31, 1792). Lawson evidently retained an interest in the new firm. On November 8, 1802, the *Telegraph and Daily Advertiser* (Baltimore) reported that William and John McFadon and Richard Lawson had dissolved their "copartnership."

22. Straight-front chests are among the most common furniture forms associated with the Bankson and Lawson shop tradition. See *Baltimore Furniture: The Work of Baltimore and Annapolis Cabinetmakers from 1760 to 1810* (Baltimore, Md.: Baltimore Museum of Art, 1947), p. 135; and Charles Montgomery, *American Furniture: The Federal Period in the Henry Francis du Pont Winterthur Museum* (New York: Viking Press, 1966), pp. 184–85, no. 141.

23. "Chinese" mullions are illustrated in the first edition of Thomas Chippendale's *Gentleman and Cabinet-Maker's Director* (1754). All of the bookcases attributed to Bankson and Lawson that have been examined by the authors are secured to their lower cases with separately attached dovetailed battens. The cornices typically have dovetailed frames, and most have friezes veneered with cross-banded mahogany and vine inlay. The pediment frames have a series of large blocks glued to the interior and are attached to the top of the upper case with screws. The upper case usually has two rectangular blocks glued to its top, which help align the cornice and hold it in place. Although the cornice moldings differ from piece to piece, most have mahogany cove elements with triangular pine or tulip laminates. Several of the most expensive examples have cornice moldings pierced with gothic arches and decorated with acorn-shaped drops, each of which is applied separately (see figs. 6, 19). The doors on bookcases typically have intricate mullions accentuated with string inlay (see figs. 5, 6, 19). The mullions are invariably tenoned into the stiles and rails rather than being set in slots that are exposed on the interior of door. Most American cabinetmakers used the latter technique, which was quicker and cheaper. The construction of the door frames is also exceptionally neat and sturdy. The rails are through-tenoned, and the joints are secured with glue and wedges rather than with pins.

24. Hepplewhite, *Cabinet-Maker and Upholsterer's Guide*, pl. 69.

25. A ca. 1768 carved chimneypiece from the Stamper-Blackwell house in Philadelphia (now in the Winterthur Museum) depicts a stag and hound in a pose similar to that inlaid on the cylinder of this desk-and-bookcase. A related stag-and-hound inlay is on the top of a tea table in a private collection. For more on the Stamper-Blackwell chimneypiece and the influence of Hercules Courtenay and carver John Pollard, see Leroy Graves and Luke Beckerdite's article

in this volume. Morrison H. Heckscher, "English Furniture Pattern Books in Eighteenth-Century America," in *American Furniture*, edited by Luke Beckerdite (Hanover, N.H.: University Press of New England for the Chipstone Foundation, 1994), p. 191.

26. A desk virtually identical to the one shown in fig. 27 is illustrated on p. 103, fig. 76, in William Voss Elder III and Jayne E. Stokes, *American Furniture, 1680–1880: From the Collection of the Baltimore Museum of Art* (Baltimore, Md.: By the museum, 1987). A similar desk is owned by the University of Virginia and displayed in Pavillion VI. A secretary-and-bookcase illustrated in Weidman, *Furniture in Maryland*, pp. 135–36, no. 96, appears to be by Bankson and Lawson or one of their journeymen. Its scalloped, satinwood-veneered skirt is similar to those on the cylinder desks noted above, and its door mullions are derived from a design shown on pl. 27 in the Society of Upholsterer's *Cabinet-Makers' London Book of Prices* (1788). Another secretary-and-bookcase with a pierced tympanum, "Chinese" mullions, and French feet with inlaid husks similar to those shown in fig. 15 is illustrated in Sotheby's, *Important Americana*, New York, January 26, 1989, lot 1496.

27. The authors have not inspected the clothespress and cannot verify its structure or the originality of the inlay on the prospect door and document drawers.

28. The *secretaire à abattant* descended in the Myer family until the Chrysler Museum acquired the house and its contents.

29. Hepplewhite, *Cabinet-Maker and Upholsterer's Guide* (1788), text for pl. 29. The tops of the sideboards attributed to Bankson and Lawson's shop (see figs. 7, 8, 32–35) are composed of thin mahogany boards with parallel laminates beneath the front, sides, and back. The tops of the serpentine and blockfront chests (figs. 2, 3) are constructed in a similar fashion. Most straight-front chests (see fig. 13) have dovetailed tops covered with veneer. Mitered strips nailed to the sides and front create the overhanging edges. These strips are generally veneered with cross-banded mahogany and inlaid with boxwood stringing, although more elaborate pieces have cross-banded satinwood. This applied overhang—which mirrors the earlier, rococo practice of applying a classical molding around the top edges of a dovetailed case—was abandoned in most American cities during the neoclassical period, but remained an integral part of Baltimore's cabinetmaking tradition well into the nineteenth century.

30. For additional commode sideboards attributed to Bankson and Lawson, see advertisement for Joe Kindig, Jr., *Antiques* 50, no. 2 (August 1946): inside front cover; and Israel Sack, Inc., *Antiques from Israel Sack Collection*, 10 vols. (Alexandria, Va.: Highland House, 1981), 1:283.

31. Robert C. Smith, "A Bill From George Seddon," *Antiques* (October 1960): 362–63. For the other bow-front sideboards attributed to Bankson and Lawson, see advertisement for Joe Kindig, Jr., *Antiques* 58, no. 1 (July 1950): inside front cover; Sotheby's, *The Garbisch Collection*, vol. 4, New York, May 23, 1980, lot 1139; Elder and Stokes, *American Furniture*, pp. 148–49, no. 113; and private collection.

32. Indenture between Bankson and Lawson and William Patterson, April 2, 1789, Baltimore County Orphan's Court Proceedings, no. 2, 1789–1792. Most apprenticeships lasted six to seven years. Although Lawson left the firm in 1792, Bankson and Wilkinson remained in business until 1796, the year Patterson first appears in Baltimore directories. Patterson married Nancy Craig at St. Paul's Episcopal Church in July 1795 (Reamy, *Records of St. Paul's Parish*, 1:89).

33. MESDA research file 10959.

34. Account of the Sale of Thomas Barrett, November 20, 1800, Baltimore County Inventories, vol. 2, folio, 688, Maryland State Archives, Annapolis. In 1803, Patterson moved to 22 Albemarle Street, where he remained until 1817.

35. Indenture between Thomas Barrett and John Lennox, February 18, 1795, Baltimore County, Maryland Orphans Court Proceedings, No. 3, 1792–1798, p. 136. Barrett married Elizabeth (maiden name unknown) prior to December 1788, when their son Thomas was born. The elder Barrett may not have been in Baltimore at the time of his and Elizabeth's marriage, since no local license or church record is known. Four Thomas Barretts emigrated from England to America between 1765 and 1770, but no connection between these individuals and the Baltimore ebonist has been established. Two individuals whose last name was Barrett lived in Baltimore County during the 1760s, and a John Barrett resided in Baltimore during the 1780s and 1790s (Henry C. Peden, Jr., *Inhabitants of Baltimore County, 1763–1774* [Westminster, Md.: Family Line Publications, 1989], p. 17). The latter was a communicant of St. Paul's Church (Reamy, *Records of St. Paul's Parish*, 1:50, 120).

36. Indenture between Thomas Barrett and John Lennox.

37. Reamy, *Records of St. Paul's Parish,* 2:23. Singleton married Elizabeth Slater in St. Paul's Church on March 20, 1793 (ibid., 1:69). U. S. Congress, "Manufactures: Communicated to the House of Representatives, April 11, 1789," in *American State Papers,* vol. 1 (Boston: T. B. Wart, 1817), pp. 5–8. *Maryland Journal and Baltimore Advertiser,* May 18, 1790. Singleton and McFadon advertised at 11 North Gay Street in the January 29, 1796, *Maryland Journal and Baltimore Advertiser.* For additional listings at that address, see the *Baltimore Town and Fell's Point Directory of 1796* and the *Baltimore Directory for 1799* (Baltimore, Md.: John Mullen, 1799). For more on McFadon's association with Richard Lawson, see n. 23. The 1790 census (taken after March) does not list William Singleton in Baltimore. He may have been one of the three males over sixteen listed with William McFadon (*First Census of the United States, 1790, Maryland* [Baltimore, Md.: Southern Book Co., 1952], p. 17). Weidman, "Baltimore Federal Furniture," p. 258, incorrectly states that McFadon was born abroad.

38. Lida Leiseuring, *Maryland Marriage Records, 1777–1799* (Baltimore, Md., 1900), n.p. Reamy, *Records of St. Paul's Parish,* 1:57, 99, 128, 159–60; 2:20. From 1796 to 1797, Singleton served as church warden and Richard Lawson was a vestryman. For a reference to the *Diana,* see the *Baltimore American,* July 14, 1804.

39. "Account of Mr. Thompson's Furniture as taken from the original bills," undated ms. (ca. 1800), Hugh Thompson Papers, ms. 990, MHS. In addition to this furniture, Thompson furnished his townhouse with lavish goods from London and Paris. *Maryland Journal and Baltimore Advertiser,* October 1, 1793. Singleton continued to purchase lumber from John McFadon and Co. in the late 1790s (John Hill, "The Furniture Craftsmen in Baltimore, 1783–1823" [M.A. thesis, University of Delaware, 1967], p. 131). The 1800 census lists three young men (ages 17–26) in addition to Singleton at his house/shop (G. Ronald Teeples, *Maryland 1800 Census* [Provo, Utah: Accelerated Indexing Systems, 1973], p. 493). In the October 1, 1793, issue of the *Maryland Journal and Baltimore Advertiser* he stated that "constant employ and liberal wages will be given to two or three good journeymen." Singleton was also a client of Thomas Barrett and owed his estate $29.80 (Account of the Sale of Thomas Barrett).

English-born cabinetmaker Gualter Hornby (b. 1755–1760, d. 1816) was also in Baltimore during the period of Bankson and Lawson's partnership; however, no documentation concerning his training, shop practices, or patrons is known. He, his wife Elizabeth (d. 1826), and at least one son, Walter, Jr. (d. 1793), arrived in the city by April 1783, when Gualter is listed as a "pauper" in the tax assessment list for East Baltimore Hundred in April of that year (*Maryland Tax List, 1783: Baltimore County* [Philadelphia, Pa.: Historic Publications, 1978]).

Hornby subsequently formed a partnership with a cabinetmaker named Turner. In the December 19, 1788, issue of the *Maryland Journal and Baltimore Advertiser,* they reported that their shop was on Gay Street and advertised "beautiful mahogany that was taken in the Time of the War." The date when the partnership disbanded is not known, but Hornby was at 6 Light Street, just about four doors north of the Bankson and Lawson shop, by 1792 (*Maryland Journal and Baltimore Advertiser,* February 5, 1792). This location was later described as 6 Light Street in Baltimore city directories. He remained at that location through 1810.

40. Jane Webb Smith, "'A Large and Elegant Assortment': A Group of Baltimore Tall Clocks, 1795–1815," in *Journal of Early Southern Decorative Arts* 13, no. 2 (November 1987): 32–103. Most of the clockmakers discussed in Smith's article did not begin working in Baltimore before Bankson and Lawson's partnership ended: William Elvins (w. 1795–1816), Charles Tinges (w. 1797–1818), Peter Mohler (1797–1827), William Thompson (w. 1796–1822), and Mountjoy and Welsh (w. 1797). Smith illustrates a tall clock case with a replaced movement by Gilbert Bigger (w. 1783–1816) on pp. 34–37, figs. 1–1d. A tall clock case with bird inlays in the hood spandrels is illustrated in an advertisement by G. K. S. Bush in *Antiques* 113, no. 6 (June 1983): 1184. The clock cases shown in figs. 40–44 and most of the examples related to them have broken-scroll pediments with tympana consisting of two scroll-sawn boards abutting a central plinth. Each section is attached to the top of the cornice molding by a series of small blocks that run end-to-end. The moldings are glued to the tympana in front and nailed from behind. At either end, they are nailed from above into the top of the cornice.

41. For more on masonic symbolism in American furniture, see F. Cary Howlett, "Admitted into the Mysteries: The Benjamin Bucktrout Masonic Master's Chair," in *American Furniture,* edited by Luke Beckerdite (Hanover, N.H.: University Press of New England for the Chipstone Foundation, 1996), pp. 199–232. For the tall clock case with figural inlay, see MESDA research file, 10, 977. The clock case and two *secretaires à abattant* have classical figures

playing a flute. Details of one *secretaire à abattant* are shown in Ronald L. Hurst and Jonathan Prown, *Southern Furniture, 1680–1830: The Colonial Williamsburg Collection* (New York: Harry Abrams for the Colonial Williamsburg Foundation, 1997), p. 369, figs. 115.6 and 115.7.

42. A Pennsylvania tall clock case with a ca. 1800 movement by Jacob Klingman (1758–1806) has a fox-and-goose inlay that is closely related to the stag and hound on the desk-and-bookcase illustrated in figs. 26 and 27. This provides further support for the argument that the inlay maker employed by Bankson and Lawson continued to work in Baltimore after the dissolution of their partnership. For an illustration of this case, see Sotheby's *Important Americana, Furniture and Folk Art,* New York, January 18, 1998, lot 1701.

43. Hurst and Prown, *Southern Furniture*, p. 125, fig. 31.1. The authors thank Deanne Levison for calling the chair illustrated in fig. 56 to their attention. For more on the side chair shown in fig. 59, see Montgomery, *American Furniture*, pp. 151–52, no. 103. According to Montgomery, these chairs descended to Tolley A. Biays, and according to oral tradition, they were made by Mr. Biays's granduncle, Baltimore cabinetmaker Warwick Price (w. 1795–1810).

44. *Columbia Herald*, May 1, 1786. Four chairs with inlaid husks and vase backs that may be part of the Bankson and Lawson shop tradition are illustrated in Christie's, *Important American Furniture, Silver, Folk Art and Decorative Arts,* June 21, 1995, New York, lot 264.

*Figure 1*   Pier table and liquor case by Edward Priestley, Baltimore, Maryland, 1827. Pier table: mahogany with yellow poplar and white pine; marble. H. 42 3/4", W. 62", D. 26 3/4". Liquor case: mahogany with yellow poplar, white pine, and mahogany. H. 20 1/4", W. 26 1/2", D. 17 1/2". (Private collection, photo, Gavin Ashworth.) Although the smooth, rounded surfaces of the liquor case contrast with the rectilinear form and carved and reeded decoration on the pier table, similar incongruities are prevalent in design book illustrations for these forms. See Thomas Hope, *Household Furniture and Interior Decoration* (1807), pls. 13, 15, 22.

*Alexandra Alevizatos Kirtley*

A New Suspect: Baltimore Cabinetmaker Edward Priestley

▼ THE PAUCITY OF documented examples of late-eighteenth- and early-nineteenth-century Baltimore furniture and manuscripts such as cabinetmakers' account books and day books has left decorative arts historians with few clues to link individual pieces with their makers, even though the city's cabinetmakers and chairmakers produced thousands of objects during that period. Most attributions to specific artisans and shops are based on widely pervasive structural and stylistic details shared by objects documented to a small number of artisans. Although this methodology can produce convincing results, it must be employed with considerable care when assessing furniture from large urban areas. In cities like Baltimore, artisans routinely moved from shop to shop taking their design and construction vocabularies with them. This migration of style and structure makes many traditional attributions to Baltimore cabinetmakers problematic.

A recently discovered receipt from Baltimore cabinetmaker Edward Priestley (1778–1837) to Talbot County, Maryland, planter Edward Lloyd VI (1798–1861) is the first document illuminating the work of this important southern tradesman. Listed on the 1827 receipt are a marble-top pier table and an accompanying liquor case (fig. 1) that remain among the furnishings in Wye House (built 1787), the Lloyd family's home in Talbot County. The mummy head supports of the pier table serve as a benchmark for attributing two sideboard tables, three sideboards, three chests of drawers, and three desks to Priestley's shop and for separating Baltimore and Philadelphia case and tables forms with this distinctive detail. Compounded from Egyptian, Gothic, and French influences, Priestley's dramatic mummy heads represent one of the most expressive and highly developed manifestations of the late neoclassical style in American furniture.

Account books and receipts reveal that Edward Lloyd VI's father Edward V (1779–1834) patronized Priestley exclusively for cabinet work between 1801 and 1825. This is significant given the cosmopolitan nature of certain segments of Maryland society. Wealthy consumers like the Lloyds were acutely aware of the latest European fashions. The Lloyds' vast resources and mercantile connections gave them access to the finest imported goods and to local tradesmen who were eager to fulfill any request. Although over 216 furniture makers worked in Baltimore during the first three decades of the nineteenth century, the Lloyds—Maryland's most culturally influential family—clearly favored Priestley.

Priestley began his career during an unprecedented period of economic growth in Baltimore (figs. 2, 3). With an excellent harbor and a vast grain-

*Figure 2*  Daniel Bowley, Esq., *Baltimore in 1752, From a Sketch Made by John Moale, Esq.*, Baltimore, Maryland, 1817. Aquatint. Dimensions not recorded. (Courtesy, Maryland Historical Society.)

*Figure 3*  W. Goodhue, Jr., *Battle Monument, Baltimore*, issued by Archer & Boilly, New York, c. 1831. (Courtesy, Winterthur Museum.)

producing hinterland, the city dominated the wheat trade in the middle Atlantic region after the Revolution. When Priestley arrived in Baltimore in 1790, the city had 13,000 inhabitants. By the time he opened his shop in 1801, the population had grown to 26,514. Nine years later Baltimore had 45,000 inhabitants, a population second only to New York.

During the late eighteenth and early nineteenth centuries, Baltimore's thriving economy attracted furniture makers from Britain, continental Europe, the West Indies, and the Atlantic seaboard. By the early 1800s, the convergence of English, Scottish, French, German, Irish, West Indian, and American traditions had given Baltimore furniture its own distinctive identity. On June 28, 1817, John Howe's Baltimore Carpet, Furniture, and Looking Glass Warehouse advertised "sideboards of Boston, New York and Baltimore styles." Established cabinetmakers and newcomers vied for the patronage of merchants, gentlemen, and professionals and endeavored to compete with furniture imported from other American cities and from abroad. It was within this climate that Edward Priestley's cabinetmaking business thrived.[1]

*Edward Priestley's Early Career and Partnership*
Edward Priestley was born in Annapolis in 1778 and arrived in Baltimore in 1790 with his mother, Mary Ann (1749/50–1835.) By 1780, Baltimore had eclipsed Annapolis socially, culturally, and economically. In 1793, New York lawyer James Kent noted that Baltimore had experienced "the most rapid growth of any town" in the United States:

> Howe's going to Phil[adelphia] in 1777 . . . diverted the [backcountry grain] . . . trade to Baltimore. The [yellow fever] Sickness in Phil[adelphia] . . . last Fall has done the same, & Baltimore this season will nearly rival Phil[adelphia] in the export of wheat & Flour. . . . [Baltimore] is built chiefly of brick. Its Houses are 3 Story-join[ed] together—are wide, & the Town appears to be better and more handsomely built than Phil. In 1760 there were not 10 brick Houses, whereas in 1787 It had 2000 Houses in the whole of which 800 were at Fell's Point, & had 152 Stores. It has grown rapidly since, & has now perhaps 13,000 Souls. It is larger than Charlestown, but does not yet equal Boston. . . . In 1760 Baltimore was 10 times inferior to Anapolis, & was a paltry Village. From 1770 it took a Spring, & grew 100 fold in 1774.[2]

Priestley probably served his apprenticeship in Baltimore between 1790 and 1801; however, the identity and location of his master remain unconfirmed. By December 1801, he had formed a partnership with cabinetmaker Samuel Minskey (1778–1819) of "Baltimore Town." The latter was the son of Annapolis carpenter Nicholas Minskey and, like Priestley, he had lost his father at an early age. Referred to as "orphans" during the period, fatherless males who apprenticed in the cabinetmaking trade generally began serving their terms at sixteen years of age. Minskey, for example, signed an indenture with Baltimore cabinetmaker Nicholas Kirby in 1794. According to furniture historian John Henry Hill, most Baltimore cabinetmaking partnerships involved unrelated tradesmen who had apprenticed with the same master. Although these partnerships rarely lasted more than three years, they allowed young artisans to combine capital to purchase tools and materials and rent shop space. It is therefore quite plausible that Priestley also apprenticed with Kirby.[3]

Priestley and Minskey's shop was located at 79 Water Street between the main commercial street and the bustling wharves in Baltimore Town (fig. 4). Their neighbors were cooper Griffith Evans and John Stickney & Company's turpentine distillery. Further east on Water Street were fellow cabinetmaker William Camp (1773–1822) and the firm of Coleman & Taylor. In 1802, Priestley and Minskey published their first and only advertisement, thanking the public for "the liberal encouragement" they had received. Their stock included sideboards, "secretaries and bookcases," fall-front desks, "circular and straight front bureaus," circular and "sash corner" card tables, "Northumberland" dining tables, oval and square pembroke tables, and

Priestley's shop | Philpot's Bridge

*Figure 4* Warner & Hanna's *Plan of the City and Environs of Baltimore,* engraved by Francis Shallus, Philadelphia, 1801. Dimensions not recorded. (Courtesy, Winterthur Museum.) In 1801, Baltimore and its environs included Baltimore-Town, Fell's Point, and Jones Town. Warehouses were located close to the water, which was the city's economic nucleus, and commercial establishments were situated to the north and concentrated around Baltimore (or Market) Street.

square and circular basin stands, all available at "the most reduced prices." Although Priestley and Minskey described themselves as "chair-makers" on one occasion, it is doubtful that they made much seating furniture. Evidence suggests that they subcontracted chair work to specialists including Francis Younker (fl. 1807–1833) and Jacob Daley (fl. 1804–1848). This practice was common in the furniture-making trades in most urban centers.[4]

Like many of their contemporaries, Priestley and Minskey engaged in the furniture export trade. On December 15, 1802, the *Georgia Republican and State Intelligencer* reported that "the ship *Comet* . . . from Baltimore" had just arrived in Savannah with a cargo of "excellent mahogany furniture" and "a few fancy chairs. . . . Any person Wishing to purchase bedsteads, or any article in the above line" could be "supplied in a few weeks by Edward Priestly, At Johnson and Robertson & Co.'s old Compting Hou[se]." The fancy chairs mentioned in this advertisement support the notion that Priestley and Minskey farmed out orders for seating furniture. Several Baltimore chairmakers specialized in the production of "fancy chairs." Matthew McColm (fl. 1803–1850), for example, worked just down the street from Priestley and Minskey and shipped fancy chairs to Savannah. Baltimore chairmakers John and Hugh Finlay (fl. 1799–1834) and Jacob Daley also exported fancy chairs and all three were acquainted with Priestley.[5]

In the January 1, 1803, issue of the *Columbian Museum and Savannah Ad-*

*vertiser*, Priestley stated that he was returning to Baltimore and wished to dispose of his remaining secretaries, bureaus, portable desks, card tables, oval pembroke tables, candle stands, bedsteads, and Windsor chairs. He also offered to execute subsequent orders "in the best manner" and deliver the furniture "in Savannah, at Baltimore prices." The latter phrase suggests that Priestley's furniture was less expensive than that imported from New York, Salem, and Philadelphia and that his Savannah patrons recognized it. The proximity of Baltimore to Savannah may have given Priestley a competitive edge. His shipping costs must have been less than those of many northern cabinetmakers who engaged in the furniture export trade.[6]

In 1806, Priestley and Minskey moved their shop to Baltimore Street at Philpot's Bridge, which spanned Jones Falls and linked Baltimore Town to Fell's Point and Old Town or Jones Town. The *Baltimore Directory* for 1804 described Baltimore Street as the "principal" one in the city. It extended from east to west, was over a mile long, and provided access to 430 warehouses, stores, and dwellings. Ship passengers arriving in Baltimore disembarked at the wharves in Fell's Point. To enter the commercial center of Baltimore Town, visitors passed through Fell's Point and crossed Philpot's Bridge. The first shop on the left was Priestley and Minskey's. This location—on a busy thoroughfare in the center of Baltimore's cabinetmaking community—provided excellent exposure to both newcomers and established elites. It also gave Priestley and Minskey access to tradesmen from whom they could commission piecework or specialized forms such as chair frames.[7]

Priestley and Minskey took four apprentices between 1801 and 1807. John Johnson began his term in October 1801. Merchant Mark Pringle, whose business was east of Priestley and Minskey on Water Street, was a party in the agreement. As a respected and prominent member of Baltimore society, Pringle often guaranteed people's credit. Priestley and Minskey's remaining apprentices signed indentures in 1807—George Plaines in May and John Bringman and Joseph Hutton in October. Like Priestley and Minskey, all of their apprentices were orphans.[8]

On March 18, 1803, Priestley and Minskey signed a petition circulated by the Cabinet-Makers and Manufacturers of Mahogany in the City of Baltimore. This petition, which was approved by the city on March 22, advocated more stringent requirements for inspecting and grading mahogany. Among the nineteen cabinetmakers and firms that joined the appeal were William Camp; Walter Crook; Michael Jenkins; James Martin; James Davidson; Coleman & Taylor; Nathaniel Hynson, Sr.; Warrick Price; Law & Denmead; and Stitcher & Clemmens. After only three years of being in business, Priestley and Minskey were allied with the most prosperous cabinetmakers in Baltimore.[9]

On November 20, 1807, the *Federal Gazette* reported that Priestley and Minskey had dissolved their partnership and that Priestley intended to continue the cabinetmaking business at 4 Baltimore Street—a location he maintained until his death in 1837. Minskey established a cabinetmaking business around the corner on Saint Patrick's Row. He remained there until 1812, when he returned to Anne Arundel County.[10]

## Priestley's Cabinet Shop, 1807–1837

During his career, Priestley adapted to stylistic and economic changes by modifying his business practices and the furniture forms he produced. This flexibility enabled him to compete with other Baltimore cabinetmakers as well as with furniture imported from abroad. Priestley advertised only twice, yet documents reveal that he enjoyed the patronage of Maryland's most prominent families. Recommendations and referrals by satisfied customers undoubtedly contributed to his success.

On November 20, 1807, the Baltimore *American and Commercial Daily Advertiser* reported that Priestley had on hand "an elegant assortment of furniture" along with "a quantity of St. Domingo and Bay MAHOGANY, fit for Cabinet Makers and House Carpenters." The furniture forms listed in the advertisement duplicated those offered by Priestley and Minskey years earlier, with the exception of a "Pedestal end Side Board, With a pair of Superb Vase Knife Cases." A subsequent advertisement that appeared in the *Baltimore Evening Post* and *Baltimore Whig* provided a more detailed description of Priestley's stock:

> Pedestal end SIDE BOARDS, kidney, commode and straight do.; SECRETARY and BOOK CASES; WARDROBES; BUREAUS of different shapes; Card Tables; North-Umberland Dining Tables, in setts; pillar and claw Breakfast Tables; oval and square ditto; Wash-stands of all kinds; Work Tables; Portable Desks; fashionable Sophas; and Mahogany Bedsteads, complete with Steps, Poplar do.[11]

Priestley's statement that these items were among "a great variety" of furniture "on hand at his manufactory" is significant. Although he clearly maintained a large stock in trade, Priestley did not operate a warehouse or separate wareroom like many of his competitors. Baltimore directories consistently refer to his business as a "cabinetmaking shop."[12]

The range of forms specified in Priestley's advertisements and his reference to other furniture "in this line" suggest that he employed a large and highly skilled workforce. Several of his contemporaries relied heavily on apprentice labor. William Camp, for example, took fifty-three apprentices between 1801 and 1822 and Jacob Daley took eighteen between 1804 and 1816. By comparison, only four apprentices bound to Priestley appear in Baltimore records from 1807 to 1837. Although his workforce clearly included unregistered apprentices, Priestley's shop apparently had a higher percentage of journeymen and indentured tradesmen.[13]

The renowned cabinetmaker John Needles (1786–1878) began his Baltimore career in Priestley's shop. According to Needles's autobiography, he arrived in Baltimore in 1808 and worked for Priestley for six months before signing an indenture with William Camp. Although Needles already had served a five-year apprenticeship with James Neale (fl. 1780–1810) of Easton, his skills may not have met Priestley's requirements. Needles subsequently established his own shop, which flourished from 1810 to 1852.[14]

From 1816 to 1817, Priestley employed journeyman Henry Lusby (1782–1867), who had completed an apprenticeship with Annapolis cabinetmaker John Shaw (1745–1829) in 1811. Lusby and Priestley remained friends long after severing their business ties. When respiratory problems forced Lusby to close his cabinetmaking business, Priestley and turner William Roney (1782–1844) wrote a letter to the city of Baltimore stating that Lusby's "arduous military duties" affected his lungs, making him unable to work near mahogany dust. City officials accepted their plea and made Lusby a hay weigher for Baltimore in 1818.[15]

Because Priestley is not listed in any federal census from 1800 to 1830, it is impossible to determine the number or status of individuals living in his house and working in his shop. At his death, he owned "one Negro named Henry about 30 years old to serve about 3 years . . . $150.00." It is possible that Henry was in the process of purchasing his freedom by working for Priestley.[16]

At least two independent tradesmen worked in Priestley's shop. The precise nature of their business arrangement is not known, but it is possible that these artisans provided Priestley with piecework or specialized forms in lieu of rent. In 1810, chairmaker Francis Younker began advertising that he made and exported fancy chairs out of Priestley's shop. Younker established his own shop in Old Town in 1824, the same year that upholsterer John L. Scott began working at Priestley's address. The sharing of premises was relatively common among Baltimore furniture makers. Chairmaker Matthew McColm worked out of Coleman & Taylor's shop from 1800 to 1804 and upholsterer Armistead Green worked out of John Needles's Hanover Street cabinetmaking manufactory from the late 1820s to the 1840s.[17]

Although most of the tradesmen who worked in Priestley's shop remain anonymous, the approximate size of his workforce can be inferred from the number of workbenches he owned at a given time. During the eighteenth and nineteenth centuries, shop masters were responsible for furnishing their workmen's benches. Laborers rarely shared their workspaces despite the fact that benches were quite expensive. Considering the number of apprentices, journeymen, and indentured tradesmen associated with him, Priestley must have had at least a half-dozen benches within one or two years of opening his shop. In 1823, he purchased thirty-one workbenches from William Camp's estate, and at his death in 1837 he owned twelve. This suggests that Priestley's workforce ranged from approximately six to more than thirty individuals.[18]

*Priestley's Ancillary Businesses*
Unlike many of his contemporaries who endeavored to expand their businesses by opening warehouses or engaging in the furniture export trade, Priestley invested in lumber, real estate, railroad stock, nail manufacturing, and wharf and ship construction. Several of these ventures, in turn, broadened his market for raw materials and furniture. In the end, these investments generated twice the income of Priestley's cabinet shop. When he died in 1837, Priestley owned twelve shares of Baltimore & Ohio railroad stock and six city lots. The combined value of these investments comprised 63 percent of his estate, which totaled $20,523.37. The remaining 37 percent included a huge stock of lumber, finished and unfinished furniture, tools, cabinetmaking supplies, and personal effects (see appendix).[19]

Priestley may have become involved in Baltimore's iron industry as early as 1807, when he appeared before the chancery court as a trustee for the estate of blacksmith Duncan McCollum. In November of that year, the *American and Commercial Daily Advertiser* reported that Priestley had sold McCollum's real estate for fourteen hundred dollars and that he was able to settle the blacksmith's debts. By 1820, Priestley had entered into partnership with Enoch and Elizabeth Betts, who operated a nail manufactory in Old Town, just over Philpot's Bridge from Priestley's shop. The Betts supplied nails to many Baltimore furniture makers.[20]

Priestley made his first foray into the lumber business on November 20, 1807, when he advertised mahogany in the *American and Commercial Daily Advertiser*. Three years later, he and cabinetmakers Walter Crook and Michael Jenkins offered "18,000 feet of 'bay' mahogany . . . particularly selected for the London market." Early tradesmen often pooled their resources to acquire large quantities of lumber or other materials. In 1816, Priestley, Jenkins, Crook, and William Camp purchased 260 mahogany logs from the ship *John Hamilton*. In a subsequent advertisement, they reported that the logs were particularly well suited for cabinetmakers owing to their superior grain and color. After 1816, Priestley financed his own lumber deals. His advertisements in Baltimore and Washington newspapers offered discounts to any purchasers who would pick up their lumber from the wharves where it was unloaded. Priestley's references to "good table wood" and "hand rail mahogany in prime order" reveal that he understood the properties of various types of timber and was able to provide the best materials for his clients.[21]

Most of Priestley's shipbuilding and wharfing ventures took place across Philpot's Bridge in Old Town. In the July 21, 1809, issue of the *Whig*, he reported that he owned a new packing machine for sealing the horizontal planks in ships and advertised for a workman to operate it. He also offered to lease the machine on terms as "low or lower . . . than any other in the City." Priestley took work orders for wharf carpenters William Fisher in 1810 and Jehu Brown in 1815. Fisher advertised that he owned the latest in piling machines, "with iron hammers in complete order," whereas Brown offered a wide variety of timbers for wharfing. Priestley may have loaned both men the capital to purchase their machinery and materials in hopes of generating more business for their joint ventures. At the very least, Priestley's various businesses gave him access to merchants, ship captains, and other individuals who could help him acquire and transport lumber and market his furniture in other locales.[22]

Priestley's real estate holdings were his most significant and lucrative investment. His advertisements for dwellings, commercial spaces, and ground lots first appear in Baltimore newspapers in 1810. That same year, he enrolled his properties on Front Street in a fire insurance policy from the Baltimore Equitable Society. Using rental income, Priestley periodically acquired additional property. In 1834 he purchased eight adjacent dwellings on Forest and Boglap Streets in Old Town. Many of Priestley's tenants and debtors were tradesmen, including cabinetmaker Levin Pritchett, cooper Joseph Armiger, carpenter Joseph Stubbs, carpenter Hiriam Tolson, and wharfer James Thompson (see appendix).[23]

*Priestley's Clients*

Although the nature of the debts owed to Priestley's estate was not usually specified, the names on the list reveal a great deal about the status of his clients and colleagues. Fellow tradesmen were probably indebted to him for credit he had extended or for goods they had purchased from his shop, whereas most of his tenants simply owed their last month's rent. The responsibility for recovering the debts fell on Priestley's executors—chairmaker and friend Jacob Daley, printer and publisher Thomas Murphy, and attorney Reverdy Johnson. The executors divided the debts into three categories: "Sperate," "Doubtful," and "Desperate." Priestley's debtors were dispersed throughout Baltimore with the heaviest concentration being in the neighborhood around his shop and home, just northeast of 4 Baltimore Street. The most numerous debtors were fellow cabinetmakers and artisans involved in other woodworking trades.

Lumber dealers on the list were H. Herrington, Job Smith, John Wilson, William H. Bates, Griffith Evans, J. Sleppy, Edward Dowling, and Timothy Richards. Each lived near Priestley and owed him a fairly insignificant sum. Herrington was obligated to pay his fifty-dollar debt in lumber.[24]

The cabinetmakers and chairmakers indebted to Priestley were dispersed throughout Maryland. Washington G. Tuck, for example, was an Annapolis cabinetmaker, as was Daniel Dashiell, who had trained with William Camp in Baltimore. By contrast, cabinetmaker Joseph J. Thomas lived and worked near Priestley and is likely the same Joseph Thomas who became a turner in the late 1830s and early 1840s. Other cabinetmakers on the list are James Askey, James Billington, Henry Dukehart, George McCoull, Levin Pritchett, Charles Suter, and Samuel Thompson. Billington's debt of $405.33 was the largest of any cabinetmaker on the list. Chairmakers who owed Priestley money included Jacob Daley, John Robinson, and Francis Younker's former apprentice, James Pennington.

Priestley's list of debtors documents his involvement with other artisans in the furniture-making trades as well as merchants and businesses that catered to them. Thomas C. Sholes was a principal in Davis & Sholes Upholsterers; Robert L. Porter and John A. Diffenderfer were hardware merchants; Edward Lynch of Lynch & Craft was a merchant specializing in paint; and Edward Patterson of J., W., & E. Patterson was an iron merchant. Debts owed by commission merchants and auctioneers also represent a significant portion of Priestley's estate.[25]

Priestley's clients included many socially prominent and politically powerful individuals from Maryland and the District of Columbia. President and Mrs. James Madison ordered a pair of card tables and a breakfast table from Priestley in 1815. Edward Lloyd V and Edward Lloyd VI were proprietors of Maryland's largest plantation. Edward V, who served as governor, congressman, and senator, was related to many of Priestley's other patrons including the Goughs, Carrolls, and Nicholsons. Like many of their social peers and relatives, Edward V and Edward VI purchased most of their furniture from Priestley rather than from northern, French, or English cabinetmakers. Charles Carnan Ridgely (1760–1829), for example, purchased

$264.62 worth of mahogany furniture from Priestley for his house Hampton in 1812.[26]

Lawyer and judge Roger Brook Taney (1777–1864) owed Priestley $30.25. Taney was admitted to the Maryland bar in 1799 and subsequently served as attorney general and secretary of the treasury during President Andrew Jackson's administration. In 1835, Taney succeeded John Marshall (1755–1835) as chief justice of the United States.[27]

The estate of Baltimore merchant Robert Oliver (1757–1834) also appears on Priestley's list of debtors. Among the wave of British merchants who arrived in the city after the Revolution, Oliver immediately established a lucrative business with Hugh Thompson and his brothers. Oliver dealt with European and Asian merchants and later profited from investments in real estate and railroads. His 1834 estate, which was valued at over $357,000, included a townhouse in Baltimore and two country seats, Green Mount and Harewood. All of Oliver's homes were filled with elaborate silver and furniture, some of which may have come from Priestley's shop.[28]

Baltimore banker George Brown owed Priestley's estate twenty-four dollars, although the latter's executors noted that the debt was probably unrecoverable. Brown's father Alexander (1764–1834) founded the banking firm of Alexander Brown & Sons in 1800. A sideboard with mummy heads similar to those on furniture from Priestley's shop was in Alexander's house, Mondawmin, just outside the city.[29]

John Glenn (d. 1835), a distinguished Baltimore attorney and judge for the United States District Court in Maryland, owed Priestley $49.25. Glenn owned a country house near Catonsville and a townhouse in Baltimore. The sideboard illustrated in figure 29 may have been among the original furnishings of one of these houses. It evidently descended to his granddaughter Letitia (1864–1910), who married Charles Biddle (1857–1923) in Baltimore on April 4, 1888. The piece remains in the Biddle's home Andalusia, located just north of Philadelphia.[30]

A few of the entries in Priestley's list of debtors note the furniture forms involved. Charles Carroll Ridgley's estate owed twenty-four dollars for a coffin for his infant son and Henry B. Chew owed thirty-one dollars for a coffin for his wife Harriet (Ridgley). The price of Priestley's coffins evidently varied based on their size, materials, and detail. Robert Scroggs's coffin, for example, cost only twelve dollars. Monsieur Pageott and Baron de Beher each owed sixteen dollars for a chair, and Mrs. H. Armstrong owed ten dollars for a bedstead.[31]

*Priestley's Inventory*

Priestley's inventory provides a patent view of a large Baltimore cabinetmaking shop from the early nineteenth century (see appendix). The document begins with household furnishings, which included a secretary-and-bookcase, bureau-and-bookcase, card table, pier table, wardrobe, sideboard, sofa, eight-day clock, and sixty-eight books, valued at fifteen dollars. Considering Priestley's extensive use of sophisticated English and French details, it is likely that furniture design books were among these volumes. To lay out these designs,

Priestley and his workmen used "patterns and cullings," a group of which were valued at five dollars by his executors.

Although the size of Priestley's shop evidently diminished during his later years, he owned several sets of tools, twelve workbenches, four glue pots, and a variety of specialized implements at his death. His inventory also lists hinges for card tables, regular tables, beds, French beds, portable desks, and "Duro" chairs, and an assortment of castors, screws, bolts, and handles. To finish the furniture, he had three types of varnish totaling eighty-three gallons. The ochre listed on Priestley's inventory may have been used for "pinking"—a slightly opaque red wash commonly found on eighteenth- and nineteenth-century British and American furniture. Pinking most often appears on the inside backboards of desk-and-bookcases and on the secondary surfaces of writing and dressing compartments. The hardware in Priestley's inventory included glass knobs, bedstead caps, plated handles, and brass ferrets—strips or tapes—for bedposts. This last item and three pieces of furniture attributed to Priestley's shop indicate that he occasionally used brass ornament on his furniture, a feature not commonly associated with Baltimore cabinetmaking.

Like many cabinetmakers, Priestley performed a considerable amount of undertaking work. His inventory lists three cooling boards, thirteen coffin plates, black muslin, and 22,000 brass nails. He also owned a variety of upholstery materials including 200 pounds of curled hair, 20 pounds of duck feathers, duck cloth, and over 215 yards of hair cloths, bed cords, sacking bottoms, and mattresses.

The finished and unfinished furniture listed in Priestley's inventory provides a more extensive view of his shop's production than the objects listed here. Beds, which were the most numerous furniture form, included examples described as "high post" (eleven), "low post" (fifteen), "French" (seven), "trundle" (four), "cradle" (ten), and "crib" (four). The appraisers also divided the tables into several categories: undescribed or "pine" tables (fourteen), "dining" tables (four), "sett [of] extension tables" (one), "breakfast" tables (one), "centre" tables (two), pairs of "card" tables (five), "dressing" tables (one), and "pier" tables (one). Washstands, candlestands, workstands, and trays with stands accounted for nineteen of the forms in Priestley's inventory. Case pieces comprised the smallest group of related forms and included five bureaus, three wardrobes, three desks, three sideboards, and one pedestal sideboard.

Priestley evidently was selling chairs in 1837, although it is impossible to determine whether they were commissioned by him or made in his shop. His inventory lists "chairs," "easy chairs," "bed chairs," "rocking chairs," a "close stool," a "music stool," and "Duro chairs"—a form that does not appear under that name in any manuscripts, inventories, design books, or price books discovered to date. References to "book arms for Duro chairs" and "screws for Duro chairs" in Priestley's inventory suggest that the term "Duro" may have been a corruption of *du roi*. If so, Priestley's "Duro chairs" may have been French-styled chairs with reclining backs and a book support attached to the seat rail or arm rail. Similar examples were illustrated in

Rudolph Ackermann's *Repository of Arts, Literature, Commerce, Manufactures, Fashions, and Politics* (1809–1829)—described as "Pocock's Reclining Patent Chair"—and John Claudius Loudon's *Encyclopedia of Cottage, Farmhouse and Villa Architecture and Furniture* (1833).[32]

*Priestley's Furniture*
The identification of furniture from Priestley's shop is complicated by several factors. At least four styles attained widespread popularity during his career, and he and his tradesmen undoubtedly adapted their work in response to changing tastes, cultural attitudes, and economic conditions. In addition, over 237 cabinetmakers worked in Baltimore between 1800 and 1837, many of whom produced forms similar to Priestley's. Because he employed many journeymen over a long period of time, construction details are only marginally useful in identifying furniture from Priestley's shop. Only when these features are considered in conjunction with documentary evidence can convincing attributions be made.

Receipts and payments made to Priestley provide information on the forms he produced, the prices he charged, and the people who patronized him. The pair of card tables and breakfast table that Priestley sold President and Mrs. James Madison must have been very elaborate for they cost eighty dollars and forty-five dollars, respectively. Even though the Madisons were ardent francophiles, their budget and political acumen may have influenced their decision to patronize an American artisan rather than purchase imported furniture. On May 5, 1815, their agent George Boyd wrote, "There can be no doubt but [furniture] . . . may be had more fashionable and cheaper [in Baltimore] . . . than in . . . [Washington] or George Town, and I only wait your commands to go there and purchase it." Several days later Boyd purchased a dozen fancy chairs from John and Hugh Finlay and the card tables and breakfast table from Priestley, who evidently had the tables on hand since he delivered them within two weeks.[33]

Although rarely acknowledged by decorative arts historians, direct French influences were pervasive in early-nineteenth-century Baltimore furniture. Several English merchants who traded with Maryland planters during the colonial period moved to France during the 1770s and 1780s. Most maintained their transatlantic connections, exporting furnishings, fabrics, and clothing to wealthy Americans, who were becoming increasingly enamoured of French goods. French merchants also opened businesses in Baltimore after the Revolutionary War, and in 1789, the French government established a consul in Baltimore for Maryland, Virginia, and the newly formed District of Columbia. French immigrants arrived in increasing numbers after the fall of Santo Domingo in 1793 and created a Frenchtown in the western section of Baltimore. Some of these newcomers were undoubtedly tradesmen well versed in the latest Parisian styles.[34]

Baltimore consumers had embraced French styles years before the Madisons ordered their tables from Priestley. Furniture made by French emigré Charles Honoré Lannuier (fl. 1803–1819) in New York descended in the Bosley family of Baltimore and a complete set of Pierre de la Mésangère's *Col-

*lection des Meubles et Objets de Goût* (1802–1835) was in the library at Hampton. When fancy chairmaker and furniture decorator Hugh Finlay returned from Europe in 1810, he advertised that he had acquired "a number of Drawings, from furniture in the first houses of London and Paris, which enable [my firm] . . . to make the most approved articles in their line." Several forms and decorative motifs and much of the punched brass ornament on Baltimore painted furniture have direct French parallels.[35]

The appraisers of Priestley's estate described furniture in his cabinet shop as "French," probably owing to his production of continental-inspired forms and his use of metal appliqués. Priestley's inventory lists seven "French" beds, six "Duro" chairs, and thirty-four brass ferrets, and three pieces of furniture attributed to his shop have brass moldings, which are common on French furniture. Priestley's ability to work in the French style undoubtedly appealed to francophiles such as the Madisons and the French consul to America, Chevalier Marter, as well as to cosmopolitan Marylanders such as the Lloyds, Carrolls, and Ridgleys.[36]

Four pieces of Edward Lloyd V's furniture can be attributed to Priestley's shop based on entries in the former's account book and his exclusive patronage of Priestley between 1801 and 1825. In March 1812 and November 1813, Lloyd recorded payments of $670.25 for "Priestley's Bill" and $123.62 "By Edw$^d$ Priestley," respectively. Although the furniture made by Priestley is not identified in these entries, it apparently included a dining table, Grecian sofa, pillar-and-claw card table, desk, and pedestal sideboard. All of these forms date from the early 1810s and correspond to those advertised by Priestley.[37]

The dining table (fig. 5) has book-matched mahogany leaves, thick reeded legs, and columnar pillars with truncated urns, features that occur on related forms from several other Baltimore shops. The slope of the legs and abbreviated shape of the urn turnings differ significantly from those on contemporary tables from New York, Boston, and Philadelphia. When all three sections are assembled, the dining table extends over thirteen feet. Its monumental size and rich materials complemented the other furnishings in the dining room, which included two enormous carved and gilded pier glasses that descended from Edward Lloyd III and three girandoles that Edward V ordered from England in 1810.[38]

Most of the construction details of the dining table are relatively generic, but two features differ from other Baltimore examples. The area between the legs at the base of each pillar is steeply chamfered, and the glue blocks inside the table frame are chamfered at their outer edge and beveled at the top and bottom. Identical blocks are on the pier table that Priestley made for Edward Lloyd VI in 1827 (see fig. 19).[39]

Possibly one of a pair, the pillar-and-claw card table illustrated in figure 6 has stylistic details associated with furniture made in New York, Philadelphia, and Boston, but its form is distinctly Baltimore. Its skirt is unusually deep and its core consists of four laminates, as opposed to the two or three smaller ones commonly found on northern examples. Similarly, the legs on the Lloyd table are dovetailed to a pillar rather than to a plinth. The sides of

*Figure 5*  End of a three-part dining table attributed to Edward Priestley, Baltimore, Maryland, 1810–1815. Mahogany with yellow poplar and oak. H. 28 3/4", W. 164" (all three sections), D. 56 3/4". (Private collection; photo, Gavin Ashworth.)

*Figure 6*  Card table attributed to Edward Priestley, Baltimore, Maryland, 1810–1815. Mahogany with yellow poplar, white pine, oak, and beech. H. 28 3/4", W. 36", D. 17 1/2". (Private collection; photo, Gavin Ashworth.)

*Figure 7* Detail of the top and pillar of the card table illustrated in fig. 6. (Photo, Gavin Ashworth.) The top has wedge-shaped mahogany veneers that eminate from a half-round mahogany panel.

*Figure 8* Detail of the leg molding and carving on the card table illustrated in fig. 6. (Photo, Gavin Ashworth.)

the legs have a slight bulge that creates a central spine, an unusual feature on both northern and southern work. The flat underside of the legs and cyma shaping at the base of the pillar are vestigial eighteenth-century details. Most urban cabinetmakers abandoned these features on card tables during the 1790s. The urn on the pillar of the card table (fig. 7) is not truncated like those on most Baltimore examples, although its shape does have parallels in earlier Annapolis work. A table with a similar base is illustrated in the *Catalogue of the Celebrated Dr. William H. Crim Collection of Genuine Antiques* (1903).[40]

The design of the carving on the knees of the card table is conventional, but the execution is idiosyncratic (fig. 8). Most of the "eyes" (the tear drop-shaped openings in front of the convex folds) between the leaves are skewed and the size of the lobes remains relatively constant from top to bottom rather than diminishing in a naturalistic manner. The quality of this carving does not approach the best work associated with Priestley's shop, strongly suggesting that he employed more than one hand.

Grecian sofas such as the one illustrated in figure 9 were almost ubiquitous in fashionable Baltimore homes. Like most early-nineteenth-century

*Figure 9* Sofa attributed to Edward Priestley, Baltimore, Maryland, 1810–1815. Mahogany with yellow poplar. H. 35", W. 96", D. 24½". (Private collection; photo, Gavin Ashworth.)

*Figure 11* Detail of the carving on the crest rail of the sofa illustrated in fig. 9. (Photo, Gavin Ashworth.)

*Figure 10* Detail of the seat frame construction of the sofa illustrated in fig. 9. (Photo, Gavin Ashworth.)

*Figure 12* Circa 1900 photograph showing a sideboard attributed to Edward Priestley, Baltimore, Maryland, 1810–1815. (Private collection; photo, Gavin Ashworth.)

Baltimore sofas, the Lloyd example is constructed in three sections—back, seat frame, and slip seat—and reinforced with braces attached to the front and rear seat rails (fig. 10). The braces are not hollowed as they are on most Baltimore sofas, including those documented to William Camp, but in other respects the construction and design of their work is similar. In typical Baltimore fashion, the Lloyd sofa has reeding on the crest, front seat rail, and legs, and arm volutes that terminate in roundels. The flower and leaf decoration on the crest rail (fig. 11) appears to be by the same hand that carved the preceding card table (fig. 6, 8). The surfaces of the leaves and petals have broad flutes and shading cuts made with a parting tool—features that make the carving "read" well from a distance.[41]

The sideboard that Edward Lloyd V commissioned from Priestley was destroyed about 1915, but it is visible in a photograph of the dining room at Wye House taken about fifteen years earlier (fig. 12). Pedestal-end forms became popular in Britain during the late eighteenth century and remained fashionable in the English-speaking world for more than a quarter century. Thomas Sheraton's *Cabinet-Maker and Upholsterer's Drawing Book* (1793) featured a design for one with "vase knife cases" and noted that "the pedestal parts . . . may be separate and then screwed to the sideboard." Priestley's shop began producing pedestal-end sideboards by 1807, when he advertised an "elegant" example "with two superb vase knife cases." The Lloyd's pair of British knifecases were displayed on the pedestals of their sideboard.[42]

The writing desk illustrated in figure 13 has feet similar to those on the sideboard. Although the form is more commonly associated with New Eng-

*Figure 13*  Writing desk attributed to Edward Priestley, Baltimore, Maryland, 1810–1815. Mahogany with yellow poplar and white pine. H. 36", W. 36", D. 17³⁄₄". (Private collection; photo, Gavin Ashworth.)

land—particularly coastal Massachusetts and New Hampshire—at least four writing desks with strong Maryland histories are known. Priestley used the term "portable desks" to describe this form, which was logical considering the construction of examples attributed to his shop. The desk sections are made as separate units and their bottom boards are dovetailed to blocks attached to the sides of the table below (fig. 14). Writing desks must have been popular with Maryland consumers. Priestley advertised the form in 1807, and examples are listed in his 1837 inventory.[43]

Baltimore Quaker Joseph Townsend (1756–1841) owned a writing desk (fig. 15) similar to Edward Lloyd V's. Townsend founded the Baltimore Equitable Society (1794) and his company insured Priestley's shop against fire. Townsend's house at 18 Baltimore Street was one block from Priestley's shop and catty-corner from the cabinetmaker's house on Harrison Street. A diary written by Townsend's son Richard (1804–1879) reveals that Joseph Townsend and Priestley were friends.[44]

The Townsend desk diverges from the Lloyd example in having its drawers situated above the writing compartment rather than inside the case and legs with spiral reeding. As on many contemporary Baltimore pieces, the

*Figure 14*   Detail showing the attachment of the desk and table sections of the writing desk illustrated in fig. 13. (Photo, Gavin Ashworth.)

*Figure 15*   Writing desk attributed to Edward Priestley, Baltimore, Maryland, 1810–1815. Mahogany with yellow poplar and white pine. H. 37", W. 32", D. 32¼". (Courtesy, Baltimore Equitable Society; photo, Gavin Ashworth.)

*Figure 16*   Detail showing the attachment of the desk and table sections of the writing desk illustrated in fig. 15. (Photo, Gavin Ashworth.)

*Figure 17* Section of handrailing by Edward Priestley, Baltimore, Maryland, 1826. (Photo, Gavin Ashworth.)

*Figure 18* Detail of the base construction of the liquor case illustrated in fig. 1. (Photo, Gavin Ashworth.)

reeding terminates in Gothic cusps. Although the case and drawer construction of the two writing desks is similar in many respects, the methods used to attach the desk sections differ significantly. On the Townsend example, the desk is glued to a medial brace tenoned to the front rail and dovetailed to the rear rail of the table section (fig. 16). In addition, the rear rail of the table section extends up and is nailed to the sides of the desk. Structural variations such as those mentioned above are commonly found in the work of large shops that employed several tradesmen over an extended period of time.

Like many of his contemporaries, Priestley furnished his clients with architectural components as well as furniture. On September 6, 1826, he billed Edward Lloyd V $7.60 for two feet of planed mahogany, five unturned mahogany newels, three unturned poplar newels, "30 feet Mahogany for [a] Hand Rail," and "30 chests drayage." Installed in the central passage in Wye House, Priestley's handrailing (fig. 17) features bold cyma and astragal moldings and a deep cove for a smooth, firm hold. These moldings differ from those of the flanking chair rail, which is original to the house and dates about 1787. Since Edward V ordered a "passage chandelier" in 1826, it is possible that the new handrail replaced an earlier one with candle arms. Priestley evidently had trouble securing payment for this work. On June 4, 1827, he billed Edward Lloyd VI for the architectural fixtures ordered by his father, along with two bedsteads and the surviving pier table and liquor case.[45]

During the summer of 1827, Edward VI was in the process of furnishing his residence at Wye Heights, an old Lloyd family property adjacent to Wye House. He received the land and a circa 1721 house from his father prior to his marriage to Alicia McBlair (1806–1838) of Baltimore on November 30, 1827. On July 22, 1827, Annapolis joiner Jeremiah L. Boyd billed Edward Lloyd V for interior and exterior work at Wye Heights. The architectural components specified in this extensive document suggest that Edward V paid to have the house converted from an eighteenth-century relic into a fashionable Greek revival structure. Edward VI and his family lived at Wye Heights until 1834, when they moved to Wye House after his father's death.[46]

The liquor case and pier table illustrated in figure 1 are undoubtedly the ones listed in Priestley's June 4, 1827, bill to Edward Lloyd VI:

| | |
|---|---|
| To Frame for Marble Slab | 33.00 |
| Mahogany Bedstead | 38.00 |
| Casted Maple Do. | 25.00 |
| Liquor Case | 35.00 |
| 2 Matresss 53 and 59½     112½ & 62½ | 69.37 |
| 11 yards Bed tick 17 casted Making Matress | 18.87 |
| Framing 2 Dressing Glasses | 10.00 |
| Cot and Tray | 5.54 |
| | $234.24 |

Inspired by Roman sarcophagi, the liquor case is constructed of sawn and joined mahogany boards that are screwed to a white pine base frame (fig. 18). The top, sides, front, and back are veneered with crotch mahogany, whereas the outer face of the base frame is veneered with less figured wood.

*Figure 19* Detail of the glue blocks on the pier table illustrated in fig. 1. (Photo, Gavin Ashworth.)

*Figure 20* Detail of the carved mummy head on the right front leg of the pier table illustrated in fig. 1. (Photo, Gavin Ashworth.)

*Figure 21* "Indian or Bearded Bacchus" designs illustrated on plate 57 of Thomas Hope's *Household Furniture and Interior Decoration* (1807). (Courtesy, Winterthur Library, Printed Books, and Periodical Collection.)

*Figure 22* Design for a chimney piece illustrated on plate 52 of Abraham Swan's *The British Architect or, The Builder's Treasury of Staircases* (1758). (Courtesy, Winterthur Library, Printed Books, and Periodical Collection.)

The interior is fitted with partitions for twelve bottles, and the feet retain their original casters, which allowed the liquor case to be moved easily from its storage spot underneath the pier table.[47]

The pier table, or "frame for a marble slab," is one of the most ornate pieces documented to Priestley's shop. It has mahogany legs with carved "mummy" heads, thick reeding, turned moldings and feet, and a mahogany-veneered yellow poplar frame. The back, side, and front rails are tenoned to the legs, and each joint is reinforced with a vertical white pine glue block (fig. 19). The blocks are chamfered on the outside edge and beveled at the top to reduce the surface area that supports the marble, thus making it more stable. Although no bill for the slab is known, the Lloyds purchased marble mantels, hearths, steps, and grave monuments from Baltimore stonecutter Thomas Towson throughout the 1820s.[48]

The exquisitely sculpted mummy heads (fig. 20), or "Persians," on the front legs of the pier table are taken from illustrations of Bacchus on plates 37 and 57 (see fig. 21) in Thomas Hope's *Household Furniture and Interior Decoration* (1807). Priestley deviated from Hope's designs by crowning his heads with stylized folds bound with a crisscross ribbon rather than with turbans. Priestley's design may have been inspired by pulvinated friezes illustrated in architectural design books (see fig. 22) such as Abraham Swan's *British Architect* (1758), or by examples that he had seen. Nineteenth-century designers and tradesmen were versatile in their adaptation of mummy head motifs. Examples similar to Priestley's appear on a variety of furniture forms depicted in Charles Percier and Pierre-François-Leonard Fontaine's *Recueil des Decorations Interieures* (1801), Pierre de la Mésangère's *Collection des Meubles et Objets de Goût* (1802–1835), and George Smith's *Collection of Designs for Household Furniture and Interior Decoration* (1808). *The New-York Book of Prices for Manufacturing Cabinet and Chair Work* (1817) lists mummy heads as an option for a "French Sideboard."[49]

Mummy imagery is usually associated with the Egyptian style, a late phase of neoclassicism that was especially popular for dining-room furnishings. As decorative arts historian Donald L. Fennimore has shown, Egyptian columns are the ultimate source of reeded supports—legs, pillars, columns—on many pieces of nineteenth-century American furniture. The legs of the pier table, for example, are reminiscent of the bundled stone reeds used to support Egyptian architectural monuments such as the temples at Luxor. By contrast, the Greeks and Romans relied solely on plain, fluted, or counter-fluted pillars. Thomas Sheraton's *Cabinet Dictionary* (1803) noted that "reeding appears the only ornament that has escaped the notice of the ancients."[50]

The date of Edward Lloyd VI's pier table demands a reevaluation of the period typically associated with the Egyptian style in America. Most scholars have argued that the taste for Egyptianalia in Baltimore reached its peak around 1820 owing to the influence of William Camp, who died in 1822. The pier table, in fact, has been attributed to Camp's shop on more than one occasion. Priestley's bill to Lloyd and Fennimore's research, however, indicate that the Egyptian style flourished well into the 1830s. A Philadelphia sideboard with twinned caryatids based on plate 95 in Smith's *Collection of Designs for Household Furniture* supports this theory. It bears the label of Joseph Barry and Joseph Krickbaum, who were in partnership from 1831 to 1833.[51]

The pier table made by Priestley serves as a cornerstone for separating his work from that of Barry, Krickbaum, and other American artisans who produced similar forms. Two sideboard tables, three sideboards, three chests of drawers, and three desks have carved heads by the same artisan responsible for those on the Lloyd table. The modeling and shading techniques are the same, and the heads vary only slightly in composition.[52]

The sideboard table illustrated in figure 23 is most similar to the pier table (fig. 1). Their rail and stile panels, astragal moldings, veneer treatment, and feet are essentially the same, and both tables feature front legs with similarly carved heads and rear legs, with reeding "bound" with a double astragal collar. The folds and fringe on the heads are identical, although those on the sideboard table have two additional tassels. The design of the ribbon above and around the faces also differs, as does the modeling and shading of the eyebrows.[53]

*Figure 23*  Sideboard table attributed to Edward Priestley, Baltimore, Maryland, 1825–1835. Mahogany with yellow poplar, oak, and mahogany. H. 39³/₄", W. 82¹/₄", D. 27¹/₂". (Private collection; courtesy, Hirschl and Adler Galleries.)

A sideboard in a private collection, another formerly owned by Dr. William H. Crim (fig. 24), and a similar example in the Baltimore Museum of Art (fig. 25) have therms with mummy heads on the pedestals. The heads (fig. 26) on the latter sideboard have angular features, wavy goatee hair, and turbans with plain crisscross ribbon that surrounds the face. Because the therms are engaged rather than freestanding like the legs on the pier and sideboard tables, the drapery below the mummy heads has only five tassels—three on the front and two on the exposed side. Tapered therms with anthropomorphic feet appear on sideboard tables illustrated in plates 94 and 95 of Smith's *Collection of Designs for Household Furniture* and described in *The New-York Book of Prices*. The brass moldings on the sideboard at the Baltimore Museum of Art (fig. 25) are similar in size and shape to the mahogany astragals on the Crim example and on pieces documented and attributed to Priestley's shop.[54]

*Figure 24*  Sideboard attributed to Edward Priestley, Baltimore, Maryland, 1825–1835. Dimensions and woods not recorded. The sideboard was lot no. 107 in O. A. Kirkland's *Catalogue of the Celebrated Dr. William H. Crim Collection of Genuine Antiques* (1903).

*Figure 25*  Sideboard attributed to Edward Priestley, Baltimore, Maryland, 1825–1835. Mahogany with yellow poplar, yellow pine, and mahogany. H. 46 3/4", W. 82 1/4", D. 27 1/2". (Courtesy, Baltimore Museum of Art.) The sideboard is comprised of three dovetailed cases that rest on a joined frame. The right pedestal is fitted with a round revolving bottle holder.

*Figure 26*  Detail of a mummy head on the sideboard illustrated in fig. 25.

*Figure 27* Desk attributed to Edward Priestley, Baltimore, Maryland, 1825–1835. Mahogany, satinwood, and ebony with yellow poplar, white pine, and mahogany. H. 56 3/4", W. 54", D. 22 1/4". (Courtesy, Maryland Historical Society; photo, David Prencipe.)

*Figure 28* Detail of the mummy head and therm on the right side of the desk illustrated in fig. 27.

A desk (fig. 27) that reputedly descended in the Owings family of Baltimore and one owned by the late Andy Warhol were not made for a dining room, the prescribed placement for Egyptianalia. Both have veneered cylinder lids that open to reveal a writing compartment with satinwood drawers, pigeon-hole valances, and colonettes supporting a central arch. The squared therms on either side of the Owings desk (fig. 28) are decorated with acanthus carving rather than the reeding that is on the Warhol desk. Although the design and execution of the leafage is related to that on Edward Lloyd V's card table (fig. 8) and sofa (fig. 11), the quality of the acanthus carving on the desk is superior. The leaves on the sides of the therms drop from scroll volutes, a design often found on architectural trusses. Given the fact that Priestley's shop did architectural work, it is conceivable that he made furniture to complement interior details in his patrons' homes. The mummy heads on the desk (fig. 28) are similar to others in the group (figs. 20, 23, 24, 26) with a few minor exceptions: the drapery has only four tassels; the goatee hair is more open and less detailed, and there is no rosette at the juncture of the crisscross ribbon. These variations are primarily stylistic, however. The mummy heads on the Warhol desk are less sophisticated but conform to the same basic pattern.[55]

A marble-top sideboard table (fig. 29) that belonged to Charles and Letitia (Glenn) Biddle has freestanding squared therms related to the engaged ones on the Owings desk. The tripartite reeding echoes details on the therms of the preceeding sideboards (figs. 24, 25), and the mummy heads (fig. 30)

*Figure 29*  Sideboard attributed to Edward Priestley, Baltimore, Maryland, 1825–1835. Mahogany with yellow poplar and white pine; marble. H. 40", W. 82 1/4", D. 24". (Courtesy, Andalusia Foundation; photo, Gavin Ashworth.)

*Figure 30*  Detail of a mummy head on the sideboard illustrated in fig. 29. (Photo, Gavin Ashworth.)

*Figure 31* Chest of drawers attributed to Edward Priestley, Baltimore, Maryland, 1825–1835. Mahogany. Secondary woods and dimensions not recorded. (Courtesy, Sotheby's.)

have precisely sculpted facial features that vary only slightly from other examples documented and attributed to Priestley's shop (figs. 20, 23, 24, 26, 28). The goatees are deeply carved and the individual tufts of hair are clustered more tightly than those on other mummy heads in the group. The drapery festoons below the heads are gadrooned rather than fringed (see figs. 20, 30), although the tassels are positioned at the corners of the therms as they are on the Owings desk (fig. 28). On the Biddle sideboard table, the capitals of the rear legs are smaller versions of the shafts of the therms—a design conceptually related to the legs of the Lloyd pier table. Like the sideboard shown in figure 25, the Biddle example is further ornamented with brass moldings.[56]

The remaining mummy head pieces in the Priestley group are a pair of bow front chests of drawers (see fig. 31). These are the only objects attributed to his shop that have "twinned" or oppositely facing heads. The composition of the twins draws on the same imagery as the other heads, and the square shafts have three reeds and end in human feet just as they do on the sideboards and desk illustrated in figures 24, 25, 27, and 29. The case—with a bowed or, as Priestley advertised, "circular" front—has parallels in contemporary Baltimore work.[57]

The stock dimensions of the mummy heads and therms are remarkably consistent given the variety of case and table designs in the group. All of the heads are nine inches high, three inches wide, and three inches deep, and all were carved from four-inch stock. The legs and supports are one piece of mahogany and are consistently eighteen inches high, except for the legs of the sideboard table shown in figure 23, which have separate feet and are 12 3/4 inches high.[58]

The carver responsible for the mummy heads was probably an employee of Priestley's shop. There is no conclusive evidence that he ever subcontracted work to the "carvers and gilders" in Baltimore, most of whom were looking glass makers and retailers. Unpublished research conducted by furniture historian Sumpter Priddy reveals that some of the itinerant immigrant stone masons and sculptors commissioned to work on architectural edifices advertised that they also worked in stucco and wood. Most of these artisans were Italian and French natives who worked for short periods of time in Washington, D.C., and Virginia, and are known to have passed through Baltimore, working on public monuments such as the Battle Monument (see fig. 3), the Washington Monument, and the Catholic cathedral. It is possible that Priestley hired one or more of these emigrés to ornament his case pieces and tables. The harmonious integration of the mummy heads, therm shafts, and other details on the case pieces and tables documented and attributed to his shop, suggests that Priestley was intimately involved in the design and production process throughout his career.

Priestley was fifty-nine when he died in 1837. His last will and testament mentions only his sons, Edward, aged five, and Howard, aged three. Priestley's obituary, probably written by Thomas Murphy, his executor and the publisher of the *Baltimore American*, noted that he:

> Came to Baltimore about . . . 1790, a friendless orphan boy with an aged and helpless mother, to whose support and comfort he devoted his life with the most exemplary filial piety, until her death, which took place only two years ago. By unremitting industry, and unwavering integrity, he secured a competency, and was much respected by a numerous circle of acquaintances. Possessed of a strong mind, a warm heart, and ardent feelings, he was a last friend, a good neighbor, and a useful citizen. His hand was ever open to relieve the distressed, and many a widow and orphan, when they hear of his death, will have to shed a tear to his memory. He met with an accident about two weeks ago, which no doubt hastened his death—returning home between his shop and dwelling, he fell and broke his arm—fever ensued—and he is now no more.[59]

Priestley's career has been sorely overlooked because no signed or labeled examples of his work are known; yet he was clearly a pivotal figure in Baltimore's cabinetmaking community. As a native of Annapolis, he was one of many craftsmen who introduced vestiges of eighteenth-century design and workmanship, most of which reflected English—and specifically London—traditions. He arrived in Baltimore during a period of great economic prosperity and achieved success through his own fortitude and business acumen. He secured a spot on the city's most commercial street, forged ties with merchants, artisans, and professionals, and engaged in a variety of business ventures, some of which proved more lucrative than his trade.

Although scholars have long believed that Philadelphia styles exerted a dominant influence on Baltimore furniture during the early nineteenth century, the work associated with Priestley and his competitors presents a much more complex story. The unique character of Baltimore neoclassical furniture reflects the cross-fertilization of styles from many cultural backgrounds and traditions—those of England, Ireland, Scotland, Germany, France, Annapolis, Philadelphia, Boston, and Portsmouth, to name but a few. Priestley's success lay in his ability to accommodate the diverse tastes of his patrons and respond to different styles and changing economic trends.[60]

ACKNOWLEDGMENTS   For assistance with this article, the author thanks James A. Abbott, David Atkinson, James Biddle, Gretchen T. Buggeln, Stiles Tuttle Colwill, Billie Conkling, Jeannine Disviscour, William Voss Elder III, Donald L. Fennimore, Brock Jobe, Lynne Dakin Hastings, the staff of Hirschl and Adler, Townsend D. Kent, Roger D. Kirtley, Timothy C. Naylor, Sumpter Priddy, R. J. Rockefeller, Martha Rowe, Page Talbott, Neville Thompson, Robert F. Trent, Gregory R. Weidman, and Sharon Woodard. I am especially grateful to Mrs. R. Carmichael Tilghman for allowing me to study so extensively the Lloyd family objects at Wye House.

1. Lloyd papers, ms. 2001, Maryland Historical Society, Baltimore (hereafter cited as MHS). The Lloyds' patronage of furniture craftsmen is detailed in Alexandra A. Alevizatos, "'Procured of the best and Most Fashionable Materials:' The Furniture and Furnishings of the Edward Lloyd Family, 1750–1850" (M.A. thesis, University of Delaware, 1999). The Lloyds purchased a small amount of furniture from Annapolis cabinetmakers John Shaw (in 1801, 1804, 1809, and 1811) and Washington G. Tuck. They also purchased coffins and farm implements from Easton, Maryland, cabinetmakers James and Joseph Neale. Other Baltimore cabinetmakers patronized by the Lloyds were fancy furniture makers John and Hugh Finlay and chairmakers John Oldham, William Singleton, and Jacob Daley. The value of the objects purchased from the aforementioned artisans was minimal. *Federal Gazette* (Baltimore), June 28, 1817.

2. Priestley's obituary in the March 14, 1837, issue of the *Baltimore American* states that his mother Mary Ann was forty-one and "aged and helpless" in 1790. The age given for her was incorrect for she was eighty-five at her death in 1835. Mary Ann Priestley (Priestly, Pressley) was listed as the ship's nurse for the colonial frigate *Defence* and as a widow with no wealth in the 1783 tax assessment for Annapolis, Maryland. See Appendix B in Edward C. Papenfuse, *In Pursuit of Profit: Annapolis Merchants in the Era of the American Revolution (1763–1805)* (Baltimore: Johns Hopkins University Press, 1975.) As quoted in "A New Yorker in Maryland in 1793 and 1824," *Maryland Historical Magazine* 47, no. 2 (June 1952): 139. Kent also noted that Baltimore had the most elegant dancing assembly room in the United States. The building containing this room also housed the Library Company of Baltimore, which owned furniture design books. Many Baltimore cabinetmakers were members of the Library Company.

3. *The Baltimore Directory* (Baltimore: Warner & Hannah Publishers, 1800–1801), p. 22. No residence for Edward Priestley or his mother is listed until 1802. Presumably they lived with a relative or friend prior to that date. Two other Priestleys are documented in Maryland during the late eighteenth and early nineteenth centuries. James Priestley, principal of the Baltimore Academy, lived on St. Paul Street from 1798 to 1808. Perrigrine Priestley lived in Talbot County (*Baltimore Directory* [Baltimore: James Robinson, 1804]). "Baltimore Town" referred to the area west of the Jones Falls. Baltimore Town was distinguished from Fell's Point, which was east of the Jones Falls on the water, and Old Town or Jones Town, which was east of the Jones Falls and north of Fell's Point. Court Proceedings of Baltimore County, liber wb3, folio 36, Maryland State Archives (hereafter cited as MSA), Annapolis. John Henry Hill, "Baltimore Furniture Craftsmen, 1783–1824" (M.A. thesis, University of Delaware, 1968), p. 47. The only record of Kirby is the indenture between him and Minskey.

4. The *Telegraph and Daily Advertiser* (Baltimore), October 18, 1802. Hill, "Baltimore Furniture Craftsmen," p. 99. Chairmaking did not include large sofas, such as classical Grecian sofas that were constructed of three separately joined frames. See Margaret Burke Clunie, "Salem Federal Furniture" (M.A. thesis, University of Delaware, 1976). Priestley and Minskey never referred to themselves as warehousemen, although they clearly maintained a stock in trade. Furniture warehouses first appeared in Baltimore in 1784, when London-trained cabinetmaker Richard Lawson and his partner John Bankson advertised their own stock along with imported furniture. Most Baltimore cabinetmakers working before the War of 1812 did not maintain large inventories.

5. Although Minskey may have profited from the firm's involvement in the furniture export trade, Priestley's name appears exclusively in the Savannah advertisements and he evidently

oversaw this aspect of the business. See Gregory R. Weidman, *Furniture in Maryland, 1740–1940: The Collection of the Maryland Historical Society* (Baltimore: Maryland Historical Society, 1984), pp. 76, 87. McColm worked as an independent tradesman in the cabinetmaking shop of Coleman & Taylor.

6. This venture represents Priestley's only documented foray into the furniture export trade. Considering his subsequent involvement in the coastal lumber trade, it is possible that he continued to export furniture. Philadelphia cabinetmaker Joseph B. Barry (fl. 1797–1833) also endeavored to sell furniture in Savannah. His venture, which began in October 1798, lasted only one month. In February 1803, Barry opened a shop at 130 Baltimore Street in Baltimore. The following month, he moved his business to Light Street near Priestley and Minskey. Barry closed his Baltimore shop early in 1804. Having failed to break into other markets, Barry also began selling lumber. Donald L. Fennimore and Robert T. Trump, "Joseph B. Barry, Philadelphia Cabinetmaker," *Antiques* 135, no. 5 (May 1989): 1215–17.

7. Baltimore Street was also known as Market Street. Priestley's advertisement in the *Georgia Republican and State Intelligencer* continued to run weekly through April 18, 1803. James Robinson, *The Baltimore Directory for 1804* (Baltimore: Warner & Hanna Publishers, 1804), p. 1. Priestley and Minskey's Baltimore Street shop had been occupied by cabinetmaker James Davidson (fl. 1783–1806) from 1796 until his death in 1806. *Baltimore American*, November 3, 1806. After Davidson's death, his wife Margaret attempted to maintain the cabinetmaking business but eventually sold the shop to Priestley and Minskey. Their business was enhanced by two chairmakers—Jacob Daley and Francis Younker (fl. 1807–1833). Both had apprenticed to Richard Sweeney (fl. 1796–1837), one of the local chairmakers associated with James Davidson. Daley and Younker moved into Sweeney's shop shortly after Davidson moved his business to Old Town in 1807. Daley was a trustee of Priestley's estate and the guardian of his children. Younker is listed as a chairmaker at 4 Baltimore Street from 1810 to 1824. Evidently he was producing and selling chairs from Priestley's shop. Hill, "Baltimore Furniture Craftsmen," pp. 62, 64, 105, 159. For more on Jacob Daley and Richard Sweeney's apprentices, see Nancy Goyne Evans, *American Windsor Chairs* (New York: Hudson Hills Press for the Winterthur Museum, 1996), pp. 164–72, 690, 712. Daley had more apprentices than any one chairmaker in Baltimore. Although he worked for several prominent Maryland patrons including the Lloyds, Daley only marked a few chairs, and his career remains fairly obscure.

8. Orphan's Court Proceedings of Baltimore County (1798–1803), liber 4, folio 206, MSA. Pringle may have guaranteed Priestley and Minskey when they first sought capital and support for their business. See Stuart Weems Bruchey, *Robert Oliver, Merchant of Baltimore, 1783–1819* (Baltimore: Johns Hopkins University Studies in Historical and Political Science, series 74, no. 1, 1956), p. 125; and J. Thomas Scharf, *Chronicles of Baltimore* (Baltimore: Turnbull Brothers, 1874), pp. 230, 288. Orphan's Court Proceedings of Baltimore County (1805–1808), liber 6, folio 220, MSA. Orphan's Court Proceedings of Baltimore County (1805–1808), liber 6, folio 270, MSA. Hutton and Plaines were the only apprentices who subsequently established their own cabinetmaking shops. Only 13 percent of all apprentices bound to Baltimore cabinetmakers between 1783 and 1824 became shop masters. For more on apprenticeship agreements in Baltimore, see Hill, "Baltimore Furniture Craftsmen," p. 47.

9. Hill, "Baltimore Furniture Craftsmen," pp. 140–41.

10. Minskey took orphan Morgan Hill as an apprentice in 1810. Minskey died on March 14, 1819, leaving a wife and three young children. His obituary appeared in the *Baltimore American* on April 1, 1819. No furniture or orders pertaining to Priestley and Minskey are known; however, Edward Lloyd V was dealing with Priestley during his partnership with Minskey.

11. *American and Commercial Daily Advertiser* (Baltimore), November 20, 1807. This is the first reference to Priestley selling lumber. *Baltimore Evening Post*, August 12, 1808; *Whig*, August 24, 1808.

12. Many Baltimore cabinetmakers opened warehouses during Baltimore's economic boom following the War of 1812. William Camp maintained a wareroom on Concord Street and John Howe maintained the Baltimore Carpet, Furniture and Looking Glass Warehouse on Calvert Street. The profusion of advertisements for furniture warehouses suggests that many cabinetmakers increased their labor force in order to mass-produce stock items. *Federal Gazette* (Baltimore), June 28, 1817. In the *Baltimore Directory and Register for 1814–15* (Baltimore: J. C. O'Reilly, 1814) Priestley's business is referred to as a "chair and cabinetmaking shop."

13. Priestley took William Sefton, a seventeen-year-old orphan, in February 1808 (Orphan's Court Proceedings of Baltimore County [1805–1808], liber 6, folio 305, MSA); John Howlett, a

fourteen year old, in March 1808 (Baltimore County Register of Wills [Indentures], 1806–1808, folio 423); and brothers Henry and William Stewart, aged sixteen and eighteen, respectively, in April 1808 (Orphan's Court Proceedings of Baltimore County [1805–1808], liber 6, folio 316, MSA). Howlett ran away in 1814, eight months before his term ended (*American and Commercial Daily Advertiser*, March 18, 1815). Hill, "Baltimore Furniture Craftsmen," pp. 45, 62. From June 1807 to October 1808, Priestley housed, fed, clothed, and employed James Hasitland, receiving sixty dollars from the latter's "benefactor" Edward Lloyd V. In an 1808 letter to Lloyd, Priestley expressed his desire to take Hasitland as an apprentice. Hasitland's status remains unclear, but he may have been a slave, free black, or indentured white (Lloyd Papers, ms. 2001, microfilm reel 25, MHS). Similarly, no official apprenticeship document survives for Levin Pritchett (Prichard). In 1818, Priestley advertised that Pritchett ran away from his shop where he was "an apprentice to the Cabinet Business" (*American and Commercial Daily Advertiser*, March 26, 1818). Priestley and Pritchett must have reconciled for Priestley subsequently extended Pritchett credit and leased him property. Priestley advertised for "three or four laborers" in the July 21, 1809, issue of the *Whig*. He also reported that he had "on hand a large quantity of mahogany furniture which he will dispose of on accommodating terms."

14. "John Needles (1786–1878): An Autobiography," edited by Edward Needles Wright, *Journal of Quaker History* 58, no. 1 (Spring 1969): 13.

15. The letter is in the Municipal Archives, City of Baltimore, Bureau of Legislative Reference, ms. 1805 (364), February 15, 1816. For more on Lusby, see Alevizatos, "The Furniture and Furnishings of the Edward Lloyd Family," pp. 73–74, 216–17. Priestley and Roney served together in the War of 1812.

16. There are several plausible explanations for Priestley's not appearing on the federal censuses taken in 1800, 1810, 1820, and 1830. Although unlikely, he may simply have been overlooked. Alternatively, Priestley may have distrusted the federal government and intentionally eluded the census takers. See Priestley's letter to the editor in the *Baltimore Whig*, June 12, 1813. The author thanks her sister Dorothy for suggesting legal reasons why Priestley may have avoided the census.

17. *Matchett's Baltimore Directories,* (Baltimore: R. J. Matchett, 1820–1840). Scott is listed at Priestley's address in *Matchett's Baltimore Directory for 1824* (Baltimore: R. J. Matchett, 1824). Hill, "Baltimore Furniture Craftsmen," pp. 54, 89, 108, 126. In 1826, Priestley hired William Roney to turn the newel posts he supplied for Wye House. Although no documentation survives, Priestley may also have patronized carver and gilder James Fraser who worked out of 2 Baltimore Street in 1812.

18. Sale of William Camp, January 3, 1823, account of sales, Baltimore County, liber wb8.

19. Priestley's estate included 91,113 feet of various types of plank; 3,666 feet of mahogany veneer; 200 feet of satinwood veneer; 506 feet of mahogany logs; and 2 slabs of wood. The plank included pine, mahogany, cherry, poplar, bay wood, and "mixed."

20. *American and Commercial Daily Advertiser,* November 20, 1807. Chancery Court of Baltimore City, liber 116, p. 527, MSA, Annapolis. Hill, "Baltimore Furniture Craftsmen," p. 151.

21. *American and Commercial Daily Advertiser,* February 23, 1811; March 12, 1816; and December 4, 1819.

22. The *Whig* (Baltimore), July 21, 1809. For Fisher's notice, see *American and Commercial Daily Advertiser,* March 30, 1810. For Brown's notice, see *Federal Gazette*, March 18, 1815.

23. Boglap Street no longer exists in Baltimore. The author thanks Sharon Woodward, president of the Baltimore Equitable Society, for providing information on Priestley's policy. Priestley maintained the policy until his death in 1837.

24. William H. Bates was a coachmaker, Griffith Evans was a cooper, J. Sleppy and Edward Dowling were carpenters, and Timothy Richards was a wheelwright.

25. Although Priestley could have sold furniture through commission merchants and auctioneers, it is more likely that the debts to his estate reflect purchases by the principals of the companies specified. The only businesses that owed Priestley money were the Merchants Bank and Friendship Fire Company, of which Priestley was a member. Richard Lemmon, the auctioneer at Robt. Lemmon & Co., and James Gittings of Merryman & Gittings had open accounts, as did commission merchants James Thompson of O'Donnell's Wharf, Lambert Gittings, Hugh Bolton of Stewart & Bolton, and Charles Karthaus, who imported wares and sold pianos made by John Gieb at his merchant house. Karthaus, Kurtz & Co.; Joseph Tucker; and William Barr and James Armour all owned dry goods merchant shops at 73, 59, and 53 Baltimore Street, respectively. *American and Commercial Daily Advertiser*, June 9, 1819.

26. Edward Lloyd V served as a United States congressman from 1806 to 1808, as governor of Maryland from 1809 to 1811, and as a United States senator from 1819 to 1826. As the sixth proprietor of Wye House, he was the largest producer of wheat in Maryland when he died in 1834. Edward V's brother-in-law Joseph Hopper Nicholson (1770–1817) owed Priestley $43.50 when he died in 1817. Edward V paid his debt (Lloyd Family Account Book, 1803–1820, private collection, Wye House, Talbot County, Maryland). A United States congressman from 1800 to 1806, Nicholson chaired the 1812 meetings of the Democratic citizens of Baltimore, in which they drafted letters to Congress in support of a war with England. Priestley shared the same opinions and expressed his heartfelt support for the French (*Baltimore Whig*, June 5, 1813). The author thanks Gregory R. Weidman for sharing her research on the Ridgley's furniture and patronage.

27. Scharf, *Chronicles of Baltimore*, p. 431.

28. Ibid., pp. 209, 472. For more information on Oliver's merchant business, see Bruchey, *Robert Oliver, Merchant of Baltimore*. Two of Oliver's executors—his brother Thomas Oliver and merchant Robert M. Gibbes—were clients of Priestley. Baltimore County Inventories, 1835, pp. 425–45.

29. See Scharf, *Chronicles of Baltimore*, p. 468. Fancy furniture purchased by the Browns from John and Hugh Finlay remains in the collections of descendants. For more on furniture commissioned by the Brown family, see Gregory R. Weidman and Jennifer F. Goldsborough, eds., *Classical Maryland, 1815–1845* (Baltimore: Maryland Historical Society, 1993), pp. 92–96.

30. Glenn's house and furnishings were vandalized during the 1835 riots (precipitated by ideas espoused during the Democratic Convention) in Baltimore. He was reimbursed over $37,000 for the damage to his home and furnishings (Scharf, *Chronicles of Baltimore*, p. 476). Another debtor who sustained considerable damages during the riot was Priestley's attorney Reverdy Johnson, whose mansion on Monument Square was one of the grandest in the city. Johnson escaped injury by fleeing to Fort McHenry. The city of Baltimore reimbursed him over $40,000 (ibid., pp. 489, 516).

31. Many other prominent attorneys, accountants, doctors, merchants, gentlemen, and ship captains were among Priestley's debtors. Some of the amounts were quite large. Accountant John Barrington owed his estate $580 for a note due in 1834 and H. O. Diffenderfer owed $496, payable in iron bar. Smaller debtors included Dr. Ashton Alexander, Dr. Barr, bank cashier Jacob Bier, Captain John Chase, Miss Chew, Dr. D. H. Clendenin, merchant J. Cornthwaite, Samuel J. Donaldson, Charles W. Dorsey, Dr. Michael Diffenderfer, attorneys W. H. Gatchell and Upton Scott Heath, attorney Reverdy Johnson, printer Sheppard C. Leakin, Captains Joshua Mezick and James Philips, conveyancer Beale Spurrier, Henry Thomson, and insurer Joseph Townsend.

32. The author thanks Robert F. Trent for suggesting that "Duro" could be a corruption of *du roi* and for sharing his information on French chairs. See Pauline Agius, *Ackermann's Regency Furniture and Interiors* (Wiltshire, Eng.: Crowood Press, 1984), p. 72. John Claudius Loundon, *An Encyclopedia of Cottage, Farm, and Villa Architecture and Furniture* (London: Longman, Orme Brown, Green, & Longmans, 1839), pl. 1913.

33. In March 1808, Priestley charged Dr. Thomas C. Walker forty dollars for a "small commode sideboard" (Craddock Papers, ms. 196, MHS)—a form he advertised five months later. *The Whig*, August 24, 1808. In 1817, Priestley sold Maryland planter Harry Dorsey Gough a mahogany cradle for the enormous sum of ten dollars (Harry Dorsey Gough Papers, MHS). Gough's home, Perry Hall, was in Harford County, Maryland. Hill, "Baltimore Furniture Craftsmen," p. 214. Katherine Conover Hunt, "The White House Furnishings of the Madison Administration, 1809–1817" (M.A. thesis, University of Delaware, 1971), pp. 46–49, 61. The author thanks Tara Gleason for this reference. Presidential commissions elevated the reputation of Priestley as well as those of contemporaries William Camp and John and Hugh Finlay. Other cabinetmakers who received similar commissions were William Palmer of New York and John Aiken of Philadelphia.

34. These merchants included Messrs. Moubos, Latil, Zacharie, Pascault, Dumeste, and Delaporte. Scharf, *Chronicles of Baltimore*, p. 209. Alevizatos, "The Furniture and Furnishings of the Edward Lloyd Family," pp. 41, 162, 164. When the Marquis de Lafayette visited Baltimore in July 1824, his secretary, Monsieur Levasseur, recorded that the city's residents possessed an air of "elegance and delicacy of manners" that typified "the amiable union of American frankness and French ease." In his description of Baltimoreans' patronage of the fine arts, Levasseur mentioned two French artisans, Monsieur Giles, the director of the Basilica Cathedral's choir,

and Maximilien Godefroy, architect of the Unitarian Church—"a masterpiece of elegance and simplicity" (Raphael Semmes, *Baltimore As Seen by Visitors, 1783–1860* [Baltimore: Maryland Historical Society, 1953], pp. 63–65). These immigrant artisans undoubtedly had an influence on Baltimore tastes. Edward Lloyd V was Lafayette's host in Maryland.

35. The Bosley's Lannuier suite is in the Maryland Historical Society. See Peter M. Kenny, Frances F. Bretter and Ulrich Leben, *Honoré Lannuier: Cabinetmaker from Paris* (New York: Metropolitan Museum of Art, 1998), pp. 133–35. Finlay's notice appeared in the *Baltimore American*, December 19, 1810, as quoted in Weidman, *Furniture in Maryland*, p. 77. Hugh Finlay visited Europe two years before Joseph Barry. Like the Madisons, Priestley was an ardent francophile. He served as a private in the War of 1812 and supported the French cause in newspaper editorials. In the June 2, 1813, issue of the *Baltimore Whig*, he described Captain John Roberts as a "viper" who "would rather see Baltimore burn by the British than saved by the French." In the June 18, 1813, issue of the *Federal Republican and Commercial Gazette* (Georgetown, Maryland), Roberts subsequently accused Priestley of being a coward and calumniator because Priestley did not sign his name to his editorial in the *Baltimore Whig*. The author thanks Martin L. Russell of the American Antiquarian Society for helping locate this editorial. Weidman and Goldsborough, *Classical Maryland*, figs. 121–28.

36. Chevalier Marter's name appears on Priestley's list of debtors.

37. Wye House is currently the home of the twelfth consecutive generation of the Lloyd family, eight of whom have lived in the 1787 Wye House structure that survives today. Lloyd Family Account Book, 1803–1820. See Alevizatos, "The Furniture and Furnishings of the Edward Lloyd Family," appendix c.

38. For complete construction and condition notes on all of the Lloyd furniture, see Alevizatos, "The Furniture and Furnishings of the Edward Lloyd Family," appendix d. The pier glasses date ca. 1750 and were ordered for Edward Lloyd III's house. Edward IV installed them in his newly built Wye House in 1788. Edward V ordered the girandoles through London merchant Thomas Eden in 1810. Because Eden sent six girandoles, rather than the three requested, the Lloyds sold three to Robert Oliver. See Alevizatos, "The Furniture and Furnishings of the Edward Lloyd Family," pp. 34, 35, 177–79, and 311–14. For labeled or otherwise documented Baltimore tables with similarly reeded and truncated bases, see William Voss Elder III and Jayne Stokes, *American Furniture, 1680–1880: From the Collection of the Baltimore Museum of Art* (Baltimore: Baltimore Museum of Art, 1987), pp. 139–40, no. 105; Weidman and Goldsborough, *Classical Maryland*, p. 115, fig. 140.

39. The laminations of the D-ends and small braces of the frame are yellow poplar and the swing rails and large medial braces are oak. Each massive pillar is supported by four legs that are dovetailed and reinforced with an iron brace below. A sharply angled chamfer does not appear on work documented and attributed to other Baltimore cabinetmakers such as John Needles and Anthony Jenkins. See Elder and Stokes, *American Furniture*, pp. 139–40, no. 105, and Weidman and Goldsborough, *Classical Maryland*, p. 115, figs. 140–42.

40. The base of the Lloyd family card table is similar to those on several tables illustrated in Edgar G. Miller, Jr., *American Antique Furniture: A Book for Amateurs,* 2 vols. (Baltimore: Lord Baltimore Press, 1937), 2, nos. 1355, 1394, 1419, 1446, and 1450. Much of the furniture in Miller was from Baltimore-area collections and a high percentage of Maryland pieces are represented. Northern tables with cabriole legs typically have plinths (see New-York Society of Journeymen Cabinet Makers, *The New-York Book of Prices for Cabinet & Chair Work* [1802], pl. 5, no. 3). Like Edward Lloyd V's card table, many examples from Boston, New York, and Philadelphia have radiating veneers and a "swelled" top. Baltimore cabinetmakers also made tables with "swelled" tops, thus this feature is not particularly useful in attributing furniture to Priestley's shop. For more on card table shapes, see Benjamin Hewitt, Patricia E. Kane, and Gerald W. R. Ward, *The Work of Many Hands: Federal Card Tables in America* (New Haven, Conn.: Yale University Art Gallery, 1981), pp. 68, 118. English card tables also influenced the design of Baltimore examples (Gregory R. Weidman, "Furnishing the Museum Rooms of the William Paca House," *Antiques* 110, no. 1 [January 1977]: 165, fig. 1). O. A. Kirkland Auctioneers, *Catalogue of the Celebrated Dr. William H. Crim Collection of Genuine Antiques,* Baltimore, April 22–May 2, 1903, lot 774. Crim was a Baltimore physican and one of the earliest American collectors. Most of the urns on Baltimore tables are plain rather than reeded. A Baltimore breakfast table with a reeded urn is illustrated in Miller, *American Antique Furniture*, fig. 1419.

41. For the documented Camp examples, see Weidman, *Furniture in Maryland*, p. 164, no. 127.

42. Judging from surviving examples, early-nineteenth-century Maryland consumers preferred pedestal-end sideboards (Hill, "Baltimore Furniture Craftsmen," pp. 208–29).

43. For other writing desks, see Decorative Arts Photographic Collection (hereafter cited as DAPC), accs. 72.335 and 87.235, Winterthur Museum. Weidman and Goldsborough, *Classical Maryland*, p. 137, no. 168; and Alevizatos, "The Furniture and Furnishings of the Edward Lloyd Family," pp. 367–71, cat. 25.

44. Townsend came to Baltimore from Doylestown, Pennsylvania. In 1837, Richard Townsend wrote, "Edward Priestley, who from our earliest years, had carried on the Cabinet-making, between our house, and the bridge, died at his house . . . on the 12th." Works Progress Administration of Maryland, trans., *The Diary of Richard H. Townsend*, vol. 1, (Baltimore: WPA, 1934), p. 198. Copies of the diary are at the Enoch Pratt Library and the Maryland Historical Society in Baltimore. The author thanks Mrs. Townsend Daniel Kent and Mrs. Billie Conkling for information on the Baltimore Equitable Society and for leading her to Richard Townsend's diary.

45. Lloyd Papers, ms. 2001, reel 27, MHS. Although Priestley's workmen cut the moldings on the handrail, he hired William Roney to turn the newels. On September 8, 1826, Roney billed Lloyd for turning five mahogany newels, three poplar newells, five mahogany drops, and three poplar drops. All of the documents pertaining to Priestley and Roney are transcribed in Alevizatos, "The Furniture and Furnishings of the Edward Lloyd Family," appendix c. Nineteenth-century architectural treatises and builders' guides document the complex and labor-intensive process of designing and manufacturing hand-railing. For more on this subject, see John Hall, *A New and Concise Method of Hand-Railing* (Baltimore: J. Murphy, 1840). In 1832, Priestley wrote Edward Lloyd VI, again seeking payment for the newels and handrail he made for Edward's father six years earlier. The handrail was for Wye House rather than Edward VI's residence at Wye Heights. The handrails for the latter are listed in a July 1827 bill from Jeremiah Boyd to Edward VI. Lloyd Papers, ms. 2001, reel 27, MHS.

46. Boyd's bill lists fences, a roof, cornices, architraves, balusters, pilasters, and column capitals, pillars, and bases for the porches. His interior work included cornice moldings, drops, carpet sills, windowsills, jib doors, windows with "lights of gothic sashes," walnut doors, mantels, mahogany paneling, spandrel paneling, risers, steps, bracket returns, and mahogany and walnut newels, handrails, and balusters. Lloyd Papers, ms. 2001, reel 27, MHS. Between June and November 1827, Edward Lloyd VI ordered a pair of gilded looking glasses, 2,992 pounds of green leather for upholstery, two dozen stair rods, and over 268 yards of carpeting and Venetian rugs from Baltimore merchants John Hastings and Joseph Blackwood. Lloyd Papers, ms. 2001, reel 28, MHS.

47. Lloyd Papers, ms. 2001, reel 27, MHS.

48. Ibid.

49. According to Vitruvius, male heads were termed "Persians" whereas female heads were called "caryatids" (Vitruvius, *The Ten Books on Architecture*, trans. by Morris Hicky Morgan, [1914; reprint ed., New York: Dover, 1960], pp. 7–8). Translations of his *Ten Books on Architecture* were widely available during the eighteenth and nineteenth centuries. Thomas Hope and Thomas Sheraton did not use this terminology, nor did any American cabinetmaker known to the author. Hope referred to the male variety as "different heads of the Indian or bearded Bacchus" (p. 49). The term "mummy" heads is used here because that is the most common designation in American cabinetmakers' price books. Vitruvius also used the term "therm" to designate the support below a head when the latter is used as a capital. Sheraton's *The Cabinet Dictionary* (1803) refers to any tapered support as a "therm." I have followed this usage because most American price books use the term "therm" in a manner similar to Sheraton. The author thanks Donald L. Fennimore for pointing out the original definitions of Persians and caryatids. The central doorway of the Mathias Hammond House (built ca. 1774) in Annapolis has a pulvinated frieze carved with oak leaves and bound with a crossed ribbon. Charles Percier and Pierre-Francois-Leonard Fontaine, *Recueil des Decorations Interieures* (1801), pls. 40, 51; Pierre de la Mésangère, *Collection des Meubles et Objets de Goût* (1802–1835), pls. 19, 22, 39, 50, 283; and George Smith's *Collection of Designs for Household Furniture and Interior Decoration* (London, 1808), pls.91–95. *The New-York Book of Prices* (1817), p. 72. Priestley was a member of The United Society of Journey Cabinet & Chair Makers of the City of Baltimore. In January 1817, they agreed to produce furniture based on rates published in a book of prices. Regretably, no Baltimore price book has been discovered (Hill, "Baltimore Furniture Craftsmen," p. 32).

50. Donald L. Fennimore, "Egyptian Influence in Early Nineteenth-Century American Furniture," *Antiques* 137, no. 2 (May 1990): 1194. As the reeding on the Grecian sofa shown in figure 9 suggests, aspects of the Egyptian style are present in many pieces of late neoclassical Baltimore furniture.

51. Ibid. The Barry and Krickbaum sideboard is a promised gift to the Philadelphia Museum of Art. The author thanks Jack Lindsey for information on this piece. Joseph B. Barry produced furniture in the Egyptian taste similar to Priestley's. The careers of both men spanned basically the same period, they catered to an elite clientele, and made similar forms—Grecian sofas, chests of drawers, pedestal sideboards, and mummy-headed decorations. The strong visual characteristics linking the pieces documented and attributed to Priestley's shop differ from those associated with Barry. The Philadelphia cabinetmaker's heads are much more rectilinear, possibly reflecting his reliance on designs illustrated in pls. 19 and 15 in Thomas Hope's *Household Furniture and Interior Decoration* (1807) and in pls. 91–95 in Smith's *Collection of Designs for Household Furniture*. Priestley's more curvaceous and sculptural heads derive from Hope's illustrations of Bacchus (pls. 37 and 57) as well as disparate architectural designs. Barry's heads invariably surmount squared therms and are usually twinned; that is, the heads are paired and face in opposite directions as on the sideboard shown in pl. 95 in Smith's *Collection of Designs for Household Furniture*. The design and orientation of Barry's mummy heads reveal a stricter reliance on published sources and less creativity than those associated with Priestley's shop. Both men were, however, familiar with the aforementioned design books as well as Percier and Fontaine's *Recueil des Decorations Interieures* and la Mésangère's *Collection des Meubles et Objets de Goût*. Although no direct link between Priestley and Barry is known, future research will probably reveal a connection. For more on furniture documented and attributed to Barry, see Fennimore and Trump, "Joseph B. Barry, Philadelphia Cabinetmaker": 1213–25.

52. Several objects with carving related to Priestley's survive (e.g., a sideboard at Colonial Williamsburg, a sideboard in the Physick House in Philadelphia, and a sideboard table at the Baltimore Museum of Art), but there is not sufficient evidence to attribute them to his shop. The carving on this group is less regimented than that documented and attributed to Priestley's shop. A sideboard that descended in the Alexander Brown family and reputedly came from his house Mondawmin also has similar carving, but its location is unknown.

53. The reeding on the sideboard table is slightly deeper than that on the pier table. The mahogany gallery on the sideboard table is set into a rabbet in the top. Hirschl and Adler Galleries purchased the table at Briggs Auction House in Booths Corner, Pennsylvania, in January 1998 and subsequently added the historically accurate glass and silver knobs to the drawers.

54. See Weidman and Goldsborough, *Classical Maryland*, p. 133, fig. 63. *The New-York Book of Prices* refers to "tapered therms with mummy heads and feet." Elder and Stokes, *American Furniture, 1680–1880*, pp. 154–55, no. 117.

55. See Weidman, *Furniture in Maryland*, pp. 140–41, no. 100. Although not documented as clients of Priestley, several social contemporaries of the Owings, such as their neighbors the Walkers, commissioned furniture from him. Another desk that appears to be from Priestley's shop is in a private collection.

56. The author thanks William Voss Elder III for sharing his knowledge of Maryland furniture and genealogy and informing her of the sideboard at Andalusia. The black paint is over mahogany and may not be original. According to family tradition, Letitia Glenn owned the sideboard table prior to her marriage to Charles Biddle. A Baltimore Grecian sofa with the same history also survives at Andalusia. The design, construction, carved ornament, and history of the sideboard provide compelling evidence for attributing it to Priestley's shop.

57. Sotheby's, *Americana and European and American Paintings, Drawings and Prints: The Andy Warhol Collection*, vol. 5, April 29 and 30, 1989, lot 3172. For related case pieces, see Weidman, *Furniture in Maryland*, p. 124, no. 79; and Weidman and Goldsboro, *Classical Maryland*, p. 135, fig. 165.

58. The shaft of the sideboard table sold by Hirschl and Adler is $12^{3}/_{4}$ inches. X-radiography would reveal whether the legs had been shortened. The dimensions and construction of other components on the sideboards, sideboard tables, pier table, and desk are also similar. The feet, for example, are uniformly four inches high. Several structural features also link the sideboards, sideboard tables, pier table, and desk. Three of the pieces have layout designs inscribed on their secondary surfaces. The rear rails of the sideboard tables illustrated in figures 23 and 29 have an inscribed drawing of the panel of the center front drawer. All of the drawers examined by the author are constructed in the same manner. The dovetail joints are long and thin, and the

drawer bottoms are chamfered at the front and sides, set into grooves, and nailed up into the drawer back. The bottoms are reinforced with thin poplar glue blocks attached end-to-end at each side, and the blocks are covered with a thin glue strip. Although this method of drawer construction has been associated with the shops of John Needles and William Camp, it also occurs on furniture from Philadelphia, New York, and Boston. In the absence of other supporting evidence, it is not a reliable means of attributing work to a specific maker. Needles worked with Priestley for six months before joining Camp's shop. Although it is conceivable that Needles introduced Priestley's structure to Camp's shop, it is more likely that the aforementioned drawer construction was already well established in Baltimore's cabinetmaking community. The mummy heads on a sideboard in the collection of the Colonial Williamsburg Foundation and a sideboard table in the Baltimore Museum of Art are closely related to those on the Lloyd pier table and can be categorized as a Priestley subgroup. Although these mummy heads are more freely and floridly carved, they are based on the same compilation of designs as the more severely carved mummy heads in the primary group of Priestley pieces. These two pieces lack only the benchmark of a documented Priestley piece. A sideboard known only in a photograph and a chest of drawers in a private collection have another variation of the mummy head. On the sideboard, the mummy is a bearded man whose head is draped in a sumptuous and fringed textile. On the chest of drawers, the colonette capitals are illusionary males with long, wavy mane-like hair and beards. For both of the above-mentioned subgroups, the compelling argument that they are products of Priestley's shop centers on the case designs, which are similar to his. Each has mitered panels, cockbeaded drawers, gothic arch paneled doors, and inwardly steeped front rails. However, different cabinetmakers labeled case pieces that resemble each other stylistically. Ronald L. Hurst and Jonathan Prown, *Southern Furniture 1680–1830: The Colonial Williamsburg Collection* (Williamsburg: Harry N. Adams for the Colonial Williamsburg Foundation), pp. 525–29, no. 159; Elder and Stokes, *American Furniture, 1680–1880*, pp. 156–57, no. 118; DAPC acc. 74.6100; and private collection.

59. *Baltimore American,* March 14, 1837.

60. Philadelphia influences are evident in pre-Revolutionary Baltimore furniture, particularly in work documented and attributed to Gerrard Hopkins (fl. 1767–1800). He and one-time partner Robert Moore (fl. 1771–1787) were Philadelphia-trained cabinetmakers who moved to Baltimore in the 1760s. During the 1790s, Philadelphia influences were displaced by a variety of cabinetmaking traditions introduced by European immigrants. James Weston Livingood, *The Philadelphia-Baltimore Trade Rivalry, 1780–1860* (Harrisburg, Pa.: Pennsylvania Historical and Museum Commission, 1947), pp. 11–13.

# Appendix

*Inventory of Edward Priestley, March 22, 1837*

| | | |
|---|---|---:|
| 1 Secretary and bookcase | | 60.00 |
| 1 Card table | | 10.00 |
| 1 Sofa | | 25.00 |
| 1 Mahogany Stand | | 4.00 |
| 1 Do Pier Table | | 10.00 |
| 1 Fender | | 2.00 |
| 1 Pair of Andirons | | 2.00 |
| 1 Pair Shovel and tongs | | 2.00 |
| 1 Doz, Rush bottom chairs | @ 75 ¢ | 9.00 |
| 1 Mahogany chair | | 2.00 |
| 1 Carpet | | 6.00 |
| 1 Rug | | 2.00 |
| 3 Blinds | @ $1 each | 3.00 |
| 1 Mahogany wardrobe | | 40.00 |
| 1 Do bedstead | | 5.00 |
| 1 Hair Matrafs | | 8.00 |
| 2 Bolsters | 50 ¢ each | 1.00 |
| 2 Pillows | 50 ¢ each | 1.00 |
| 4 Blankets | $1.50 each | 6.00 |
| 2 Bed Spreads | $2.00 each | 4.00 |
| 6 Sheets | 75 each | 4.50 |
| 2 Table cloths | $5.00 each | 10.00 |
| 1 Beareau | | 10.00 |
| 1 Toilet Glafs | | 1.00 |
| 1 Beareau and bookcase | | 20.00 |
| 68 Books | | 15.00 |
| 1 Pier Glafs | | 5.00 |
| 1 Close Stool | | 1.00 |
| 1 Chimney Board | | 1.00 |
| 1 Toilet | | 1.00 |
| 11 Table Spoons silver} | | |
| 11 Tea Spoons silver} | 31 ounces @ $1 pr Oz | 31.00 |
| 1 Ladle silver} | | |
| 2 Bedsteads | @ 2.50 per piece | 5.00 |
| 1 Small bed | | 5.00 |
| 1 Matrafs | | 2.00 |
| 3 Sheets | @ 50 cts | 1.50 |
| 3 Blankets | | 1.50 |
| 1 Bedstead | | 3.00 |
| 1 Matrafs | | 1.00 |
| 1 Lot of Wadding | | 1.50 |
| 1 Hatrack | | 5.00 |

| | | |
|---|---|---|
| 1 Mahogany sideboard | | 20.00 |
| 1 Sofa | | 6.00 |
| 1 Eight day clock | | 35.00 |
| 2 Mahogany tables | | 10.00 |
| 1 Do cupboard | | 8.00 |
| 1 Raut Stand | | 2.00 |
| 1 Drefsert do | | 3.00 |
| 1 Pair Andirons | | 3.00 |
| 1 Fender | | 1.00 |
| 1 Sett of Castors | | 8.00 |
| 1 Lott of Crockery ware | | 10.00 |
| 5 Waiters | 20 ¢ each | 1.00 |
| 3 Mantle Ornaments | @ 33 1/3 ¢ each | 1.00 |
| 1 Looking glafs | | 5.00 |
| 2 Candle sticks 50 4 each | | 1.00 |
| 1 Mahogany table | | 2.00 |
| 1 Lot of tin ware | | 2.50 |
| 6 Painted brickets | @ 25 ¢ each | 1.50 |
| 2 Coffee mills | @ 50 ¢ each | 1.00 |
| 3 Tea kettles | @ 33 1/3 ¢ each | 1.00 |
| 3 Dutch ovens | $1.00 | 3.00 |
| 2 Frying pans | 50 ¢ each | 1.00 |
| 1 Spider | | .50 |
| 1 Gridiron | | .50 |
| 1 Sadle | 25 ¢ each | .50 |
| 1 Lot of Pot hooks and Tormenters | | .50 |
| 1 Mahogany knife box | | 1.00 |
| 3 Doz. knives and forks | @ 1.00 per do | 3.00 |
| 1 Basket | | .50 |
| 1 Safe | | 2.00 |
| 8 Stone jars | 25 ¢ each | 2.00 |
| 1 Bread tray | | 1.00 |
| 2 Meat tubs | 25 ¢ each | .50 |
| 1 Tray and stand | | 1.00 |
| 2 Pin tables | @ 50 ¢ each | 1.00 |
| 1 Cloaths horse | | .50 |
| 1 Bench | | .25 |
| 1 Wood horse and saw | | 1.00 |
| 1 Drefs glafs | | .50 |
| 1 Low post bedstead | | 5.00 |
| 1 Feather bed | | 6.00 |
| 4 Blankets | 37 ¢ each | 1.50 |
| 2 Pictures | 25 ¢ each | .50 |
| 3 Old chairs | 25 ¢ each | .75 |
| 2 Wash tubs | 37 1/2 ¢ each | .75 |
| 1 Shovel | | .25 |
| 2 Barrels of Vinegar | 2 $ per barrel | 2.00 |
| 39000 feet of pine plank | @ $15 per 1000 feet | 585.00 |
| 1 Wheel barrow | | 1.50 |
| 1 Wood axe | | .75 |
| 1 French Mahogany bedstead | | 12.00 |
| 1 Duro chair | | 8.00 |
| 1 Screw | | 2.00 |
| 1 Pin table | | 1.00 |
| 1 Gold Watch | | 25.00 |

| | | |
|---|---|---:|
| 1 Pair Gold Spectacles | | 8.00 |
| 1400 feet of pine plank | @ 15 $ per 100 feet | 210.00 |
| 1200 feet of Maple | @ $2    Do | 24.00 |
| 3000 feet Inch poplar | 1 1/2¢  per foot | 45.00 |
| 775 feet mixed boards | 1 1/2¢  per foot | 11.62 |
| 1600 feet do  do | 1 1/2¢  per foot | 24.00 |
| 340 Do bay wood | 10 ¢  per foot | 34.00 |
| 70 Do     Do | 12 1/2¢ | 8.75 |
| 1 Lott of Mahogany cuttings | | 10.00 |
| 126 feet Mahogany | @ 12 1/2¢ | 15.12 |
| 106 feet pine | 2 ¢ | 2.12 |
| 1000 feet Inch poplar | 1 1/2 | 15.00 |
| 200   Do     Do    Pine | 1 1/2¢ per foot | 3.00 |
| 178   Do       Mahogany | 12 1/2¢ | 22.25 |
| 633   Do          Do | a 3 ¢ | 63.30 |
| 966   feet     venear | 6 ¢ | 57.96 |
| 360   Do       Do | 4 | 14.40 |
| 150   Do       Do | 5 | 7.50 |
| 490   Do       Do | 8 | 39.20 |
| 1 Lot Satin wood | 300 feet @ 9 ¢ | 27.00 |
| 1       Do Mahogany venear | | 4.00 |
| 1 Do  50 feet Do    Do | 6 ¢ | 3.00 |
| 100 feet      Do    Do | 4 ¢ | 4.00 |
| 200   Do    Do    Do | 3 ¢ | 6.00 |
| 150   Do    Do    Do | 4 ¢ | 6.00 |
| 150   Do    Do    Do | 3 ¢ | 4.50 |
| 150   Do    Do    Do | 3 ¢ | 6.00 |
| 200   Do    Do    Do | 3 ¢ | 6.00 |
| 150   Do    Do    Do | 3 ¢ | 4.50 |
| 350   Do    Do    Do | 3 ¢ | 7.50 |
| 1 Lot of venier cuttings | | 3.00 |
| 200   feet    Do   Do | @ 6 ¢ | 12.00 |
| 1 Lot Mahogany Cuttings | | 5.00 |
| 100 feet of Maple | @ 4 ¢ | 4.00 |
| 9 Low post bedsteads | $3 | 27.00 |
| 4 Setts high post Do | 50 ¢ | 2.00 |
| 7 Setts of Stumps  feet | 50 ¢ | 3.50 |
| 2 Setts french posts | 37 1/2 | .75 |
| 1 Pine table | | 1.00 |
| 1 Poplar cradle | | 2.50 |
| 1 Barrel of Glue 150 lbs at 10¢ | | 15.00 |
| 1 Do Red Ochre | | 1.00 |
| 2 Kegs | | .75 |
| 25 lbs Nails  6 1/2 | | 2.50 |
| 1 old bedstead | | 1.00 |
| 3 Pair cooling boards | 66 2/3 ¢ | 2.00 |
| 1 Box window glafs | | 1.00 |
| 30 Bed pans | @ 25 ¢ | 7.50 |
| 8 Doz wrapping mats | 1.00 $ per doz | 8.00 |
| 3 old work benches | | 3.00 |
| 200 feet pine boards | @ 2 ¢ | 24.80 |
| 1 Lot of glue | | 18.00 |
| 2 Poplar Cradles | $2.25 | 4.50 |
| 2 Trundle bedsteads | @ 2 $ | 4.00 |
| 1 Mahogany Crib | | 8.00 |

| | | |
|---|---|---:|
| 2 Small Mahog. tables | 1 $ | 2.00 |
| 1 Mahog. wash stand | | 2.50 |
| 2 Do Cradles | @ 4$ | 8.00 |
| 1 Drefsing box | | 1.00 |
| 1 Do Table | | 5.00 |
| 1 Pair book chairs duro | | 4.00 |
| 3 Frames | @ 25 ¢ | .75 |
| 6 Bed pans | @ 25 ¢ | 1.50 |
| 1 Venear Saw | | .50 |
| 1 Furnace | | .25 |
| 3 Demijohns | 8 ¢ | .25 |
| 1 Box unfinished work | | 2.00 |
| 1 Bedstead, unfinished | | 20.00 |
| 1 Lott varnish pots and brushes | | 1.50 |
| 2 ottomans each | 5$ | 10.00 |
| 2 Hatracks unfinished | @ 7$ | 14.00 |
| 2 Mahog. rocking chairs | @ 8$ | 16.00 |
| 2 Do Workstands | 12$ | 24.00 |
| 2 Do Cradles | $3.75 | 7.50 |
| 2 Do Beaureau | @ 14$ | 28.00 |
| 6 Poplar bedsteads | @ $5.50 | 33.00 |
| 1 Stove | | 4.00 |
| 3 Old tables | | .25 |
| 1 Do desk | | .25 |
| 18 Gall.s varnish | @ $1.25 | 22.50 |
| 35 do do | @ 1.75 | 61.25 |
| 30 do do | @ 1.25 | 37.50 |
| 7 Demijohns | @ 43 ¢ | 3.00 |
| 2 Benches | @ 4$ | 8.00 |
| 1 Sideboard, unfinished | | 10.00 |
| 2 Sofas | do @ 7.50 | 15.00 |
| 1 Lott Mahog. hair stuff | | 6.00 |
| 1 Stove | | 3.00 |
| 4 Glue pots | @ 1.00 | 4.00 |
| 1 Portable desk | | 17.00 |
| 1 Bar of Iron | | .50 |
| 1 Sofa, unfinished | | 7.00 |
| 7 Work benches | 1.75 | 12.25 |
| 1 Sideboard, unfinished | | 15.00 |
| 2 Mahog. breakfast tables | $7.50 | 15.00 |
| 2 Pair card tables | @ $28 | 56.00 |
| 3 Iron Clamps | @ $3 | 9.00 |
| 2 Doz hand screws | @ 4$ per doz | 8.00 |
| 1 Lott tools | | 6.00 |
| 1 Lott patterns and cullings | | 5.00 |
| 5 small iron clamps | 60 ¢ | 3.00 |
| 2 Arm chairs | $15 | 30.00 |
| 1 Sideboard | | 40.00 |
| 114 feet Mahogany | @ 6 ¢ per foot | 6.84 |
| 215 feet Do | @ 4 ¢ | 8.60 |
| 330 Do Do | @ 10 ¢ | 33.00 |
| 65 Do Do | @ 5 ¢ | 3.25 |
| 50 Do Do | @ 3 ¢ | 1.50 |
| 59 Do Do | @ 5 ¢ | 2.94 |
| 188 Do Do | @ 6 ¢ | 11.28 |

| | | | |
|---|---|---|---|
| 250 Do | Do | @ 6¢ | 15.00 |
| 50 Do | Do | @ 8¢ | 4.00 |
| 1000 Do | Do | @ 10¢ | 100.00 |
| 270 Do | Do | @ 6¢ | 16.20 |
| 500 Do | Do | @ 7¢ | 35.00 |
| 553 Do | Do | @ 14¢ | 77.42 |
| 325 Do | Do | @ 14¢ | 45.55 |
| 732 Do | Do | @ 15¢ | 109.80 |
| 360 Do | Maple | @ 1 1/2¢ | 5.46 |
| 600 feet | Do | @ 1 1/2¢ | 6.00 |
| 450 Do | Do | @ 2 1/2¢ | 11.25 |
| 700 Do | Do | @ 1¢ | 7.00 |
| 300 Do | Mahogany | @ 6¢ | 18.00 |
| 506 Do | Logs Do | @ 13¢ | 583.78 |
| 65 Do | Do | @ 3¢ | 1.95 |
| 100 Do | Do | @ 5¢ | 5.00 |
| 128 Do | Do | @ 7¢ | 7.96 |
| 163 Do | Do | @ 10¢ | 16.30 |
| 472 Do | Do | @ 12¢ | 56.64 |
| 476 Do | Do | @ 10¢ | 47.60 |
| 65 Do | Do | @ 8¢ | 4.80 |
| 406 Do | Do | @ 15¢ | 62.40 |
| 100 Do | Do | @ 13¢ | 13.00 |
| 124 Do | Do | @ 13¢ | 16.12 |
| 76 Do | Do | @ 7¢ | 5.32 |
| 315 Do | Do | @ 15¢ | 47.25 |
| 1916 Do | Do | @ 9¢ | 187.70 |
| 285 Do | Do | @ 10¢ | 28.50 |
| 260 Do | Do | @ 15¢ | 39.00 |
| 320 feet | Mahogany | @ 15¢ | 51.20 |
| 414 Do | Do | @ 18¢ | 74.52 |
| 422 Do | Do | @ 8¢ | 33.76 |
| 1112 Do | Do | @ 16¢ | 177.92 |
| 320 Do | Do | @ 9¢ | 28.80 |
| 371 Do | Do | @ 13¢ | 48.23 |
| 1990 Do | Do | @ 12¢ | 238.80 |
| 816 Do | Do | @ 11¢ | 89.96 |
| 442 Do | Do | @ 11¢ | 48.62 |
| 136 Do | Do | @ 14¢ | 19.09 |
| 40 Do | Do | @ 6¢ | 2.40 |
| 200 Do | Do | @ 7¢ | 14.00 |
| 250 Do | Do | @ 6¢ | 15.00 |
| 2 Lot Slabs | Do | | 2.25 |
| 165 feet | Do | @ 11¢ | 18.15 |
| 1315 Do | Do | @ 6¢ | 78.90 |
| 242 Do | Do | @ 8¢ | 19.36 |
| 288 Do | Do | @ 10¢ | 28.80 |
| 627 Do | Do | @ 10¢ | 62.70 |
| 100 Do | Do | @ 12¢ | 12.00 |
| 36 Do | Do | @ 12¢ | 4.32 |
| 28 Do | Do | @ 8¢ | 2.24 |
| 44 Do | Maple | @ 4¢ | 1.76 |
| 113 Do | Mahogany | @ 13¢ | 15.29 |
| 217 Do | Do | @ 10¢ | 21.70 |
| 700 Do | Do | @ 9¢ | 63.00 |

| | | | |
|---|---|---|---:|
| 728 Do | Do | @ 8¢ | 58.24 |
| 350 Do | Do | @ 12¢ | 42.00 |
| 714 Do | Do | @ 12¢ | 85.68 |
| 133 Do | Do | @ 8¢ | 10.64 |
| 270 Do | Do | @ 8¢ | 21.60 |
| 230 Do | Do | @ 9¢ | 20.70 |
| 258 Do | Do | @ 7¢ | 18.06 |
| 206 Do | Do | @ 9¢ | 18.54 |
| 268 Do | Do | @ 10¢ | 26.80 |
| 290 Do | Do | @ 12¢ | 34.80 |
| 76 feet of | Mahogany | @ 10¢ | 7.60 |
| 8500 Do | Cherry | @ 1 1/2¢ | 127.50 |
| 4500 Do | Poplar | @ 1 1/2¢ | 67.50 |
| 810 Do | Scantling | @ 1 1/2¢ | 12.15 |
| 3 Mahog. | Wardrobes | @ $40 | 120.00 |
| 3 Do | Beareaus | @ $15 | 45.00 |
| 1 Do | Pier Table | | 35.00 |
| 1 Do | ped. Sideboard | | 30.00 |
| 2 Do | Sideboard | @ $30 | 60.00 |
| 3 Wash stands, marble tops | | @ 12 $ | 36.00 |
| 1 Drefing beaureau | | | 35.00 |
| 1 Do | box | | 5.00 |
| 2 Wash stands | | $7 | 14.00 |
| 2 Mahog. do | | $5 | 10.00 |
| 2 Do cradles | | $6 | 12.00 |
| 1 Poplar do | | | 2.00 |
| 4 Mahog. breakfast tables | | $8 | 32.00 |
| 7 Do  Tables | | $12 | 84.00 |
| 3 Do  Cribs | | $10 | 30.00 |
| 1 Maple french post bedstead | | | 8.00 |
| 6 Mahogany  do  do | | $14 | 84.00 |
| 1 Poplar  do  do | | | 4.00 |
| 2 Trundle bedsteads | | $2 | 4.00 |
| 4 Lowpost poplar bedsteads | | $3.50 | 14.00 |
| 1 Maple do | | | 6.00 |
| 4 Mahog. high post  do | | 28$ | 112.00 |
| 3 Poplar   do  do | | 6 $ | 18.00 |
| 2 Trays with Stands | | 2 $ | 4.00 |
| 1 Centre table marble slab | | | 30.00 |
| 2 Duro chairs | | $8 | 16.00 |
| 1 Bed chair | | | 3.00 |
| 34 Brafs ferrets for bed posts | | @ 4¢ | 1.36 |
| 1 Pine table and box | | | .75 |
| 1 Do | Do | | .50 |
| 1 Lot of Pine | | | .75 |
| 1 Desk | | | 1.00 |
| 2 Old chairs | | @ 25¢ | .50 |
| 22 New sacking bottoms | | 1 $ | 22.00 |
| 38 Quires of Sand paper | | 12 1/2¢ | 4.75 |
| 47 Papers of Sprigggs | | @ 8¢ | 3.76 |
| 10 Socks | | @ 75¢ | 7.50 |
| 43 Grofs wood Screws | | @ 40 | 17.20 |
| 2 1/2 Yds. Green Cloth | | @ 2 $ | 5.00 |
| 10,000 Brafs Nails | | @ 30¢ | 30.00 |
| 13 Coffin plates | | 12 1/2¢ | 1.62 |

| | | |
|---|---|---|
| 9 Lounge Screws | @ 12 1/2¢ each | 1.12 |
| 26 Screws for duro chairs | @ 6 | 1.56 |
| 13 Hooks | @ 3¢ | .39 |
| 24 Brafs Hooks | @ 3¢ | .72 |
| 9 Pair Iron Hinges | @ 6 1/2 | .56 |
| 37 Pair but do | 6 1/2 ¢ | 2.25 |
| 8 Pair Table fustnings | @ 12 1/2 | 1.00 |
| 37 Pair Card table hinges | 8¢ | 2.96 |
| 1 Handscrew tap | | 4.00 |
| 15 Sett bed screws | @ 19¢ | 2.95 |
| 4 Sockett castors | @ 1.50 | 6.00 |
| 10 Sett French Castors | @ 87 1/2 ¢ | 8.75 |
| 16 Brafs bolts | @ 6 1/4 ¢ | 1.00 |
| 1 Pair plated handles | | .50 |
| 1 Lot portable desk mountings | | 3.00 |
| 1/2 a box Candles | | 1.50 |
| 2 Doz Table hinges | @ 1.00 | 2.00 |
| 3 Setts Iron castors | @ 75¢ | 2.25 |
| 2 lbs wax | @ 25¢ | .50 |
| 5 bed cords | @ 10¢ | .50 |
| 3 Sacking bottoms | $1.00 | 3.00 |
| 1 Lott Iron handles | | 1.00 |
| 1 Do bedstead caps | | .25 |
| 102 Castors | @ 3 ¢ | 3.06 |
| 6 Yds. Muslin | @ 12 1/2 ¢ | .75 |
| 11 Doz Glafs knobs | @ 37 1/2 ¢  per dozen | 4.12 |
| 2 Boxes odds and ends | | 4.00 |
| 1 Box of Trimmings | | 1.00 |
| 1 Pair Tongs | | .25 |
| 1 Do Andirons | | .25 |
| 1 Shovel | | .25 |
| 1 Wash stand | | .50 |
| 1 Bacin | | .25 |
| 1 Pitcher | | .25 |
| 20 lbs of Feathers | 35¢ | 7.00 |
| 47 1/2 Yds Hair Cloth 16 Inch | @ $1 | 47.75 |
| 27     do do do    15 do | @ 87 1/2 | 27.72 |
| 15     do do do    17 do | @1.05 | 15.75 |
| 46 1/2 do do do    17 do | @ 1.05 | 48.82 |
| 34     do do do    30 do | @ 1.50 | 51.00 |
| 2     yds do do    26 do | @ 1.00 | 2.00 |
| 5     do do do    26 do | @ 1.00 | 5.00 |
| 1     do do do    20 do | | .87 |
| 1     do do do    16 do | | .50 |
| 4     yds do do    28 do | @ 1.25 | 5.62 |
| 3     do do do    26 do | @ 1.00 | 3.00 |
| 29 1/2 do do do | 1.12 1/2 | 35.18 |
| 37     do   Duck | @ 18¢ | 6.66 |
| 25     do   Smeing | 10¢ | 2.50 |
| 36     do do | 8¢ | 2.88 |
| 25     do   Black Muslin | @ 8¢ | 2.00 |
| 200 lbs    Curled hair | @ 20¢ | 40.00 |
| 25 Papers of Tacks | @ 6 1/2 | 1.55 |
| 12000 Brafs Nails | 25¢ | 3.00 |
| 1 Damaged plate | | .50 |

| | | |
|---|---|---|
| 1 Lott of Wire | | 1.00 |
| 4 Sacking bottoms | 75¢ | 3.00 |
| 2 lbs Curled hair | 30¢ | .60 |
| 1 Beda twin and linen | | 1.50 |
| 1 Stove | | 2.00 |
| 1 Pine table | | .75 |
| 1 Duro chair | | 2.00 |
| 1 Sett Scales and weights | | 1.00 |
| 1 Trussel | | .25 |
| 4 Sacking bottoms 504 | | 2.00 |
| 1 Mahog. rocking chair | | 12.00 |
| 12 Do    chairs | $6 | 72.00 |
| 4 Easy    do | 10¢ | 40.00 |
| 1 Bed chair | | 4.00 |
| 1 Mantle Glafs | | 6.00 |
| 1 Small Sofa | | 15.00 |
| 1 Sett extension tables | | 45.00 |
| 1 Pair Eliptic do | | 15.00 |
| 1 Do  Do   Do pillar and claw | | 30.00 |
| 2 Pair card tables | @40$ | 80.00 |
| 3 Dineing tables | @12$ | 36.00 |
| 4 Breakfast pillar and claw | 18$ | 72.00 |
| 3 Wash stands | @10$ | 30.00 |
| 1 Centre table | | 18.00 |
| 3 Candle stands | @3$ | 9.00 |
| 2 Music Stools | @5$ | 10.00 |
| 1 Close Stools | @7$ | 14.00 |
| 1 Tray and Stand | | 1.00 |
| 1 Chest | | .50 |
| 3 Wheel barrows | $2.50 | 7.50 |
| 1 Hand barrow | | 2.00 |
| 1 Wood Axe | | .25 |
| 1 Coop | | 1.50 |
| 1 Cooking Stove and pots &c | | 15.00 |
| 17 Chairs  yellow and black | @25¢ | 4.25 |
| One Negro man named Henry about 30 years old to serve about 3 years | | 150.00 |
| 12 Shares in the Baltimore and Ohio rail road stock @ 35$ per Share | | 420.00 |
| A certain lot of ground, situate on the West side of Front St. in the City of Baltimore; binding on said street about 26 feet and running back about 150 feet more or lefs with all the improvements thereon being a three story brick building 25 feet fronton said street, running back 20 feet with a backbuilding 42 feet by 15 feet, the whole of the saidlot, being subject to a ground rent of 52 $ per annum | | $2700.00 |

A certain lot of ground, situate on the North side of Douglafs St. in the City of Baltimore commencing 49 feet from Friendship Street, running West 33 feet, North West parallel to Friendship St. 50 feet more or lefs to an alley three feet wide then Easterly bounding on the Southeastmost side of said alley and parallel to Douglafs Street 35 feet and then Southesterly by a straight line to the place of beginning with all the improvements thereon, being two~small frame houses fronting 35 feet on Douglafs Street, the whole of the said lot being subject to a ground rent of $ 24.53 per annum                700.00

A certain lot of ground situate on the SouthWest corner of Water and Concord Street In the city of Baltimore fronting on Water Street

23 feet running back on Concord St 60 feet more or lefs with all the improvements thereon being a two Story brick building 23 feet more or lefs on Water St and running back parallel with Concord St 16 feet 6 inches more or lefs, Two one Stpry brick buildings fronting on Concord St 36 feet and running back 23 feet, the whole of the said lot being subject to a ground rent of 100 Dollars per annum          1800.00

A certain lot of ground situate on the Southermost side of Plowman Street in the City of Baltimore, at the distance of forty feet Westerly from the corner formed by the intersection of the Southernmost side of Plowman St and the Westernmost side of Albemarle St, and running thence Westerly bounding on the Southernmost side of Plowman Street, seventy two feet more or lefs~ to a point distant thirty eight feet Easterly from the corner formed by the intersection of the Southernmost side of PlowmanStreet, and the Eastermost side of Front Street then Southerly parallel to Albemarle Street ninety feet more or lefs to lot number 189 then Easterly at right angles, with the last foregoing course, and bounding on said lot number 189 seventy two feet more or lefs to intersect a line drawn Southerly parallel to Albemarle St. from the beginning and then reversing the said line so drawn and bounding thereon Northerly to the place of beginning with all the improvements thereon fronting on Plowman street with a two story brick building being a frame building in the rear, also a frame building used as a saw pitt, also fronting on Plowman Street, the whole of the said lot being subject to a ground rent of $8.89          2200.00

A certain lot of ground situate on the North Side of Pitt Street in the City of Baltimore commencing 20 feet from the South East corner formed by the intersection of Pitt and East Street, thence running Westerly 20 feet then Northerly 89 feet 6 inches, then Easterly 40 feet to East Street, then Southerly 49 feet to the place of beginning, with all the improvements thereon being a two Story brick building on the North Side of Pitt Street, extending back thirty three feet 6 inches. A two Story brick dwelling fronting on the West side of East Street, near the North side of Pitt Street 13 feet 6 inches covering half a small alley, extending back 37 feet, with a two Story brick dwelling at the North end thereof, a two Story brick dwelling fronting on the West side of East Street, near the North side of Pitt Street, 13 feet 6 inches and extending back 24 feet the whole of the said lot being subject to a ground rent of 50 $ per annum          2800.00

One fifth of two thirds of a certain lot ground Situate on the North West corner of Howard and Fayette Streets in the City of Baltimore fronting on Howard Street 34 feet more or lefs, and running back to waggon alley 80 feet more or lefs, with all the improvements thereon, being two two Story brick building fronting on Howard Street 34 feet more or lefs by 30 feet deep more or lefs, the whole subject to a ground rent of 7 Dollars per annum          800.00

$20,458.76

We the subscribers do certify that the aforegoing is a True and just Inventory and valuation of all and Singular the goods and chattels and personal Estate Of the said Edward Priestley deceased, so far as the same Have come to our sight and knowledge, and as valued and Appraised by us in Dollars and cents, according to the best Of our skill and judgement. In Testimony of all of which, we hereunto subscribe our seals.
        Charles Suter

Nich$^S$ Stansbury  Appraisers

Amount of Appraisement as above $20,458.76
Cash in FranklinBank of Balt. t the time of the deceased's death 64.61
Whole amount of inventory $20,523.37
Tho$^S$ Murphy}
Jacob Daley}                Executors
Reverdy Johnson}
Baltimore County Ss on the 22$^d$ day of March 1837 came . . .

*Source:* Edward Priestley Inventory, March 22, 1837, vol. DMP 46, pp. 343–55, WK 1096 to 1097, Maryland State Archives.

*Tabulation of Furniture Forms and Materials Listed in Edward Priestley's Inventory*

| | |
|---|---|
| High post bedsteads | 11 |
| Low post bedsteads | 15 |
| French bedsteads | 7 plus 2 posts for French beds |
| Trundle bedsteads | 4 |
| Cradles | 10 |
| Cribs | 4 |
| Tables | 14 (variously pine or old) |
| Dining tables | 4 plus one sett extension tables |
| Breakfast tables | 10 |
| Center tables | 1 plus one with marble slab |
| Card tables | 5 pairs |
| Pier tables | 1 |
| Chairs | 14 |
| Easy chairs | 4 |
| Bed chairs | 2 |
| Sofas (finished) | 0 |
| Duro chairs | 2 plus one pair with book arms |
| Rocking chairs | 3 |
| Ottomans | 2 |
| Desks | 2 plus one portable |
| Sideboards | 3 |
| Pedestal sideboards | 1 |
| Wardrobes | 3 |
| Bureaus | 5 plus one dressing bureau |
| Washstands | 11 |
| Candlestands | 3 |
| Workstands | 2 |
| Dressing Table | 1 |
| Dressing Box | 1 |
| Box | 1 |
| Trays with Stands | 3 |
| Close Stool | 1 |
| Music Stool | 2 |
| Frames | 3 |
| Chest | 1 |

*Tabulation of Unfinished Work Listed in Edward Priestley's Inventory*
1 box unfinished work

1 Bedstead unfinished
2 hatracks
1 sideboard
2 sofas
1 sofa
7 setts stumps (for bedsteads)

*Edward Priestley's List of Debtors*

An Inventory of All the Deb[ts] due to Edward Priestley late of Baltimore County deceased as appears by the books and papers left by the deceased or which have come to the knowledge of J. Daley, T. Murphy and R. Johnson Executors:

|  | Sperate | Doubtful | Desperate |
|---|---|---|---|
| H. Herringon note dated the 21[st] Dec[r] 1836 at 6 mo[s] |  | $50.00 | To be paid in lumber |
| A Huckett due bill for |  | 19.02 |  |
| J. Barrington on note at 60 days dates 2[d] Sept 1834 for |  | 580. |  |
| Daniel Dashiell on note at 6 mo. dates Annapolis May 4[th] 1835 for |  | 40. |  |
| James Gaw on not at 8 months dated 12[th] October 1836 for |  | 90.48 |  |
| Joseph J. Thomas on note at 3 months dated January 1[st] 1836 for |  | 62.86 |  |
| Joseph J. Thomas on note at 5 months dated January 1[st] 1836 for |  | 62.86 |  |
| James Gaw on note dated Oct. 12[th] 1836 at 6 months for |  | 89.61 |  |
| Robt. L. Porter and James Askey on note at 6 months dated March 11[th] 1835 for |  | 50.47 | An acct. in bar |
| James Askey and Robert L. Porter on note dated March 11[th] 1835 at 12 months for |  | 51.94 | An acct. in bar |
| Charles R. Carroll on Open acct. for coffin | 24 |  |  |
| Sam.[l] J. Donaldson on Open account | 8.75 |  |  |
| Thomas Murphy on Open Account | 2 |  |  |
| Joshua Dorsey on Open acct; |  |  | 61.25 |

|  | Sperate | Doubtful | Desperate |
|---|---|---|---|
| Will. H. Bates on Open acct; | | | 19. |
| Geo. J. Brown on Open acct; | | | 24. |
| Mrs. Hanna on Open acct; balance | | | 54.50 |
| Blakey on Open acct; | | 16.50 | |
| John Wilson on Open acct. | .25 | | |
| James L. Hawkins on Open account | .50 | | |
| Richard Caton do do | 14.12 | | |
| Thomas S. George do do | | 18 | |
| H. D. G. Carroll do do | | 1.50 | |
| Olivia Gill do do | 15. | | |
| R. M. Gibbes do do | 2.12 1/2 | | |
| Geo. W. Andrews do do | 101.02 | | An acct in bar |
| Samuel Cox do do | | | 227.88 |
| S. C. Leakin do do | 2.50 | | |
| John Barrington do do | 26.94 | | Discount paid on note |
| Mrs. M<sup>c</sup>Lanahan do do | 2.25 | | |
| Edward Lloyd do do | | .75 | |
| Capt. Fitch do do | | 11. | |
| Joshua Mezick do do | | | 20. |
| Levin Pritchett do do | | 4.44 | |
| Capt. John Chase on Open account | | | |
| Mifs Chew do do | 12. | | |
| Edward Patterson do do | 16. | | |
| J. Pennington do do | .75 | | |
| Mon: Pageott | 1 Chair | 16. | |
| Mifs Osbourn | | 3.50 | |
| James Gittings on Open acct. | | 3.75 | |
| Benjamin Boles do do | | | 89.69 |
| Willowby Lewis do do | 99.61 | | Acct. in bar |
| Richard Lemmon do do | 5.75 | | |
| Henry B. Chew, coffin &c | 31. | | |
| Groffith Evans, mending Stand | | .50 | |
| Edward Lynch, Open acct. | 26.87 | | |
| Benjamin Deford | 1.87 | | |
| U.S. Heath Esqr Pedistle Stand | 30. | | |

|  |  | Sperate | Doubtful | Desperate |
|---|---|---|---|---|
| J.S.Gittings on Open acct. |  | 5.12 |  |  |
| Thomas Pinkney |  | 55. |  |  |
| Capt. James Philips | do | 17. |  |  |
| James Billington | do | 405.33 |  | An a/c in bar |
| Mrs. H. Armstrong | bedstead |  | 10. |  |
| George Wimmell open acct. |  | 42. |  |  |
| J. Sleper | do |  |  | 16. |
| W. H. Gatchell | do | 18 |  |  |
| Doct. Barr | do |  |  | 70.75 |
| Lambert Gittings | do | 4.37 1/2 |  |  |
| John Hoffinan | do | 16. |  |  |
| Andrew Leakin | do | 1.50 |  |  |
| Merchants bank | do | 4.50 |  |  |
| Hugh Bolton | do | 21. |  |  |
| Timothy Richards | do | 35.15 |  |  |
| James Dadelli | do |  |  | 45.92 |
| Archibald Stirling | do | 84.75 | An acct. in bar |  |
| Friendship Fire Co. | do | 2.55 |  |  |
| Baron de Beher | one chair |  | 16. |  |
| Chevalier Marter | do |  | 16. |  |
| Isaac Cooper | do |  |  | 89.88 |
| D. H. Clandenin | do | .62 1/2 |  |  |
| Mrs. Granmer | do |  | 4.87 |  |
| Henry Dukehart | do | 2.50 |  |  |
| John H. Atkinson | do |  | 22. |  |
| C. L. Lavine | do |  | 74.25 |  |
| John Diffenderffer | do | 3. |  |  |
| Ann Bartley | do |  | 15. |  |
| Mifs Claggett | do | 95. |  |  |
| J. Cornthwaite | do |  | 4.87 1/2 |  |
| Doct. A. Alexander | do | 4. |  |  |
| Geo. G. Bewer | do |  | 18. |  |
| Martin Harnifs | do |  |  | 66.17 |
| James Thompson | do | .50 |  |  |
| Robt. A. Scroggs coffin |  | 12. |  |  |
| Charles W. Kathhouse | do | 2.75 |  |  |

|  |  | Sperate | Doubtful | Desperate |
|---|---|---|---|---|
| Henry Carrol | do | 25. | | |
| Esther Evans | open acct. | 15. | | |
| Thomas Littleton | open acct. | 116.92 | | |
| Mrs. Dukehart | do | .75 | | |
| Mrs. C. Spencer | do | 82. | | Acct. in bar cash pd. |
| Wm. Menifee | do | 69.88 | | On loan from Mrs. Spencer |
| Wm. Barr | do | 18. | | |
| Mrs. Jane Martin | do | | 7. | |
| Daniel Brown | do | | 17.75 | |
| Thomas C. Sholes | do | 9.19 | | Acct. in bar |
| Sam.[l] G. Hyde | do | 102.33 | | |
| Jacob Bier | do | 1. | | |
| James Armour | do | 20. | | |
| John J. Dwiding | do | 10. | | |
| Doct. J. C. White | do | 4.37 | | |
| Job Smith | do | 4. | | |
| Edward Dowling | do | 22. | | |
| Capt. H. A. Thompson | do | 29.75 | | |
| H. O. Diffenderffer | do | 496. | | Acct. in bar for work |
| Rachael Stokes | do | | | 13.50 done in Shop |
| Beal Spurrier | do | 18.25 | | |
| Thomas Oliver | do | .75 | | |
| Mrs. W. Harrison | do | 23. | | |
| Capt. S. Smith | do | 7.25 | | |
| Eliza Torry | do | | 42. | |
| Joseph Townsend | do | .50 | | |
| Charles W. Dorsey | do | 6.87 | | |
| Geo. W. Teakle | do | 259. | | |
| Sarah H. Porter | do | 5.27 | | |
| Executors R. Oliver | do | 4.25 | | |
| R.B. Taney | do | 30.25 | | |
| Joseph Tucker | do | 2. | | |
| Mary Tinges | do | 72.63 | | Acct. in bar money lent E. Priestley |
| John Robinson | do | | 29. | |
| Henry Thomson | do | 11.10 | | |
| John M[c]Tavish | do | 2.25 | | |

|  |  | Sperate | Doubtful | Desperate |
|---|---|---|---|---|
| Estate Lavachi | do | 50. | | |
| Sam.¹ Thomson | do | 50.87 | | Acct. in bar |
| Jacob Daley | do | 193. | | |
| D.ʳ M. Diffenderffer | do | 22.50 | | Acct. in bar |
| Rob. M.ᶜLanahan | do | | | 73.29 |
| Joseph Thomas | do | | 21.73 | |
| Washington G. Tuck | do | | | 47.43 |
| Sam.¹ T. Thomson | do | 18. | | |
| John Stewart | do | 541.12 | | Acct. in bar |
| Charles Suter | do | 10. | | |
| John Glenn | do | 49.25 | | |
| George M.ᶜCoull | | | 48.27 | |
| James Thompson | rent | 80. | | |
| Mrs. Magarth | rent | | 74. | |
| Hager Scott | rent | | 75. | |
| Emily Martin | rent | | 30. | |
| Benjamin Custin | rent | | | 40. |
| Ann Tice | rent | | | 25. |
| Hiriam Tolson | rent | | | 80. |
| Henry Williams | rent | | 24. | |
| Frances Baley | rent | | | 32. |
| Sam.¹ Howard | rent | | | 33. |
| Richard Lewis | rent | | | 39. |
| James Duncan | rent | | 52. | |
| James Clark & Son | rent | | | 66.17 |
| William Orr | rent | 30. | | |
| Shadrack Jackson | rent | | 15. | |
| William Earnest | rent | | | 16. |
| Joseph Armiger | rent | | 8. | |
| John Wilson | rent | | | 14. |
| Levin Pritchet | rent | | 32. | Acct. in bar |
| G. Primrose | rent | | 15. | |
| Joseph Stubbs | rent | 30. | | |
| | | $3847.75 | $462.40 | $1329.01 |

| | |
|---|---:|
| Amount of Sperate Debts as Above | $3847.75 |
| Amount of Doubtful Debts as Above | 462.40 |
| Amount of Desperate Debts as Above | 1329.01 |
| Whole Amount of Debts due to the deceased | Dollars 5659.16 |

Tho$^s$ Murphy }
Reverdy Johnson } Ex$^{rs}$
Jacob Daley }

Baltimore County Ss On the 26$^{th}$ day of September 1837 came Thomas Murphy, Jacob Daley and Reverdy Johnson, Executors of Edward Priestley deceased and made Oath on the holy Evangely of Almighty God that the aforegoing is a true and just Inventory of the Debts due to the said deceased, which have come to their knowledge and that they will well and truly charge themselves with all and every such debt or debts as shall come to their hands or pofsefsion Sworn to in Open Court

Test. D. M. Perine, Register of Will for Balt$^o$ County

*Source*: Edward Priestley Debtor List, September 26, 1837, no. CM155, vol. DMP 47, pp. 6–10, WK 1096 to 1097, Maryland State Archives.

*Figure 1* Charles Willson Peale, *John Cadwalader Family*, 1771. Oil on canvas. 51 1/2" × 41 1/4". (Courtesy, Philadelphia Museum of Art.)

*Figure 2* Charles Willson Peale, *Lambert Cadwalader*, 1770. Oil on canvas. 51" × 41". (Courtesy, Philadelphia Museum of Art.)

*Leroy Graves and Luke Beckerdite*

New Insights on John Cadwalader's Commode-Seat Side Chairs

▼ FEW PIECES OF American furniture have received as much attention and acclaim as the commode-seat rococo side chairs commissioned by Philadelphia merchant John Cadwalader and his wife Elizabeth (Lloyd) (fig. 1). Only seven chairs from the set are known, but there may have been between sixteen and twenty originally. They appear to have been completed by September 1, 1770, when Charles Willson Peale received payment in full for portraits of John Cadwalader's brother Lambert (fig. 2) and parents Thomas and Hannah.[1]

The chair illustrated in figure 3 may be the one depicted in Peale's portrait of Lambert Cadwalader. The underside of the shoe is numbered "I," and the carving on the back and seat rails (fig. 4) is more detailed and more carefully rendered than that on the other surviving chairs (see figs. 5, 6). This disparity suggests that the chair shown in figure 3 may have been submitted for approval before work began on the remainder of the set. Because its carved details and upholstery evidence are clear and relatively unambiguous, this chair serves as a benchmark for reexamining aspects of the set's manufacture, upholstery, and context.[2]

In 1927, furniture historian Samuel W. Woodhouse published one of the commode side chairs and attributed it to Philadelphia cabinetmaker Benjamin Randolph. Since then, scholars have pointed to cabinetmaker Thomas Affleck and carvers Hercules Courtenay, John Pollard, Nicholas Bernard, and Martin Jugiez as possible makers. Most of these later attributions have cited bills, waste book entries, and inventories pertaining to Cadwalader's house and furnishings, but few have reconciled these documents with the physical evidence on the chairs.[3]

The production of elaborate sets or suites of furniture required a great deal of cooperation between the patron and maker. Although John and Elizabeth probably approved drawings of the chairs, Lambert may have assumed responsibility for the completion of the set. During the fall of 1769, he supervised work on John and Elizabeth's townhouse while the couple attended to her ailing father in Maryland. John's waste book notes that he reimbursed Lambert £94.15 for "B. Randolph['s] acct for Furniture" and £30 for "2 marble Slabs etc. had of C. Coxe." It is impossible to attribute the chairs to Randolph's shop based solely on the £94.15 entry, but that sum would have been sufficient for a large set.[4]

Circumstantial evidence strongly suggests that the chairs are products of Randolph's shop. The acanthus leaves on the rails and knees (see figs. 4, 7) are by the same hand that carved two side chairs with Randolph's label (see

*Figure 3* Side chair, Philadelphia, ca. 1769. Mahogany with white cedar. H. 36 3/4", W. 21 3/4" (seat), D. 17 7/8" (seat). (Courtesy, Chipstone Foundation; photo, Hans Lorenz.)

*Figure 4* Detail of the carving on the front rail of the side chair illustrated in fig. 3.

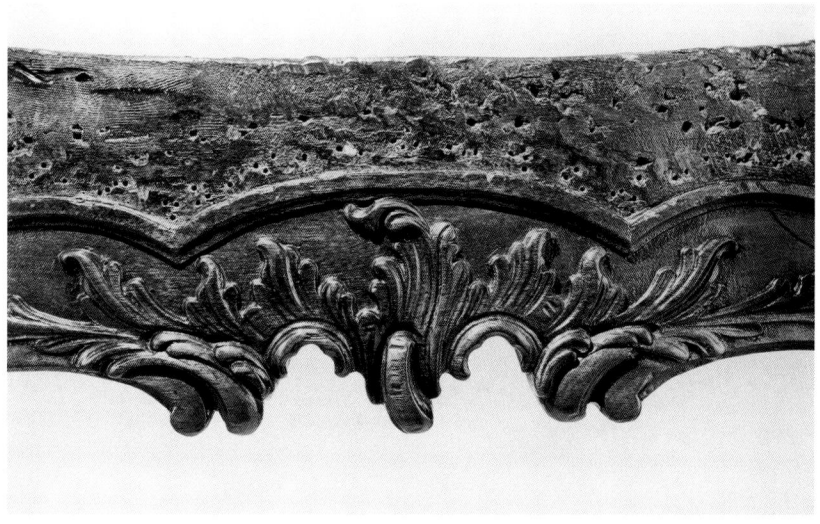

*Figure 5* Side chair, Philadelphia, ca. 1769. Mahogany with white cedar. H. 37$^{1}/_{16}$", W. 21$^{3}/_{4}$" (seat), D. 18" (seat). (Courtesy, Colonial Williamsburg Foundation; photo, Hans Lorenz.)

*Figure 6* Detail of the carving on the front rail of the side chair illustrated in fig. 5. The tradesmen who made the chairs in this set used a combination of planes, chisels, files, and scrapers to prepare the upholstery surfaces on the front and side rails. Because the front rails are serpentine, they used a curved toothing plane to finish the area for the foundation upholstery (approx. 1"–1$^{1}/_{4}$" at the top) and chisels, files, and scrapers to prepare the surface below. On the side rails, they used a standard smoothing plane to finish the area for the foundation upholstery and chisels, files, and scrapers below.

*Figure 7*  Detail of the knee carving on the side chair illustrated in fig. 3.

*Figure 8*  Side chair with the label of Benjamin Randolph, Philadelphia, ca. 1770. Mahogany. H. 38³⁄₈", W. 23³⁄₄", D. 19". (Courtesy, Museum of Fine Arts, Boston, M. and M. Karolick Collection, © 2000, all rights reserved.)

*Figure 9*  Detail of the knee carving on the side chair illustrated in fig. 8.

figs. 8, 9). The carving on the Cadwalader chairs is also related to architectural work from the parlors of the Stamper-Blackwell house in Philadelphia (now installed in the Winterthur Museum) (fig. 10) and the Thomas Ringgold house in Chestertown, Maryland (now installed in the Baltimore Museum of Art) (fig. 11). These interiors feature details (see figs. 12, 13) taken from Thomas Johnson's *A New Book of Ornaments* (1762) (see figs. 14, 15). Philadelphia carvers Hercules Courtenay and John Pollard probably introduced these rococo designs. Courtenay apprenticed with Johnson before immigrating to the colonies in 1765. He began his Philadelphia career as an indentured tradesman in Randolph's shop, where he worked with London-trained carver John Pollard. Courtenay established his own shop by the summer of 1769. On September 17, 1770, he billed John Cadwalader £81.2.1 for architectural carving, including a "Tablet the Judgement of Hercules" valued at £8.10.[5]

Pollard was the principal carver in Randolph's shop during the late 1760s and early 1770s. As such, he probably supervised several apprentices and journeymen. Because the ornament on the chairs differs significantly from work attributed to Courtenay and the other major carvers active in Philadelphia during the period, Pollard and his associates in Randolph's workforce are the most likely candidates as carvers of Cadwalader's commode-seat chairs. The

*Figure 10*  View of the Stamper-Blackwell parlor. (Courtesy, Winterthur Museum.)

*Figure 11*  View of the Ringgold parlor. (Courtesy, Baltimore Museum of Art.) The Ringgold house was one of two residences on Maryland's eastern shore with architectural carving imported from Philadelphia. The other is Cloverfields in Queen Anne's County. Philadelphia carvers shipped architectural carving as far south as Charleston, South Carolina.

*Figure 12*  Detail of the center tablet on the chimneypiece in the Stamper-Blackwell parlor. The scrolls and leaves framing the central scene are taken from the tablet design illustrated in fig. 14.

*Figure 13*  Detail of one of the frieze appliqués on the chimneypiece in the Ringgold parlor. This frieze appliqué is based on the design shown in fig. 15, but it is inverted.

*Figure 14*  Design for a tablet illustrated in Thomas Johnson, *A New Book of Ornaments* (1762). The only complete copy of this publication is in the Victoria and Albert Museum. It consists of six patterns "Designed for Tablets & Friezes for Chimney-Pieces."

*Figure 15*  Design for a frieze illustrated in Thomas Johnson, *A New Book of Ornaments* (1762).

*Figure 16* Detail of the acanthus carving on the left stile of the side chair shown in fig. 3.

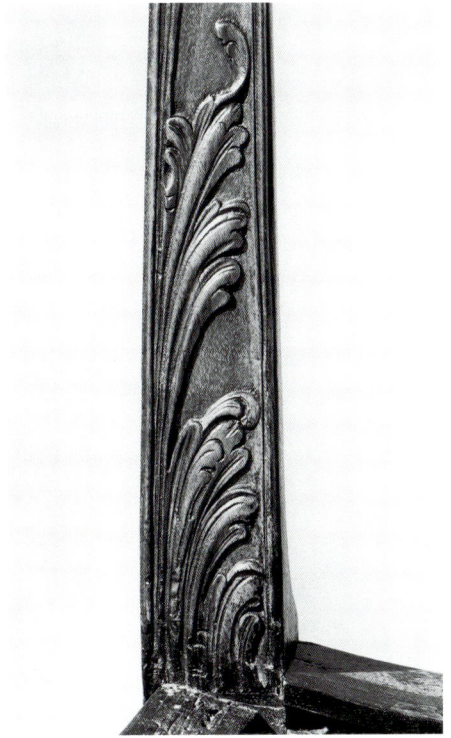

*Figure 17* Pier table, Philadelphia, 1765–1769. Mahogany with yellow pine; marble. H. 32 3/8", W. 48", D. 23 1/4". (Courtesy, Metropolitan Museum of Art; John Stewart Kennedy Fund.) Two large scrolls are missing from the lower edge of the table.

*Figure 18* Detail of the carved figure in the center of the table illustrated in fig. 17.

chairs clearly represent the work of at least two carvers. In accordance with accepted eighteenth-century practice, the most accomplished tradesman worked on the stiles, crest, and back—the components nearest the eye.[6]

The carving on the backs of the chairs is most like that on the tablets and frieze appliqués in the Stamper-Blackwell and Ringgold parlors. All of these designs feature acanthus leaves with intricately curled tips and deeply modeled surfaces (see figs. 12, 13, 16). The foliage on the tablets and leaves below the central husk on the crests of the chairs rank among the finest American carving in the rococo style. The only Philadelphia carving that surpasses this work is on a pier table attributed to Pollard (fig. 17). This table, which also belonged to Cadwalader, may be one of the "2 marble Slabs etc." that Lam-

*Figure 19*  Design for a pier glass and table illustrated on pl. 152 in the third edition of Thomas Chippendale's *Gentleman and Cabinet-Maker's Director* (1762). (Courtesy, Winterthur Museum.)

bert purchased from Charles Coxe for £30 in 1769. Like the architectural carving, the table has details (see fig. 18) taken from British design books (see fig. 19), specifically the third edition of Thomas Chippendale's *The Gentleman and Cabinet-Maker's Director* (1762). Randolph and his tradesmen undoubtedly had access to a copy. His trade card includes imagery borrowed from the *Director*, and Randolph was a member of the Library Company of Philadelphia, which owned a copy of the third edition by 1769. However, the overt British design of the table, architectural carving, and commode-seat chairs suggests that they reflect the imagination of an immigrant tradesman such as Pollard rather than a native-born entrepreneur such as Randolph. The latter was a lumber merchant before his investment in a successful privateering venture enabled him to hire the workforce for a cabinet shop.[7]

Cadwalader's commode-seat chairs were the genesis of an elaborate suite of furniture made for the townhouse he and his wife purchased from Samuel Rhodes in 1769. At the time of their marriage in 1768, Elizabeth Lloyd's personal wealth exceeded £11,000. A cash advance of £2,500 made by her father, Edward III, allowed the couple to purchase the townhouse and begin converting it into what one observer called "a grand and elegant" residence. Cadwalader made over £374 in unspecified payments to house joiner Thomas Nevell, which suggests that Nevell made and installed new architectural components throughout the house. The Cadwaladers' residence also contained over £360 worth of architectural carving, including a variety of moldings, trusses, architrave flowers, frieze appliqués, and sculptural busts and tablets. Among the carvers who worked on this project were Hercules Courtenay, Nicholas Bernard, Martin Jugiez, and, in all probability, John Pollard. Randolph's shop had the largest account, providing £252.16.1 worth of carving.[8]

Several pieces of furniture made by Thomas Affleck and carved by James Reynolds and by the firm of Bernard and Jugiez were designed to be en suite with Cadwalader's commode-seat chairs. Between October 13, 1770, and January 14, 1771, Affleck's shop made over eighteen pieces of furniture for Cadwalader. Included were two mahogany commode sofas "for the Recesses" valued at £16, "one Large ditto" valued at £10, "an Easy Chair to Sute ditto" valued at £4.10 (fig. 20), two commode card tables valued at £10, and four firescreens valued at £10. During the same time frame, Reynolds and Bernard and Jugiez were also occupied with other commissions from Cadwalader. In October 1770, Bernard and Jugiez billed Cadwalader £28.10.7½ for architectural carving. Three months later, Reynolds charged him £140.18.1 for several

*Figure 20*  Easy chair attributed to Thomas Affleck, Philadelphia, 1771. Mahogany with yellow pine, white oak, white cedar, black walnut, and tulip poplar. H. 45". (Courtesy, Dietrich Americana Foundation.) The carving on this chair is attributed to the shop of Nicholas Bernard and Martin Jugiez.

large carved and gilded looking glasses, picture frames, and 539 yards of papiér-maché borders described as "Palmyra Scrowl" and "Leaf & Reed."⁹

The commode-seat chairs were clearly part of a unified decorative scheme that included the suite made by Affleck and that extended to the architectural carving and fabrics used in each of Cadwalader's principal rooms. Bills pertaining to the textile furnishings in Cadwalader's house shed light on the probable number, upholstery, and placement of the commode-seat chairs. On October 18, 1770, Philadelphia upholsterer Plunkett Fleeson charged Cadwalader £13.13 for "covering 32 chairs over rail finish'd in canvis." The following January, the upholsterer made seventy-six Saxon blue French check cases with blue and white fringe for these chairs and others that Cadwalader had either purchased or inherited from his father-in-law. The commode-seat chairs were subsequently fitted with covers made of blue and yellow silk damask that Cadwalader ordered from London merchants Rushton & Beachcroft. In January 1772, Philadelphia upholsterer John Webster billed Cadwalader £18.7.10 for making the curtains for four windows and for upholstering twenty chairs and three sofas with these fabrics. A subsequent entry in Cadwalader's waste book provides additional information on Webster's work, noting that the payment was for "Curtains in [the] front & back Rooms, Covers to Settees & Covers to Chairs in front & back Rooms." The curtains and covers in the front room were blue and the ones in the back par-

*Figure 21*  Detail of one of the webbing sites on the seat rails of the chair illustrated in fig. 3. Each site is indicated by a cluster of nail holes approximately 1⁷⁄₈" wide.

lor were yellow to match the colors of each room's walls and Wilton carpets. An "Inventory of Contents Remaining in [the] Cadwalader House" taken in 1786 lists two blue damask window curtains, a blue damask settee cover, ten blue damask chair covers, two yellow silk damask window curtains, ten yellow silk damask chair bottoms, and "1 cover of a settee for do."¹⁰

Although the records pertaining to the upholstery of Cadwalader's seating furniture are both detailed and extensive, the physical evidence on the commode-seat chairs documents a history of coverings more complicated than previously thought. All of the side chairs examined for this article had six strips of webbing, three nailed to the side rails and three to the front and rear rails (fig. 21). Fleeson would have pulled the front-to-rear strips much tighter than the other webbing in order to maintain the shape of the seat frame. After attaching the webbing, he nailed a layer of "canvis" to the top face of the seat rails to provide a foundation for the stuffing. The next procedure involved attaching upholstery rolls made of "curled hair" wrapped

*Figure 22*  Detail of the right leg of the chair illustrated in fig. 3, showing file marks from the removal of the upholstery peak. The peaks on the commode-seat chairs were approximately 1/2" high.

in canvas. Fleeson evidently stitched the rolls to the foundation canvas and nailed them to the upper edge of the front and side rails. Upholstery peaks (fig. 22) that extended above the seat rail at the outer corner of each front leg established the height of the rolls and profile of the seat (fig. 23*a*). The front rolls were uniform in height, but the ones on the side rails tapered from approximately 1/2" at the front to 1/4" at the rear. Once the rolls were attached, Fleeson stitched the first layer of hair in place. After building up the cavity with successive layers of hair, he attached the top canvas (fig. 23*b*). This was a critical step, because Fleeson had to pull the canvas from back to front as he nailed it in place. Only by keeping the canvas in constant tension could he maintain a sharp sweeping edge along the front rail.[11]

*Figure 23*  Detail of the front seat rail of the chair illustrated in fig. 5, showing nailing patterns for securing the (*a*) upholstery roll and (*b*) top canvas.

Fleeson charged 8s 6d for covering each of the chairs. Evidently this price included materials, since his bill does not include any additional charges for webbing, canvas, hair, tacks, thread, or tape. He probably returned the chairs to the cabinetmaker after January 28, 1771, when he recorded charges for making their slipcovers. Ultraviolet photography and microscopy indicate that the finish on the chairs was applied after the foundation upholstery (figs. 24, 25). Another Philadelphia side chair (figs. 26, 27), which may also be a product of Randolph's shop, had its foundation upholstery and finish applied in the same sequence. Not surprisingly, its rail flouresces like those on the Cadwalader set.[12]

Evidence suggests that the slipcovers made by Fleeson and Webster fit rather snugly against the seat rails. Both sets of covers probably had shaped lower edges that conformed to the carved strapwork on the front and side rails. The narrow fringe stitched to the edges of the covers may have hung above or just over the carving.

*Figure 24* Ultraviolet photograph showing the front rail of the chair illustrated in fig. 5. The area covered by the foundation upholstery flouresces differently from that covered by finish.

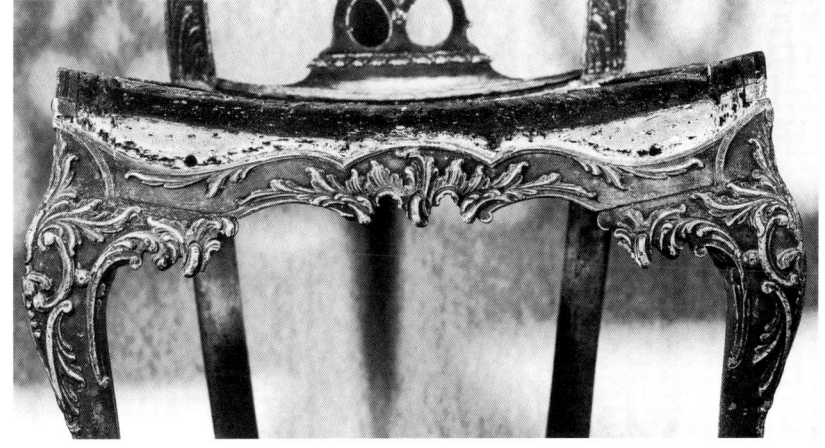

*Figure 25* Ultraviolet photograph showing the front rail of the chair illustrated in fig. 3. The area of the seat rail covered by the foundation upholstery flouresces differently from that covered by finish.

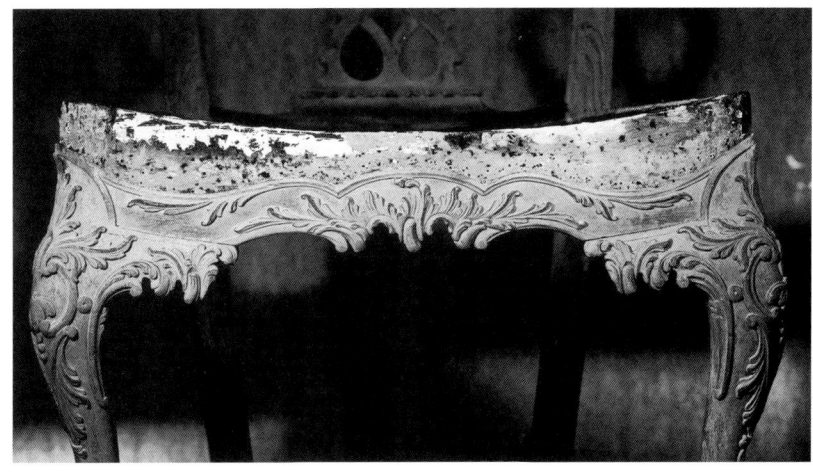

*Figure 26* Side chair, Philadelphia, 1765–1775. Mahogany with tulip poplar. H. 41 1/2", W. 27", D. 15 1/2". (Courtesy, Colonial Williamsburg Foundation; photo, Hans Lorenz.)

*Figure 27* Detail of the front seat rail of the chair illustrated in fig. 26. The area covered by the foundation upholstery flouresces differently from that covered by finish.

*Figure 29*  Detail showing how the slipcovers of the commode-seat chairs would have been tied off.

*Figure 28*  Detail showing two of the six spoon bit holes used for tying on the slipcover of the chair shown in fig. 5.

With the exception of the chair illustrated in figure 3, all the commode-seat examples have two holes drilled with a spoon bit in the front and side rails (see fig. 28). These holes appear to have been intended for tying on slipcovers, but it is impossible to determine if they are original. A strip of tape or cord attached to the covers would have been inserted through the holes at the back of each side rail and tied off in the middle. The remaining cords would have been tied off at each front corner (see fig. 29).[13]

Although at least one set of slipcovers remained in the Cadwalader house until 1786, the chairs were subsequently fitted with fixed upholstery. The front and side rails have clear imprints from a row of brass nails with square, tapered shanks and heads approximately 1/2" in diameter. The nailing follows the curves of the carved strapwork, but varies from a maximum height of 1/2" to a low of 3/16" (figs. 30, 31). The unevenness in this pattern suggests that one set of slipcovers—probably the damask ones made by Webster—may have been reused. The fringe stitched to the lower edge would have made inconsistencies in the nail pattern almost imperceptible (fig. 32), and the tacks used to secure the edges of the covers adjacent to the carving would have been hidden (fig. 33).

*Figure 30*  Detail of the nailing line for fixed upholstery on the front rail of *(left)* the chair illustrated in fig. 3 and *(right)* the chair illustrated in fig. 5.

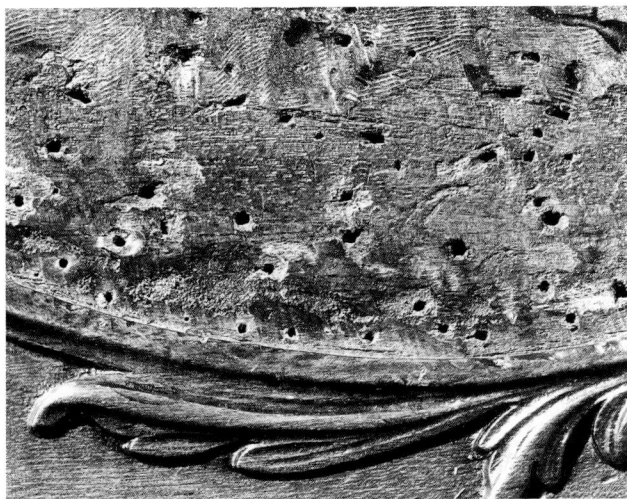 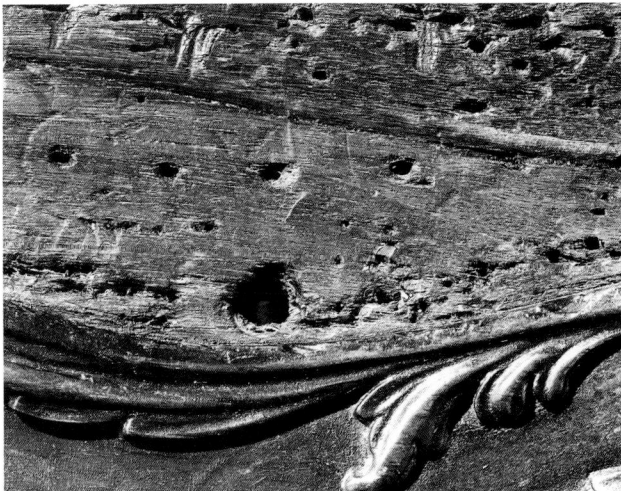

*Figure 31* Detail of the nailing line for fixed upholstery on the side rail of (*left*) the chair illustrated in fig. 3 and (*right*) the chair illustrated in fig. 5.

*Figure 32* Detail of the side chair illustrated in fig. 5 showing how the fringe of a reused slipcover would have been nailed to the side rail.

*Figure 33* Detail of the tacking evidence adjacent to the carved strapwork on the rails of the seat of the side chair illustrated in fig. 5.

By the fall of 1772, the Cadwaladers had nearly completed the furnishing of their townhouse. Their residence there was shortlived, however, owing to Elizabeth's death in 1776 and John's service in the Revolutionary War. During the British occupation of Philadelphia, Generals William Howe and

William Knyphausen commandeered Cadwalader's house. The latter made a relatively detailed list of the furnishings, most of which appear in the 1786 inventory.[14]

During the late 1770s and early 1780s, Cadwalader, his new wife Willimina Bond, and their children spent much of their time at Shrewsbury Farm in Kent County, Maryland. On January 8, 1786, he wrote Richard Tilghman that he could no longer afford to maintain two households. John died of pneumonia the following month. Willimina subsequently moved back to Philadelphia, having been left life tenancy in the townhouse "together with all the . . . furniture." She lived in the house until September 1787, when she leased it to her brother Phineas Bond. Willimina and her family moved into a house at 35 Union Street; presumably she took most of the furnishings with her. They remained in her possession until 1819, when Willimina moved to England.[15]

Although it is impossible to determine precisely when or why the commode-seat chairs were fitted with fixed covers, the brass nails used to attach them and other physical evidence on the seat rails suggest that the alteration occurred during the late eighteenth century. By 1786, several of the objects commissioned by John and Elizabeth Cadwalader had fallen into disrepair. The front garret contained "10 old mahogany chairs many broke," a damaged washstand, and two trunks containing the damask window curtains, fabric for mending them, ten blue damask chair "covers," and ten yellow damask chair "bottoms." These references, Willimina's moves, and her family's reduced finances support the theory that the slipcovers were reused, probably after she moved to Union Street.[16]

ACKNOWLEDGMENTS   For assistance with this article the authors thank Colonial Williamsburg photographers Hans Lorenz and Craig McDougal and furniture conservators Mark Kutney and Alan Miller.

1. John Cadwalader Waste Book, box 8, General John Cadwalader section (hereafter cited GJCS), Cadwalader Papers, Historical Society of Pennsylvania, Philadelphia, p. 53. The payment to Peale was for "2 minature & 3 portrait Paintings in full." For more on the sitters, see Nicholas B. Wainwright, *Colonial Grandeur in Philadelphia: The House and Furniture of General John Cadwalader* (Philadelphia: Historical Society of Pennsylvania, 1964), pp. 108–11, 114–15. Some scholars have argued that the chair in Lambert's portrait is from a different set because it has plain stiles; however, evidence suggests otherwise. Peale's portrait of the John Cadwalader family depicts one of the commode front tables owned by Cadwalader. The table and chair in the paintings show similar degrees of artistic license when compared with the actual objects. For more on these portraits, see ibid., pp. 108–11, 114–15.

2. All of Cadwalader's commode-seat side chairs are numbered on the underside of the shoe. On the chair shown in figure 3, the number was made with a chisel using converging angled cuts. The chair illustrated in fig. 5 has the number 11 on the rear seat rail under the shoe.

3. Samuel W. Woodhouse, Jr., "Benjamin Randolph of Philadelphia," *Antiques* 11, no. 5 (May 1927): 366–71; and Samuel W. Woodhouse, Jr., "More About Benjamin Randolph," *Antiques* 17, no. 1 (January 1930): 21–25. For more recent studies of these chairs, see *Philadelphia: Three Centuries of American Art* (Philadelphia: Philadelphia Museum of Art, 1976), pp. 113–15; Philip D. Zimmerman, "A Methodological Study in the Identification of Some Important Philadelphia Chippendale Furniture," in *American Furniture and Its Makers*, edited by Ian M. G. Quimby (Chicago: University of Chicago Press for the Winterthur Museum, 1978), pp. 193–208; and Mark J. Anderson, Gregory J. Landrey, and Philip D. Zimmerman, *Cadwalader Study* (Winterthur, Del.: Winterthur Museum), pp. 8–13.

4. Wainwright, *Colonial Grandeur*, pp. 22. Wainwright notes that Cadwalader purchased a painted high-post bedstead, window cornices, and rods and hooks from Randolph in September 1769. Part of the £94.15 payment to Randolph may have been for this work (Wainwright, *Colonial Grandeur*, p. 38).

5. For more on the chairs with Randolph labels, see Philip D. Zimmerman, "Labeled Randolph Chairs Rediscovered," in *American Furniture*, edited by Luke Beckerdite (Hanover, N.H.: University Press of New England for the Chipstone Foundation, 1998), pp. 81–99. Luke Beckerdite, "Philadelphia Carving Shops, Part III: Hercules Courtenay and His School," *Antiques* 131, no. 5 (May 1987): 1052-63. Ringgold had business dealings with John Cadwalader (Thomas Ringgold and Co. to John Cadwalader, October 21, 1769–December 9, 1770, GJCS) and an account with Benjamin Randolph. Randolph's account book contains a debit entry under Ringgold's name "To Shop £23.6.6" (Pennsylvania-Philadelphia Account Book, 1768–1787, Rare Books and Manuscripts Division, New York Public Library, p. 144). For more on Courtenay's apprenticeship, see Morrison H. Heckscher, *American Furniture in the Metropolitan Museum of Art II, Late Colonial Period: The Queen Anne and Chippendale Styles* (New York: Random House, 1985), p. 24. Courtenay signed the Non–Importation Agreement in 1765 (*Philadelphia: Three Centuries*, p. 111), the same year he began work in Randolph's shop (Benjamin Randolph Receipt Book, 1763–1777, Winterthur Museum). Randolph made several payments on Courtenay's account. The carver's term probably expired by May 19, 1768, when he married Mary Shute (*Philadelphia: Three Centuries*, p. 111). Courtenay advertised independently in the August 7, 1769, issue of the *Pennsylvania Gazette*. His bill for architectural carving in Cadwalader's house is in Incoming Correspondence, Bills, and Receipts, 1770, box 2, folder 17, GJCS and is reproduced in Wainwright, *Colonial Grandeur*, p. 12.

6. Pennsylvania-Philadelphia Account Book, 1768–1787, passim. For more on the styles of other major Philadelphia carvers, see Luke Beckerdite, "Philadelphia Carving Shops, Part I: James Reynolds," *Antiques* 125, no. 5 (May 1985): 1120-33; Luke Beckerdite, "Philadelphia Carving Shops, Part II: Bernard and Jugiez," *Antiques* 128, no. 3 (September 1985): 498-513; and Luke Beckerdite, "Philadelphia Carving Shops, Part III: Hercules Courtenay and His School," pp. 1044–63. Plates 1–5 in Matthias Lock's *The Principles of Ornament, or the Youth's Guide to Drawing of Foliage* (1769), illustrate the principle of placing more complex designs closer to the eye. Similarly, Thomas Sheraton's *Cabinet Dictionary* (1803), states:

> Figures, foliage, and flowers are the three great subjects of carving; which, in the finishing, require a strength of delicacy suited to the height or distance of the object from the eye. . . . It requires some command of the mind, for the carver to work so close as to suit considerable height or distance; in which case, his eye, in working at so short a distance, must not govern him . . . but his judgement must take the lead, and constantly suggest to him the folly of finishing, in a tender manner, those flowers, and foliage . . . which are only to be viewed at a distance.

In architectural carving, apprentices and less experienced journeymen often worked on cornice moldings, brackets, and flowers, whereas master carvers and more accomplished journeymen focused their attention on chimneypiece appliqués and other prominent components. A ceremonial chair in St. Peter's Church in Philadelphia has an elaborately carved back with acanthus leaves that are very similar to those on the backs of the Cadwalader commode-seat chairs. The carved details on the ceremonial chair are more carefully rendered, like those from the Ringgold and Stamper-Blackwell parlors.

7. Cadwalader Waste Book, p. 63. Morrison H. Heckscher, "English Furniture Pattern Books in Eighteenth-Century America," in *American Furniture*, edited by Luke Beckerdite (Hanover, N.H.: University Press of New England for the Chipstone Foundation, 1974), p. 185. The author thanks Charles Hummel for the information on Randolph's venture.

8. This estimate of Elizabeth Lloyd's wealth does not include her land on Maryland's eastern shore, seventy-eight slaves, one hundred horses, and livestock (Wainwright, *Colonial Grandeur*, p. 3). In 1774, John Adams wrote, "we visited a Mr. Cadwallader a Gentleman of large Fortune, a grand and elegant House and Furniture." Ibid., pp. 11, 13, 19–20, 33, 104. Thomas Nevell worked on several important Philadelphia buildings, including Captain John McPherson's house, Mount Pleasant, in Fairmount Park (Thomas Nevell Account Book, Rare Book Collection, University of Pennsylvania). For more on these carvers and their work for Cadwalader, see Beckerdite, "Bernard and Jugiez," 502–5; and Beckerdite, "Hercules Courtenay," p. 1051. The bills for all of these carvers are either reproduced or transcribed (Randolph) in Wainwright, *Colonial Grandeur*.

9. Thomas Affleck to John Cadwalader, April 18, 1771, box 2, folder 18, GJCS. Affleck's bill requested payment for eighteen pieces of furniture, two knife trays, bed and window cornices, and services from October 13, 1770, to January 14, 1771. Notations at the bottom of the bill indicate that Affleck subcontracted the carving on these pieces to James Reynolds and the shop of Bernard and Jugiez. Affleck's bill, which totaled £119.8, is reproduced in Wainwright, *Colonial Grandeur*, p. 44. Bernard and Jugiez's receipted bill, dated February 13, 1771, is in box 2, folder 18, GJCS. Reynolds's receipted bill, dated June 29, 1771, is in box 2, folder 20, GJCS. The bills from both carving firms are reproduced in Wainwright, *Colonial Grandeur*, pp. 29, 46.

10. The bills from Fleeson, Webster, and Rushton & Beachcroft (the London company that provided the silk fabrics, fringe, and tape) are reproduced in Wainwright, *Colonial Grandeur*, pp. 40–41, 59, 61. For more on the wall colors and carpets in Cadwalader's house, see ibid., passim. Cadwalader owned a second suite of furniture with hairy paw feet and straight rails. Examples are in the Winterthur Museum, Stratford Hall, and the Philadelphia Museum of Art. The chairs and matching card tables in the second suite may have sat in the small front parlor, which had green walls. Assuming that there were twelve chairs in this suite and twenty commode-seat chairs, that would account for the thirty-two that Fleeson covered over the rail. Although chair "bottoms" could be interpreted as slipseats, this term probably referred to slipcovers. The use of two terms in the inventory may result from its having been taken by John Cadwalader's sister Rebecca and his brother-in-law Samuel Meredeth. Three copies of the inventory survive, and they vary slightly. The 1786 inventory also lists one mahogany dining table, one marble slab [table], and one card table in the "small front parlor"; one marble slab [table], one card table, and ten mahogany chairs, in the "back parlor"; one large settee, one small settee, one card table, ten mahogany chairs in the "front parlor"; one small settee in the "entry" on the second floor; six mahogany chairs with chintz "furniture" in the "back chamber" on the second floor; six mahogany "carpet bottom" chairs in the "front chamber" on the second floor; two old chairs and six mahogany chairs in the "front room" on the third floor; and two green covers for card tables, one large easy chair, and ten old mahogany chairs "many broke" in the "front garrett" on the third floor (ibid., p. 73).

11. Although Fleeson's name is used in conjunction with the upholstery on the commode-seat chairs, journeymen probably did much if not all of the work. Wainwright, *Colonial Grandeur*, pp. 40–41

12. Ibid., pp. 40–41. Colonial Williamsburg conservator Mark Kutney performed the finish microscopy.

13. The side chair illustrated in fig. 3 may have left the Cadwalader family as early as the 1780s. Recent research by Jennifer Olshin suggests that the chair passed from the Cadwalader family to David Lewis (1766–1840), who lived on "Second Street north of Spruce" (Christie's, *Important American Furniture, Folk Art and Chinese Porcelain*, October 14, 1999, lot no. 174, p. 89). Lewis may have purchased the chair from Cadwalader's second wife, Willimina, or from one of John's children. (For more on Willimina and the Cadwalader children, see Wainwright, *Colonial Grandeur*, pp. 72–77.) If this history is correct, it supports the theory that the slipcovers were originally tied off at the rear stiles and that the holes in the rails are additions. Screws have been inserted in some of the holes, possibly to attach a deck for spring upholstery. A circa 1720 armchair attributed to James Moore has seat covers tied off in a similar manner (Geoffrey Beard, *Upholsterers and Interior Furnishings in England* [New Haven: Yale University Press for the Bard Graduate Center, 1997], p. 176, fig. 151-4).

14. Wainwright, *Colonial Grandeur*, pp. 61–67.

15. Ibid., pp. 68–77.

16. Ibid., pp. 72–73.

*Martha H. Willoughby*

Patronage in
Early Salem:
The Symonds Shops
and Their Customers

▼ DISPLAYING DISTINCTIVE geometric moldings, architectural appliqués, and mannerist carving, a group of furniture attributed to the Symonds shops of Salem, Massachusetts, documents the transfer of seventeenth-century British styles to New England. While previous studies of this group have focused on the products of these shops and the identities of individual tradesmen associated with them, the histories of several objects reveal networks of patronage based upon family and religious ties. Like the Townsends and Goddards of eighteenth-century Newport, the principal joiners in the Symonds shops capitalized on these and other connections to dominate the furniture-making trade in Salem.[1]

Several cupboards, chests, and cabinets now attributed to the Symonds shops appeared in early studies of Essex County furniture. In 1938, furniture historian Irving P. Lyon included several examples from the group in a series of articles on Ipswich, Massachusetts, joiner Thomas Dennis. Several decades later, Helen Park attributed two of the pieces illustrated by Lyon to Salem, citing their histories of descent in local families and that town's preeminent position as the economic and furniture-producing center of Essex County. The first scholar to recognize that these objects were part of a "Salem school" was Benno Forman. He concluded that joiner John Symonds (ca. 1595–1671) was the most likely progenitor of this tradition, based on the unfinished furniture, tools, and turned components listed in his inventory. Forman also noted that the careers of John Symonds and his sons James (1633–1714) and Samuel (1638–1722) encompassed the dates ascribed to the furniture. In addition to identifying chamber tables, chairs, and other forms from the Symonds shops, Robert F. Trent strengthened Forman's attribution by linking the furniture to architectural woodwork from John Symonds's hometown, Great Yarmouth, in Norfolk, England. Embellished with geometric moldings, corbels, and interlacing S-scrolls, the interior paneling of the Star Hotel in Great Yarmouth has many of the same details found on furniture attributed to the Symonds shops. Trent also identified the group's mannerist design sources and chronicled the evolution of various forms through the last decades of the seventeenth century.[2]

Eight pieces of furniture—four cabinets, three chests, and a cupboard—attributed to the Symonds shops have histories or physical evidence connecting them to their original owners. Three of the cabinets bear dates and the initials of a married couple that correspond to only one husband and wife living in Essex County at the time. Forman traced the initials on two of these examples to Thomas Buffington (1639–1728) and Sarah Southwick

*Figure 1* Cabinet attributed to the Symonds shops, Salem, Massachusetts, 1676. Red oak, red cedar, black walnut and soft maple (by microanalysis). H. 17 1/4", W. 17", D. 9 7/8". (Courtesy, Winterthur Museum; photo, Gavin Ashworth.)

(1644–1733) of Salem (fig. 1) and Ephraim Herrick (1638–1693) and Mary Cross (1640–1693) of Beverly, Massachusetts (fig. 2). Neither object has a provenance, thus the identification of their original owners rests solely upon their initials. A recently discovered cabinet (fig. 3) has the initials of Joseph Pope (1650–1712) and Bathsheba Folger (1652–1726), whose identities were uncovered by their late-twentieth-century descendants, the last family members to own the piece. The fourth cabinet (fig. 4) is initialed "TH," and, like the Herrick and Pope cabinets, it is dated 1679. This piece evidently

170  MARTHA H. WILLOUGHBY

*Figure 2* Cabinet attributed to the Symonds shops, Salem, Massachusetts, 1679. Red oak, black walnut, eastern red cedar, and soft maple with white pine (by microanalysis). H. 17³/₄", W. 17¹/₄", D. 9³/₄". (Courtesy, Metropolitan Museum of Art, gift of Mrs. Russell Sage; photo, Gavin Ashworth.)

belonged to Thomas Hart (d. 1731) of Lynnfield, Massachusetts, and passed to his brother Samuel's family upon Thomas' death.[3]

The chest illustrated in figure 5 probably belonged to John Trask (1678–1737) and Hannah Osborne (1679–1721) of Salem. It descended through three generations of their family to William Blake Trask (1812–1906) (fig. 6), who donated the piece to the New England Historical and Genealogical Society in 1902. An article by William published a year earlier shows the chest (fig. 7) in the house of his great-great-great grandfather, William (1640–1691).

*Figure 3* Cabinet attributed to the Symonds shops, Salem, Massachusetts, 1679. Red oak, black walnut, soft maple (by microanalysis), and cedar with pine. H. 16 3/8", W. 17", D. 9 1/2". (Courtesy, Peabody Essex Museum; photo, Gavin Ashworth.)

Given the similarities between this example and a related chest dated 1701 (fig. 8), it is more likely that John Trask commissioned his chest (fig. 5) around the time of his marriage than that he inherited it from his father.[4]

Another one-drawer chest (fig. 9) attributed to the Symonds shops belonged to Lyman and Elizabeth Osborne during the late nineteenth and early twentieth centuries (fig. 6). Furniture historians have speculated that it descended from Lyman's ancestor Samuel Osborne (1675–1750), but the original owner was probably his brother John (1671–1744) or sister Hannah, who married John Trask. A nineteenth-century inscription—"Hannah Osborne 1831"—on the underside of the lid indicates that the chest came down in a branch of Elizabeth's family.[5]

A note in the chest illustrated in figure 10 suggests that its original owners

*Figure 4* Cabinet attributed to the Symonds shops, Salem, Massachusetts, 1679. Red oak, white oak, black walnut, and soft maple with white pine (by microanalysis). H. 16¾", W. 17⁵⁄₁₆", D. 5⅝". (Courtesy, Winterthur Museum; photo, Gavin Ashworth.)

were Nathaniel (1670–1749) and Rebecca (Conant) (1671–1760) Raymond of Beverly, Massachusetts, and that the piece descended through female lines for five generations. Historian Laurel Thatcher Ulrich has shown that eighteenth-century New England women often inherited objects that "preserved their personal identity" and "ratified their connection with their family of origin." Although furniture, needlework, and silver emblazoned with initials and dates are the most conspicuous examples of objects that "preserve lineages through time," unmarked items with oral or written histories often performed the same function.[6]

According to its late-nineteenth-century owner, Harriet Putnam Fowler, the cupboard illustrated in figures 11 and 12 descended from Lieutenant Stephen Putnam (1694–1772) and his wife and first cousin, Miriam Putnam

*Figure 5* Chest attributed to the Symonds shops, Salem, Massachusetts, 1680–1705. Red oak and unidentified woods. H. 30", W. 47 1/2", D. 21 3/4". (Courtesy, Israel Sack, Inc.)

(b. 1698). This history is supported by the listing of the "old Fashion Cubbard" valued at eighteen shillings in Stephen's inventory. Undoubtedly an inherited item, the cupboard could have been made for Stephen's father, Deacon Benjamin Putnam (1664–1715), or grandfather, Lieutenant Nathaniel Putnam (1619–1700). Alternatively, Miriam's father, John Putnam (1667–1736), or grandfather, Captain John Putnam (1627–1710), could have commissioned it.[7]

The owners of four of the objects attributed to the Symonds shops—the Popes, Buffingtons, Osbornes, and tangentially the Trasks—were closely affiliated through marriage and religious associations. The progenitors of the first three families were Quakers persecuted during the late 1650s and 1660s. As early as 1656, the General Court of the Massachusetts Bay Colony attempted to suppress the sect by imprisoning English Quakers arriving in Boston. In response to growing conversions, the court enacted numerous laws forbidding attendance of "Quaking" meetings and housing of visiting Friends. The penalties imposed on Quakers and their allies became increasingly brutal and included fines, whipping, mutilation, banishment, and hanging.[8]

With the impending arrival of English Quakers in 1657, Salem officials passed laws nearly as oppressive as those instituted in Boston. Several Friends were arrested for attending a meeting at the house of Nicholas Phelps in 1658. Among the persecuted were Joshua Buffum (1635–1705) and Lawrence (d. 1660) and Cassandra Southwick (d. 1660), whose granddaughter owned the cabinet illustrated in figure 1. All were whipped and imprisoned in Boston because there was no jail in Salem at the time. Buffum and the Southwicks continued to participate in Quaker meetings after their release and were promptly reincarcerated. Refusing to renounce their beliefs, they were

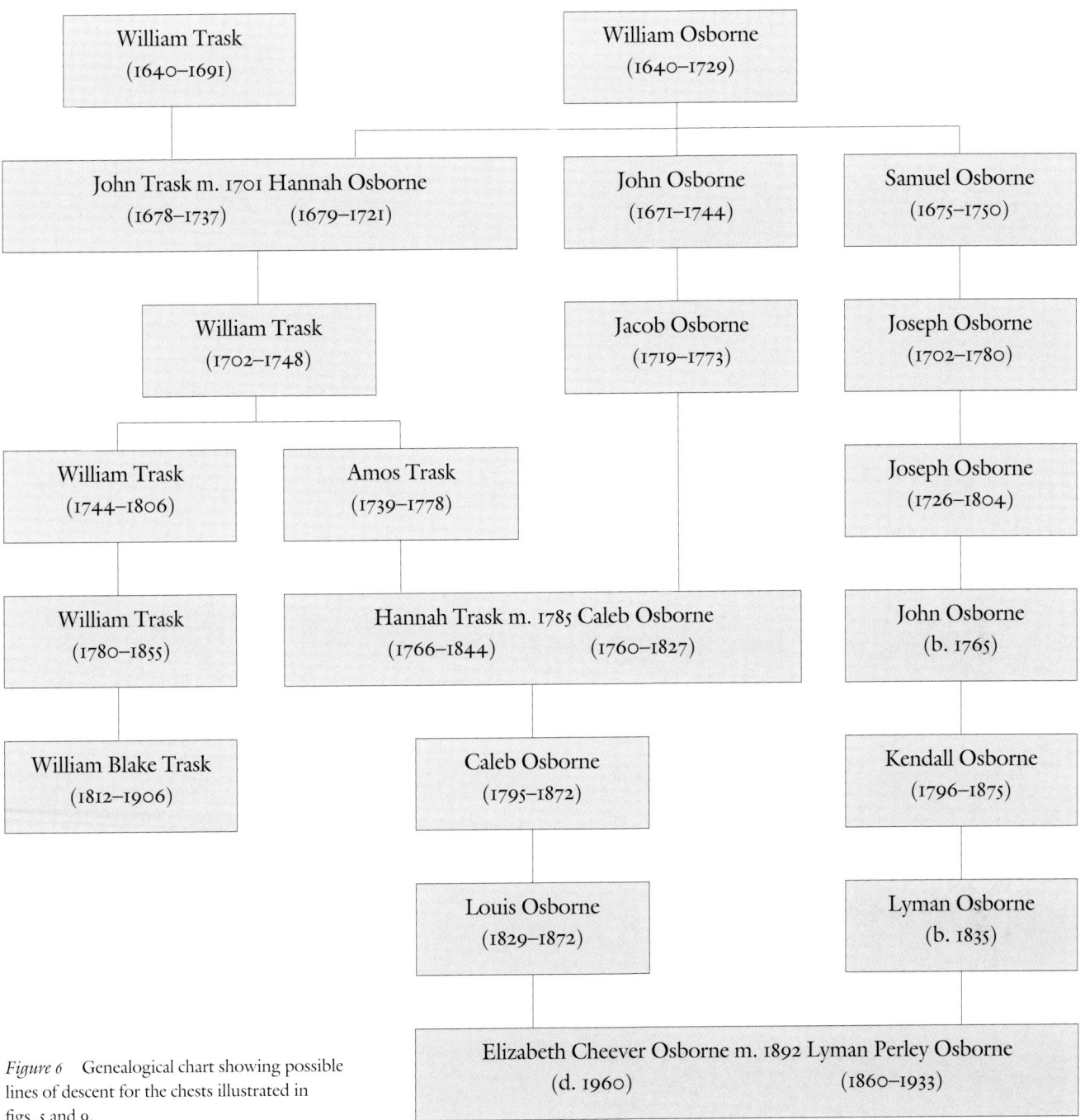

*Figure 6* Genealogical chart showing possible lines of descent for the chests illustrated in figs. 5 and 9.

banished under the threat of death. All three fled to Shelter Island, off the coast of Long Island, where Lawrence and Cassandra died in 1660. Buffum returned to Salem in 1661 and received fines throughout the decade for not attending a recognized church.[9]

Although they escaped arrest, Joseph (1607–1667) and Gertrude (Shattuck) Pope also attended the meeting at Nicholas Phelps's house and, like Buffum, they received fines throughout the 1660s. At least five of their children married into Quaker families. The cabinet illustrated in figure 3 commemorates the 1679 marriage of Joseph Pope, Jr., and Bathsheba Folger,

*Figure 7* Photographs of the Trask homestead showing the chest illustrated in fig. 5. Built by William Trask in 1680, the house was owned by lineal descendants of his son John in the nineteenth century and was presumably part of the real estate inherited by John upon his father's death in 1691. Reprinted from William Blake Trask, "Captain William Traske and Some of His Descendants," *New-England Historical and Genealogical Register* 55 (July 1901), opposite p. 321.

*Figure 8* Chest attributed to the Symonds shops, Salem, Massachusetts, 1701. Oak, maple, mahogany, and red cedar (by microanalysis). H. 31¼", W. 47¾", D. 20⅝". (Courtesy, Concord Museum, gift of Russell Kettell; photo David Bohl.)

daughter of Nantucket Quaker Peter Folger. Joseph, Jr.'s, sisters Damaris (b. 1643) and Hannah (b. 1648) married brothers Joshua and Caleb (1650–1731) Buffum, respectively. Like his brother, Caleb was one of the more devout Quakers in Salem. He donated land for a Quaker meetinghouse in 1690 and for a burial ground in 1718.[10]

Business associations also linked the Pope and Buffum families. In 1677, Joshua Buffum charged Joseph Pope, Jr., five shillings for "a chist for Samuel Pope." Joseph, Jr., paid his debt with "191 fut of pine bord," a common type of exchange in seventeenth-century New England. In the same year, Buffum hired Pope and ten other men to help him move the Salem town meetinghouse.[11]

Sarah Buffington, one of the first owners of the cabinet illustrated in figure 1, was the daughter of John (1624–1672) and Sarah (Tidd) Southwick, both of whom received fines for not attending a sanctioned church during the 1660s. Although Sarah Buffington's husband Thomas is not listed as a Quaker in Salem records, he is identified as a Friend in Buffington family accounts and all of the couple's children were members of the sect. Their eldest son, Benjamin (b. 1699), was the second husband of Caleb Buffum's daughter, Hannah.[12]

The Osborne family had ties to the Quaker community through William Osborne's (1640–1729) wife, Hannah Burton (1640–1721) and their children's marriages. During the 1660s, Hannah was fined for not attending a recognized church, as was her father, Captain John Burton (d. 1684), and brother John (b. 1640). Her father accompanied Lawrence and Cassandra Southwick's son Josiah (1632–1693) on an exploratory journey to Rhode Island during the beginnings of Quaker persecution in 1657. The Osborne family's relationship with the Southwicks continued through the late 1600s and early 1700s with the marriages of William and Hannah's sons Samuel

*Figure 9*  Chest attributed to the Symonds shops, Salem, Massachusetts, 1680–1705. Oak and maple with pine. H. 31", W. 45 1/2", D. 20". (Courtesy, Peabody Essex Museum.)

*Figure 10*  Chest attributed to the Symonds shops, Salem, Massachusetts, 1680–1700. Oak and maple with pine (by microanalysis). H. 30 1/8", W. 46 3/8", D. 22 1/4". (Courtesy, Winterthur Museum.)

and John to sisters Eleanor (1674–1702) and Mercy (b. 1676) Southwick, daughters of Daniel Southwick (1637–1719) and granddaughters of Lawrence and Cassandra. Like his brother Josiah, Daniel Southwick adhered to his parents' Quaker beliefs and was fined throughout the 1660s. William and Hannah Osborne's sons also married daughters of Joshua and Caleb Buffum. After Mercy Southwick's death, John Osborne married Hannah Buffum (b. 1677), daughter of Caleb Buffum, and Samuel Osborne's daughter, Elizabeth (b. 1699), married Joshua Buffum (b. 1681), eldest son and namesake of the defiant Quaker carpenter.[13]

Although not a Quaker, William Trask (1640–1691) was intimately connected to the Friends community in Salem. His daughter Mary (b. 1683) married John Southwick, who may have been a grandson of Lawrence and

*Figure 11* Cupboard attributed to the Symonds shops, Salem, Massachusetts, 1680–1700. Oak, maple, and walnut with pine. H. 58 3/4", W. 45", D. 21". (Courtesy, Peabody Essex Museum.)

Cassandra, and several of his nieces and nephews married Quakers. The genealogical record is unclear, but William Trask may also have been the brother of Henry (d. 1689), a Quaker who married Lawrence and Cassandra Southwick's daughter Mary. Henry and Mary were imprisoned in Boston in 1659 and 1660 and repeatedly fined during the following decade.[14]

William Trask had extensive business dealings with Joshua Buffum. He and his brother John frequently employed Buffum to do carpentry work on their homes and mills and repaid their debts with large quantities of Indian corn. Like Joseph Pope, Jr., Trask was one of several men hired by Buffum to move the town meetinghouse in 1677.[15]

Joshua and Caleb Buffum may have been peripherally connected to the Symonds shops. Although Salem records invariably refer to them as carpenters, both men evidently made furniture. Joshua Buffum's account book, for example, contains debit entries for inexpensive forms such as the "chist for Samuel Pope." In 1856, Caleb Buffum's great-great-great grandson and namesake reported seeing "several articles such as chests, etc. which . . . [the elder Caleb] made." According to the younger Caleb (b. 1816), his

*Figure 12* "The Putnam (Enclosed) Court Cupboard," Putnam Leaflets, vols. 1–2, 1896–1897, Peabody Essex Museum. This is a late-nineteenth-century photograph of the cupboard shown in fig. 11. (Courtesy, Peabody Essex Museum.)

great-grandfather Joshua Buffum (1719–1793) recalled visiting a shop where the elder Caleb worked. Like the Symonds, the first generation Buffums hailed from Great Yarmouth and it is likely the families knew each other before immigrating. Both John Symonds and Robert Buffum (ca. 1590–1669) had their children baptized in St. Nicholas Church in Great Yarmouth during the early 1630s. Robert owned land adjoining Symonds's property in Salem. By 1700, these tracts had passed to the next generation. Joshua and Caleb Buffum owned agricultural land on either side of James Symonds's fields, and all three men had houses in town. James Symonds's house and shop were near the wharves and Joshua's and Caleb's homes were next to each other at the western end of town. At the very least, the Buffums may have encouraged fellow Quakers to patronize their neighbors. The Symondses were not Friends and their only familial connection to the sect was the marriage of James Symonds's daughter Ruth to Josiah Southwick.[16]

Three pieces attributed to the Symonds shops demonstrate few or no ties to the Quaker community. Associated through marriage and geographic proximity, the original owners of the cabinet and chest illustrated in figures 2 and 10—Ephraim and Mary Herrick and Nathaniel and Rebecca Raymond—had farms and land in Beverly bordering the Royal Side section of Salem. A petition devised by Rebecca's grandfather Roger Conant, one of the earliest settlers of Salem, reveals the common heritage of Beverly's first families. After the town was incorporated in 1668, Conant reported that some individuals were referring to Beverly as "Beggarly" and asked the court to change the name to Budleigh, his native town in Devonshire. Nathaniel and Rebecca's parents and Ephraim Herrick supported the petition. Like the Conants, Raymonds, and Herricks, many of Beverly's early settlers were from England's West Country.[17]

Thomas Hart, who lived in Lynnfield, Massachusetts, on the western side of Salem, was also related to Ephraim Herrick, albeit through a relatively circuitous route. Men from both families married daughters of Dr. Zarubbabel Endicott (1635–1684), the son of Salem's founder John Endicott (1589–1665), a staunch opponent of the Quakers. Endicott's daughter Sarah married Thomas Hart's brother Samuel, and his daughter Mary married Ephraim Herrick's brother Joseph. The Endicott family also provides a link to the Symonds family since the physician's grandson, Zarubbabell Endicott, Jr., married Grace Symonds, the daughter of Samuel.[18]

All of the Symonds shop's known patrons were middle- to upper-class members of the region's farming community. With few ties to any of the aforementioned families, the Putnams were the wealthiest. Brothers Nathaniel and John Putnam, either of whom could have commissioned the cupboard shown in figure 11, were taxed ten and nine shillings, respectively, in 1683. With only 23 inhabitants paying 8 shillings or higher, the Putnams were in the top 5 percent of 700 tax-eligible residents listed in Salem. As historian Jonathan Chu has noted, the average tax rate for 1683 was 2.8 shillings.[19]

Joseph Pope, Thomas Buffington, William Osborne, and William Trask all paid taxes of 2.8 shillings or more. The Herricks, Raymonds, and Harts lived outside Salem and do not appear on the tax list; however, their probate documents indicate that they were within the same economic strata. Ephraim Herrick's inventory, taken in 1693, totaled £483.7. By contrast, the average estate valuation in Salem was £330 between 1661 and 1681. The earliest probate data for the Raymond and Hart families is from the eighteenth century, but it suggests that the original owners of the cabinet and chest illustrated in figures 2 and 10 were relatively prosperous. Nathaniel Raymond left an estate valued at £1396 in 1749 and Thomas Hart's sister-in-law, Sarah (Endicott) Hart, a widow whose family inherited his cabinet (fig. 2), was worth over £459 when she died in 1732.[20]

Not represented among the known patrons of the Symonds shops are members of the merchant and artisan classes living in Salem's town center. Although many of these urban inhabitants may have purchased furniture in Boston, it is likely that some commissioned work from the Symonds shops. The Putnam cupboard (fig. 11) and the cabinets illustrated in figures 1–4

*Figure 13* Chest of drawers attributed to the Symonds shops, Salem, Massachusetts, 1675–1700. Oak with pine. H. 38 3/4", W. 40 1/4", D. 21 3/8". (Courtesy, Museum of Fine Arts, Boston; bequest of Charles Hitchcock Tyler.)

reflect the sophistication of Salem's furniture makers and consumers, but chests like the ones shown in figures 5 and 8–10 were provincial adaptations of urban forms. As furniture historians Benno Forman and Robert F. Trent have shown, Boston joiners began making chests of drawers during the 1630s. Although inventories of Salem merchants and mariners list chests of drawers as early as 1676, consumers in outlying agricultural areas were often slower to adopt new forms, as the single-drawer chests suggest. Many of the chests of drawers attributed to the Symonds shops (see fig. 13) may have been owned by Salem's urban elite.[21]

The individuals and objects discussed in this essay illustrate only a few of the myriad avenues connecting seventeenth-century artisans to their patrons and their community. Who tradesmen knew, either directly or indirectly, was often as important as what they made. The Symonds family's links to Quakers, members of "established" churches, prominent farmers, and Salem's urban elite enabled them to dominate the furniture-making trades in Salem during the last quarter of the seventeenth century.

1. For more on the Townsends and Goddards, see Jeanne Vibert Sloane, "John Cahoone and the Newport Furniture Industry," in *New England Furniture: Essays in Memory of Benno Forman*, edited by Brock Jobe (Boston: Society for the Preservation of New England Antiquities, 1987); Margaretta M. Lovell, "'Such Furniture as Will Be Most Profitable': The Business of Cabinetmaking in Eighteenth-Century Newport," *Winterthur Portfolio* 26, no. 1 (Spring 1991):

52–56; and *American Furniture,* edited by Luke Beckerdite (Hanover, N. H.: University Press of New England for the Chipstone Foundation, 1999), passim.

2. Irving P. Lyon, "The Oak Furniture of Ipswich, Massachusetts, Part V," *Antiques* 33, no. 2 (June 1938): 322–25; and Irving P. Lyon, "The Oak Furniture of Ipswich, Massachusetts, Part VI," *Antiques* 34, no. 2 (August 1938): 79–81. Helen Park, "The Seventeenth-Century Furniture of Essex County and Its Makers," *Antiques* 78, no. 4 (October 1960): 350–55. Benno M. Forman, "The Seventeenth-Century Case Furniture of Essex County, Massachusetts, and Its Makers" (M.A. thesis, University of Delaware, 1968), pp. 42–50. Robert F. Trent, "The Symonds Joinery Shops of Salem and Their Works," *The Peabody Museum of Salem Antiques Show* (Salem, Mass.: Peabody Museum, 1981), pp. 33–36. *New England Begins: The Seventeenth Century,* edited by Jonathan L. Fairbanks and Robert F. Trent, 3 vols. (Boston: Museum of Fine Arts, Boston, 1982), 2: 279–80, 288–89, nos. 274, 285, and 3: 526–28, nos. 484, 485. Robert F. Trent, "The Symonds Shops of Essex County, Massachusetts," *The American Craftsman and the European Tradition, 1620–1820* (Minneapolis, Minn.: Minneapolis Institute of Arts, 1989), pp. 23–41.

3. Althought the initials "TH" were thought to have referred to a Thomas Hart residing in Ipswich, Benno Forman discovered that the twentieth-century owner of the cabinet, Eben Parsons, was a direct descendant of Samuel Hart (d. 1731), brother of Thomas Hart of Lynnfield. Forman, "The Seventeenth-Century Case Furniture of Essex County," pp. 111–13. Winterthur Museum object files 58.526 and 57.540, Winterthur, Delaware. Trent, "The Symonds Shops of Essex County," pp. 34–35. Christie's, *The Joseph and Bathsheba Pope Valuables Cabinet,* New York, January 21, 2000.

4. Because members of the Trask and Osborne families intermarried in 1701 and 1785, it is impossible to determine the chests' lines of descent. The modern designations "Trask" chest (fig. 5) and "Osborne" chest (fig. 9) derive from the names of the last family owners—William Blake Trask and Lyman and Elizabeth Osborne. Forman, "The Seventeenth-Century Case Furniture of Essex County," pp. 108–10. William Blake Trask, "Captain William Traske and Some of His Descendants," *Genealogical Register* 55, (July 1901), pp. 321–38. Sidney Perley, *The History of Salem, Massachusetts,* 3 vols. (Salem, Mass.: By the author, 1924–1928), 1: 322. Sotheby's, *Important Americana,* New York, January 24–27, 1990, lot 1243. Israel Sack, Inc., *American Antiques from Israel Sack Collection,* 10 vols. (Alexandria, Va.: Highland House, 1992), 10: 2544. The Trask chest (fig. 5) was first displayed at the Museum of Fine Arts, Boston, in 1870 and was on loan there from 1912 to as late as 1968. The chest sold at auction in 1990 and is now in the collection of Israel Sack, Inc.

5. Perley, *History of Salem,* 1: 323; Forman, "The Osborne Family Chest Re-Discovered," *Historical New Hampshire* 26, no. 1 (Spring 1971): 27–30. Donated to the New Hampshire Historical Society as part of the Prentis collection in 1957, the Osborne chest was recently acquired by the Peabody Essex Museum in Salem.

6. Object file 58.525, Winterthur Museum. In the early twentieth century, the chest belonged to Emily G. Patch, Nathaniel and Rebecca (Conant) Raymond's great-great-great-granddaughter. The note states that the chest was owned by "Mary Raymond's mother" and delineates its descent. Genealogical research corroborates the history. Frederick Odell Conant, *A History and Genealogy of the Conant Family* (Portland, Me.: Privately printed, 1887), pp. 128–31; Samuel Raymond, comp., *Genealogies of the Raymond Families of New England 1630 to 1886* (New York: J. J. Little & Co., 1886), p. 123. Laurel Thatcher Ulrich, "Furniture as Social History: Gender, Property, and Memory in the Decorative Arts," in *American Furniture,* edited by Luke Beckerdite (Hanover, N. H.: University Press of New England for the Chipstone Foundation, 1993), pp. 53–66.

7. Harriet Putnam Fowler, "History of the Old Putnam Cupboard," *The Historical Collections of the Danvers Historical Society* 36 (1948), pp. 53–58. Trent, "The Symonds Shops of Essex County," p. 36. For the Putnam family genealogy, see Perley, *History of Salem,* 2: 109–11. Charred surfaces on the cupboard indicate that it was in a fire. Although Putnam family tradition maintains that the piece was rescued from a fire in the home of Deacon Benjamin Putnam, Harriet Putnam Fowler has shown that the younger John Putnam's house caught fire in 1709 and raised the possibility that the cupboard descended in Miriam's family. In 1895, Harriet Putnam Fowler donated the cupboard to the Essex Institute. Fowler, "History of the Old Putnam Cupboard," p. 54.

8. For a thorough account of Quaker persecution in Salem, see Perley, *History of Salem,* 2: 242–75.

9. For a detailed description of Joshua Buffum's defiance, see Owen A. Perkins, comp., *Buf-

*fum Family*, 2 vols. (Smithtown, N. Y.: Privately printed, 1985), 2: 7–11. Jonathan M. Chu, *Neighbors, Friends or Madmen: The Puritan Adjustment to Quakerism in Seventeenth-Century Massachusetts Bay* (Westport, Conn.: Greenwood Press, 1985), pp. 125–75. Chu lists all of Salem's known Quakers in the years in which they were fined, in an appendix on pages 169 and 170. Joseph Pope, Sr., received fines in 1658, 1662, and 1666 and Gertrude Pope received fines in 1658, 1660, 1661, 1662, 1663, 1664, 1665, 1666, and 1669. For more on the Pope family, see Henry Wheatland, "Notice of Some of the Descendants of Joseph Pope of Salem," in Charles Henry Pope, *A History of the Dorchester Pope Family 1634–1888* (Boston: By the author, 1888). For more on Peter Folger, see Florence Bennett Anderson, *A Grandfather for Benjamin Franklin: The True Story of a Nantucket Pioneer and His Mates* (Boston: Meador Publishing Company, 1940).

10. The Pope and Buffum families intermarried extensively in the eighteenth century. Joseph Pope, Jr., and Joshua Buffum's grandchildren Enos Pope (1721–1813) and Lydia Buffum (1726–1781) married in the Quaker meeting house in Salem in 1749. Their marriage certificate bears the signatures of members of the Southwick, Osborne, Gaskill, Boyce, and Needham families, all of whom were descendants of seventeenth-century Salem Quakers (Marriage certificate of Enos Pope and Lydia Buffum, Salem, 1749, Enos Pope Papers, Phillips Library [hereafter cited as PL], Salem, Massachusetts).

11. Joshua Buffum Account Book, 1672–1705, PL, p. 14 and end leaves; Perkins, *Buffum Family*, 2: 15. Joseph Pope, Jr.'s son Nathaniel (1679–1711) owned land bordering Joshua Buffum's property and was a witness to his will in 1705.

12. Ralph M. Buffington, *The Buffington Family in America* (Houston, Tx.: Clara Dunagan Rhame, et al., 1965), pp. 293a–98. About 1770, Benjamin and Hannah Buffington moved to the Quaker community of Swansea, Massachusetts, where their descendants remained members of that faith until the mid-nineteenth century. *Encyclopedia of Massachusetts: Biographical-Genealogical* (New York: American Historical Society, 1917), pp. 338–39. Thomas and Sarah Buffington's grandson James Buffington (1707–1773) attended the Quaker wedding of Enos and Lydia (Buffum) Pope (marriage certificate of Enos Pope and Lydia Buffum).

13. Chu, *Neighbors, Friends or Madmen*, appendix 1, pp. 169–70. William Osborne and Hannah Burton were married in 1672. Perley, *History of Salem*, 2:246.

14. Trask, "Captain William Traske and Some of His Descendants," pp. 321–38. Quakers John Hill and Joseph Boyce witnessed the will of William Trask's father. Chu, *Neighbors, Friends or Madmen*, appendix 1, pp. 169–70.

15. Joshua Buffum Account Book, pp. 50, 54–57, 118. Almost identical to the Trask and Osborne examples, the Dodge family chest bearing the initials and date "MT/1701" (fig. 8) could be another example of Symonds shop furniture belonging to this sphere of patronage. If the date corresponds to a marriage, it is possible the chest was made for Mary Kitchin who married John Turner in that year. She is the only individual recorded in Salem whose initials and date of marriage correspond to those on the chest and her uncle and aunt, John and Elizabeth Kitchin, were Quakers. The Dodge chest is now in the collections of the Concord Museum. See David F. Wood, ed., *The Concord Museum: Decorative Arts from a New England Collection* (Concord, Mass.: Concord Museum, 1996), pp. 6–7, cat. 3; and Chu, *Neighbors, Friends or Madmen*, appendix 1, pp. 169–70.

16. Joshua Buffum Account Book, passim. Caleb Buffum, "An Account of the Buffum Family by Caleb Buffum Written in 1856, Re-written in 1875," Buffum Family Papers, PL, p. 7. Walter Goodwin Davis, *Massachusetts and Maine Families in the Ancestry of Walter Goodwin Davis*, 3 vols. (Baltimore, Md.: Genealogical Publishing, 1996), 3: 399. Walter N. Buffum, "Notes Relating to Robert Buffum and His Children," Buffum Family Papers, PL. Sidney Perley, "Northfields, Salem, in 1700," *Essex Institute Historical Collections* 49 (1913), pp. 356–67; map, William W. K. Freeman, comp., "Part of Salem in 1700 from the Researches of Sidney Perley" (Salem, Mass.: James Duncan Phillips, 1933).

17. For Roger Conant's petition, see Raymond, comp., *Genealogies of the Raymond Families*, pp. 116–17. Cousins of Ephraim and Mary Herrick and Nathaniel and Rebecca Raymond also intermarried. Rebecca's uncle Exercise Conant was an appraiser of Ephraim Herrick's estate and an overseer of his will, as was William Raymond, Nathaniel's uncle. Will and Inventory of Ephraim Herrick, October 9, 1693, Essex County Probate Records (hereafter cited as ECPR), no. 13124, Massachusetts State Archives, Boston.

18. Perley, *History of Salem*, 1: 90–91, fn. 5; 2: 256, 267–69. Richard P. Hallowell, *Quaker Invasion of Massachusetts* (Boston: Houghton, Mifflin, and Co., 1883), pp. 40, 191–93.

19. Chu, *Neighbors, Friends or Madmen*, pp. 128, 145–46, fn. 12.

20. As only about 25 percent of estates were probated and the average sum of £330 refers only to probated estates, the actual average value would have been considerably lower (ibid.). For a complete list of the 1683 tax, see Perley, *History of Salem*, 3: 419–22. Will and Inventory of Ephraim Herrick; Will and Inventory of Nathaniel Raymond, January 29, 1750, ECPR, no. 23277; Will and Inventory of Sarah Hart, June 25, 1733, ECPR, no. 12601.

21. Benno M. Forman, "The Chest of Drawers in America, 1635–1730: The Origins of the Joined Chest of Drawers," *Winterthur Portfolio* 20, no. 1 (Spring 1985), pp. 1–30. Trent, "The Symonds Shops of Essex County," pp. 27–28. For chests of drawers attributed to the Symonds shops, see Lyon, "The Oak Furniture of Ipswich, Massachusetts, Part VI," pp. 80–81, figs. 56–59; Richard H. Randall, Jr., *American Furniture in the Museum of Fine Arts, Boston* (Boston: By the museum, 1965), pp. 30–33, cat. 25; and Trent, "The Symonds Shops of Essex County," p. 38.

*Elizabeth A. Fleming*

Cultural Negotiations:
A Study of the
New Mexican *Caja*

▼ IN TRADITIONAL Native American lore, the coyote plays the role of ubiquitous trickster. As an agent of disorder, this animal symbolizes the belief that imperfection gives the world its dynamism and liveliness. With Hispanic settlement in New Mexico from the seventeenth century on, the word "coyote" expands in use to identify mixed-race individuals, themselves signifiers of change and diversification. The author's guise in this article will be that of the coyote who challenges entrenched notions about Spanish colonial furniture within the broader field of American decorative arts.[1]

Just as there is an Anglo bias to early American historiography, which emphasizes looking to New England for a sense of the past, there is a New England bias to American decorative arts scholarship. One result is that scholars and collectors have developed subjective ranking systems that often ignore the complexities and nuances of other regional styles, technologies, and tastes. The Spanish and Native American influences manifest in the style and structure of New Mexican *cajas* (see figs. 1, 2) are the products of an environment that differed radically from that of colonial New England. This disparity is apparent in the decoration and construction of furniture (see fig. 3).[2]

Two distinct types of *cajas* serve as the focal point for this article. The first type consists of dovetailed board chests with low-relief carving depicting heraldic devices such as lions, pomegranates, vines, and rosettes (see figs. 4, 5). Some historians have suggested that these chests originated in the southern Río Abajo area of New Mexico, but their evidence is inconclusive. The second type of *caja*, which features mortise-and-tenon joinery and geometric chip-carving (see figs. 1, 6), is associated with the Taos–Santa Cruz region of northern New Mexico.[3]

Our perceptions regarding early New Mexico have been dominated by the theme of conquest and exploitation. One of the most widely held beliefs is that the Hispanics, under the jurisdiction of the Spanish Crown and Catholic Church, arrived in New Mexico in 1598 and immediately and methodically began to dislocate and annihilate the Native American population. This oversimplified viewpoint erroneously assumes a separation of indigenous and European cultures analogous to that in New England. Another widely accepted notion maintains that a mentality of "making do" with available materials prevailed on the Spanish colonial frontier and resulted in a rather primitive material culture. This misconception results from equating the New Mexican experience with that of European colonists in the New England wilderness.

*Figure 1*  *Caja*, New Mexico, 1760–1800. Pine. H. 30", W. 55", D. 19". (Courtesy, Sotheby's.)

*Figure 2*  Detail of the side of the *caja* illustrated in fig. 1.

*Figure 3*  Chest, Hadley-Hatfield area of Massachusetts, ca. 1710. Oak with pine. H. 45", W. 36", D. 19³⁄₄". (Courtesy, Chipstone Foundation; photo, Gavin Ashworth.)

A more accurate interpretation of the seventeenth- and eighteenth-century Spanish occupation of New Mexico, particularly after the Pueblo Revolt of 1680 and Spanish reconquest in 1692, balances the military and religious forces imposed on the Pueblos with Hispanic dependency on Native

*Figure 4* Caja, New Mexico, 1760–1800. Pine. H. 23", W. 47", D. 21". (Courtesy, Colorado Springs Fine Arts Center, Taylor Museum.)

*Figure 5* Caja, New Mexico, 1760–1800. Pine. H. 22½", W. 34½", D. 17¼". (Courtesy, Sotheby's.)

Americans for survival. Rather than eradicating indigenous culture, Hispanic traditions intermingled with those of the Pueblos and were integrated on a variety of fronts, particularly marriage, trade, and craft traditions. Native Americans provided major population infusions into Spanish communities. In the first New Mexican settlement expedition of 1598, only 13 of 131 soldiers arrived with spouses. By 1776, the estimated Spanish population had grown to over ten thousand, as compared to eight thousand Pueblo

*Figure 6* Caja, New Mexico, 1760–1800. Pine. H. 32¹/₂", W. 37¹/₂", D. 17". (Courtesy, Sotheby's.)

Indians. This growth was made possible not by Hispanic women making the trek to the northern frontier over the two centuries, but by the integration of Native Americans into Hispanic communities through marriage, enslavement, and mercenary opportunities. The 1790 census of Albuquerque records that 69 percent of the marriages surveyed were between different racial groups.[4]

Just as distinct racial communities mixed freely, goods were regularly exchanged between the Spanish and Native American populations. Although dependent on Indian products such as corn, textiles, and furs for their livelihood and sustenance, Europeans often exploited Native American labor and values. The notion of "making do" is therefore also inappropriate to the northern frontier of New Spain. Upon entering the Rio Grande Valley, the Spanish encountered village-dwelling agriculturists and artisans who possessed firmly entrenched communal and cultural traditions, well-evolved languages, and permanent communities constructed of adobe and timber. Unlike many of the Indians first encountered in Mexico or on the East Coast, the Pueblos were *gente vestida* (clothed people): "[M]ost if not all the men wore cotton blankets and on top of these a buffalo hide. Some covered their privy parts with small cloths, very elegant and finely worked. The women wore . . . turkey-feather cloaks."[5]

Frontier survival entailed harnessing the existent Pueblo culture. The building of Franciscan missions, for example, involved Pueblo labor and native technologies including transverse clerestory windows and façade orientation to the east or southeast, as opposed to the European tradition of west-facing façades. In addition, archaeological evidence shows that the Franciscans commissioned Pueblo potters to make ceramic vessels in European forms such as chalices and soup bowls. Eager to capitalize upon the Pueblo artisan economy they first encountered, the Franciscans also trained the Pueblo Indians in new trades including textile weaving and woodworking.[6]

From the outset, the Spanish colonial settlements began to develop a unique Hispanic-Pueblo material culture. The two traditions had differing, but equally complex, relationships to the land. Spanish culture was tempered both by the New Mexican environment and by physical distance from its epicenter—Madrid. In contrast, the New Mexican landscape was a spiritual and sacred center for the Pueblo Indians. It gave birth to their people and was at the core of their religious beliefs. Notwithstanding this disparity in orientation, both the Spanish and the Pueblo relationships to New Mexico were grounded in their respective histories. A characterization of the Spanish colonial frontier might thus center on its adherence to a broad spectrum of religious and cultural traditions—both of Old-World Spain and of ancient Pueblo and nomadic Native American tribes. This revered connection to and reliance upon tradition establishes New Mexico as a very different colonial frontier from New England, which was economically linked to the mother country but was settled by those who wanted to escape Old-World religious and cultural constraints.[7]

The traditional orientation of eighteenth-century New Mexico was manifested in the strength of religion, the coexistence of cultures, and the material nature of Spanish colonial objects. Both Christianity and Native American spiritualism were vibrant institutions on the frontier during the eighteenth century. Led by Don Diego de Vargas, the reconquest of New Mexico in 1692 was driven by the missionary impulse of the Catholic Church and the Spanish government's need to thwart French and British expansion in the area. Vargas's triumphal reentry into Santa Fe involved not only carrying a wooden statue of "Our Lady of the Conquest," but also a ceremonial kissing of the cross by both Vargas and Pueblo leaders to indicate allegiance to the Catholic god and Spanish king. The religious zeal of the Franciscans, who relished the prospect of frontier martyrdom in the service of their god, led them to transport the cross, once again, throughout the territory—rebuilding Pueblo missions and churches and meticulously recording baptisms of Indians throughout the century. Despite the conversions to Christianity taking place, Native American religious beliefs persisted. The present-day survival of many rituals and religious stories testify to the preservation of Native American spiritualism during the eighteenth century. *Kivas*, which were the holy centers of Pueblo communities, were maintained within pueblos even though Franciscans sought to destroy them. Owing to the strength of Native American beliefs, Franciscans were forced to integrate these two faith systems. Images of the Christian god and Christian saints were modified to relate visually to Pueblo *katsina* (rain spirits) and dead ancestors, as well as to harness the power of nature-derived Pueblo symbols. Clouds, for example, became important components in New Mexican representations of saints, Jesus Christ, and God the Father (see fig. 7).[8]

*Figure 7* Saint Anthony of Padua and the Infant Jesus, Santo Domingo Pueblo, New Mexico, 1693–1710. Painted hide. 46 1/2" × 26 3/8". (Courtesy, Division of Cultural History, National Museum of American History, Smithsonian Institution.)

Ordinances drawn up in late-sixteenth-century Spain and Mexico served as the principal blueprints for New Mexican colonization through 1821. The Laws of the Indies, compiled in 1573 by King Philip II of Spain, provided instructions and mandates concerning city planning, governance systems, and interracial relations. Old-World regulations, such as the 1568 "Ordinances of the Trades of Carpenters, Joiners, and Musical Instrument Makers of the City of Mexico," directed the administration and production quality of craft guilds throughout New Spain and formally encouraged the apprenticeship of Indians. Despite divergent circumstances and distance between New Mexico and Mexico, not to mention between New Mexico and Spain, these rules led to the persistence of Old-World governing practices and served as a blueprint for managing hospitable relations with native populations. On principle, the Pueblo people were amenable to cultural coexistence according to their communal codes of conduct. Ideals of synthesis, association, and harmony guided their interaction with each other as well as with the Spanish. From a practical point of view, such an Hispanic-Pueblo alliance offered increased protection from the attacks of nomadic Native Americans and other Europeans. In both Hispanic and Pueblo realms, dependence upon value-laden systems derived from their respective traditions was a way of rationalizing the irrational and of making the unfamiliar routine.[9]

Inherent in the reverence for history in the region was an interest in preservation which, at least in the case of the Hispanic New Mexicans, was played out on a material level. Like many European chests made from the Renaissance to the seventeenth century, *cajas* are constructed of thick boards, panels, and framing members. This durable structure conforms to art historian George Kubler's notion of "strong surfaces." According to Kubler, solidity signifies abundant raw materials and is an identifying trait of colonial artisanry.[10]

The physical qualities of early New Mexican furniture encourage a more thorough analysis of the two distinct types of *cajas*—heraldic board chests and chip-carved framed chests. These chests reveal much about their makers and about values concerning recyclability, safekeeping, and adornment prevalent on the New Mexican frontier by the end of the eighteenth century. Differences in the structure and decoration of *cajas* reflect two contrasting strategies for survival on the Spanish colonial frontier. The heraldic board chests lack legs, and are isolationist in design and mobile in form. They were literally the means by which Old-World Spain and its authority were transported into the northern frontier. Supply caravans traveled from as far south as Mexico City and brought a variety of textiles, ceramics, metalwork, and even such exotic Spanish foodstuffs as almonds and olive oil. The most precious goods were stored in *cajas*, both on journeys northward and in homes. Although the framed chests with abstract chip-carved patterns served a similar storage function, their formal elements reflect integration—the intermingling of sophisticated Old-World cabinetmaking techniques and Native American decoration. With stiles extending into legs, the Hispanic *caja* form is typically fixed in place.[11]

In light of these varied impressions, the *cajas* demand a modification of Kubler's thesis regarding the interaction of central and peripheral cultures. He contends that cultures occupying a provincial edge remain insulated from other cultures that are geographically close but do not originate from the same center. While the board chests confirm his notion of the separatist tendencies of peripheral cultures, the framed chests with chip-carving suggest the opposite. They indicate that complex cultural products arise when a peripheral culture, like that of the Spanish in New Mexico, comes in direct contact with the center of another culture, in this instance that of the Pueblos.[12]

Late-eighteenth-century New Mexican *cajas* demonstrate the adeptness and flexibility of available woodworking technology as well as the social values and subsistence priorities of those who owned interior furnishings. Early woodworking in New Mexico engaged the skills and sensibilities of both Hispanic and Pueblo craftsmen. At least seven Spanish *carpinteros* arrived in New Mexico with Juan de Oñate's settlement expedition in 1598. These Hispanic artisans and their successors built missions, towns, and *haciendas*; made household necessities such as chairs, *cajas*, *trasteros* (cupboards) and *graineros* (storage cabinets); and produced spiritual objects such as *retablos* and *bultos* (carved images of saints). The Pueblo people also practiced carpentry with considerable skill. Initially trained by Franciscans in order to satisfy the needs of local missions, the Pecos and Abó pueblos became major woodworking centers as early as the seventeenth century and produced household goods and architectural components. On a fact-finding tour of the New Mexican missions in 1776, Fray Francisco Dominguez described the Indians of the Pecos pueblo as good carpenters whose skills were in great demand across the colony, from Taos to Isleta, and who thus had a high degree of economic mobility. Other eighteenth-century reports about the Pecos pueblo mention lumber prepared by local carpenters and delivered to Santa Fe, as well as made-to-order doors, window frames, and beds.[13]

New Mexican woodworkers typically had a few basic tools: an ax for felling trees; a pit saw and a hand saw for cutting timber; an adze for smoothing boards; a plane for producing finished surfaces; chisels for cutting joints and

*Figure 8*   Tusayan storage jar, New Mexico, 1100–1300 A.D. Earthenware with black-on-white decoration. H. 14". (Courtesy, Sotheby's.)

carving; an auger for boring; and knives, a grooving plane, and a compass for creating surface decoration. The diversity of formal adaptations and innovations applied to construction and ornament denote the flexibility of this woodworking technology and the production systems that grew up around it. Dramatic developments in carpentry and joinery came with the intermingling of Native American and Hispanic traditions. Seemingly similar forms, for example, often have strikingly different aesthetic traits. The dovetailed board chests illustrated in figures 4 and 5 are Spanish in both construction and decoration. Similarly, the heraldic carving and attached moldings reveal that the craftsmen were familiar with the standardized imagery and structural practices maintained by Spanish and Mexican woodworking guilds. In contrast, the carving on framed chests (see figs. 1, 6) is reminiscent of the rhythmic linear patterns on ancient Anasazi and contemporary Pueblo pottery (see fig. 8), and of architectural elements such as the stacking of adobe cube houses and the pervasive use of wooden ladders (see fig. 9).[14]

*Figure 9* Taos Pueblo, Taos, New Mexico. (Courtesy, Museum of New Mexico.) This image shows the Taos Pueblo as it appeared about 1880.

Despite their differences, many of the framed and board *cajas* are similar in basic design and proportion. New Mexican woodworkers typically used squares based on fractions of the *vara* (eighty-four centimeters) to lay out their case designs and decorative grids. The chest illustrated in figure 5, for example, is one *vara* wide and one-half *vara* deep, whereas the *caja* shown in figure 10 is one-and-one-third *vara* wide, two-thirds *vara* high, and almost two-thirds *vara* deep. Small *cajas* are almost invariably twice as wide as they are deep, whereas larger ones tend to be three times as wide as they are deep. The corner posts on standard framed *cajas* (see fig. 1) are at least as high as the chest is deep; whereas those on chests with elaborate bases are typically one-and-one-half to two times as high as the chest is deep (see fig. 6). Similarly, decoration on *cajas* generally falls into one of three basic patterns. Either the surface has been divided like a grid into seven panels (see figs. 4, 5, 10), or it holds two comparable symmetrical designs (see figs. 1, 6),

*Figure 10* Caja, New Mexico, 1760–1800. Pine. H. 22", W. 44", D. 20½". (Courtesy, Sotheby's.)

or it is a single composite scheme (see fig. 11). On every chest included in this study the maker laid out most of the decoration with a compass.[15]

These entrenched proportional systems and the prevalence of *cajas* from the seventeenth century on indicate that woodworkers produced these forms with a conscious sense of the past. As material expressions of continuity and conformity, *cajas* reflect their makers' training and owners' cultural values, wealth, and tastes. This concept also relates to the solid structure and strong visual quality of *cajas* and to their physical state today. Both the board chests and their framed counterparts give substance to Kubler's notion that "colonial surfaces . . . [have an] inner strength . . . [which] gladly accepts every kick and bruise without horrid damage." The damaged and repaired surfaces of these chests attest to their continued service within a household or community and to the need to preserve forms and raw materials on the frontier. Replaced locks, hinges, boards, supports, and lids; broken or repaired corners; and punctures filled with hay, clay, and wooden or iron pins are common on early *cajas*. These injuries and restorations are part of each piece's character, an accumulation of history both literally and figuratively.[16]

A further priority of the Spanish colonial frontier community was the safekeeping of possessions. Locks are prominent fixtures on almost every *caja* and many are beautifully wrought. Escutcheons range from circular and rectangular iron plates with punched decoration (see figs. 10, 11) to elaborate curvilinear forms (see figs. 4, 5). Metal locks with mechanisms were among the equipment of Juan de Oñate's expedition of 1598, and are be-

*Figure 11*  *Caja*, New Mexico, 1760–1800. Pine. H. 18 1/2", W. 37", D. 19". (Courtesy, Sotheby's.)

*Figure 12*  Detail of an interior wall of La Hacienda de los Martinez, Taos, New Mexico, ca. 1805. (Photo, Anthony Richardson.)

*Figure 13* Detail of the ceilings of La Hacienda de los Martinez, Taos, New Mexico, ca. 1805, showing (*left*) aspen or cottonwood *latillas* (poles) and (*right*) split cedar or pine *rajas* (boards). (Photo, Anthony Richardson.)

lieved by scholars to be one of the most common items imported into colonial New Mexico. Borderland blacksmiths installed and repaired imported locks and occasionally produced their own mechanisms. The more irregular escutcheons with punched decoration such as the one on the chest illustrated in figure 10 are most likely New Mexican manufactures. On some eighteenth-century *cajas*, the lids and areas of the façade have been chiseled away to hold imported or locally-made locks. This adaptation suggests that the integrity of the piece was secondary to the protection of its contents. The method of lock installation likewise indicates totally segregated systems of production for furniture and iron hardware. Tools, technology, and entire furniture pieces often required alteration to better withstand life in the borderlands.[17]

According to eighteenth-century probate inventories, *cajas* were typically used to store and protect valuable household goods such as red velvet capes, imported Chinese silk, Spanish embroidered ribbon, gold-plated reliquaries, pearl earrings, and silver buckles and toothpicks. Such objects must have offered a visual contrast to the typical New Mexican colonial homes, which were of simple and similar construction. Walls of sun-dried adobe bricks had built-in fireplaces, benches, and shelving and were finished with plaster (fig. 12). Ceilings with massive *vigas* (beams) supported a horizontal series of *latillas* (poles) or *rajas* (split or hand-hewn boards) (fig. 13), and lustrous waterproof floors of packed mud, straw, wood ash, and ox or cattle blood were burnished to a smooth finish with stones.[18]

*Cajas* were both serviceable and decorative objects. New Mexican *carpinteros* clearly worked for discerning consumers whose needs and demands reflected not only the physical but also the social climate of the northern frontier. *Cajas* exhibit a variety of decorative options, including schematic

*Figure 14*  *Caja*, New Mexico, 1750–1800. Pine. H. 15½", W. 33", D. 13½". (Courtesy, Sotheby's).

labor-intensive designs that incorporate rosettes, floral patterns, pomegranates, and lions (see figs. 4, 5, 10, 11); abstract geometrical patterns of rectangles, triangles, and semi-circles (see figs. 1, 6); and delicate, incised rosettes and arrowhead designs (see fig. 14). Variation in the quality of embellishment and the degree of labor invested in production indicates a sophisticated society layered with differing tastes and levels of wealth. Unifying all of these strata was a compulsion to enliven and vary the appearance of domestic spaces.

Much remains to be discovered about the origins and meanings of the motifs of the Spanish colonial frontier; however, the stylistic differences between the board and framed chests do indicate distinct tastes. The surfaces of the board chests illustrated in figures 4, 5, and 10 are divided into precise geometric units, each framed by applied moldings. The moldings and scalloped carving on the interior edge of each square and rectangle ensure that the decorative motifs are viewed as separate entities. The same four motifs, varied in placement and articulation, appear on all known chests of this type: rosettes with twelve petals; lions with crowns and faces turned toward their tails; vine-like plants with scrolled branches; and pomegranates with flanking leaves. This repetitive decoration suggests that the makers of *cajas* used templates; however, variations in motifs and the quality and quantity of carved forms indicate that different levels of skill existed within workshops and that artisans adjusted their work to accommodate their patrons' budgets. The pomegranate designs on the chest shown in fig-

*Figure 15*  *Caja*, New Mexico, 1760–1800. Pine. H. 20½", W. 38½", D. 19". (Courtesy, Sotheby's).

ure 4, for example, are quite elaborate, whereas those on the *caja* illustrated in figure 15 are crudely rendered. The latter ornament may be the work of a novice who was in the process of mastering simple, well-contained forms before advancing to more complicated floral and animal motifs.

The carved elements on the board chests (see figs. 4, 5, 10) appear to derive from a distant source. The method of hollowing rosette petals and dividing up surface space has precedents in seventeenth-century Spanish furniture (see figs. 16, 17), and the lions are clearly drawn from Spanish heraldry (fig. 18). Board chests with low-relief carving of this type would have been especially well suited for *rico* households. The *rico* class consisted of fifteen or twenty families—the wealthy New Mexican aristocracy that congregated in the cities of Santa Fe, Albuquerque, and Santa Cruz—who vig-

*Figure 16*  Refectory table, Spain, 1600–1700. Oak. Dimensions not recorded. (Courtesy, Isabella Stewart Gardner Museum, Boston.)

*Figure 17* Chest, Spain, 1600–1700. Oak. Dimensions not recorded. (Courtesy, Hispanic Society of America, New York.)

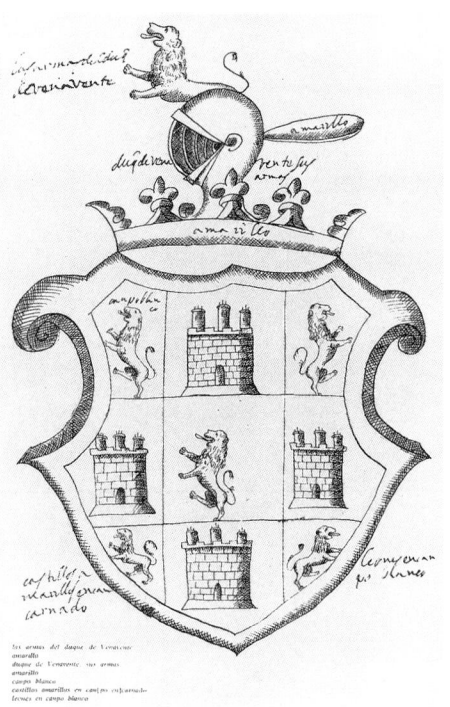

*Figure 18* Design for a coat-of-arms, Spain, *Origen y Armas de varios nobles de Espána*. (Courtesy, Biblioteca de la Universidad de Zaragoza, ms. no. 198.)

orously preserved their pure Spanish blood. The heraldic imagery on *cajas* served as a reminder of Old-World order, while the applied moldings may have expressed *rico* attitudes toward life on the frontier. Robert St. George asserts that the ubiquitous moldings on late-sixteenth-century chests from eastern Massachusetts mark settlers' reaction to the lack of order in the New World. The same can be said of the applied moldings and scalloped borders on Mexican board chests. They isolate discontinuous forms and give order to chaos.[19]

Although the surface decoration on the framed chests is very ordered, it differs from that of the board chests in being expansive. The applied moldings on the board chests conceal the dovetailed joints, whereas the mortise-and-tenon joinery on the framed chests is exposed, making it an integral part of surface decoration (figs. 1, 6). This visible joinery has Spanish precedents (see fig. 17); however, superimposed on the structure is a system of dispersed repetitive patterns that diverges from the Hispanic practice of covering surfaces with discontinuous, segregated carved designs. The chests' thick framing members have chip-carved designs resembling ladder-like squares and arrowheads, and the front and side panels have beveled edges and fields with abstract designs. This integration of non-figurative ornament and Hispanic structure suggests that the maker's decorative sensibilities developed outside Spanish tradition. Framed *cajas* like the examples shown in figures 1 and 6 are creolized forms. They express none of the isolationist attitudes manifest in many contemporary board chests.

The negotiation and exchange between Hispanic and Native American cultures become more evident when the carved decoration on framed chests is examined in light of Native American spiritual beliefs and iconography. The cosmology of the Pueblo Indians has a distinctive spatial organization

*Figure 19*  Zuni bowl, New Mexico, ca. 1890. Earthenware with polychrome decoration. H. 6½", Diam. 16½". (Courtesy, Margorie and Charles Benton, Evanston, Illinois.)

that emphasizes ascent, descent, and the four points of a compass. Within Pueblo culture, four is a sacred number. Dances are customarily repeated four times and painted imagery on Pueblo pottery includes motifs with four points (see fig. 19). The number four also relates to the Pueblos' creation myth, which recounts their emergence from the underworld. In the beginning, four pairs of warrior twins ascended ladders and climbed out of a hole in the earth's crust. Each pair set out in a different direction—north, south, east, and west—in order to discern whether the earth was ready for habitation. In *Native American Architecture*, Peter Nabokov and Robert Easton assert: "On the horizontal plane, an idealized schema of Pueblo spatial concepts might show zones of sacredness radiating out from such a 'center' shrine toward the 'houses' of the four cardinal directions."[20]

The front and side panels of a chest removed from the San Felipe pueblo in 1922 have a circular center design from which the points of four triangles expand outward (fig. 1). Recalling the Pueblo Indians' escape from and return

*Figure 20*  *Kiva* interior, Meshongnovi Hopi village, Arizona, c. 1902. (Courtesy, Field Museum.)

to the underworld, the chip-carving on the stiles and rails resembles the ladders used to get into and out of building units (see fig. 9) and *kivas*, sacred Pueblo spaces dug into the earth (see fig. 20). Other framed chests display a similar visual language. The panels on the example shown in figure 6 feature a central circle, its outer edge defined by ladderlike chip-carving. Surrounding this design are pairs of corresponding shapes that extend in four directions. In this instance, the circular "ladders" relate to a design depicting Pueblo emergence from the underworld on a circa 900–1200 bowl found in southwestern New Mexico (fig. 21). The triangular-shaped chip-carving on the frame also resembles the pointed protrusions on Navajo textiles that signify people walking (see fig. 22).[21]

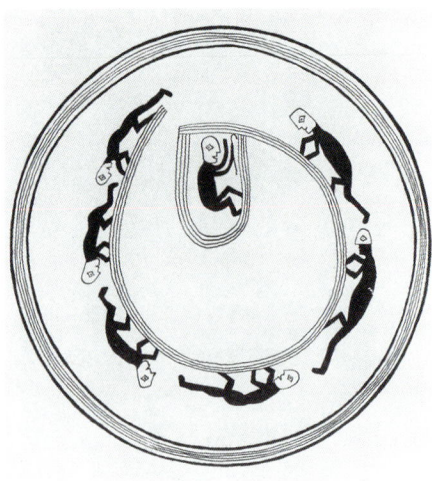

*Figure 21* Design from Mimbres bowl, New Mexico, 900–1200 A.D. Earthenware with black-on-white decoration. Dimensions not recorded. (Courtesy, Patricia Carr, *Mimbres Mythology*, 1979.)

*Figure 22* Navajo saddle blanket, New Mexico, 1880–1900. 32" × 28". (Courtesy, Museum of Indian Arts and Culture/Laboratory of Anthropology, Museum of New Mexico.)

The influence of Pueblo Indian cosmology on the decoration of *cajas* suggests three different patterns of cultural exchange on the Spanish colonial frontier. It is possible that Hispanic cabinetmakers, trained in a guild system in either Spain or New Mexico, borrowed motifs from Pueblo textiles and pottery and incorporated them into their furniture. These artisans did not ignore non-Hispanic influences, as Kubler's model would predict, but adapted to their immediate environment and the predominant, preexisting culture. The lines of artistic communication between a peripheral Hispanic culture and a central Pueblo civilization superseded those between the Hispanic periphery and its Old-World center.

It is equally plausible that Spanish-trained Pueblo *carpinteros* produced the decoration on the framed chests for Hispanic clients. Pueblo Indians were enlisted into the woodworking trade with the first Spanish settlement in New Mexico. Throughout the next two centuries, the skills of Pueblo carpenters remained in high demand and gave the craftsmen a measure of economic mobility. In light of Native American ideological priorities of harmony and preservation, the framed *cajas* might have served as a site for recording and remembering their history. As exemplified in the 1996 exhibition and catalogue *Weaving A World: Textiles and the Navajo Way of Seeing*, there is a long-standing custom of Native Americans sharing imagery and artifacts, but not meaning, with outsider cultures. The motivation behind this tradition is the conservation of principal elements of Native American culture. If Pueblo *carpinteros* did share their cosmological imagery with a Hispanic market, it implies further problems for the model of one-sided cultural transfer between the Spanish center and the New Mexican periphery. In this instance, the split relates to cultural consumption rather than production on the peripheral edge. Hispanic chest owners had adapted their sensibilities to their new environment and had grown accustomed to indigenous decorative elements within their own homes.

Spanish-trained Pueblo woodworkers may also have made framed *cajas* for Native American homes. Evidence for this includes the chests' iconography and the Pueblo practice of integrating Hispanic *hornos* (outdoor ovens), *fogons* (corner fireplaces), and other items into their daily life. It thus seems feasible that they considered the framed chest as another useful Spanish invention for Pueblo communities—appropriate not only for storage of textiles, furs, and foodstuffs, but also for storytelling. The chest illustrated in figure 1, which came out of a Pueblo household in the early twentieth century, supports this theory. If framed chests were present in Pueblo households during the eighteenth century, then the Native American population was selectively absorbing Hispanic culture.[22]

The latter two possibilities, which center around the notion that Pueblo Indians adopted new craft traditions rather than just exotic imagery, suggest that Hispanic culture was dominant on the New Mexican frontier. According to psychiatrist Frantz Fanon, native cultures typically adopt aspects of the colonizing culture to give the appearance of conforming while maintaining their own heritage:

> At the very moment when the native intellectual is anxiously trying to create a cultural work he fails to realize that he is utilizing techniques and language which are borrowed from the stranger in his country. . . . He wishes to attach himself to the people; but instead he only catches hold of their outer garments. And these outer garments are merely the reflection of a hidden life, teeming and perpetually in motion.

Cultures are thus only superficially integrated through cohabitation and the subsequent mixing of blood and traditions. Core values remain distinct, but inaccessible except as a historical point of reference.[23]

Historians have suggested that the differences between framed *cajas* and their board counterparts are regional as opposed to cultural. Several framed chests (see fig. 6) have been attributed to the Velarde region of northern New Mexico because they are similar to a chest that descended in the Valdez family there. Variations in the style and structure of *cajas* may also relate to the socioeconomic status of their owners. With their conspicuous Hispanic iconography and connotations of segregation, board chests may have appealed to affluent *ricos* who valued pure Hispanic ancestry. By contrast, framed *cajas* correspond visually to households of interracial heritage. Such homes were most prevalent in New Mexico during the eighteenth century. The framed chests are more complex objects than board chests—a manifestation of how aesthetics and cultural production evolve when injected with new ideas, traditions, and technologies.[24]

Most *cajas* are assigned late-eighteenth-century dates; however, age may also account for differences between the board and framed forms. The board chests, for example, may precede the framed chests. With their Spanish iconography, board *cajas* manifest a need for visual attachment to the Old World. They support the theory that colonists had to integrate fully within their Old-World empire before developing a common American cultural identity. By comparison, the framed chests may be the result of prolonged frontier existence wherein time was required to perfect ancient woodworking skills, to adapt to the remote location and local traditions, and to build a common integrated culture. Makers may have produced framed chests only when their clients were ready to embrace New Mexican culture.[25]

Since the arrival of Oñate's expedition in 1598, New Mexico has served as meeting ground, trading post, and war zone. Native cultures—Pueblo communities and nomadic tribes—interacted with Spanish colonists and Franciscan missionaries venturing from Mexico. After the opening of the Santa Fe Trail in 1821, American settlers arrived from the eastern United States in wagon trains and brought with them a melange of British, French, and German customs. Many historians attribute the growth of the European population and simultaneous decrease in Pueblo and other Native American residents to acculturation. According to this theory, so-called primitive cultures are modified and submerged when they come into contact with more advanced cultures. The framed *cajas* suggest that creolization is a more appropriate framework for understanding cultural interaction on the Spanish colonial frontier. As a creole culture, eighteenth-century New Mexico was neither purely Hispanic nor Native American. Its unique character was a product of the region's distant relationship to Spain and its internal social structure, which had to incorporate two separate hierarchies. Similarly, the strong surfaces, Hispanic woodworking technologies, and pueblo-oriented decoration of the framed chests result from divergent cultures adapting to each other and especially to the environment.[26]

ACKNOWLEDGMENTS   For assistance with this article, the author thanks Edward S. Cooke, Jr., Glenn Adamson, Lucy Soutter, and Luke Beckerdite. The author is also grateful to Susan Conley at the Colorado Springs Fine Art Center and Taylor Museum, David

McNeece at the Museum of New Mexico, and Skip Miller at Taos Historic Museums for their particularly devoted assistance with research and illustrations. Al Luckett and Leslie Keno deserve special recognition for making New Mexican objects available to the author.

1. Roseann S. Willink and Paul G. Zolbrod, *Weaving A World: Textiles and the Navajo Way of Seeing* (Santa Fe: Museum of New Mexico Press, 1996), p. 5. During the eighteenth century, the term "coyote" referred to a person of both Spanish and New Mexican Indian parentage, often of darker skin color. Today "coyote" identifies people who are part Hispanic and part Anglo. For a discussion of the ethnic-racial classes of New Mexico, see William DeBuys, *Enchantment and Exploitation: The Life and Hard Times of a New Mexico Mountain Range* (Albuquerque: University of New Mexico Press, 1985), p. 69; and Chris Wilson, *The Myth of Santa Fe: Creating a Modern Regional Tradition* (Albuquerque: University of New Mexico Press, 1997), pp. 41–43. See Michael J. Ettema, "History, Nostalgia, and American Furniture," *Winterthur Portfolio* 17 (1982): 135–36; and Edward S. Cooke, "Craftsmen," in *Decorative Arts and Household Furnishings in America 1650–1920: An Annotated Bibliography*, edited by Kenneth L. Ames and Gerald W. R. Ward (Winterthur, Del.: Winterthur Museum, 1989), p. 334 for a summary of the limits of American decorative arts studies.

2. As relics of a frontier culture, *cajas* typically have more period or use-related repairs and modifications than New England chests, thus complicating traditional assessments of condition relative to use. The carving on *cajas* also differs from New England work in both design and placement. New England chests rarely have carved side panels (see fig. 3), although they are common in Hispanic traditions (see fig. 17).

3. Lonn Taylor and Dessa Bokides, *New Mexican Furniture, 1600–1940* (Santa Fe: Museum of New Mexico Press, 1987), p. 23. For a general discussion and visual survey of the types of New Mexican chests, see ibid, pp. 23–24, 28–34, 40–46. My observations and analysis are principally drawn from direct experience with and extensive research on the collection of Mr. and Mrs. Al Luckett, Jr., of Santa Fe, New Mexico. See Sotheby's, *American Furniture and Decorative Arts from Spain's Northern Colonial Frontier 1700–1900, The Collection of Mr. and Mrs. Al Luckett, Jr.*, (New York: Sotheby's, January 15, 1997).

4. Wilson, *Myth of Santa Fe*, pp. 26–32, provides an overview of the interaction between Indians and Hispanics. DeBuys, *Enchantment and Exploitation*, p. 70. There was a complicated *casta* hierarchy in New Mexico in which social status was equated with ethnic ancestry and skin color. Interracial marriages could involve any combination of continental Spanish, Hispanic Mexican, Mexican Indian, New Mexican Indian, and African peoples.

5. "*Memoria* of the Castaño de Sosa Expedition," as cited in John L. Kessell, *Kiva, Cross, and Crown: The Pecos Indians and New Mexico 1540–1840* (Washington, D. C.: National Park Service, U.S. Department of the Interior, 1979), p. 55.

6. Wilson, *Myth of Santa Fe*, p. 26. Joseph Toulouse, *The Mission of San Gregorio de Abó: A Report on the Excavation and Repair of a Seventeenth-Century New Mexico Mission*, Monographs of the School of American Research 13 (Santa Fe: School of American Research, 1949), p. 19.

7. DeBuys, *Enchantment and Exploitation*, p. 9. The ideological and cultural divergence between the northern and southern colonies is framed in terms of their respective relationships to the Old World in Jonathan Prown, "'A Preponderance of Pineapples': The Problem of Southern Furniture," in *American Furniture*, edited by Luke Beckerdite (Hanover, N.H.: University Press of New England for the Chipstone Foundation, 1996), p. 7.

8. Ramón A. Gutiérrez, *When Jesus Came, the Corn Mothers Went Away: Marriage, Sexuality, and Power in New Mexico, 1500–1846* (Palo Alto: Stanford University Press, 1991), pp. 146, 154, 162–66. A table enumerating nomadic Indian baptisms during the eighteenth century is on p. 154.

9. Wilson, *Myth of Santa Fe*, p. 24. For a discussion of the particulars of the carpentry ordinances, see Taylor and Bokides, *New Mexican Furniture*, pp. 7–8. Willink and Zolbrod, *Weaving A World*, pp. 18, 24. Wilson, *Myth of Santa Fe*, p. 50. Chris L. Miller and George R. Hamell, "A New Perspective on Indian-White Contact: Cultural Symbols and Colonial Trade," *Journal of American History* 73, no. 2 (September 1986): 321; the authors discuss how societies attempt to incorporate novel historical circumstances into their cognitive world.

10. George Kubler, "Time's Perfection and Colonial Art," in *Spanish, French, and English Traditions in The Colonial Silver of North America*, Winterthur Conference Report 1968 (Winterthur, Del.: Winterthur Museum, 1969), p. 11. Raw materials like pine, however, were not necessarily abundant everywhere in New Mexico.

11. Marc Simmons, "Colonial New Mexico and Mexico: The Historical Relationship," in *Colonial Frontiers, Art and Life in Spanish New Mexico: The Fred Harvey Collection*, edited by Christine Mather (Santa Fe: Ancient City Press, 1983), pp. 71–73.

12. Kubler, "Time's Perfection," pp. 7–8.

13. In the context of New Mexico, the term *hacienda* refers to a landed estate with a central house in which rooms are built around a courtyard or series of courtyards. Fray Francisco Atanasio Dominquez, *The Missions of New Mexico, 1776*, translated and edited by Eleanor B. Adams and Fray Angelico Chavez (Albuquerque: University of New Mexico Press, 1956), p. 214. Kessell, *Kiva, Cross, and Crown*, p. 133.

14. See Taylor and Bokides, *New Mexican Furniture*, pp. 7, 23, for a more thorough account of the technical aspects of the ordinances regulating proportions, construction methods, and appropriate surface designs.

15. The use of geometric units in the layout of New England chests is discussed in Robert Blair St. George, "Style and Structure in the Joinery of Dedham and Medfield, Massachusetts, 1635–1685," *Winterthur Portfolio* 13 (1979): 20–21. Taylor and Bokides, *New Mexican Furniture*, p. 12.

16. Taylor and Bokides, *New Mexican Furniture*, p. 23. The *caja* is the furniture form most frequently cited in eighteenth-century New Mexican probate inventories held at the Spanish Archives of New Mexico, New Mexico State Record Center and Archives, Santa Fe, New Mexico. More *cajas* survive than any other colonial New Mexican furniture form. Kubler, "Time's Perfection," p. 11.

17. Marc Simmons and Frank Turley, *Southwestern Colonial Ironwork: The Spanish Blacksmithing Tradition from Texas to California* (Santa Fe: Museum of New Mexico Press, 1980), pp. 151, 153.

18. Probate Inventory of Señor Armijo, 1748, Twitchell 240, Spanish Archives of New Mexico.

19. See Angel San Vicente, Cristina Monterde, Maria Pilar Pueyo, Rosa Gutierrez, and Asuncion Blasco, eds., *Origen y Armas de Varios Nobles de España* (Zaragoza, Spain: Biblioteca de la Universidad de Zaragoza, 1983), especially p. 36 for designs of Spanish coats-of-arms that include lions similar to those on the New Mexican board chests. Robert St. George, "Style and Structure," p. 25.

20. For more information on Pueblo cosmology, see DeBuys, *Enchantment and Exploitation*, p. 21 and Peter Nabokov and Robert Easton, *Native American Architecture* (New York: Oxford University Press, 1989), pp. 348–401. Nabokov and Easton, *Native American Architecture*, p. 368.

21. Sotheby's, *Luckett Collection*, lot 156. Willink and Zolbrod, *Weaving A World*, p. 52.

22. Nabokov and Easton, *Native American Architecture*, p. 366.

23. Frantz Fanon, "On National Culture," in *Colonial Discourse and Post-Colonial Theory: A Reader*, edited by Patrick Williams and Laura Chrisman (New York: Columbia University Press, 1994), pp. 41, 46.

24. Taylor and Bokides, *New Mexican Furniture*, pp. 24, 28.

25. This theory is introduced in Timothy H. Breen, "An Empire of Goods: The Anglicization of Colonial America, 1690–1776," *The Journal of British Studies* 25, no. 4 (October 1986): 499.

26. My understanding of creolization derives from Edward Brathwaite, *The Development of Creole Society in Jamaica 1770–1820* (Oxford, Eng.: Clarendon Press, 1971), xii–xv.

# Book Reviews

Henry Petroski. *The Book on the Bookshelf*. New York: Alfred A. Knopf, 1999. x + 290 pp.; numerous bw illus., appendix, bibliography, index. $26.00.

Henry Petroski has done it again. The bard of the overlooked, the ordinary, and the taken-for-granted objects in our daily lives, Petroski has turned his attention to something almost all of us encounter on a daily basis and probably never notice: the bookshelves that we perceive, if at all, in a (literally) supporting role. But as the author says, he "looked up one evening and saw bookshelves in a different light," to our benefit.

A professor of civil engineering and of history at Duke University, Petroski has made a specialty of chronicling, in the words of the title of one of his earlier books, "the evolution of useful things," such as the pencil and the safety pin. "How often," he asks, "do we really *see* what we look at, day in and day out?" It's a fair question, and Petroski's gift is to make us see, not only the thing itself, but also its connections to the greater world of technology and of culture in which such an object is embedded.

I must confess at this point that as a librarian (and a pack-rat accumulator of books) I probably ponder bookshelves more often than some of Petroski's readers, but this tends to be on an immediate and problem-solving level. What his book does is much grander. After all, as he points out, the "stories of the evolution of the book and the bookshelf are inseparable, and both are examples of the evolution of technology." And, I must add, for readers of this journal, the story of the bookshelf is an example of the evolution of a furniture form often taken for granted.

The first "books" were scrolls (*volumeria*). They were stored, rolled up, in shelving most closely resembling the pigeonholes of a small-town post office, complete with identifying tags affixed to one end. By the Early Christian Era, however, alternate forms of recorded writing had evolved: the hand-held wax tablet (infinitely erasable) and the codex, a form of bound manuscript using papyrus as its base. The need to house both bound and rolled materials led to the development of a closed cabinet called the *armarium* (from whence came *armoire*), also called later, in France, the *presse*.

Medieval book-holdings were few and precious. Generally, monasteries were the sites with significant collections, which by our standards were scanty indeed: this explains the use, for some centuries, of locked—at times, triple-locked—low chests purpose-built for book storage. A very few of these chests survive and are illustrated here. (They also appear in the surprisingly numerous manuscript views of scholars in their studies, and in these, at times, seem to be set on frames.) Monasteries also gave rise to standing desks—lecterns positioned to allow the reader maximum use of natural light—and to the ancestors of today's carrels, originally partitioned-off sections of the garden side of cloister walkways. Over the years, the chests that held the few books a monastery or wealthy owner might hold were turned on the ends, provided with shelves, and united with lecterns. With these shelves positioned at right angles to tall windows, the library as we know it assumed its modern form, so characteristic that a library building can often be spotted at a distance simply by the arrangement of its windows or lack of them.

Along the way, Petroski delights his readers with the unexpected: the development and disappearance of the "chained" book (which any truthful librarian will admit to wishing for on occasion); the "spectator sport" of examining someone else's bookshelves; the early custom of shelving books fore-edge out, with titles written on the page ends. The ubiquitous Samuel Pepys turns out to have been a leader in the spine-outwards movement, having designed his own bookshelves and commissioned matching bindings for his very extensive library.

Petroski even touches on the disappearance of the book, in more ways than one: some books have been destroyed deliberately by their owners (the reader who tore out each page as he finished reading it being an extreme example). The advent of the e-book ("the last book") may or may not signal disappearance of another sort altogether. Petroski does not pass judgment here: the evolution of technology, we feel, will always interest him, wherever it may lead. In the meantime, he raises the readers' spirits with a delightful appendix on the many ways we can choose to arrange books on our own shelves, ranging from the common (by author) to the unexpected (by enjoyment, by color, by sentimental value).

*The Book on the Bookshelf* is not only entertaining and illuminating; it can cause the reader to look around with new eyes and a heightened appreciation of all those things we never notice but can't do without. I recommend this book—and his others as well—to those of us who take our surroundings for granted. These overlooked and neglected objects are fortunate indeed to have Henry Petroski as their historian.

Neville Thompson
Winterthur Museum

---

Donald C. Peirce. *Art & Enterprise: American Decorative Art, 1825–1917, The Virginia Carroll Crawford Collection*. Atlanta, Ga.: High Museum of Art in association with Antique Collectors' Club, 1999. 411 pp.; 235 color and 247 bw illus., glossary, bibliography, index. $60.00.

*Art & Enterprise: American Decorative Art, 1825–1917, The Virginia Carroll Crawford Collection* is a noteworthy, enormous catalogue published in conjunction with an exhibition of the same title at the High Museum of Art, Atlanta, from June 12 through September 12, 1999. Donald C. Peirce, Curator of Decorative Art, wrote the 227 illustrated entries in the book encompassing metals, glass, ceramics, a few textiles, and furniture. The spectra of styles, makers, and materials, and the geographic scope make this book an essential addition to the libraries of scholars and collectors of decorative arts as well as of interest to the general public.

The Crawford collection provides a survey of the finest artisans and designers of high-style nineteenth- and early-twentieth-century American decorative arts. The encyclopedic nature of the collection is the result of a well-conceived collecting plan guided by an intuitive staff. In the 1970s, with the High Museum's focus on the growth of its decorative arts collection, eighteenth- and nineteenth-century American objects and a collection of English ceramics were acquired. The ceramics collection was introduced in the 1988 publication *English Ceramics: The Frances and Emory Cocke Collection,* also written by Peirce. Mrs. Virginia Carroll Crawford, a magnanimous patron of the High Museum and a board member, was interested in assisting the museum in the development of an important collection. She generously endorsed former curator of decorative art Katherine Gross Farnham's enthusiasm for a time-specific collection of nineteenth-century American decorative arts. Acquisitions began under the stewardship of Farnham, assisted by New York City–based consultant David A. Hanks. While some larger institutions—the Brooklyn Museum of Art and the Metropolitan Museum of Art—and mid-sized organizations, such as the Munson-Williams-Proctor Institute of Utica, New York, had been actively collecting nineteenth-century American material since the 1950s or before, there was little competition in this area, and many stellar works of art were available at a relatively moderate cost.

The first purchase (1979) for the Crawford collection, a labeled Thomas Godey cabinet (cat. no. 63), set the tone and complied with the goal of the collection: "To represent the period from 1825 to 1917 in American decorative art with masterpieces whose superior artistic quality is matched by their historical significance" (p. 9). In 1980 Donald C. Peirce joined the staff of the High Museum as curator of decorative art, and working closely with Hanks, he has overseen the evolution of the collection. Peirce has demonstrated great sensitivity to the stated goal.

Because the High Museum lacked adequate storage and exhibition space, in the early 1980s much of the collection was warehoused in New York City. In 1983 the Crawford collection was first exhibited in the new Richard Meier–designed High Museum. In that year the first catalogue of the collection was published: David A. Hanks and Donald C. Peirce, *The Virginia Carroll Crawford Collection, American Decorative Arts, 1825–1917* (Atlanta: High Museum of Art, 1983). This ninety-four-page book, using a format similar to that of *Art & Enterprise,* highlights approximately fifty-eight objects, with an additional sixty-two objects in a black-and-white illustrated appendix.

Mrs. Crawford's benefaction continued until her death in August 1999, after more than two decades of generosity. The words of former High Museum director Gudmund Vigtel in his preface to the 1983 publication germanely describes the development of the Crawford collection: "The result of this fortuitous collaboration among benefactor, museum staff, and consultant is a collection of consistently high quality of design and extraordinary craftsmanship, of great stylistic breadth, full of delightful surprises" (pp. 6–7).

In *Art & Enterprise* Donald Peirce has mastered the exacting task of creating an academically strong and visually appealing catalogue. The articulate essays, which average one to one and a half pages in length, are accompanied by striking color images (with a few in black and white) and "tombstone" information (object name, date, maker/designer and active dates, maker's location, materials, measurements, and inscription or mark). At times an expanded essay, set off by a subheading, addresses either more than one object by a particular maker or a particular theme, such as upholstery treatments of the 1880s (pp. 216–19). A black-and-white thumbnail photograph of a label or mark supplements most entries, and in many cases, crisp photographs of details further the reader's grasp of inherent craftsmanship. Overall, the design of the book is clean and user-friendly.

*Art & Enterprise* is divided into twelve sections, generally arranged chronologically by style beginning with classicism and closing with art nouveau and arts and crafts. Four of the twelve chapters, however, encompass broader themes and date ranges—industrialization (1835–1900), patent furniture (1850s–1880s), rich cut glass (1890–1917), and designs by architects. Each stylistic division in the book considers objects from a variety of media. "Classicism, 1830s," which introduces the body of the catalogue, has eight entries in four media: silver, gilded-brass, porcelain, and wood. The individual object entries follow a general format of succinct biographical information on the maker (when known) followed by an analysis of style, form, and ornamentation. Deft descriptions encourage close examination. Focused attention leads readers to a better understanding of a maker's choice of technique and style for the selected ornamental detail.

This book is about decorative arts as art, but as exemplified in "Classicism, 1830s," Peirce's tone is one of broad-based connoisseurship. The entries, in many instances moving beyond biographical and stylistic information, add sources of influence and social history to provide greater interpretive context. In the case of argand lamps (cat. no. 4), Peirce explains the technology of the lamp, how it affected form, and the evolution of the usage of argand lamps in the United States. He adds that Thomas Jefferson admired the new, brighter-burning fixtures after arriving in Paris in 1784 as ambassador: "the first argand cylinder lamps in America may have been gifts sent by Jefferson" (p. 22). (The pair in the Crawford collection were manufactured in England and retailed in Boston.)

The following chapter, "Industrialization, 1835–1900," slightly interrupting the chronological flow of the text, addresses objects manufactured by commercial enterprises often utilizing new technology. Read comprehensively, the entries, which concentrate on glass, ceramic, and cast iron, provide insight into the unprecedented industrial growth of the American decorative arts industry during the second half of the nineteenth century. As an example, by 1876 half the glass produced in the United States was made in Pittsburgh, Pennsylvania (p. 35). An extended entry on Pittsburgh-made glass (pp. 33–35) explains that glass manufacturing and distribution flourished there due to "materials, access to fuel, the growing western market, location, and industrial enterprise" (p. 33). From such utilitarian objects as a pressed-glass window pane (cat. no. 11) and whale oil lamps (cat. no. 12) to ornamental witch balls (cat. no. 13), the articles demonstrate the range of glassware produced in Pittsburgh and other centers.

Throughout the catalogue, object entries include references to related objects elsewhere in the book. Peirce's elucidation of the complex associations among stylistic movements and among artisans enhances a reader's understanding of the myriad levels of interpretation and art historical references pervading nineteenth- and early-twentieth-century decorative arts. The entries on indoor and outdoor cast-iron furniture (pp. 46–51) not only offer the reader a well-rounded look at the cast-iron industry in the United States and illustrate why "many nineteenth-century commentators referred to their era as the age of cast iron" (p. 48), but they also demonstrate the stylistic association between cast-iron objects and related cabinetwork. The cast-iron ottoman made by M. L. Greenwood and Company of Cincinnati (cat. no. 21) embodies the rococo revival style in its sinuous outline, and the essay also refers to the high-style rococo furniture by John Henry Belter (cat. no. 44 ). Similarly, discussion of a cast-iron bench by an unknown maker (cat. no. 26) alludes to such "related . . . domestic furniture from the 1850s through the 1870s" by Alexander Roux (cat. no. 46), Daniel Pabst (cat. no. 54), and a John Jelliff–inspired maker (cat. no. 66).

One of the strengths of *Art & Enterprise* is its assimilation of contextual information. Photographic documentation varies from an image depicting an object *in situ* to original design drawings and related objects. The chapter "Gothic and Elizabethan Revivals, 1845–1865" includes a Gothic revival–style pitcher and goblet by Zalmon Bostwick (cat. no. 28). The items are rare examples of Gothic revival silver, and little is known about this New York City maker who was active only from 1846 to 1852. Complementing the essay are photographs of the marks on the bottom of the pitcher, an English stoneware piece exemplifying the design antecedent, and an American earthenware variation of the form. Comparable photographic references enhance other essays. An entry on a solar lamp (cat. no. 31) uses an 1856 image from a retail catalogue depicting like objects and a black-and-white reproduction of an 1845 painting by Henry F. Darby. The Darby portrait of the Reverend John Atwood family (in the Museum of Fine Arts, Boston) features a similar lamp on the center table.

The breadth of the objects in the Crawford collection demonstrates the application to an array of objects of motifs associated with a stylistic movement. This methodology is well illustrated in the chapters "Rococo Revival, 1845–1865" and "A New Classicism, 1855–1875." A majority of the rococo revival wares in the collection are from Philadelphia and the New York City area. The items range from an opulent silver pitcher made by R. and W. Wilson (cat. no. 38) to exuberantly carved and pierced parlor furniture attributed to John Henry Belter (cat. no. 44). In both media, the naturalistic motifs, richly fashioned in three dimensions, are some of the finest interpretations of the style. The use of classical motifs in a loose and inventive American interpretation of Egyptian themes can be seen in an ebonized armchair with carved lotus blossoms and sphinx-like arm supports (cat. no. 73). More familiar applications of Greek- and Roman-derived ornament are illustrated in the expanded essay "Union Porcelain Works" (pp. 148–55).

The next two chapters, "Patent Furniture, 1850s–1880s" and "Return to Craftsmanship, 1870s," are provocatively juxtaposed. Patent furniture, which embraced mechanical ingenuity and mass-production techniques, followed the prevalent ornamentation of the period in which it was produced. The centripetal chair (cat. no. 83) made in Troy, New York, about 1850 utilized sheet metal, bent steel, and cast iron, and it emulates the silhouette of the rococo revival style. The seven objects in "Return to Craftsmanship" demonstrate the reactions designers had to the "sinuous curves and sumptuous ... surfaces" delineated by American furniture makers since the 1840s (p. 178) and to the methodology of mass production. The austere sideboard in cat. no. 89 seems out of place in the Crawford collection until one reads how it is "nearly an exact copy" of a design published in Charles Locke Eastlake's *Hints on Household Taste in Furniture, Upholstery and Other Details* (Boston, 1872), one of the most influential treatises of its time. Peirce advances the interpretation of the sideboard by referencing it in his discussion of a richly carved sideboard in the rococo revival chapter.

"Late Century Eclecticism, 1876–1905" illustrates the diversity of stylistic influences existing toward the end of the century and reveals the broad-based approach of Peirce and Hanks toward the content of the Crawford collection. During the last quarter of the nineteenth century, designers took inspiration from international influences, such as the arts of the Middle East, as indicated in the flamboyant Tiffany and Company silver-gilt, enamel, and semiprecious-stone coffee set (cat. no. 153 and jacket detail). The heterogeneity of American culture stimulated the country's firms to create distinctly American objects; this is seen in the Texas-made steer horn chair and ottoman (cat. no. 150) and in the Tiffany and Company bowl modeled after a Native American basket (cat. no. 152).

With forty-two entries, "Art Nouveau and Arts and Crafts" is one of the largest segments of the catalogue. Few examples of art nouveau furniture are presented, but this is not surprising as few fully realized American interpretations of the movement are extant. Arts and crafts–style objects from the consummate firms and craftspeople are included: Charles Rohlfs and Craftsman Workshops furniture; Van Briggle, Grueby, and Newcomb pottery; and silver by Arthur J. Stone and the Kalo shop, to cite only a few of the makers. This chapter is one of the few to present textiles; this addition, which includes examples of floor coverings retailed from Stickley's Craftsman Workshop (cat. nos. 190–91), broadens a reader's knowledge and understanding of a domestic arts and crafts interior.

The last section of the book, heavily devoted to furniture, is entitled "Designs by Architects." These entries are as informative as all others, but a general reader may have benefited more if the entries had been included in the chronological segments of the text. The section on Alexander Jackson Davis, for example, would have added to one's understanding of the Gothic revival style. Likewise, the organic chair probably designed by the firm of Herts and Tallant and the works designed by Frank Lloyd Wright and the brothers Greene and Greene would have added depth to the art nouveau and arts and crafts chapter.

Locales and makers are comprehensively accounted for in all the chapters. *Art & Enterprise* is inclusive in its consideration of urban areas at the pinnacle of the manufacturing trades in the nineteenth and early twentieth centuries. As one expects, the northeastern states are heavily represented by the industrialized hubs of Boston, Philadelphia, Baltimore, and New York, but lesser seats of commercial trade are also included. Midwestern cabinetmaking centers such as Cincinnati and Indianapolis are portrayed by goods from the Rookwood Pottery and Wooton Desk Manufacturing Company, respectively. Smaller communities also played a significant role in the development of decorative arts: Bennington, Vermont, was home to a respected ceramic production (cat. nos. 15–17), and University City, Missouri, claimed a short-lived pottery and porcelain enterprise (cat. nos. 210–211) that attracted distinguished ceramists of the time—Taxile Doat and Samuel and Adelaide Alsop Robineau. A few objects made in Europe but retailed in the United States (at times, marked by American businesses) are also scattered in the text.

Read sequentially, the various accounts of particular makers are instructive for understanding how their work evolved. For example, in "Japanese Taste and Exotica, 1870–1910," which is especially strong in its representation of glass and ceramics, Tiffany and Company is represented in the chapter with seven entries, but the author's references in the book provide an elaboration of the company's work from the 1850s through 1907 that gives a broad understanding of the firm's designers and artisans and their output.

A brief glossary, a bibliography that distills secondary source scholarship, and an index conclude *Art & Enterprise*. Overall, the book presumes a certain level of knowledge. The glossary, therefore, is of particular assistance to readers who are new to the field. The bibliography and index are useful tools, although city names are not indexed.

*Art & Enterprise* presents an extensive survey, but a brief introductory essay for each section would have strengthened the comprehensive nature of the book. Much of the information can be gleaned by reading each entry in a specific chapter, but introductions could lay an art historical foundation, provide a place for explanations of terminology, and address topics that warrant clarification for less knowledgeable readers. For example, what is meant by a "Return to Craftsmanship," and why did it take hold in America in the 1870s? Additionally, the delineation of primary and secondary woods in the individual furniture entries would have been an added benefit to specialists.

Since the publication of the Metropolitan Museum of Art's catalogue *19th-Century America: Furniture and Other Decorative Arts* (New York: Metropolitan Museum, 1970), few publications have been so rich in scope. Many books about nineteenth-century decorative arts have focused on specific movements or themes, and these are included in Peirce's bibliography, but *Art & Enterprise* is a leader in that it includes all media. It demonstrates that while many institutions have moved away from general, collection-based catalogues, there is still merit in collection surveys.

*Art & Enterprise: American Decorative Art, 1825–1917, The Virginia Carroll Crawford Collection* is an important reference tool for seasoned curators and scholars and a textbook for burgeoning decorative arts enthusiasts. Peirce's book reflects his conscientious scholarship and his dedication to the study of American decorative arts. Indeed, the collection he continues devotedly to nurture demonstrates the *art* and *enterprise* of American craftsmanship.

Anna Tobin D'Ambrosio
Munson-Williams-Proctor Institute Museum of Art

Jack Lindsey, with essays by Richard S. Dunn, Edward C. Carter II, and Richard Saunders. *Worldly Goods: The Arts of Early Pennsylvania, 1680–1758*. Philadelphia: Philadelphia Museum of Art, 1999. xxii +266 pp.; 506 color and bw illus., checklist, appendixes, bibliography, index. $65.00.

On October 10, 1999, the exhibition "Worldly Goods: The Arts of Early Pennsylvania, 1680–1758" opened to the public at the Philadelphia Museum of Art. The show immersed visitors in an array of objects made (or sometimes used) in the Philadelphia region through the 1750s. Such striking new discoveries as the claw-and-ball-foot high chest dated 1743 and signed by "Jos. Claypoole," or the several impressive early secretaries and host of small tables commanded one's attendance and attention. The sheer visual assault of so much concentrated material encouraged repeat visits. Twelve weeks later the exhibition was dismantled and the many privately owned objects returned, leaving only insufficient memories and the catalogue. This review addresses the catalogue with an emphasis on furniture.

Jack Lindsey, the exhibition curator and chief author of the catalogue, states in his preface that "attention on the Philadelphia rococo style has resulted, until very recently, in a gap in scholarship on the earlier period in Pennsylvania" (p. xiv). "*Worldly Goods,*" he goes on to say, "is the first attempt at a broader and more complete investigation." Indeed, inadequate attention has been paid this fascinating and important time and place, which (at the very least) needs to be examined in order to understand better the learned and artistic culture and society of Philadelphia in the 1760s and 1770s. Lindsey's purpose, though, is to gather and present a comprehensive cross-section of objects that evoke or document what he characterizes as William Penn's "new social order" (p. 4). The 506 pieces of furniture, silver, base metals, glass, ceramics, textiles, scientific instruments, paintings, works on paper, and printed works he assembled burst the seams of the modest-sized, 266-page catalogue. By comparison, the Philadelphia Museum's own bicentennial exhibition catalogue *Philadelphia: Three Centuries of American Art*, consumes 665 pages to discuss 546 objects. The 1982 "New England Begins: The Seventeenth Century" exhibition at the Museum of Fine Arts, Boston, has 504 objects presented in a three-volume catalogue totaling 575 pages; and the catalogue *The Great River: Art and Society of the Connecticut Valley, 1635–1850* (1985), from the exhibit at the Wadsworth Atheneum, devotes 525 pages to 354 objects.

The catalogue divides equally into interpretive essays followed by a checklist, a listing of woodworkers, clockmakers, and silversmiths, and a bibliography. All of the objects in the exhibition are illustrated in color or black and white. A select few images are large, occasionally full-size, but the great majority—including all of the ones of interest to this reviewer—are small, typically 3 × 2½ inches or less. Fortunately, they are printed on a coated paper that maximizes available detail.

Five essays, including three by guest authors, interpret the material. Lindsey's introductory chapter characterizes Pennsylvania settlement as chaos receding in the face of evolving social order and growing prosperity. As evidence, he cites an increasingly rich and diverse material world. Philadelphians demonstrated this change through 1) more specific room use, 2) increasingly elaborate domestic and social rituals acted out with objects that were functionally more specific, and 3) greater efforts "to improve the signals sent to their neighbors and peers by their personal appearance and possessions" (pp. 4–5). Development along this path was rapid because of "natural abundance" and the "economic and investment potentials provided by the physical characteristics of the site" (p. 11). Lindsey sets this tranquil, conflict-free image of colonial settlement in stark contrast to long-term turmoil and devastation throughout Europe. Although some readers may object to this characterization, they must keep in mind that *Worldly Goods* is a celebration of "the richness and ingenuity of the aesthetic traditions and craftsmanship that made their way to the Delaware Valley" (p. 11).

In Richard S. Dunn's chapter, the author sketches a religious, political, and economic history of the region. He describes the circumstances of William Penn's founding of the colony, notes the ethnographic diversity of the region, and traces growth of the city through 1755. By that time, Philadelphia supported several intellectual and civic organizations as well as a level of commercial activity that presaged the leadership role it would play in establishing a new nation.

Edward C. Carter II writes of a similar sense of "foreshadowing," to use his term, among the scientific community of Philadelphia. Here, Carter stretches the time frame to 1769, the year in which Philadelphians, notably David Rittenhouse, participated in an international effort to observe a transit of Venus. Favorable reaction abroad to Rittenhouse's work—taking both astronomical measurements calculated to determine the distance of the earth to the sun as well as earthly measurements of longitude that were essential for navigation—indicated that scientific pursuits in Philadelphia had come of age on the world stage. Regrettably, the more engaging aspects of this story lay beyond the boundaries of the exhibition, forcing readers to be content with early but tentative contributions of such facile minds as John Logan, John Bartram, and Benjamin Franklin.

To Richard Saunders, the last guest author, early Pennsylvania painting "came of age" from 1700 to 1750, not unlike Carter's scientific community. Saunders sees more ambition than ability in these immigrant painters, noting the unfavorable circumstances of frontier life. By 1735, he suggests, circumstances improved, due both to economics and a decline in Quakerism and its accompanying reluctance to support portraiture. John Smibert's arrival from Scotland heralded a new level of achievement, reinforced by the visit in 1746 of American-born Robert Feke. Philadelphia portraiture matured with painters such as John Hesselius, John Wollaston, and William Williams. That this artistic community nurtured Benjamin West affirms its coming of age on a world stage.

Jack Lindsey's essay entitled "Pondering Balance, the Decorative Arts of the Delaware Valley," longer than the three guest essays combined, forms the heart of *Worldly Goods*. Many of the topics he presents spill into six additional decorative arts narratives, three of which introduce furniture, in the checklist section. Extrapolating from a 1751 letter in which a wealthy Philadelphia attorney expresses frustration with fitting out his new country house, Lindsey uses the concept of "balance" to introduce a theme of self-conscious awareness of beauty and refinement in the lives and homes of colonial Philadelphians. More specifically, the author speaks of "a growing worldliness" (p. 72), manifested in broad-based upward mobility, blurring (pp. 73–74) or growing (p. 78) class distinctions, and recession of Quaker leadership. Although these themes recur throughout Lindsey's work, they do not emerge as the basic interpretive message. His essay quickly assumes the shape of a more conventional decorative arts history: a discussion of domestic architecture and interiors yields to inventory studies to suggest the range of objects within these settings, and concludes with lengthy treatments of artisans in general, and furniture craftsmen, woodworking techniques, tools, and woods in particular. Along the way, the author takes special note of European sources.

In tracing Philadelphia's ethnic ties to Europe, visible in its material culture, Lindsey recognizes the Dutch so often that their influence seems second only to the English, with Welsh, German, and Swedish occupying a lower tier. Claims of Dutch influence, typically paired with English, are stated regularly in the furniture checklist narratives. In the absence of specific historical evidence supporting this assertion, the author's footnotes indicate his dependence for this interpretation upon the Dutch- English- American path of design transmission presented in "Courts and Colonies," an exhibition commemorating the tercentenary of the accession of King William of the Netherlands to the English throne. But what may illuminate on a national level (assuming away the difficulties of translating Dutch and English court styles into American bourgeois styles) does not necessarily apply in Philadelphia. Nor do repeating the assertion and substituting *kas*, the Dutch term for a wardrobe, for the commonly used German term *schrank* (cat. no. 44), make it any more reliable. In fact, Lindsey seems to have gotten caught in his own web. In analyzing a particular chair (p. 163, cat. no. 146), he likens the carved crest to "Dutch and Scandinavian vernacular carving traditions," offering no further explanation but footnoting Benno Forman's *American Seating Furniture, 1630–1730: An Interpretive Catalogue*. Yet Forman only speculates about possible Scandinavian (or North German) influences in turning and makes no mention of the Dutch.[1]

In contrast to relatively insignificant numbers of Dutch settlers in Philadelphia, waves of Scots-Irish and German immigrants entered the city in the 1720s and 1730s, respectively. In a study not referenced in the catalogue, Désirée Caldwell researched Philadelphia furniture makers from 1681 to 1755. Using a pool of 441 workers (over 200 more than recorded in the *Worldly Goods* compilation), she was able to determine some ethnic origins: 60 were German, 4 Dutch, and 1 was Dutch or German. In another study absent from footnotes and bibliography, Benno Forman explored the impact of the largest non-British ethnic group in the city in "German Influences in Pennsylvania Furniture." Impact of the Scots-Irish remains largely unexamined. *Worldly Goods* would have benefited by addressing some of these larger themes. Instead, Lindsey's characterization of wainscot chairs as "the local convergence of stylistically related yet culturally separate English, Welsh, German, Dutch, and Scandinavian traditions of construction and techniques" (p. 158) aptly represents his broader acceptance of a homogenized material world. Following this reasoning, there is no basis to describe the characteristics that distinguish a six-board chest identified as "of Swedish type" (cat. no. 17) or that typify the many Dutch influences Lindsey observes.[2]

The text displays an acceptance of conventional wisdom in areas that may need to be reexamined. Was all furniture made with line-and-berry inlay of Chester County manufacture only (p. 138)? The elegant and urbane dressing table with the date of 1724 inlaid within line-and-berry decoration in the top (cat. no. 52) is one of several objects likely made in Philadelphia. Local chairs made to compete with "Boston" chairs in the 1740s are once again presented as outmoded William and Mary–styled leather-back chairs, despite preponderant evidence that Philadelphia chairmakers responded with more fashionable Queen Anne–styled splat-back chairs. "Irish" dovetailed leg tenons have German roots and actually may have come to Ireland via late-seventeenth-century German immigrants to England.[3]

Occasional lapses in a work as far-reaching and complex as *Worldly Goods* should not discolor the whole, but numerous simple factual errors and questionable interpretations exist. Figure 120, for example, is an ink drawing that purports to show the back of the famous Slate Roof House built by Samuel Carpenter in the late seventeenth century and demolished in 1868. But this "Carpenter Mansion" looks like a different building entirely from William Strickland's ink wash of the Slate Roof House shown in figure 177 (see cat. nos. 478 and 480). None of the rooflines and chimneys seems to correspond, and no explanation of the differences is provided. The author identifies the two claw-and-ball-foot stools illustrated as figure 158 and catalogue no. 108 as part of a rare set of four documented by a 1756 bill; the two unillustrated stools are listed as owned by Winterthur Museum. However, the wary reader must check other published sources to learn that Winterthur owns a set of four stools that differ in having pad feet and are actually the documented set in question.[4]

One of the essential functions of a catalogue is to record by words and images the objects assembled for exhibition. The three other catalogues mentioned above are classics in the American furniture canon because of the information they contain. *Worldly Goods* provides only a checklist and a single, small photograph. A few photographic details are scattered through the essays. About half of the entries have a one- or two-line statement of provenance or significance. Attributions and references to bills or other documentation are not footnoted. There are neither construction notes nor statements of condition, and furniture woods are incomplete. The photograph of the great caned Thomas Lloyd armchair at Winterthur (cat. no. 137) appears to have been one taken in 1976 before restoration of arm-support losses.

The dating of objects is often an acid test of identification and significance (and value in the marketplace). Comparison of dates and date ranges for several Philadelphia Museum objects previously published in museum catalogues reveals that dating has drifted earlier, and in some instances jumped, without explanation. A clockface (cat. no. 422) by Francis Richardson, Jr., published in 1974 as ca. 1735, is re-dated ca. 1715–25, when the maker would have been ten to twenty years old. In the intervening years, this clockface also acquired cast spandrels, but no mention of the change occurs.[5]

Exhibitions such as "Worldly Goods" are enormous undertakings that consume prodigious quantities of time and money. Their complexities and scale generally limit them to large institutions of national stature, which bring not only the necessary skills and resources but also prestige, excitement, and a sense of moment. The catalogues accompanying these efforts carry weight and influence by association with the institutions and projects, in addition to their own substance and contributions. As permanent records, exhibition catalogues bear an opportunity cost: they must be done well because many years will pass before museum directors and funders agree to revisit the material or themes. Moreover, objects in private ownership will generally not be accessible except through the catalogue. Successful exhibitions and catalogues feed scholarship in the intervening years. Indeed, *Worldly Goods* brings to view many new objects that must now be worked into the corpus of Philadelphia furniture. It should inspire reexamination of this important time and place in the history and appreciation of American decorative arts.

Philip D. Zimmerman
Lancaster, Pennsylvania

1. For examples, see pp. 129, 130, 132, 134, 136, 150, 158, 160, 163, and 165.

2. Désirée Caldwell, "Germanic Influences on Philadelphia Early Georgian Seating Furniture" (M.A. thesis, University of Delaware, 1985), appendix I, pp. 88–114. Benno M. Forman, "German Influences in Pennsylvania Furniture" in *Arts of the Pennsylvania Germans*, edited by Scott T. Swank (New York: W. W. Norton for Henry Francis du Pont Winterthur Museum, 1983), pp. 102–70.

3. William Macpherson Hornor, Jr., cites this dressing table as a paradigm of Philadelphia furniture making and presents evidence of inlay work in Philadelphia in *Blue Book, Philadelphia Furniture: William Penn to George Washington* (Philadelphia: privately printed, 1935), pp. 10, 34. See also Cathryn J. McElroy, "Furniture in Philadelphia: The First Fifty Years," in *American Furniture and Its Makers: Winterthur Portfolio 13*, edited by Ian M. G. Quimby (Chicago: University of Chicago Press, 1979), pp. 69–70. See Philip D. Zimmerman, "Philadelphia Queen Anne Chairs in the Collections of Wright's Ferry Mansion," *Antiques* 149, no. 5 (May 1996): 742-43. The only statement of Irish origin known to this reviewer is a single chair, identified as Irish without substantiation, in John T. Kirk, *American Furniture and the British Tradition to 1830* (New York: Alfred A. Knopf, 1982), nos. 822–24. See Caldwell, "Germanic Influences," pp. 28–46; and Zimmerman, "Philadelphia Queen Anne Chairs," p. 739, n. 23.

4. Joseph Downs, *American Furniture: Queen Anne and Chippendale Periods* (1952; reprint, New York: Viking Press, 1967), no. 294. Both sets of stools are illustrated and discussed in Hornor, *Blue Book, Philadelphia Furniture*, p. 199, pls. 51 and 309, although the pad-foot example is described as one of a pair.

5. *The Pennsylvania German Collection* (Philadelphia: Philadelphia Museum of Art, 1982); *Philadelphia: Three Centuries of American Art* (Philadelphia: Philadelphia Museum of Art, 1976). Compare cat. nos. 6, 46, 70, 98, 110, 129, and 164. Cat. no. 112 is dated slightly later. Martha Gandy Fales, *Joseph Richardson & Family, Philadelphia Silversmiths* (Middletown, Conn.: Wesleyan University Press, 1974), p. 29.

John Morley. *The History of Furniture: Twenty-Five Centuries of Style and Design in the Western Tradition*. Boston: Little, Brown, and Co., A Bulfinch Press Book, 1999. 352 pp.; 173 color and 507 bw illus., bibliography, index. $75.00.

In an age when furniture scholarship is becoming ever more specialized, it is refreshing to see an author attempt to survey twenty-five centuries of Western style and design in a single volume, as John Morley does in *The History of Furniture*. Morley takes on the history of ornament from ancient Greek, Roman, and Egyptian times through, basically, the middle of the nineteenth century. The main focus of the work is on objects made before about 1850. However, two chapters at the end of the book deal with "The Wilder Shore of Style," by which the author means the influence of China, Japan, India, Egypt, and Africa, and "Latter-day Polarities," a reference to the dichotomy between art nouveau and twentieth-century neoclassicism.

Large in format and beautifully illustrated with a wide variety of images, *The History of Furniture* represents one of the few large-scale, serious overviews of furniture since the publication in 1965 of *World Furniture*, edited by Helena Hayward. Although Morley's new book does not entirely supplant the Hayward anthology, which has a different format and focus, it goes far beyond the less satisfactory 1992 work by H. D. Molesworth and John Kenworthy-Brown entitled *Three Centuries of Furniture in Color* (an English text written to go with illustrations first published in 1969 in Alvar Gonzalez Palacios, *Il Mobile nei Secoli*) and the more general *History of Furniture*, edited by Anne Charlish and published in 1976.

*The History of Furniture* identifies "classical" and "anti-classical" modes in ancient work and explores how "the antithesis between these two main antique schools . . . profoundly influenced interior decoration and furniture design during the centuries that followed the fifteenth-century Italian Renaissance" (p. 9). The influences of the "pointed styles"—Islamic and Gothic—are also considered as part of the backdrop against which furniture styles and designs have evolved. The origins and evolution of ornaments and motifs are examined in detail.

This is very much a book by a traditional art historian written for other traditional art historians. Its text is wide-ranging, learned, perceptive, and elegantly written, with bountiful quotations from period sources in literature, history, and the arts. Morley makes no bones about confining his focus to tracing the complicated story of motifs and sources of influence, and he is almost exclusively interested in high-style furniture. His approach is thus both traditional and, to my mind, somewhat old-school English, reminiscent, for example, of the tone of early issues of *Furniture History*. Morley is primarily concerned with the outer envelope of the object rather than with its construction, and he is unapologetic about his lack of interest in what he calls "*licenza* in exposition" (p. 7), or what some people might call social and cultural interpretation. He is not particularly interested in vernacular or rural furniture, or in the new literature on consumerism, or in furniture as evidence of material culture, or in many of the other avenues that furniture historians, especially those in America, now like to wander down. Within the parameters he has chosen to define the history of furniture, however, Morley does an excellent job of unraveling the complicated story of why furniture looks the way it does. Hereafter no one will be able to say simply that such-and-such an object was "influenced by" or "inspired by" an earlier piece without bringing to mind the subtle, intricate web of relationships that Morley has so deftly woven.

American furniture is discussed here and there in the volume, with, for instance, a Salem blockfront desk-and-bookcase on p. 157, a Meeks desk-and-bookcase (ca. 1825) on p. 217, a Belter bed on p. 253, and an arts and crafts interior on p. 249. The only concentrated section on American work is devoted to classics of twentieth-century seating (pp. 273–74). Thus students of American work will find this book of greatest use as a means for placing high-style American furniture in an international, largely Euro-centric, context.

The bibliography included in *The History of Furniture* deserves a special word of mention. Rather than being a compilation of the vast secondary literature, Morley has assembled three useful lists of primary sources. The first includes books containing antique, exotic, and Gothic sources of design, while the second cites pattern and ornament books. The last group includes a shorter list of works that have influenced taste or ideas. Again, works published in America are not included to any significant degree, but overall the bibliography is a useful reference that will be of value to students.

Even if Morley has not told the *entire* history of furniture, *The History of Furniture* is a major contribution to our understanding of the evolution of taste and of design. It seems destined to become a cornerstone in any library on furniture, American and otherwise.

Gerald W. R. Ward
Museum of Fine Arts, Boston

*Compiled by*
*Gerald W. R. Ward*

Recent Writing on
American Furniture:
A Bibliography

▼ THIS YEAR'S list includes works published in 1999 and roughly through July of 2000; as always, a few earlier publications that had escaped notice are also cited. The short title *American Furniture 1999* is used in citations for articles and reviews published in last year's issue of this journal, which is also cited in full under Luke Beckerdite's name.

For their assistance in a variety of ways I am grateful to Jonathan L. Fairbanks, Pat and Dick Warner, and Milo Naeve. Staff members of the library of the Museum of Fine Arts, Boston, the Portsmouth Athenaeum, and the Winterthur Museum Library, especially Neville Thompson, have also been helpful.

Recent scholarship on American furniture was again recognized in the past year. The Robert C. Smith Award for 1998 was presented to Peter M. Kenny of the Metropolitan Museum of Art by the Decorative Arts Society, for his two essays in the exhibition catalogue devoted to Charles-Honoré Lannuier. The catalogue of nineteenth-century furniture at the Munson-Williams-Proctor Institute in Utica, New York, edited by Anna Tobin D'Ambrosio, was also honored with an award from the Victorian Society of America.

I would be delighted to receive suggestions for titles that should be included in these annual lists. Review copies of significant works would also be much appreciated.

Abendroth, Uta, Karin Beate Phillips, Christian Pixis, and Volkard Steinbach. *World Design: The Best in Classic and Contemporary Furniture, Fashion, Graphics, and More.* Edited by Bernd Polster. San Francisco: Chronicle Books, 2000. 432 pp.; numerous color illus., chronology.

Adamson, Glenn. "California Dreaming." In *Furniture Studio: The Heart of the Functional Arts,* edited by John Kelsey and Rick Mastelli, pp. 32–42. Free Union, Va.: Furniture Society, 1999. Color and bw illus.

Adamson, Glenn. "California Spirit: Rediscovering the Furniture of J. B. Blunk." *Woodwork,* no. 59 (October 1999): 22–29. 14 color and 5 bw illus. (See also "Work and Home: A Visit with J. B. Blunk," pp. 30–31.)

Adamson, Jeremy. "Cederquist Exhibition Opens March 30th." *James Renwick Alliance Quarterly* (Winter 1999–2000): 12–13. 1 bw illus.

Albertson, Karla Klein. "Worldly Goods: The Arts of Early Pennsylvania, 1680–1758." *Antiques and the Arts Weekly* (December 17, 1999): 1, 68–71. 15 bw illus.

Albrecht, Donald, Ellen Lupton, and Steven Skov Holt. *Design Culture Now: National Design Triennial, Cooper-Hewitt National Design Museum, Smithsonian Institution.* New York: Princeton Architectural Press, 2000. 216 pp.; numerous color and bw illus., biographies, index.

Albus, Volker, et al. *Icons of Design! The 20th Century.* New York: Prestel, 2000. 184 pp.; 249 color and 125 bw illus., bibliography, index.

Alexander, John. *Make a Chair from a Tree.* Baltimore, Md.: greenwoodworking in association with Anatol Pollilo and ALP Productions, 1999. Video; 124 minutes.

"American Clock Exhibit Opens At Museum of Early Trades and Crafts." *Antiques and the Arts Weekly* (July 7, 2000): 90. 1 bw illus.

Anderson, Judy. "Rare Woodwork Joinery from the 1650s by an Early Marblehead Craftsman." *News from the Marblehead Historical Society* (Fall 1999): 4. 2 bw illus.

Andrews, Edward Deming, and Faith Andrews. *Masterpieces of Shaker Furniture.* 1966. Reprint. New York: Dover Publications, 1999. 106 pp.; illus., bibliography.

"Arthur Wesley Dow and American Arts and Crafts." *Antiques and the Arts Weekly* (December 10, 1999): 1, 68–70. 12 bw illus.

*Avery Index to Architectural Periodicals at Columbia University.* Cumulative edition. Los Angeles: Getty Research Institute, 2000 release. CD-ROM. (This new release contains all articles from earlier releases, as well as some 150,000 records converted from the card files of the Avery Library covering from the 1860s to the 1970s.)

Bakker, Keith, Patricia E. Kane, and Dawn M. Wilson. "'Finished in Gold and White': The Restoration of a Philadelphia Federal Armchair." *Yale University Art Gallery Bulletin* (1999): 93–101, 158–61. 5 color and 6 bw illus.

Baldon, Russell. "Next." In *Furniture Studio: The Heart of the Functional Arts,* edited by John Kelsey and Rick Mastelli, pp. 126–33. Free Union, Va.: Furniture Society, 1999. Color illus.

Barquist, David L. Review of Peter M. Kenny, Frances F. Bretter, and Ulrich Leben, *Honoré Lannuier, Cabinetmaker from Paris: The Life and Work of a French Ébéniste in Federal New York.* In *Studies in the Decorative Arts* 7, no. 1 (fall–winter 1999–2000): 110–14. 1 bw illus.

Beach, Laura. "Art & Enterprise: The Virginia Carroll Crawford Collection of American Decorative Arts, 1825–1917." *Antiques and the Arts Weekly* (August 27, 1999): 1, 68–70. 10 bw illus.

Beach, Laura. "Boston in the Age of Neo-Classicism, 1810–1840: Hirschl & Adler Gallery" (exhibtion review). *Antiques and the Arts Weekly* (January 14, 2000): 1, 68–73. 21 bw illus.

Beach, Laura. "Design for a New Age: American Modern, 1925–1940." *Antiques and the Arts Weekly* (June 23, 2000): 1, 68–71. 13 bw illus.

Beach, Laura. "Masterpieces of American Furniture: Munson-Williams-Proctor Institute" (exhibition and catalogue review). *Antiques and the Arts Weekly* (September 24, 1999): 1, 68–69. 9 bw illus.

Beck, Tracey Rae. "The Substance of Childhood." *Antiques* 157, no, 2 (February 2000): 324–33. 16 color illus. (Includes some children's furniture.)

Beckerdite, Luke, ed. *American Furniture 1999.* Milwaukee, Wis.: Chipstone Foundation, 1999. xiii + 319 pp.; numerous color and bw illus., bibliography, index. Distributed by University Press of New England, Hanover, N.H., and London.

"Beekman Family Games Tables Brings $910,000 At Sotheby's." *Antiques and the Arts Weekly* (January 28, 2000): 81. 1 bw illus.

Benes, Peter, ed. *Rural New England Furniture: People, Place, and Production.* Dublin Seminar for New England Folklife Annual Proceedings 1998. Boston: Boston University Scholarly Publications, 2000. 256 pp.; numerous bw illus., maps, bibliography.

Berlin, Carswell Rush. "An Important Rosewood and Cast-Iron Gueridon Attributed to Duncan Phyfe and Sons." *Antiques* 157, no. 5 (May 2000): 770–77. 10 color and 5 bw illus.

Bivins, John. "Rhode Island Influence in the Work of Two North Carolina Cabinetmakers." *American Furniture 1999,* pp. 78–108. 43 color and bw illus.

Blackburn, Roderic H. "The Crane and Ware Houses United." *Antiques* 156, no. 3 (September 1999): 310–21. 14 color illus.

Blotner, Pamela. "The Whole Tree." *Woodwork,* no. 63 (June 2000): 22–28. 14 color illus.

Bofferding, R. Louis. "Innovators of Style." *Christie's Magazine* 16, no. 7 (September/October 1999): 108–11. 6 color and 2 bw illus.

Brawer, Nicholas A. "Georgian Campaign Furniture." *Antiques* 157, no. 6 (June 2000): 924–31. 10 color and 3 bw illus.

Brown, Michael D. "Topping Off Thomas Dawes's Desk-and-Bookcase." *Antiques* 157, no. 5 (May 2000): 788–95. 6 color and 6 bw illus.

Budis, Erin M. "Sewing Desks: Gender and Appearance in Shaker Communities and the World." In *Rural New Hampshire Furniture: People, Place, and Production,* edited by Peter Benes, pp. 209–25. Boston: Boston University Scholarly Publications, 2000. 10 bw illus.

Burgard, Timothy Anglin. *The Art of Craft: Contemporary Works from the Saxe Collection.* Boston: Fine Arts Museums of San Francisco in association with Bulfinch Press/Little, Brown and Company, 1999. 270 pp.; 220 color and 50 bw illus., bibliography, index. (Includes some turned vessels and furniture.)

Burks, Jean M. Review of John Kassay, *The Book of American Windsor Furniture: Styles and Technologies.* In *American Furniture 1999,* pp. 280–82.

Busch, Akiko. *Geography of Home: Writings on Where We Live.* New York: Princeton Architectural Press, 1999. 163 pp.

Busch, Jason T. "The Briggs Family Business and Furniture: A Study of Patronage and Consumption in Antebellum Southwestern New Hampshire." In *Rural New England Furniture: People, Place, and Production,* edited by Peter Benes, pp. 138–56. Boston: Boston University Scholarly Publications, 2000. 11 bw illus.

Busch, Jason T. "Furniture Patronage in Antebellum Natchez." *Antiques* 157, no. 5 (May 2000): 804–13. 19 color and 1 bw illus.

Butler, Jon. *Becoming America: The Revolution Before 1776.* Cambridge: Harvard University Press, 2000. x + 324 pp.; bw illus., index. (Some references to furniture in chapter entitled "Things Material.")

[Carpenter, Art]. "A Master in Wood." *Woodwork,* no. 57 (June 1999): 16. 3 color illus. (Exhibition notice.)

Carpenter, Arthur Espenet. "Memoir." In *Furniture Studio: The Heart of the Functional Arts,* edited by John Kelsey and Rick Mastelli, pp. 43–49. Free Union, Va.: Furniture Society, 1999. Color and bw illus.

Cathers, David. *Stickley Style: Arts and Crafts Homes in the Craftsman Tradition.* New York: Simon and Schuster, 1999. 224 pp.

"A Chair 'Fit for a King.'" *Antiques and the Arts Weekly* (August 4, 2000): 100. 1 bw illus.

Cheney, Robert C. "Roxbury Eight-Day Movements and the English Connection, 1785–1825." *Antiques* 157, no. 4 (April 2000): 606–15. 14 color illus.

[Christie's]. *The Barbra Streisand Collection: Important American Arts & Crafts, Architectural Designs, Art Nouveau, and Works by Louis Comfort Tiffany.* New York: Christie's, November 29, 1999. Sale 9296. 195 pp.; numerous color and bw illus.

[Christie's]. *The Joseph and Bathsheba Pope Valuables Cabinet.* New York: Christie's, January 21, 2000. Sale 9426. 60 pp.; color illus., appendixes, bibliography. (Includes Robert F. Trent, "The Joseph and Bathsheba Pope Cabinet and the Symonds Shop," pp. 18–21.)

Churchill, Edwin A., and Thomas B. Johnson. "The Painted Furniture of Maine." *Antiques* 157, no. 5 (May 2000): 778–87. 13 color and 1 bw illus.

Clark, Paul, and Julian Freeman. *Design: A Crash Course.* New York: Watson-Guptill, 2000. 144 pp.; 400 color illus., glossary, index.

"The Clocks of George McFadden at the Museum of Our National Heritage." *Antiques and the Arts Weekly* (June 16, 2000): 28. 1 bw illus.

"Collecting, With a Maker's Eye." In *Furniture Studio: The Heart of the Functional Arts,* edited by John Kelsey and Rick Mastelli, pp. 85–93. Free Union, Va.: Furniture Society, 1999. Color illus. (Re collection of Garry and Sylvia Bennett.)

[Concord (Massachusetts) Museum]. "Keeping Time: Clockmaking in Concord, 1790–1835." *Concord Museum Newsletter* (Summer 2000): 1, 7. 2 bw illus.

[Concord (Massachusetts) Museum]. "A New Acquisition." *Concord Museum Newsletter* (Fall 1999): 1, 6. 1 bw illus. (Re Boston-made side chair, 1750–65, owned in Concord in the eighteenth century.)

Connell, James E. *The Charlton Standard Catalogue of Canadian Clocks.* Toronto: Charlton Press, 1999. 136 pp.; illus.

Connell, Martha Stamm. *Celebrating the Creative Spirit: Contemporary Southeastern Furniture: An Exhibition of Artist-Made Furniture.* Mobile, Ala.: Mobile Museum of Art, 1998. 62 pp.; color and bw illus.

Connors, Michael. "Danish West Indian Furniture." *Antiques* 156, no. 3 (September 1999): 338–47. 20 color illus.

Conradsen, David H. *Useful Beauty: Early American Decorative Arts from St. Louis Collections.* St. Louis: St. Louis Art Museum, 1999. 100 pp.; illus.

Conran, Sebastian, and Mark Bond. *Soma Basics: Furniture.* San Francisco: Soma Books, 2000. 128 pp.; color illus., index.

Cooke, Edward S., Jr. "Introduction: Defining the Field." In *Furniture Studio: The Heart of the Functional Arts,* edited by John Kelsey and Rick Mastelli, pp. 8–11. Free Union, Va.: Furniture Society, 1999. 6 color illus.

Cooper, Wendy A., and Tara L. Gleason. "A Different Rhode Island Block-and-Shell Story: Providence Provenances and Pitch-Pediments." *American Furniture 1999,* pp. 162–208. 60 color and bw illus.

[Cooper-Hewitt Museum]. "The Work of Charles and Ray Eames Opens October 12 at Cooper-Hewitt." *Antiques and the Arts Weekly* (September 24, 1999): 123.

Cotton, Bernard D. Review of Ronald L. Hurst and Jonathan Prown, *Southern Furniture, 1680–1830: The Colonial Williamsburg Collection.* In *Regional Furniture Society Newsletter,* no. 31 (Winter 1999/2000): 5–7. 7 bw illus.

"The Country Seat: A Cast-Iron Success Story." *Maine Antique Digest* 28, no. 9 (September 2000): 39A. 4 bw illus.

[Craftsman Farms Foundation]. "Stickley Museum Collection Grows by Three Buildings and 13 Stickley Pieces." *Antiques and the Arts Weekly* (January 14, 2000): 66. (See also *Maine Antique Digest* 28, no. 2 [February 2000]: 7A.)

[Crosby, Wesley]. "Portfolio: Wesley Crosby." *American Craft* 59, no. 5 (October/November 1999): 89. 2 color illus. (Re contemporary furniture maker.)

*Defining Craft 1: Collecting for the New Millenium.* New York: American Craft Museum, 2000. 151 pp.; numerous color illus., bibliography, index. (Includes some furniture, and essays by David Revere McFadden and Ursula Ilse-Neuman.)

*Dunbar: Fine Furniture of the 1950s.* Atglen, Pa.: Schiffer Publishing, 2000. 212 pp.; numerous bw illus.

Dunnigan, John. "Understanding Furniture." In *Furniture Studio: The Heart of the Functional Arts,* edited by John Kelsey and Rick Mastelli, pp. 12–23. Free Union, Va.: Furniture Society, 1999. 20 color illus.

Edwards, Holly, et al. *Noble Dreams, Wicked Pleasures: Orientalism in America, 1870–1930.* Princeton, N.J.: Princeton University Press in association with the Sterling and Francine Clark Art Institute, 2000. xiii + 242 pp.; numerous color and bw illus., bibliography, index. (A few references to furniture.)

Emlen, Robert P. "Shaker Furniture and Shaker Architecture in Enfield, New Hampshire: Reconstructing Material Life in Form, Time, and Place." In *Rural New England Furniture: People, Place, and Production,* edited by Peter Benes, pp. 191–208. Boston: Boston University Scholarly Publications, 2000. 11 bw illus.

"Euclidean Gestures: The Architectural Furniture of E. Weinberger and S. Schmidt." *Antiques and the Arts Weekly* (October 15, 1999): 8.

Evans, Nancy Goyne. "Politics, Enterprise, and Design: The Nature and Influence of Windsor Chairmaking in Early Federal Rhode Island." *American Furniture 1999,* pp. 48–77. 28 bw illus.

"Exploring Newbury and Newburyport Furniture." *SPNEA Newsletter,* series 78 (spring 2000): 1–2. 5 color illus.

Feld, Stuart P., with an introductory essay by Page Talbott. *Boston in the Age of Neo-classicism, 1810–1840.* New York: Hirschl and Adler Galleries, 1999. 144 pp.; numerous color and bw illus., bibliography.

Fiell, Charlotte, and Peter Fiell, eds. *Decorative Arts 50s: A Source Book.* New York: Taschen, 2000. 575 pp.; numerous color and bw illus., index.

Fiell, Charlotte, and Peter Fiell, eds. *Decorative Arts 60s: A Source Book.* New York: Taschen, 2000. 575 pp.; numerous color and bw illus., index.

Fiell, Charlotte, and Peter Fiell, eds. *Decorative Arts 70s: A Source Book.* New York: Taschen, 2000. 575 pp.; numerous color and bw illus., index.

Fish, Marilyn. *Gustav Stickley: Heritage and Early Years.* North Caldwell, N.J.: Little Pond Press. 1998. 36 pp.

Fish, Marilyn. *Gustav Stickley: 1884–1900.* North Caldwell, N.J.: Little Pond Press. 1999. 56 pp.

Foote, Timothy. "Washington Slept Here." *Smithsonian* 30, no. 9 (December 1999): 36+. 3 color illus.

[Ford, Richard]. "Portfolio: Richard Ford." *American Craft* 59 (August–September 1999): 69. 2 color illus. (Re contemporary furniture maker.)

Fox, Robert, and Anthony Turner, eds. *Luxury Trades and Consumerism in Ancien Régime Paris: Studies in the History of the Skilled Workforce.* Aldershot, Hampshire, England: Ashgate Publishing, 1998. 360 pp.

Frelinghuysen, Alice Cooney. "Emily Johnston de Forest." *Antiques* 157, no. 1 (June 2000): 192–97. 10 color and 3 bw illus.

*Furniture History* 35 (1999): 1–172. Numerous color and bw illus.

*Furniture Society* [newsletter] 3, no. 2 (October 1999): 1–12. bw illus.

[Furniture Society]. *The Furniture Society 1999 Conference Program/Resource Directory.* Free Union, Va.: Furniture Society, 1999. 208 pp., index.

"Gallery." *Woodwork,* no. 56 (April 1999): 48–53. 14 color illus. (Re contemporary objects by Michael Schultz, Anne Shutan, Dolly Spragins, and others.)

"Gallery." *Woodwork,* no. 57 (June 1999): 44–49. 11 color illus. (Re contemporary furniture by Kelly Stockton of Bow, Washington, and the Minnesota Woodworkers Guild of Minneapolis.)

"Gallery." *Woodwork,* no. 59 (October 1999): 42–49. 24 color illus. (Re contemporary furniture and woodwork by various makers.)

"Gallery." *Woodwork,* no. 60 (December 1999): 24–27. 14 color illus. (Re contemporary furniture and woodwork by various makers.)

"Gallery." *Woodwork,* no. 61 (February 2000): 57–61. 16 color illus. (Re contemporary furniture and woodwork by various makers.)

"Gallery." *Woodwork,* no. 62 (April 2000): 36–42. 24 color illus. (Re contemporary furniture and woodwork by various makers.)

"Gallery." *Woodwork,* no. 63 (Junel 2000): 42–47. 22 color illus. (Re contemporary furniture and woodwork by various makers.)

"Gallery of Studio Furniture: Juried Work from Members of the Furniture Society." In *Furniture Studio: The Heart of the Functional Arts,* edited by John Kelsey and Rick Mastelli, pp. 24–31, 50–57, 94–101. Free Union, Va.: Furniture Society, 1999. Numerous color illus.

Garrett, Wendell. Editorial. *Antiques* 157, no. 5 (May 2000): 759. 1 color illus.

Gelertner, Mark. *A History of American Architecture: Buildings in Their Cultural and Technological Context.* Hanover, N.H., and London: University Press of New England, 1999. xxii + 346 pp.; 298 bw illus., maps, line drawings, glossary, bibliography, index.

Gilborn, Craig. *Adirondack Camps: Homes Away from Home, 1850–1950.* Syracuse, N.Y.: Syracuse University Press, 2000. 352 pp.; 16 color and 311 bw illus., appendixes, bibliography, index. Copublished with the Adirondack Museum.

Gladwell, Brian. "Putting it Together." In *Furniture Studio: The Heart of the Functional Arts,* edited by John Kelsey and Rick Mastelli, pp. 119–25. Free Union, Va.: Furniture Society, 1999. Color illus.

Gomez-Ibanez, Miguel. "Antiques of Tomorrow" (exhibition review). In *Furniture Studio: The Heart of the Functional Arts,* edited by John Kelsey and Rick Mastelli, pp. 139–41. Free Union, Va.: Furniture Society, 1999. 3 color and 1 bw illus.

Gordon, Glenn. "Three Shows in Chicago." *Woodwork,* no. 58 (August 1999): 50–55. 12 color illus.

Green, Nancy E., et al. *Arthur Wesley Dow (1857–1922): His Art and His Influence.* New York: Spanierman Gallery, 1999. 272 pp.; numerous color and bw illus., chronology, index. (Includes some arts and crafts furniture.)

Gustafson, Eleanor H. "Museum Accessions." *Antiques* 157, no. 1 (January 2000): 42. 4 color illus. (Re acquisitions by the Metropolitan Museum of Art.)

Gustafson, Eleanor H. "Museum Accessions." *Antiques* 157, no. 5 (May 2000): 684. 4 color illus. (Re furniture acquisitions by four museums.)

Gustafson, Eleanor H., ed. "Collectors' Notes." *Antiques* 156, no. 2 (August 1999): 142–44. 2 color and 4 bw illus. (Re comments by Ulysses Dietz concerning the attribution of Victorian furniture to either John Jeliff and Co. or the firm of M. and H. Schrenkeisen.)

Hance, Dawn D. "Rutland's Early Clockmakers Lord and Goddard." *NAWCC Bulletin* 41, no. 4 (August 1999): 485–91. 11 bw illus., bibliography.

Harrod, Tanya. *The Crafts in Britain in the Twentieth Century.* New Haven: Yale University Press in association with the Bard Center for Graduate Studies in the Decorative Arts, New York, 1999. 496 pp.; 222 color and 284 bw illus., index.

Harwood, Barry R. Review of Christian G. Carron, et al., *Grand Rapids Furniture: The Story of America's Furniture City.* In *American Furniture 1999,* pp. 282–88.

Hawkins, David. *Close Encounters with Antique Furniture: A Restorer's Story.* Traverse City, Mich.: Rhodes & Easton, Sage Creek Press, 1999. 180 pp.; illus.

Hays, John, and Martha Willoughby. "In Perfect Form." *Christie's Magazine* 16, no. 7 (September/October 1999): 116–19. 3 color illus., line drawing.

Headley, Mack. "Eighteenth-Century Cabinet Shops and the Furniture-Making Trades in Newport, Rhode Island." *American Furniture 1999,* pp. 17–47. 23 color and bw illus., appendix.

[Headley-Whitney Museum, Lexington, Kentucky]. "Inlaid Kentucky Furniture Exhibition in February at Headley-Whitney Museum." *Antiques and the Arts Weekly* (January 21, 2000): 73.

Heckscher, Morrison H. "Natalie K. Blair's 'Museum Rooms' and the American Wing." *Antiques* 157, no. 1 (January 2000): 182–85. 8 color and 1 bw illus.

Hershey, Connie. "Birdcages and Pad Feet: Walnut Tea Tables from Southeastern Pennsylvania." In *Boxes, Vessels, & Spuns: Trappings and Trimmings for Tea* (catalogue of the eighteenth annual Chester County Historical Society antiques show), pp. 18–21. West Chester, Pa.: Chester County Historical Society, 2000. 4 bw illus., bibliography.

"Herter Brothers Meet Norman Bates." *Maine Antique Digest* 28, no. 3 (March 2000): 11A. 2 bw illus.

Hession, Jane King, Rip Rapson, and Bruce N. Wright. *Ralph Rapson: Sixty Years of Modern Design.* Afton, Minn.: Afton Historical Society Press, 1999. 235 pp.; numerous bw illus.

Hewett, David. "The 1999 Edition of *American Furniture*" (book review). In *Maine Antique Digest* 28, no. 6 (June 2000): 22D. 1 bw illus.

Hewett, David. Review of John Obbard, *Early American Furniture: A Practical Guide for Collectors.* In *Maine Antique Digest* 28, no. 5 (May 2000): 22D. 1 bw illus.

[Historic Deerfield]. "Historic Deerfield Acquires Hurst Collection." *Antiques and the Arts Weekly* (January 28, 2000): 75. 2 bw illus.

Holmes, Roger. "From a Distance." In *Furniture Studio: The Heart of the Functional Arts,* edited by John Kelsey and Rick Mastelli, pp. 58–67. Free Union, Va.: Furniture Society, 1999. Color and bw illus.

Hunting, Mary Anne. "Living with Antiques: Rosemary Lodge in Water Mill, New York." *Antiques* 158, no. 1 (July 2000): 104–113. 15 color and 8 bw illus.

Hurst, Ronald L. "Refurnishing the Randolph House . . . Again?" *The Colonial Williamsburg Interpreter* 20, no. 3 (special edition 1999): 37–42. 7 color and bw illus.

Hurst, Ronald L. "Retrieving the Past from the Peyton Randolph House." *Colonial Williamsburg* 21, no. 6 (December 1999/January 2000): 10–17. 14 color illus.

Israel, Barbara. *Antique Garden Ornament: Two Centuries of American Taste.* New York: Harry N. Abrams, 1999. 256 pp.; numerous color and bw illus., catalogue, appendixes, bibliography, index.

"It's Not All Wood." In *Furniture Studio: The Heart of the Functional Arts,* edited by John Kelsey and Rick Mastelli, pp. 102–9. Free Union, Va.: Furniture Society, 1999. Color illus.

Jaffee, David P. "Artisan-Entrepreneurs in Worcester County, Massachusetts." In *Rural New England Furniture: People, Place, and Production,* ed. Peter Benes, pp. 100–18. Boston: Boston University Scholarly Publications, 2000. 8 bw illus.

Jaffee, David P. *People of the Wachusett: Greater New England in History and Memory, 1630–1830.* Ithaca, N.Y.: Cornell University Press, 2000. xiii + 360 pp.; 21 maps, 2 figures, 13 bw illus., 7 tables, bibliography, index. (Some references to rural furniture.)

Johnson, J. Stewart. *American Modern, 1925–1940: Design for a New Age.* New York: Harry N. Abrams in association with the American Federation of Arts, 2000. 192 pp.; 142 color and 30 bw illus., checklist, biographies, glossary, bibliography, index.

Johnson, Kathleen Eagen. "Cross Roads and Cross Rivers: Diversity in Colonial New York." *Antiques and the Arts Weekly* (November 26, 1999): 1, 68–70C. 16 bw illus.

"The Joseph and Bathsheba Pope Valuables Cabinet." *Maine Antique Digest* 28, no. 3 (March 2000): 38D. 1 bw illus.

Kane, Patricia E. "The Palladian Style in Rhode Island Furniture: Fly Tea Tables." *American Furniture 1999,* pp. 1–16. 15 color and bw illus.

Kaplan, Wendy. "The Simple Life: The Arts and Crafts Movement in Great

Britain." *Antiques* 156, no. 4 (October 1999): 476–83. 13 color and 1 bw illus.

Keno, Leslie, and John Nye. "American Heirlooms." *Sotheby's Preview* 12, no. 1 (January 2000): 56–59. 4 color illus.

Kelsey, John, and Rick Mastelli. *Furniture Studio: The Heart of the Functional Arts*. Free Union, Va.: Furniture Society, 1999. 144 pp.; numerous color and bw illus., index.

Kenny, Peter M. "R. T. H. Halsey: American Wing Founder and Champion of Duncan Phyfe." *Antiques* 157, no. 1 (January 2000): 186–91. 9 color and 2 bw illus.

Kirsch, Francine. "The Americanization of Marquetry." *Woodwork*, no. 57 (June 1999): 50–59. 13 color illus.

Komanecky, Michael. "Augsburg Collectors' Cabinets." *Antiques* 156, no. 2 (August 1999): 176–83. 13 color illus.

Krashes, David. "The South Shaftsbury, Vermont, Painted Wooden Chests." In *Rural New England Furniture: People, Place, and Production*, ed. Peter Benes, pp. 226–35. Boston: Boston University Scholarly Publications, 2000. 10 bw illus.

Kronick, Richard L. Exhibition review of "Ralph Rapson: Sixty Years of Modern Design," Minneapolis Institute of Arts, 27 March–23 May 1999. In *Journal of the Society of Architectural Historians* 59, no. 1 (March 2000): 100–103.

Langsner, Drew. Review of John Alexander, "Make a Chair from a Tree" (video). In *Woodwork*, no. 63 (June 2000): 18. 1 color illus.

Lavine, John. "Some Thoughts on Collecting." *Woodwork*, no. 58 (August 1999): 68–71. 10 color illus.

Ledes, Allison Eckardt. "Current and Coming: American Clocks." *Antiques* 157, no. 4 (April 2000): 524, 528. 2 color illus.

Ledes, Allison Eckardt. "Current and Coming: American Orientalism." *Antiques* 157, no. 6 (June 2000): 846. 2 color illus.

Ledes, Allison Eckardt. "Current and Coming: The Gothic Revival in England and America." *Antiques* 157, no. 5 (May 2000): 672, 674. 2 color illus.

Ledes, Allison Eckardt. "Current and Coming: Neoclassical Boston." *Antiques* 156, no. 6 (December 1999): 766, 768, 770. 1 color illus. (Re exhibition at Hirschl and Adler Galleries in New York City.)

Ledes, Allison Eckardt. "Current and Coming: Newbury and Newburyport Furniture." *Antiques* 157, no. 6 (June 2000): 850, 852. 3 color illus.

Ledes, Allison Eckardt. "Current and Coming: Sitting Revolutionized." *Antiques* 156, no. 4 (October 1999): 388, 390. 3 color illus. (Re exhibition of the work of Charles and Ray Eames at the Cooper-Hewitt Museum.)

Lefrançois, Thierry. "The Musée du Nouveau Monde in New Rochelle, France." *Antiques* 157, no. 3 (March 2000): 438–47. 15 color illus.

Leier, Ray, Jan Peters, and Kevin Wallace. *Contemporary Turned Wood: New Perspectives in a Rich Tradition*. 128 pp.; numerous color illus. Madison, Wis.: Hand Books Press, 1999. Distributed by Popular Woodworking Books, Cincinnati, Ohio.

Lindsey, Jack L. "Art, Science, and Patronage in Early Philadelphia." *Antiques* 156, no. 4 (October 1999): 492–99. 16 color illus.

Lindsey, Jack L., with essays by Richard S. Dunn, Edward C. Carter II, and Richard Saunders. *Worldly Goods: The Arts of Early Pennsylvania, 1680–1758*. Philadelphia: Philadelphia Museum of Art, 1999. xxii + 266 pp.; 506 color and bw illus., checklist, appendixes, bibliography, index.

Little, Nina Fletcher. *Country Arts in Early American Homes*. 1975. Reprint, Boston: Society for the Preservation of New England Antiquities, 1999. xviii + 221 pp; 20 color and 190 bw illus., index. (With a new foreword by Wendell D. Garrett.)

*Living with Form: The Horn Collection of Contemporary Crafts*. Little Rock, Ark.: Bradley Publishing in cooperation with the Arkansas Art Center, 1999. vii + 215 pp.; numerous color illus., catalogue, bibliography, index.

Locklair, Paula. "New in the MESDA Collection." *The Luminary* (Newsletter of the Museum of Early Southern Decorative Arts) 21, no. 1 (Spring 2000): 6–8. 7 bw illus. (Includes worktable, ca. 1800, from Athens, Georgia; side chairs, 1735–45, from Virginia; pembroke table, 1785–95, from Charleston, South Carolina; and other furniture.)

[Los Angeles County Museum of Art]. "LACMA Exhibition to Explore the Career and Work of Charles and Ray Eames." *Antiques and the Arts Weekly* (June 23, 2000): 40. 3 bw illus.

Lovell, Margaretta M. Review of Philip Zea, *Useful Improvements, Innumerable Temptations: Pursuing Refinement in Rural New England, 1750–1850*. In *American Furniture 1999*, pp. 276–80.

[Lyman Allyn Museum]. "Lyman Allyn Acquires Rare Side Chair." *Maine Antique Digest* 27, no. 11 (November 1999): 10A. 1 bw illus.

McFadden, Tom. "Two Shows on the Northcoast." *Woodwork*, no. 60 (December 1999): 54–59. 24 color illus.

McInnis, Maurie D., et al. *In Pursuit of Refinement: Charlestonians Abroad, 1740–1860*. Columbia: University of South Carolina Press, 1999. xix + 352 pp.; numerous color and bw illus., bibliography, index.

[McKie, Judy Kensley]. *The Furniture Art of Judy Kensley McKie, August 11–September 18, 2000*. East Hampton, N.Y.: Pritam & Eames, 2000. Unpaged; color illus., bibliography. (Includes short essay by Michael W. Monroe.)

Maddex, Diane. *50 Favorite Furnishings by Frank Lloyd Wright*. New York: Smithmark, 1999. 128 pp.; numerous color and bw illus., bibliography, index.

"Margolis: A Family of Furniture Makers." *Maine Antique Digest* 28, no. 6 (June 2000): 4D. 4 bw illus.

Marshall, Jason. "Restoration Debate: The Conservator's Point of View." *Woodwork*, no. 61 (February 2000): 62–67. 10 color illus.

Martin, Ann Smart. *Makers and Users: American Decorative Arts, 1630–1820, from the Chipstone Collection*. Madison, Wis.: Elvehjem Museum of Art, University of Wisconsin–Madison, 1999. 71 pp.; 16 color and 126 bw illus., index.

Martin, Loy D. "A Critical Discourse: Tradition and Continuity." *Woodwork*, no. 61 (February 2000): 72–76, 12 color illus.

Martin, Loy D. "Embedded Energies." In *Furniture Studio: The Heart of the Functional Arts,* edited by John Kelsey and Rick Mastelli, pp. 76–84. Free Union, Va.: Furniture Society, 1999. Color illus. (Re collection of Dorothy and George Saxe.)

Martin, Terry. "Gentle Strength: The Work of Betty Scarpino." *Woodwork*, no. 61 (February 2000): 24–30. 17 color illus.

Matheson, Susan. *Modern Gothic: The Revival of Medieval Art.* New Haven: Yale University Art Gallery, 2000.

May, Stephen, "Picturing Old New England: Image and Memory." *Antiques and the Arts Weekly* (August 20, 1999): 1, 68–69. 18 bw illus.

Mayer, Lance, and Susan Schoelwer. "Colorful Survivors." *Antiques and the Arts Weekly* (October 15, 1999): 1, 68–69. 6 bw illus.

Meiland, David. "Miles Karpilow: A Craftsman's Journey." *Woodwork*, no. 60 (December 1999): 28–37. 25 color and 7 bw illus.

[Metropolitan Museum of Art]. "The American Wing, Metropolitan Museum of Art: 75 Years." *Antiques* 157, no. 1 (January 2000): 168–233. Numerous color and bw illus. (Special issue with eleven articles, several of which are cited elsewhere.)

[Metropolitan Museum of Art]. "The Metropolitan Museum of Art Celebrates the American Wing." *Antiques and the Arts Weekly* (December 10, 1999): 65. 3 bw illus.

[Metropolitan Museum of Art]. "Recent Acquisitions: A Selection, 1998–1999." *Metropolitan Museum of Art Bulletin* 57, no. 2 (Fall 1999): 50+. (Includes some furniture.)

"Million-Dollar American Furniture Auction Prices." *Maine Antique Digest* 28, no. 2 (February 2000): 10A.

[Milwaukee Art Museum]. "Boston Tea Table/Walnut Desk Added to Milwaukee Art Museum's Collection." *Antiques and the Arts Weekly* (May 12, 2000): 92.

Moore, C. Eugene. *Inspiring Interiors 1950s: From Armstrong.* Atglen, Pa.: Schiffer Publishing, 1999. 160 pp.; 253 color illus.

Morley, John. *The History of Furniture: Twenty-Five Centuries of Style and Design in the Western Tradition.* Boston: Little, Brown, and Co., A Bulfinch Press Book, 1999. 352 pp.; 173 color and 507 bw illus., bibliography, index.

Morrison, Jasper, ed. *International Design Yearbook 14.* New York: Abbeville Press, 1999. 232 pp.; numerous color illus., biographies.

Moure, Nancy Dustin Wall. *California Art: 450 Years of Painting and Other Media.* Los Angeles: Dustin Publications, 1998. 560 pp.; 475+ color illus., 45 bw illus., timeline, bibliography, index. (Includes some California furniture.)

[Mount Vernon]. "Mount Vernon Acquires Chair from Washington's Mansion." *Antiques and the Arts Weekly* (April 14, 2000): 10.

Murdoch, Tessa. Review of Christopher Gilbert, *Furniture at Temple Newsam House and Lotherton Hall,* vol. 3. In *Studies in the Decorative Arts* 7, no. 1 (fall–winter 1999–2000): 114–17.

"Museum of Early Trades and Crafts Opens Timepiece Exhibit." *Antiques and the Arts Weekly* (June 16, 2000): 60.

Naeve, Milo M. "Keys for Collectors and Connoisseurs: The A, B, C, Ds." In *SOFA New York: Sculpture, Objects, and Functional Art,* pp. 26–31. New York: Expressions of Culture, Inc., 2000. 4 color and 1 bw illus. (See also *Decorative Arts Society Newsletter* 8, no. 2 [Summer 2000]: 6–9.)

Nasstrom, Heidi. Review of Anna Tobin D'Ambrosio, ed., *Masterpieces of American Furniture from the Munson-Williams-Proctor Institute.* In *American Furniture 1999,* pp. 293–300.

[National Museum of American History]. "National Museum of American History Receives Ellicott Family Tall Clock." *Antiques and the Arts Weekly* (January 7, 2000): 16.

Nelson, Robert E., ed. *Directory of American Toolmakers: A Listing of Identified Makers of Tools Who Worked in Canada and the United States before 1900.* South Dartmouth, Mass.: Early American Industries Association, 1999. 1,184 pp.

[New Hampshire Historical Society]. "Furniture Show Opens at New Hampshire Historical." *Antiques and the Arts Weekly* (August 13, 1999): 92O. (Re exhibition of contemporary furniture.)

Nelson, Susan S. "Capt. Abraham Knowlton, Joiner, and the Seminal Woodworkers of Ipswich, Massachusetts." In *Rural New England Furniture: People, Place, and Production,* edited by Peter Benes, pp. 42–59. Boston: Boston University Scholarly Publications, 2000. 8 bw illus.

"New Hampshire Furniture Masters Plan Exhibit/Auction." *Antique and the Arts Weekly* (June 9, 2000): 21. 1 bw illus.

Nylander, Jane C., with Diane L. Viera. *Windows on the Past: Four Centuries of New England Homes.* Boston: Bulfinch Press/ Little Brown, and Company, 2000. 208 pp.; 220 color and 38 bw illus., bibliography, index.

Obbard, John. *Early American Furniture: A Practical Guide for Collectors.* Paducah, Ky.: Collector Books, 2000. 335 pp.; numerous line drawings, bibliography.

Oda, Noritsugu. *Danish Chairs.* San Francisco: Chronicle Books, 1999. 224 pp.; illus.

Ola, Per, and Emily D'Aulaire. "Taking the Measure of Time." *Smithsonian* 30, no. 9 (December 1999): 52+. 19 color illus. (See, especially, the Joseph Ellicott tall clock recently acquired by the National Museum of American History.)

Oughton, Frederick. *Grinling Gibbons and the English Woodcarving Tradition.* Fresno, Cal.: Linden Publishing Co., 1999. 224 pp.; illus.

Pacey, Arnold. *Meaning in Technology.* Cambridge, Mass.: MIT Press, 1999. viii + 264 pp.; 3 illus., bibliography.

Patton, Sharon F. *African-American Art.* Oxford History of Art. New York: Oxford University Press, 1998. 319 pp.; 133 color and bw illus., bibliography, timeline, index.

[Peabody Essex Museum]. "Museum Acquires an Important Seventeenth-

Century American Cabinet." *Peabody Essex Museum* (May/June 2000): 20. 2 color illus.

[Peabody Essex Museum]. "Museum Claims Tiny Treasure." *Antiques and the Arts Weekly* (January 28, 2000): 67. 1 bw illus. (Re Salem valuables cabinet of 1679.)

Peck, Amelia. "Robert de Forest and the Founding of the American Wing." *Antiques* 157, no. 1 (January 2000): 176–81. 1 color and 7 bw illus.

Peirce, Donald C. *Art & Enterprise: American Decorative Art, 1825–1917, The Virginia Carroll Crawford Collection.* Atlanta, Ga.: High Museum of Art in association with Antique Collectors' Club, 1999. 411 pp.; 235 color and 247 bw illus., glossary, bibliography, index.

Petroski, Henry. *The Book on the Bookshelf.* New York: Alfred A. Knopf, 1999. x + 290 pp., numerous bw illus., appendix, bibliography, index.

Pierce, Kelly. "Joe Leonard: Into the Future, Looking Back." *Woodwork*, no. 56 (April 1999): 20–29. 11 color illus.

Pierce, Kelly. "Mark Arnold: Revisiting the Golden Age of American Furniture." *Woodwork*, no. 58 (August 1999): 22–30. 13 color illus.

*Postprints of the Wooden Artifacts Group, Presented at the 26th Annual Meeting of the American Institute for Conservation, Alexandria, Virginia, June 1998.* N.p.: Wooden Artifacts Group, American Institute for Conservation, [1999]. 59 pp.; bw illus., index to WAG articles by author, 1986–98. (Anthology of eight articles; see especially David Bayne, "Painted Rush Seats"; Pamela Kirschner, "Frank Lloyd Wright Furniture: A Technical Study of Objects from the Darwin Martin House"; Harry A. Alden, "Scientific Limitations of Microscopic Wood Analysis of *objets d'art*.")

Prown, Jonathan. "Introduction." *American Furniture 1999*, pp. xi–xiii.

Rachlin, Harvey. *Jumbo's Hide, Elvis's Ride, and the Tooth of Buddha: More Marvelous Tales of Historic Artifacts.* New York: Henry Holt and Co., 2000. xi + 372 pp.; bw illus., bibliography, index. (Includes brief chapters on John Folwell's "rising sun" Chippendale-style chair at Independence Hall and U. S. Grant's brass smoking stand.)

*Regional Furniture: The Journal of the Regional Furniture Society* 13 (1999): 1–122. Numerous bw illus.

*Regional Furniture Society Newsletter*, no. 31 (Winter 1999/2000): 1–17. bw illus.

Roberts, Derek. *Mystery, Novelty, and Fantasy Clocks.* Atglen, Pa.: Schiffer Publishing, 1999. 288 pp.; illus.

Roberts, Margaret. "Northern Forms: The Scots in America, by Mary Ann Apicella." *Regional Furniture Society Newsletter*, no. 31 (Winter 1999/2000): 15.

Rodermann, Patricia A. *Patterns in Interior Environments: Perception, Psychology, and Practice.* New York: John Wiley, 1999. 253 pp.; 4 color and 150 bw illus., bibliography, index.

Rouland, Steven, and Linda Rouland. *Knoll Furniture: 1938–1960.* Atglen, Pa.: Schiffer Books, 1999. 160 pp.; 271 color and bw illus.

[Sack, Harold]. "Harold Sack, Expert on American Furniture, Dies." *Antiques and the Arts Weekly* (July 14, 2000): 66. 2 bw illus.

[Sack, Harold]. "Harold Sack." *Antiques and the Arts Weekly* (July 21, 2000): 1, 68–71. 7 bw illus.

[Sack, Harold]. "Harold Sack." *Maine Antique Digest* 28, no. 8 (August 2000): 3A–4A. 1 bw illus.

Safford, Frances Gruber. "The Hudson-Fulton Exhibition and H. Eugene Bolles." *Antiques* 157, no. 1 (January 2000): 170–75. 5 color and 6 bw illus.

Sardar, Zahid. *San Francisco Modern: Interiors, Architecture, and Design.* San Francisco: Chronicle Books, 1998. 204 pp.; illus.

Sassone, Adriana Boidi, et al. *Furniture: From Rococo to Art Deco.* Koln: Benedikt Taschen Verlag, 2000. 815 pp.; 1,300+ color and bw illus., appendix, glossary, bibliography, index.

Schimmelman, Janice. *Architectural Books in Early America: Architectural Treatises and Building Handbooks Available in American Libraries and Bookstores through 1800.* 1985. 2d rev. ed, New Castle, Del.: Oak Knoll Press, 1999. 235 pp.

"Seated in Style at Drake University." *Antiques and the Arts Weekly* (October 15, 1999): 36.

"Shaker Chair Exhibition at Shaker Museum." *Antiques and the Arts Weekly* (August 20, 1999): 63.

Siegel, Kathran. "A Bridge Between Art and Life" (exhibition review). In *Furniture Studio: The Heart of the Functional Arts*, edited by John Kelsey and Rick Mastelli, pp. 136–38. Free Union, Va.: Furniture Society, 1999. 7 color illus.

[Simpson, Tommy]. "Installation By Tommy Simpson at the American Craft Museum." *Antiques and the Arts Weekly* (July 28, 2000): 104–I. 1 bw illus.

Simpson, Tommy. *Two Looks to Home: The Art of Tommy Simpson.* Introduction by Pam Koob. A Bulfinch Press Book. Boston: Little, Brown and Company, 1999. 166 pp.; numerous color illus.

[Skiles, Munder]. "Reinventing the Garden Seat: John Danzer Shows Off Munder Skiles." *Antiques and the Arts Weekly* (June 16, 2000): 40. 2 bw illus.

Smith, Robert. "Adventures at the Edge: The Work of Peter Maynard." *Woodwork*, no. 62 (April 2000: 24–31. 21 color illus.

[Society for the Preservation of New England Antiquities]. "A Model of Domestic Efficiency." *SPNEA* (Newsletter), series 76 (Fall 1999): 5. 1 color illus. (Re Hoosier cabinet at Castle Tucker.)

[Society for the Preservation of New England Antiquities]. "SPNEA Exhibits Newbury Furniture." *Antiques and the Arts Weekly* (April 21, 2000): 102. 4 bw illus.

"Society of American Period Furnituremakers." *Woodwork*, no. 59 (October 1999): 18–19. 2 color illus.

Solis-Cohen, Lita. "American Wing Celebrates 75 Years." *Maine Antique Digest* 27, no. 12 (December 1999): 8A. 1 bw illus.

Solis-Cohen, Lita. "Boston in the Age of Neoclassicism." *Maine Antique Digest* 28, no. 1 (January 20000): 8A. 2 bw illus.

Solis-Cohen, Lita. "Rare Pembroke Table Sold by Sack." *Maine Antique*

*Digest* 28, no. 3 (March 2000): 9A. 2 bw illus.

Solis-Cohen, Lita. "That Classy Classical Style." *Maine Antique Digest* 28, no. 9 (September 2000): 10A.

Solis-Cohen, Lita. "Worldly Goods: The Arts of Early Pennsylvania." *Maine Antique Digest* 27, no. 10 (October 1999): 11A. 1 bw illus.

Soros, Susan Weber. *The Secular Furniture of E.W. Godwin with Catalogue Raisonné*. New Haven: Yale University Press in association with the Bard Graduate Center for Studies in the Decorative Arts, New York, 1999. 320 pp.; 240 color and 120 bw illus., appendix, bibliography, index.

Soros, Susan Weber, ed. *E.W. Godwin: Aesthetic Movement Architect and Designer*. New Haven: Yale University Press in association with the Bard Graduate Center for Studies in the Decorative Arts, New York, 1999. 400 pp.; 320 color and 80 bw illus.

Thomas, David C., and Peter Benes. "Amzi Chapin: A New England Cabinetmaker Singing and Working in the South and Trans-Appalachian West." In *Rural New England Furniture: People, Place, and Production*, ed. Peter Benes, pp. 76–99. Boston: Boston University Scholarly Publications, 2000. 8 bw illus.

Treadway Gallery. *The 1950s/Modern Price Guide: Furniture*. 2 vols. Cincinnati, Ohio: Treadway Gallery in association with the John Toomey Gallery of Oak Park, Illinois, 1999. 232 p.; illus. 242 pp.; illus.

"Treasure: The President's Grandfather." *Harvard Magazine* 102, no. 3 (January–February 2000): 112. 1 color illus. (Re clock collection at Harvard.)

Trent, Robert F. "Introduction." In *Rural New England Furniture: People, Place, and Production*, edited by Peter Benes, pp. 7–12. Boston: Boston University Scholarly Publications, 2000.

Trent, Robert F. "New Insights on Early Rhode Island Furniture." *American Furniture 1999*, pp. 209–23. 21 color and bw illus.

Trent, Robert F., and Peter Follansbee. "Repairs Versus Deception in Essex County Cupboards, 1830–1890." In *Rural New England Furniture: People, Place, and Production*, edited by Peter Benes, pp. 13–28. Boston: Boston University Scholarly Publications, 2000. 9 bw illus., glossary.

Updike, John. "Fun Furniture." In *More Matter: Essays and Criticism*, pp. 716–20. New York: Alfred A. Knopf, 1999. 2 bw illus. (Review of "New Handmade Furniture" exhibition at the Museum of Fine Arts, Boston; first published in *Art & Antiques*.)

Upton, Dell. *Architecture in the United States*. New York: Oxford University Press, 1998. 335 pp.; 189 color and bw illus., maps, timeline, bibliography, index. (The thematic approach of this volume—focusing on community, nature, technology, money, and art—may be of interest to historians of furniture.)

"Using Dolphins as a Decorative Motif." *Antiques and the Arts Weekly* (April 21, 2000): S10–S11. 2 bw illus.

[Virginia Museum of Fine Arts]. "Virginia MFA Announces New Acquisitions." *Antiques and the Arts Weekly* (April 7, 2000): 50. 4 bw illus. (Re a Philadelphia high chest, ca. 1745–50, and a ca. 1830 octagonal tilt-top table by Charles Koones of Alexandria, Virginia.)

[Virginia Museum of Fine Arts]. "Virginia MFA Announces New Acquisitions." *Antiques and the Arts Weekly* (July 7, 2000): 56. 1 bw illus. (Includes screen, 1881–82, by Louis Comfort Tiffany and Associates.)

Voorsanger, Catherine Hoover. "Collecting the Nineteenth Century for the American Wing." *Antiques* 157, no. 1 (January 2000): 198–203. 10 color and 1 bw illus.

[Wadsworth Atheneum]. "Recent Acquisitions . . ." *Newsletter of the Decorative Arts Society* 7, no. 2 (Fall 1999): 14. (Re Massachusetts chest, 1685–1705, branded GB and with initials EB, related to the Parmenter cupboard.)

Wahlberg, Holly. *1950s Plastic Design: Everyday Elegance*. Atglen, Pa.: Schiffer Publishing, 1999. 112 pp.; numerous color and bw illus., bibliography, index.

Walsh, Judith. "The Language of Flowers in Nineteenth-Century American Painting." *Antiques* 156, no. 4 (October 1999): 518–31. 15 color illus., table. (Contains detailed chart delineating the "[M]eanings in the language of flowers in America," citing various meanings given in period books and dictionaries, that will be of interest to historians of inlay and painted furniture.)

Ward, Gerald W. R. "'America's Contribution to Craftsmanship': The Exaltation and Interpretation of Newport Furniture." *American Furniture 1999*, pp. 224–48. 10 color and bw illus.

Ward, Gerald W. R., comp. "The Furniture of Rural New England: A Selected Bibliography." In *Rural New England Furniture: People, Place, and Production*, edited by Peter Benes, pp. 236–51. Boston: Boston University Scholarly Publications, 2000.

Ward, Gerald W. R., comp. "Recent Writing on American Furniture: A Bibliography." *American Furniture 1999*, pp. 301–310.

[Wenham (Massachusetts) Museum]. "Please Be Seated Furniture Exhibit at Wenham Museum January 22." *Antiques and the Arts Weekly* (January 14, 2000): 20.

West, James T. "John Winkley, New Hampshire Clockmaker." *NAWCC Bulletin* 41, no. 4 (August 1999): 437–51. 27 bw illus., 2 line drawings, table.

White, Frank G. "Sterling, Massachusetts: An Early-Nineteenth-Century Seat of Chairmaking." In *Rural New England Furniture: People, Place, and Production*, edited by Peter Benes, pp. 119–37. Boston: Boston University Scholarly Publications, 2000. 10 bw illus.

Wilhide, Elizabeth. *Living With Modern Classics: The Chair*. New York: Watson-Guptill, 2000. 80 pp.; 125 color illus.

Wilkie, Angus. "Barbra Streisand: The Passionate Collector." *Christie's Magazine* 16, no. 8 (November 1999): 58–65. 7 color and 1 bw illus.

Willoughby, Martha. "The Accounts of Job Townsend, Jr." *American Furniture 1999*, pp. 109–61. 9 color and 3 bw illus., 3 tables, 2 appendixes.

Willoughby, Martha. "Brave New World: The Story of the Joseph and Bathsheba Pope Valuables Cabinet." *Antiques and the Arts Weekly* (January 14, 2000): 42. 2 bw illus.

Wilson, Kristina. "Icons of High Modernism" (review of Paola Antonelli et al., *Sitting on the Edge: Modernist Design from the Collection of Michael and Gabrielle Boyd*). In *Furniture Studio: The Heart of the Functional Arts,* edited by John Kelsey and Rick Mastelli, pp. 134–35. Free Union, Va.: Furniture Society, 1999. 2 color illus.

Wilson, H. Weber. *Antique Hardware Price Guide.* Krause Publications, 1998. 230 pp.; 400+ color and bw illus.

[Winterthur Museum]. *Kids! 200 Years of Childhood.* Winterthur, Del.: Winterthur Museum, 1999. 34 pp.; color and bw illus. Distributed by University Press of New England, Hanover, N.H. and London.

[Winterthur Museum]. "Kids! 200 Years of Childhood: Winterthur Museum." *Antiques and the Arts Weekly* (July 30, 1999): 1, 76–78. 13 bw illus. (Re exhibition at Winterthur through February 18, 2001.)

Wohlauer, Gilian Shallcross. *MFA: A Guide to the Collection of the Museum of Fine Arts, Boston.* Boston: Museum of Fine Arts, Boston, 1999. 400 pp.; numerous color illus., index. (Includes some furniture.)

Wolverton, Nan. "Bottomed Out: Female Chair Seaters in Nineteenth-Century Rural New England." In *Rural New England Furniture: People, Place, and Production,* edited by Peter Benes, pp. 175–90. Boston: Boston University Scholarly Publications, 2000. 5 bw illus.

Wood, David F. "Cabinetmaking Practices in Revolutionary Concord: New Evidence." In *Rural New England Furniture: People, Place, and Production,* edited by Peter Benes, pp. 29–41. Boston: Boston Unversity Scholarly Publications, 2000. 4 bw illus.

Wood, David F. "Concord, Massachusetts, Clockmakers." *Antiques* 157, no. 5 (May 2000): 760–69. 13 color illus.

[Yale University Art Gallery]. "'Please Be Seated'": Public Seating from the Yale University Art Gallery Collection." *American Craft* 59 (August–September 1999): 48–51. 8 color illus.

Zea, Kimberly King. "Cheaper by the One-sixth Dozen: Vermont's Patterson Chair Company." In *Rural New England Furniture: People, Place, and Production,* edited by Peter Benes; pp. 157–74. Boston: Boston University Scholarly Publications, 2000. 10 bw illus.

Zea, Philip. "The Serpentine Furniture of Colonial Newport." *American Furniture 1999,* pp. 249–75. 27 color and bw illus.

Zea, Philip. "William Lloyd and the Workmanship of Change." In Benes, *Rural New England Furniture,* pp. 60–75. 9 bw illus.

Zimmerman, Philip D. "Dating Dunlap-Style Side Chairs." *Antiques* 157, no. 5 (May 2000): 796–803.

Zimmerman, Philip D. Review of Myrna Kaye, *There's a Bed in the Piano: The Inside Story of the American Home* and Galen Cranz, *The Chair: Rethinking Culture, Body, and Design.* In *American Furniture 1999,* pp. 288–93.

# Index

Ackermann, Rudolph, 112
Adam style: Baltimore and, 34–35(&fig. 3). *See also* Robert and J. Adam style
Advertisements: "Colonial" (Potthast Brothers, Inc.), 33(fig.); Edward Priestley furniture, 106
Affleck, Thomas, furniture of, 153, 160, 167(n9)
Africa, 1
Aiton, Thomas, 60, 94(n4)
Albuquerque, N.Mex., 197
Alexander Brown & Sons, 110
Ambler, Mary, 60
*American and Commercial Daily Advertiser,* 106
*American Antique Furniture: A Book for Amateurs* (Miller), 46, 132(n40)
American decorative arts, nineteenth- and early-twentieth-century, 206–11
*American Seating Furniture, 1630–1730: An Interpretive Catalogue* (Forman), 214
Ames, Kenneth L., on colonial revival style, 32
Andalusia house, 110, 134(n56)
Anderese, Nicholas, 22, 30(n19)
Annapolis, Md., 109, 127
"Anti-classical" modes, influences of, 217–18
Antique dealers, Baltimore, 35
*Antiques,* 33
Apple, 12(fig. 22)
Appleton, Charles-Louis, 19
Appleton, Henri, 19
Appleton, John, 19
Appleton, John-James, 19
Appleton, Margaret (Gibbs), 19
Appleton, Nathaniel, 19
Appleton, Nathaniel, Jr., 19
Appleton bookcase, compared to Moore bookcase, 22
Apprenticeships, 103, 105, 106, 129(n7), 129(n13), 156
Architectural books, 22–23
Architectural woodwork, 95(n12), 156, 160, 167(n6)
Architecture: influences on Baltimore neoclassical style, 119(&fig. 7), 130(n17); influences on Newport colonial style, 4, 5(fig. 5), 6(figs.), 7(&fig. 12), 9(fig.17), 10(figs.)
Armchair(s): James Moore, 168(n13); Potthast Bros., Inc., 35(&fig. 6), 40, 41(figs.)
Armstrong, H., 110

Arrow, James, 95(n12)
*Art & Enterprise: American Decorative Art, 1825–917, The Virginia Carroll Crawford Collection* (Peirce) (rvw), 206–11
Art nouveau style, twentieth-century neoclassicism and, 217
Askew, William, 75
Askey, James, 109
Attributions: to Benjamin Randolph, 153, 156; to Christopher Townsend, 13, 17; to Job Townsend, 12, 13; to John Townsend, 17; to Townsend brothers, 17(&fig. 32)
Atwood family, 209
Auctions: colonial revival style and, 45; Crim collection, 57(n28)

Bailey, Constant, 3
Baltimore: British influences on, 59, 60, 76–77, 127; city plan of, 104(fig.); colonial revival style, 31, 32; European influences on, 135(n60); exports to Savannah, 104; French style influences on, 112, 113, 131(n34); history of, 59–60, 101–2, 128(n2); neoclassical style, 60, 62, 68–69, 71, 75, 76, 82, 83, 84(fig. 38), 85, 92–93, 94(n6), 101, 127, 134(n50); paintings of, 102(figs.); Philadelphia influences on, 127; pre-Revolutionary furniture, 135(n60); sketches of, 59(&fig.), 102(fig. 2)
*Baltimore American,* 127
Baltimore Carpet, Furniture, and Looking Glass Warehouse, 102, 129(n12)
Baltimore carvers and gilders, 127
*Baltimore City Directory,* 35
Baltimore Equitable Society, 118
*Baltimore Magazine,* 49
Baltimore Museum of Art, 49, 55, 122, 134(n58), 156
Baltimore price book, 133(n49)
Banister, John, 2
Bankson, Andrew (father), 71–72
Bankson, John, 71–72, 95(n14), 96(n21); furniture of, 70
Bankson, Sarah (Allen) (mother), 71–72
Bankson and Lawson: bookcases, 96(n23); card table, 91(&fig. 51); chairs, 92; chest of drawers, 61(fig.); chests, 96(n22); clothespress, 79(fig.); desk-and-bookcase, 69(fig.), 76(fig. 26), 77; desks, 78(&fig.); factories, 73,

95(n11); furniture of, 80–82, 81(figs.), 91, 97(n26), 97(n29); *secretaires à abattant,* 61, 62(fig.), 78, 80, 90(&fig. 49), 94(n5), 97(n28); sideboards, 61, 64(fig. 7), 65(fig. 8), 80–82, 80(figs.), 81(figs.), 82(fig. 35), 97(n29); warehouse, 72–73

Bankson and Lawson school: chairs, 91, 92(&fig. 53), 93(&figs.), 99(n43); clock cases, 85(&fig. 40), 86(figs.), 99(n42)

Barker, William, 16

Baroque design, and New York, 12–13, 14

Barrett, Elizabeth, 97(n35)

Barrett, Thomas, 83, 84, 97(n35)

Barrett, Thomas (son), 97(n35)

Barry, Joseph B., 132(n35); cabinet shop of, 129(n6); furniture of, 121–22

Basin stand, 30(n20)

Battle Monument, 102(fig. 3), 127

Bedsteads, of Pueblo artisans, 191

Belter, John Henry, furniture of, 209

Bench(es), rococo revival, 209

Bennington, Vt., 211

Bernard, Nicholas, carving of, 153, 160

Bernard and Jugiez, carving of, 160

Berry & Son. *See* J. W. Berry & Son

Biays, Tolley A., 99(n43)

Biddle, Charles, 110, 134(n56)

Biddle Letitia (Glenn), 110, 134(n56)

Bigger, Gilbert, 98(n40)

Billington, James, 109

Bjerkoe, Ethel Hall, 29(n11)

Blockfront style, 61(&fig.), 68(fig. 18), 97(n29)

Bond, Phineas, 166

Bookcases, library: Bankson and Lawson, 77; Potthast Bros., Inc., 55. *See also* bookshelves

*Book of Architecture* (Gibb), 23

*Book on the Bookshelf, The* (Petroski) (rvw), 205–6

Bookshelves, history of, 205–6

Border patterns, shell motif, 26(fig. 43)

Bosley family, 112, 132(n35)

Boston, Mass., Newport colonial style and, 2–3, 23

Bostwick, Zalmon, 209

Bowfront style, Baltimore and, 81(fig. 34), 82(&fig. 35)

Boyce, Joseph, 183(n14)

Boyce family, 183(n10)

Boyd, George, on Baltimore furniture, 112

Breakfront(s), of Potthast Bros., Inc., 35(&fig. 6)

Brice House, 49

Bringman, John, apprenticeships of, 105

*British Architect* (Swan), 121

British influences: on Baltimore, 59, 60, 61–62, 66–68, 68, 70, 94(n8), 127; on Newport colonial style, 2, 19, 21(fig. 36), 23; on Potthast Bros., Inc., 46(&fig. 30)

Brooklyn Museum of Art, 49, 207

Brown, Alexander, 110

Brown, George, 110

Brown & Sons. *See* Alexander Brown & Sons

Buffington, Benjamin, 176, 183(n12)

Buffington, Hannah (Buffum), 176, 183(n12)

Buffington, James, 183(n12)

Buffington, Sarah (Southwick), 169–70, 176

Buffington, Thomas, 169–70, 176, 180

Buffington family, 174

Buffum, Caleb, 176, 178, 179

Buffum, Caleb (younger), 178–79

Buffum, Damaris (Pope), 176

Buffum, Elizabeth (Osborne), 177

Buffum, Hannah (Pope), 176

Buffum, Joshua, 177

Buffum, Joshua (elder), 174, 176, 178, 179, 183(n10), 183(n11)

Buffum, Joshua (younger), 179

Buffum, Robert, 179

Buffum family, 183(n10)

Bureau tables: Christopher Townsend, 25(&fig. 41), 26(fig. 42); Edmund Townsend, 26(fig. 44); Job Townsend, 25(&fig. 41), 26(fig. 42); John Townsend, 26(fig. 44); Newport colonial style, 23, 25(&fig. 41), 26(fig. 42)

Burton, John, 176

Burton, John (elder), 176

Cabinet shop(s): Bankson and Lawson, 75; Benjamin Randolph, 156, 160; Christopher Townsend, 3(&fig.); Coleman and Taylor, 129(n5); Edward Priestley, 103, 105, 106–7, 118, 129(n12); Francis Younker, 107; George Plaines, 129(n8); Henry Lusby, 107; Jacob Daley, 129(n7); John Needles, 106, 107; John Shaw, 106; Joseph B. Barry,

129(n6); Joseph Hutton, 129(n8); Matthew McColm, 129(n5); Potthast Bros., Inc., 31, 36(&fig. 9), 44(&figs.), 45, 52(fig. 41), 53; Priestley and Minskey, 103, 104(fig.), 105, 129(n7); Samuel Minskey, 103, 105; Seddon and Sons, 70; William Camp, 103

*Cabinet Dictionary, The* (Sheraton), 133(n49), 167(n6)

*Cabinet-Maker and Upholsterer's Guide, The* (Hepplewhite), 56(n5), 59, 61, 77, 91, 92, 95(n15)

*Cabinet-Maker and Upholsterer's Drawing Book, The* (Sheraton), 56(n5), 68, 78, 91, 117

Cabinet-Makers and Manufacturers of Mahogany in the City of Baltimore, 105

*Cabinet-Makers' London Book of Prices,* 61

*Cabinet-makers of America, The* (Bjerkoe), 29(n11)

Cabinet(s), of Thomas Godey, 207

Cadwalader, Elizabeth (Lloyd) (first wife), 153, 160, 165, 167(n8); painting of, 152(fig. 1)

Cadwalader, John, 153, 166; inventory of, 161, 168(n10); painting of, 152(fig. 1)

Cadwalader, Lambert, 152(fig. 2), 153

Cadwalader, Willimina (Bond) (second wife), 166, 168(n13)

Cadwalader commode front table, 152(fig. 1), 166(n1)

Cadwalader commode-seat side chair(s), 152(figs.), 153–66, 154(figs.), 155(figs.), 162(&figs.), 166(n1), 167(n6), 168(n13)

*Cajas,* and Spanish colonial style, 185–202, 186(fig. 1), 187(figs.), 188(fig.), 190(fig.), 191(fig.), 193(fig.), 194(fig. 11), 196(fig.), 197(fig. 16), 198(figs.), 199(fig.)

Caldwell, Désirée, on ethnic origins of Philadelphia furniture, 214

Camp, William, 121; cabinet shop of, 103; furniture of, 36(&fig. 10), 56(n11), 134(n58); warehouses, 129(n12)

Campbell, Robert, 23

Card table(s): Bankson and Lawson, 91(&fig. 51); Edward Priestley, 113, 114(fig. 6), 115(&figs.), 124, 132(n40); Potthast Bros., Inc., 55(&fig. 47), 58(n38)

Carroll, Charles, Jr., 40, 47

Carroll, Harriet (Chew), 47

Carroll family, 47, 113

230 INDEX

Carter, Edward C., II, on Philadelphia, 213
*Cartouches de Différentes Inventions* (Rabel), 67
Carvers: of Baltimore, 127; Bernard and Jugiez, 160; Hercules Courtenay, 77, 96(n25), 153, 156, 160, 167(n5); James Reynolds, 160–61, 167(n9); John Pollard, 153, 156, 160; Martin Jugiez, 153, 160; Nicholas Bernard, 153, 160
Carving: Baltimore neoclassical style, 77, 83, 115(&fig. 7), 116(fig. 11), 117, 124, 126, 127, 130(n17); colonial revival style, 48(&figs.); Newport colonial style, 19, 23; Philadelphia rococo style, 153, 155, 159; rococo style, 158(figs.), 159(&fig. 16), 167(n6); Spanish colonial style *cajas*, 185, 186(fig. 1), 187(figs.), 188(fig.), 193(fig.), 197
Casey, Samuel, 19(&fig. 34)
Cast-iron furniture, Crawford collection and, 208–9
*Catalogue of the Celebrated Dr. William H. Crim Collection of Genuine Antiques* (Kirkland), 37(fig. 13), 115
Catholic cathedral, 127
Chair(s): eclecticism and, 210; export trade, 3; Herts and Tallant, 210; Hispanic artisans, 191; Potthast Bros., Inc., 34(fig. 4), 35(&figs.), 38, 38(&figs.), 39(fig. 17), 40(fig. 19), 46(fig. 31), 47(&figs.), 48(&figs.), 55, 57(n28), 58(n38); rococo revival style, 209. *See also by specific style*
Champan, Israel, 4
Charles Rohlfs and Craftsman Workshops, 210
Charleston, inlay construction and, 62, 74
Charlish, Anne, 217
Chest(s): Bankson and Lawson, 60(fig. 2), 61(&fig.); colonial style, 185, 186(fig. 3); Jos. Claypoole, 212; Symonds shops, 169–71(&figs.), 172(&figs.), 173(fig.), 174(&fig.), 176(&figs.), 177(figs.), 180, 181(fig.), 182(n6), 182(n7). See also *cajas*
Chests of drawers: Bankson and Lawson, 66–67(fig. 13); Job Townsend, Jr., 30(n21); Long Island style, 12(fig. 22), 13(fig. 23); Potthast Bros., Inc., 36, 54, 56; William Camp, 36(fig. 10), 56(n11)
Chew, Harriet (Ridgley), 110
Chew, Henry B., 110
Chicago, Ill., mass production and, 52

Chimney Corner Antiques, 52
China table, 30(n20)
Chippendale, Thomas, 56(n5), 160
Chippendale style, 33, 38, 46
Christie's, 57(n32), 99(n44)
Chrysler Museum, 97(n28)
Chu, Jonathan, on Salem taxes, 180
Cincinnati, Ohio, and nineteenth- and early-twentieth-century cabinet-makers, 210–11
*City and Country Builder's and Workman's Treasury of Designs, The* (Langley), 23
"Classical" modes, influences of, 217–18
Classicism style, Crawford collection and, 208
Claypoole, Jos., furniture of, 212
Clock case(s): Bankson and Lawson school, 85(figs.), 86(figs.), 99(n42); John Goddard, 23; William Patterson, 82–83(fig. 36)
Clockmakers, 85, 98(n40)
Clothespress(es), Bankson and Lawson, 78, 79(fig.)
Coffee table(s), 46
Coleman and Taylor, 107, 129(n5)
*Collection des Meubles et Objets de Goût* (la Mésangère), 112–13, 121, 134(n51)
*Collection of Designs for Household Furniture and Interior Decoration* (Smith), 121–22, 134(n51)
*Colonial Furniture: The Superb Collection of the Late Howard Reifsnyder*, 45
*Colonial Furniture of New England, The* (Lyon), 33
Colonial revival style: Mt. Vernon and, 50–51; Potthast Bros., Inc. and, 31–59, 56(n8)
Colonial style: European influences on, 203(n7); Newport, 3–4(fig.), 5(fig. 5), 6(figs.), 8(figs.), 9(figs.), 10(&figs.), 19–20, 19(fig. 34), 21(fig. 36), 23, 28, 33
Colonial Williamsburg, 49, 134(n58)
Colony House (Newport), 3–4, 5(figs.), 6(figs.), 7(&figs.)
*Columbian Museum and Savannah Advertiser*, 104
Columns/capitals, 19, 21(fig. 38), 52(&fig. 42), 80(fig. 30), 89(fig. 47)
Combs and Jenkins, 96(n21)
Conant, Exercise, 183(n17)
Conant, Roger, 180
Conant family, 180
Concord Museum, 183(n15)

Construction methods: Baltimore neoclassical style furniture, 60–61, 82, 94(n8), 94(n9); Baltimore neoclassical style inlays, 62, 68–69, 68(figs.), 78; Baltimore rococo style tables, 132(n40); Bankson and Lawson furniture, 96(n23), 97(n29); Bankson and Lawson school clock cases, 85; Benjamin Randolph chairs, 153, 154(fig. 4), 156; Cadwalader chair upholstery, 166, 168(n13); Christopher Townsend furniture, 13–14, 16–17(&figs.), 21(fig. 37), 22, 25, 30(n20); Edward Priestley furniture, 113, 115, 117–19, 118(figs.), 120(fig. 19), 121, 122(&fig.), 132(n38), 132(n39); Hispanic colonial chests, 203(n2); Job Townsend tables, 11–12(fig. 21), 13–14, 13(fig. 24), 15; John Webster upholstery, 164; Long Island style chest, 13(&fig. 23); Newport colonial style tables, 7(figs.); Plunkett Fleeson upholstery, 161–62, 163(figs.), 164(&figs.), 165(&figs.), 168(n11), 168(n12), 168(n13); Potthast Bros., Inc. furniture, 52(fig. 41), 53–54(&figs.); Rappahannock River Basin legs, 15(fig. 27); Spanish colonial style *cajas*, 185, 186(fig. 1), 188(fig.), 190, 92–93(&fig.), 194(fig.), 196–97, 198(&fig. 17), 203(n2); William Camp sofas, 117
Continental Memorial Hall, 48
Corinthian capital, 89(fig. 47)
Cornelius, Charles Over, 57(n32)
Courtenay, Hercules: carving of, 77, 96(n25), 153, 156, 160, 167(n5); shop of, 156
Courtenay, Mary (Shute), 167(n5)
Coxe, Charles, 160
Cox family, 12
Crawford, Virginia Carroll, 207
Crawford collection, 206–11
Crim, William H., 36, 37(fig. 13), 58(n38), 122, 132(n40)
Crim chair, 38(&fig. 14), 39(fig. 16), 40(fig. 19), 58(n38)
Cupboard(s): Newport colonial style, 4, 7(fig. 12); Symonds shops, 173–74, 178(fig.), 179(fig.), 180, 182(n7)
Cylinder-front style, 77, 78(&fig.)


Daley, Isaac, 129(n7)
Daley, Jacob, 109, 128(n1): cabinet shop of, 129(n7); furniture of, 104

Darby, Henry F., 209
Dashiell, Daniel, 109
*Das Neue Baltimore,* 36, 56(n10)
Davidson, James, furniture of, 129(n7)
Davidson, Margaret (wife), 129(n7)
Davis, Alexander Jackson, 210
De Beher, Baron, 110
De Mille, Cecil B., 44
Delaplaine, Samuel, 13, 29(n13)
Dennis, Thomas, 169
Design(s): Baltimore neoclassical style, 68–69, 73(fig.), 101; classicism style, 209; Edward Priestley furniture, 110–13, 115; Newport colonial style, 23; sources for, 45; Spanish colonial style chests, 185–202, 186(fig. 1), 187(figs.), 188(fig.), 190(fig.), 191(fig.), 193(fig.), 194(fig. 11), 196(fig.), 197(fig. 16), 198(figs.), 199(figs.). *See also under specific styles*
*Designs for Household Furniture* (Shearer), 61
Desk-and-book-case(s): Bankson and Lawson, 69(fig.), 76(fig. 26), 77, 78(fig.); Christopher Townsend, 10, 18(fig.), 19–20(&fig. 34), 21(fig. 36), 22, 29(n17), 30(n20), 30(n21); history of, 205; Job Townsend. Sr., 3, 10, 20(fig.)
Desk(s), 69–70: Bankson and Lawson, 61, 76(fig. 26), 78(&fig.); Christopher Townsend, 28; Edenton (North Carolina), 28(fig.); Edward Priestley, 124(&figs.); Edward Townsend, 30(n19); Job Townsend, Jr., 30(n19); monasteries and, 205
Dining table(s): Edward Priestley, 113, 114(fig. 5); Potthast Bros., Inc., 35(&fig. 6), 54(&fig. 46), 55, 58(n38)
Doat, Taxile, 211
Dodge chest, 176(fig.), 183(n15)
Dominguez, Fray Francisco, 191
Doors: Baltimore neoclassical, 63(fig.), 64(fig. 6), 69(fig.), 78, 84(fig. 38), 96(n23); Newport colonial style, 19, 21(fig. 36)
Doric columns, 19, 21(fig. 38)
Dougherty, John, 60, 94(n4)
Dover Inlay, 54
Downing, Antoinette F., on Christopher Townsend, 4
Drawers: Bankson and Lawson, 60(fig.), 61(fig.), 67(&fig. 16), 68; Bankson and Lawson school, 94(n9); Christopher Townsend, 18(fig.), 19–20, 22(fig. 39), 25(&fig. 41), 26(fig. 42), 30(n21); Edmund Townsend, 26(fig. 45); Edward Priestley, 119, 134(n58); Job Townsend, 25(&fig. 41), 26(fig. 42); John Townsend, 26(fig. 44); Long Island style, 13(fig. 23)
Dressing table(s): Job Townsend, 13(fig. 24), 15; Job Townsend, Sr., 12(&fig.); Newport colonial style, 14; Rappahannock River Basin, 14, 15(&fig. 26); Ward family, 16
Dukehart, Henry, 109
Dumbarton House, 49
Duncan Phyfe style, 33
Dunne, Richard S., on Philadelphia, 213
Du Pont, Henry Francis, 45

Eastlake, Charles Locke, 210
Easton, Ann Bull, 3
Easton, Nicholas, 3
Easton, Robert, on Pueblo designs, 199
Easton's Point, 2(fig.), 3
Easy chair, of Thomas Affleck, 160(&fig. 20)
Eclecticism style, and Tiffany and Company, 210
Economy, of Rhode Island, 1–3
Eddis, William, 60
Edenton N.C., 28(fig.)
Edmunds, James, 35, 56(n8)
Egyptian style: Crawford collection and, 209; influences on Baltimore, 121, 124, 134(n50); influences on Edward Priestley, 101
Elvins, William, 98(n40); clock movements of, 85, 86(figs.)
Empire revival style, 33
*Encyclopedia of Cottage, Farmhouse and Villa Architecture and Furniture* (Loundon), 112
Endicott, Grace (Symonds), 180
Endicott, John, 180
Endicott, Zarubbabel, 180
Endicott, Zarubbabel, Jr., 180
*English Ceramics: The Frances and Emory Cocke Collection* (Peirce), 207
Enoch Pratt House, 55
Essex County, 169
Essex Institute, 182(n7)
European cultural influences: on Baltimore, 59, 135(n60); on colonial style, 189, 203(n7); on Philadelphia, 214–15, 216(n6)
Exports: from Baltimore, 59; Coleman and Taylor, 129(n5); Edward Priestley, 105, 129(n5), 129(n6); Joseph B. Barry, 129(n6); Matthew McColm, 129(n5); Newport colonial style, 3; Priestley and Minskey, 104; Savannah and, 105. *See also* imports; trade

Factories, Bankson and Lawson, 73, 95(n11)
Fancy chair(s): Finlay brothers, 104; Francis Younker, 107; Jacob Daley, 104; Matthew McColm, 104; Priestley and Minskey, 104
Faneuil Hall Hardware, 54
Fanon, Frantz, on interactions between cultures, 201
Farnham, Katherine Gross, 207
*Federal Gazette,* 105
Feet: Bankson and Lawson, 60(fig.), 61(fig.), 62(fig.), 67(fig. 15), 68(&fig. 18), 69(fig.), 82, 85; French forms, 66(fig. 13), 67(fig. 14), 68; Newport colonial style, 2(fig. 45), 12(figs.), 15(fig. 28), 16(&fig.), 17(&fig. 31), 26(fig. 44); Potthast Bros., Inc., 38, 40
Feke, Robert, 213
Finlay, Hugh, 112, 113, 128(n1), 132(n35); furniture of, 104
Finlay, John, 112, 128(n1); furniture of, 104
Flanigan, J. Michael, 30(n20)
Fleeson, Plunkett, upholsterers, 161–62(&figs.), 168(n10), 168(n11)
Folger, Peter, 176
Fontaine, Pierre-François-Leonard, 121, 134(n51)
Ford, Henry, 45
Forman, Benno, 182(n3), 214; on Boston joiners, 181; on Salem school, 169; on Symonds shop, 169
Fowler, Harriet Putnam, 173, 182(n7)
Francophiles, 113, 132(n35)
Fraser, James, 130(n17)
French, 127
French stylistic influences: on Baltimore, 112, 113, 131(n34); on Edward Priestley, 101, 113; neoclassical style and, 79–80
Friezes, 121(&fig.)
*Furniture History,* 217

*Furniture of Our Forefathers, The* (Singleton), 33
*Furniture Treasury* (Nutting), 33

Garvan, Francis, 38, 45
Gaskill family, 183(n10)
Gateleg table(s), 10
*Gentleman and Cabinet-Maker's Director, The* (Chippendale), 56(n5), 160(&fig. 19)
*Georgia Republican and State Intelligencer*, 104
German-Americans, 56(n2)
Gibb, James, 23
Gibbes, Robert M., 131(n28)
Gilders, 127, 130(n17)
Gillow firm, 68
Glenn, John, 110, 131(n30)
Goddard, Hannah (Townsend), 23
Goddard, John, 22; furniture of, 27(fig. 46), 28
Godey, Thomas, furniture of, 207
Gonzalez Palacios, Alvar, 217
Gordon, William, 95(n14)
Gothic revival style, and the Crawford collection, 209, 210
Gothic style, influences on Edward Priestley, 101
Gough, Harry Dorsey, 131(n33)
Grand Rapids, Mich., mass production and, 52
*Great River: Art and Society of the Connecticut Valley 1635-1850, The*, 212
Great Yarmouth, 179
Greek motifs, 115(&fig. 9), 209
Green, Armistead, 107
Greene and Greene, 210
Greenfield Village, 49
Greenwich Hospital Chapel, 95(n12)
Greenwood and Company. *See* M. L. Greenwood and Company
Gusler, Wallace, on furniture construction, 22

Hagen, Earnest F., furniture of, 32
Halsey, R. T. H., 57(n32)
Hammond-Harwood House, 48, 49
Hampton house, 75, 110, 113
*Handbook of the American Wing* (Halsey and Cornelius), 57(n32)
"Hand made" production, 52, 53. *See also* mass production

Hanks, David A., 207
Hardware, 54, 68
Hart, Samuel, 171, 180, 182(n3)
Hart, Sarah (Endicott), 180
Hart, Thomas, 171, 180, 182(n3)
Hart family, 180
Hasitland, James, 129(n13)
Hayward, Helena, 217
Hepplewhite, George, 56(n5), 59, 61, 91, 92, 95(n15); on sideboards, 81; on writing tables, 77
Hepplewhite style, 33, 46; table(s), 54(&fig. 46)
Herrick, Ephraim, 170, 180
Herrick, Joseph, 180
Herrick, Mary (Cross), 170, 180
Herrick, Mary (Hart), 180
Herrick family, 180, 183(n17)
Herts and Tallant, 210
Hessalius, John, 213
High chests: Long Island style, 12(fig.22), 13(&fig. 23); Newport colonial style, 14, 15(fig. 28), 16, 23, 24–25(fig. 40)
High Museum of Art, 206, 207
Hill, Henry John, on apprenticeships, 103
Hill, John, 183(n14)
*Hints on Household Taste in Furniture, Upholstery and Other Details* (Eastlake), 210
Hispanic artisans: furniture of, 191, 203(n2); Pueblo culture and, 188–90, 191(fig.), 192(fig.), 199(&figs.), 200(&figs.), 201; Spanish colonial style, 198
*History of Furniture, The* (Charlish, ed.), 217
*History of Furniture: Twenty-Five Centuries of Style and Design in the Western Tradition, The* (Morley) (rvw), 217–18
Homewood house, 40–42, 47, 49
Hope, Thomas, 121, 133(n49), 134(n51)
Hopkins, Gerrard, 135(n60)
Hornby, Gualter, 60, 94(n4)
*Household Furniture and Interior Decoration* (Hope), 121, 134(n51)
*House in Good Taste, The* (Wolfe), 33
Howe, John, 102; and warehouses, 129(n12)
Howe, William, 165–66
Howlett, John, 129(n13)
Hunt, Benjamin, 16
Huntboard(s), 35(&fig. 6)

Hurd, John, 19
Hurst, Ronald L., on Irish influences, 14
Hutton, Joseph: apprenticeships, 105; cabinet shop of, 129(n8)

*Il Modile nei Secoli* (Gonzalez Palacios), 217
Immigrants: classic revival style and, 32; European, 135(n60); French, 112, 127, 131(n34); Italian, 127; neoclassical style and, 61, 68, 77
*Important American Furniture, Silver, Folk Art, and Decorative Art* (Christie's), 57(n32), 99(n44)
*Important American Furniture and Folk Art* (Sotheby's), 29(n17)
Imports, 60, 75, 194. *See also* exports; trade
Indianapolis, Ind., 210–11
Industrialization, Crawford collection and, 208
Initials/inscriptions: Symonds shops, 169–71, 172–73, 176(fig.), 177(fig. 10). *See also* labels/brands/numbers
Inlay(s): Baltimore neoclassical style, 62, 63(fig.), 64(fig. 6), 65(fig. 8), 66–67(&figs.), 69(fig.), 72(fig.), 73(fig.), 74(&fig. 23), 76(fig. 25), 77(fig.), 78(&fig.), 80(&fig. 31), 84, 85, 86(fig. 42), 87(fig. 44), 88(fig. 45), 89, 90(fig. 50), 91(&figs.), 92(&figs.), 93(fig. 55), 96(n23), 96(n25), 98(n40), 99(n42); colonial revival style, 49(&fig. 36), 54, 55(fig. 47); Newport colonial style, 13(fig. 23)
"Interesting Facts: Inside Secrets of Selecting Furniture Correctly" (Potthast Bros., Inc.), 31, 52, 53, 54
Inventories: Edward Priestley, 110–12, 136–46; John Cadwalader, 161, 168(n10)
Ipswich, Mass., 169
Irish, 14, 60
Italians, 127

J. W. Berry & Son, 52, 53
Jamestown Tercentenial Exhibition, 40–42
Japanese motifs, and Tiffany and Company, 211
Jelliff, John, 209
Johnson, John, apprenticeships of, 105
Johnson, Reverdy, 109

Johnson, Thomas, 77, 156
Jos. Claypoole, furniture of, 212
Jugiez, Martin, carving of, 153, 160

Kalo shop, 210
Kenmore house, 49
Kent, James, on Baltimore, 103
Kenworthy-Brown, John, 217
Key, Francis Scott, 40
Key chair(s), 40, 41(fig. 21)
Kirby, Nicholas, 103
Kirkland, O. A., 37(fig. 13), 115
Kitchin, Elizabeth, 183(n15)
Kitchin, John, 183(n15)
Klingman, Jacob, 99(n42)
Knabe and Company, 35, 52
Knyphausen, William, 166
Krickbaum, Joseph, furniture of, 121–22
Kubler, George, on colonial artisanry, 190, 193, 203(n10)

L. & J. G. Stickley, furniture of, 56(n2)
Labels/brands/numbers: Benjamin Randolph, 153, 156(&figs.); Cadwalader commode-seat side chairs, 153, 154(figs.), 155(fig. 5), 166(n2); William Patterson, 82, 83(fig. 37). *See also* initials/inscriptions
Labels/inscriptions: Christopher Townsend, 15(fig. 28); John Seymour, 45
Labor, distribution of, 3, 22
Lafayette, Marquis de, on Baltimore, 131(n34)
Langley, Batty, 23
Lannuier, Charles Honoré, 112
Lannuier suite, 132(n35)
Lawson, Agnes (Simpson) (mother), 95(n11)
Lawson, Richard, 60, 84, 94(n4), 95(n11), 96(n21); furniture of, 70, 76; painting of, 71(fig.)
Lawson, Stephen (father), 95(n11)
Legs/knees: Baltimore neoclassical style, 81(fig. 33), 82; colonial revival style, 38, 39(fig. 17), 40(fig. 19); Newport colonial style, 7(fig. 11), 13(&fig. 13), 14(&fig.), 15(&figs.), 16–17(&fig. 30), 16(&fig.)
Lennox, John, 84, 97(n35)
Leopold, Harry B., 32

Letterbook, Abraham Redwood, on patrons, 29(n11)
Lewis, David, 168(n13)
Liberto, Enrico, 52, 53
Lightfoot, Philip, 91
Lindsey, Jack, 212
Liquor case, of Edward Priestley, 100(fig.)
Lloyd, Alicia (McBlair), 119
Lloyd, Edward, III, 113, 160
Lloyd, Edward, V, 101, 109, 129(n10), 129(n13), 131(n26), 131(n34)
Lloyd, Edward, VI, 101, 109, 113, 119, 133(n45)
Lloyd family, 113, 117
London. *See* British
*London Cabinet Book of Prices, The* (Society of London Upholsterers), 56(n5)
*London Tradesman, The* (Campbell), 23
Long Island style, influences on Job Townsend, Sr., 12(fig.22)
Louis XV style, 68
Loundon, John Claudius, 112
Lovell, Margaretta, on Newport cabinetmakers, 3, 30(n25)
Lusby, Henry, cabinet shop of, 107
Lyon, Irving P., on Essex County furniture, 169
Lyon, Irving Whitehall, on American antique furniture, 33

M. L. Greenwood and Company, furniture of, 209
Madison, Dolly, 109, 112, 113
Madison, James, 112, 113
Mahogany, 10–11(fig. 20), 26(&figs.), 49(&fig. 36), 68, 75, 94(n9), 96(n23), 105
Map, of Newport, 2(fig.)
Marter, Chevalier, 113, 131(n37)
Martin, Joseph, 16
Maryland, 47, 101. *See also under specific cities*
Maryland Building, 41(fig. 22), 57(n15)
Maryland Historical Society, 32, 55, 58(n38), 132(n35)
Maryland Institute College of Art, 44
Maryland State House, 40–41(&figs.)
Mass production: Baltimore neoclassical style, 53, 129(n12); colonial revival style, 52; Newport colonial style, 1, 3, 22, 28, 30(n25); rococo revival style, 209–10

*Master Craftsmen of Newport* (Moses), 17
Mathias Hammond House, 133(n49)
McColm, Matthew, 107; cabinet shop of, 129(n5); furniture of, 104
McCormick, James, 60, 94(n4)
McCoull, George, 109
McFadon, John, 84, 85, 96(n21)
McFadon, William, 96(n21)
McLoughlin, William G., on socioeconomics, 1
McPherson, John, 167(n8)
Melvil, Thomas, 4
Meredeth, Rebecca (Cadwalader), 168(n10)
Meredeth, Samuel, 168(n10)
Mésangère, Pierre de la, 112–13, 121, 134(n51)
Metropolitan Museum of Art, 16, 49–50, 57(n32)
Miller, Edgar G., on Potthast Bros., Inc., 46–47
Miller, Edgar G., Jr., 132(n40)
Miller, Edith (Davison), 35
Miller's chair(s), 35, 56(n8)
Minskey, Nicholas (father), 103
Minskey, Samuel, cabinet shop of, 103, 105
Mission style, 42, 56(n2)
Mohler, Peter, 98(n40)
Moldings: Baltimore neoclassical style, 64(fig. 6), 69(fig.), 96(n23), 98(n40), 119, 122, 126; Newport colonial style, 18(fig.), 19, 21(figs.), 22(&fig. 38), 25(&fig. 41), 30(n20); Spanish colonial style, 196, 198
Molesworth, H. D., 217
Mondawmin, 110
Montgomery Ward, 52
Monticello house, 49
Moore, Cornelius C., 22
Moore, James, furniture of, 168(n13)
Moore, Robert, 135(n60)
Moore bookcase, compared to Appleton bookcase, 22
Morel, Nicholas, 95(n12)
Morley, John, 217
Moses, Michael, 17; on Goddard, 23
Mountjoy and Welsh, 98(n40)
Mount Clare house, 49
Mount Pleasant house, 167(n8)
Mount Vernon house, 49, 50–51
Mummy head design, 120(fig. 20), 121, 122(&fig.), 123(figs.), 124(&fig. 28), 125(fig 30), 126, 133(n49), 134(n51)

234  INDEX

Mundy, Richard, 10
Munson-Williams-Proctor Institute, 207
Murphy, Thomas, and Edward Priestley, 109, 127
Museum of Fine Arts, Boston, 49
Museum of the Daughters of the American Revolution, 48
Muth, Mary-Lee Carroll, 48, 57(n29)
Myer, Moses, 80
Myer family, 97(n28)

Nabakov, Peter, on Pueblo designs, 199
*Native American Architecture* (Nabakov and Easton), 199
Native American culture: Spanish colonial style and, 188–90, 198–99, 201; Tiffany and Company and, 210
Neale, James, 128(n1)
Neale, Joseph, 128(n1)
Needham family, 183(n10)
Needles, John: apprenticeships of, 106; cabinet shop of, 106, 107; furniture of, 134(n58)
Neoclassical style: Baltimore, 60, 62, 68–69, 71, 75, 76, 82, 83, 84(fig. 38), 85, 92–93, 94(n6), 101, 127, 134(n50); French influences on, 79–80; Philadelphia, 101. *See also* classicism style
Neoclassicism, twentieth-century art nouveau style and, 217
Nevelle, Thomas, 160, 167(n8)
*New Book of Ornaments, A* (Johnson), 156
*New England Furniture at Winterthur* (Richards and Evans), 30(n20)
New England Historical and Genealogical Society, 171
New Hampshire Historical Society, 182(n5)
New Mexico: history of, 183–90, 194(fig. 12), 195(&fig.), 202, 203(n4), 204(n16); Spanish colonial style, 185–202
Newport: British influences on, 19, 21(fig. 36); colonial style, 3–4(fig.), 5(fig. 5), 6(figs.), 8(figs.), 9(figs.), 10(&figs.), 19–20, 19(fig. 34), 21(fig. 36), 23, 28; history of, 1; map of, 2(fig.)
New York, 23, 32, 112, 131(n33). *See also under specific cities*
*New York Book of Prices for Manufacturing Cabinet and Chair Work, The*, 121, 122, 134(n54)
Nicholson, Joseph Hopper, 131(n26)

*19th-Century America: Furniture and other Decorative Arts*, 211
Non-Importation Agreement of 1765, 167(n5)
Nutting, Wallace, on American antique furniture, 33

Oldham, John, 128(n1)
Oliver, Robert, 110
Oliver, Thomas, 131(n28)
Oñate, Juan de, 191, 193, 202
*One Hundred and Fifty New Designs* (Johnson), 77
On carving, Thomas Sheraton, 167(n6)
"Ordinances of the Trades of Carpenters, Joiners, and Musical Instrument Makers of the City of Mexico," 190
Ornaments, in Edward Priestley case pieces and tables, 127
Osborne, Eleanor (Southwick), 177
Osborne, Elizabeth, 172
Osborne, Hannah (Buffum), 177
Osborne, Hannah (Burton), 176, 183(n13)
Osborne, John, 172
Osborne, John (elder), 177
Osborne, Lyman, 172
Osborne, Mercy (Southwick), 177
Osborne, Samuel, 172, 176–77
Osborne, William, 176, 180, 183(n13)
Osborne chest, 177(fig. 9), 182(n5)
Osborne family, 172, 174, 176, 183(n10); genealogy chart, 175(fig.)
Ottoman(s), of M. L. Greenwood and Company, 209
Owings family, 124, 134(n55)
Oyster Bay, N.Y., influences on Newport colonial style, 3, 12

Pabst, Daniel, 209
Pageott, Monsieur, 110
Paintings/drawings: Baltimore, 59(&fig.), 102(figs.), 104(fig.); Christopher Townsend's house, 3(fig.); Crim chair, 39(fig. 16); Elizabeth Cadwalader, 152(fig. 1); Job Townsend, Sr., 19, 20(fig.); John Cadwalader, 152(fig. 1); Lambert Cadwalader, 152(fig. 2); Newport town plan, 2(fig.); Potthast Bros., Inc., 36, 37(fig. 11), 45(&fig.), 49(&fig. 35), 53(fig. 44), 54–55(&fig. 49), 54(fig. 45); Potthast Bros., Inc. chest of drawers, 36, 37(fig. 12); Potthast Bros., Inc. sideboard, 55(fig. 48); Richard Lawson, 71(fig.)
*Palladio Londonensis* (Salmon), 22
Park, Helen, on Essex County furniture, 169
Parsons, Eben, 182(n3)
Patch, Emily G., 182(n6)
Patrons, individual/institutional: Abraham Redwood, 10; Ann Willing, 70; Bankson and Lawson, 75; of Bankson and Lawson, 75; of Benjamin Randolph, 167(n5); Buffington family, 174; of Christopher Townsend, 3, 10; Continental Memorial Hall, 48; Dodge family, 183(n15); Dolly Madison, 109; Edward Lloyd, V, 109, 129(n10); Edward Lloyd, VI, 101, 109; of Edward Priestley, 101, 109–10, 129(n10); of Finlay brothers, 131(n33); Francis Garvan, 45; Hammond-Harwood House, 48; Henry Ford, 45; Henry Francis du Pont, 45; Isaac Stelle, 10; of Jacob Daley, 129(n7); of Job Townsend, 3; of John Aiken, 131(n33); John Cadwalader, 153, 167(n5); joiners and, 29(n11); Lloyd family, 128(n1), 129(n7); Madison family, 131(n33); Mark Pringle, 105, 129(n8); Osborne family, 174; Pope family, 174; of Potthast Bros., Inc., 36, 48; of Symonds shops, 169–81, 183(n15); Thomas Ringgold, 167(n5); Trask family, 174; William Bingham, 70; of William Camp, 131(n33); William H. Crim, 36; William Palmer, 131(n33)
Patterson, William, 83, 97(n32), 97(n34); furniture of, 82–83(fig. 36)
Peabody Essex Museum, 182(n5)
Peale, Charles Willson, painting by, 152(fig. 1), 153
Pediments: Baltimore neoclassical style, 73(fig.), 74(&fig. 23), 78, 83, 85, 87(fig. 44), 88(fig. 46), 89, 98(n40); Newport colonial style, 19, 21(fig. 36), 22
Peggy Stewart House, 49
Peirce, Donald C., 206
Pennington, James, 109
Pennsylvania, 99(n42). *See also* Philadelphia
Pepys, Samuel, 206
Percier, Charles, 121, 134(n51)
Perry Hall, 131(n33)

"Persians." *See* Mummy head designs
Petroski, Henry, 205
Phelps, Nicholas, 174
*Philadelphia: Three Centuries of American Art*, 212
Philadelphia Museum of Art, 45, 49, 134(n51), 168(n10), 212
Philadelphia, Pa.: Chippendale style, 38; colonial revival style, 45; European influences on, 214–15, 216(n6); furniture export trade, 129(n6); history of, 212–13; influences on Baltimore, 135(n60); mid-eighteenth century furniture, 212; rococo style, 127, 153, 156
*Philip Flayderman Collection: Historic American Furniture, The*, 45
Photographs/lithographs: of Potthast Bros., Inc., 31(&fig.), 36(fig. 9); of Potthast suite, 35(fig. 6); of the Senate chamber of the Maryland Building, 42(&figs.); of Trask homestead, 176(figs.); of William H. Crim, 37(fig. 13)
Phyfe, Duncan, furniture of, 32
Pier table(s): Edward Priestley, 100(fig.), 101(&fig.), 119, 120(fig. 19), 121, 134(n58); John Pollard, 159–60(&figs.)
Pine, 203(n10)
Plaines, George: apprenticeships of, 105; cabinet shop of, 129(n8)
Plaw, John, 71
Pleasant Hill, 35(&fig. 6)
Polk, Charles Peale, 95(n11), painting by, 71(fig.)
Pollard, John: carving of, 96(n25), 153, 156, 160; furniture of, 159–60(&figs.)
Pope, Bathsheba (Folger), 170, 175–76
Pope, Enos, 183(n10), 183(n12)
Pope, Gertrude (Shattuck), 175
Pope, Joseph, 170, 175, 180
Pope, Joseph, Jr., 175, 178, 183(n10)
Pope, Lydia (Buffum), 183(n10), 183(n12)
Pope, Nathaniel, 183(n11)
Pope family, 174, 183(n10)
Port Royal, Va., 91
Potthast, Berthold, 44
Potthast, Frank J., 44
Potthast, George J., 44
Potthast, John, Sr., 31(&fig.), 32, 35
Potthast, Michael, 44
Potthast, Theodore, Sr., 31(&fig.), 35, 45
Potthast, Theodore J., 44, 48–49
Potthast, Vincent, 31(&fig.), 35, 36(fig. 8), 44

Potthast, William, 31(&fig.), 35, 36(fig. 7), 44, 45
Potthast, William A., 44
Potthast Brothers, Inc.: cabinet shops, 36(&fig. 9); furniture of, 31–58, 34(fig. 4), 35(figs.), 38(fig. 14), 39(figs.), 41(fig. 21), 46(figs.), 47(fig.), 48(fig. 32), 50(figs.), 51(figs.), 54(fig. 46), 57(n32), 58(n38)
Potthast family, 42
Pratt-Keyser Building, 55
Prentis collection, 182(n5)
Price, Warwick, 99(n43)
Prices: Bankson and Lawson furniture, 73; Bernard and Jugiez carvings, 160(&fig. 20); Christopher Townsend desk-and-bookcase, 10; colonial revival style furniture, 36, 43; Edward Priestley furniture, 112, 119, 131(n33); Hercules Courtenay carvings, 156; James Reynolds, 160–61; Job Townsend furniture, 3, 12; John Pollard furniture, 160; John Webster upholstery, 161; Newport colonial style, 16; Plunkett Fleeson upholstery, 161–62(&figs.); Potthast Brothers, furniture, 45; Symonds shops cupboard, 174; Thomas Affleck furniture, 160
Priddy, Sumpter, on specialization and emigrés, 127
Priestley, Edward: cabinet shop of, 103, 105, 106–7, 118, 129(n12); card table, 113, 114(fig. 6), 115(&figs.), 124, 132(n40); desk, 124(&figs.); dining table, 113, 114(fig. 5); drawers, 119, 134(n58); furniture of, 101, 105, 106, 111–13, 113, 115, 117–19, 121–22, 124, 126–27, 129(n13); inventory of, 110–12, 136–46; investments/estate of, 107–10, 130(n19), 130(n24), 130(n25), 131(n31), 146–51; liquor cases, 100(fig.), 119(&fig. 18), 121; lumber business, 129(n11); sideboards/commodes, 110, 116(fig. 12), 122(&fig.), 123(figs.), 124, 125(fig. 29), 126, 134(n56), 134(n58); sofas, 115(&fig. 9), 116(fig. 11), 116(figs.), 117, 134(n56); writing desks, 117–18(&fig.), 118(figs.)
Priestley, Edward (son), 127
Priestley, Howard, 127
Priestley, Mary Ann (mother), 103, 128(n2)
Priestley and Minskey: cabinet shop of,

103, 104(fig.), 105, 129(n7); furniture of, 103–4
Pringle, Mark, 105, 129(n8)
Pritchett, Levin, 108, 109, 129(n13)
Pueblo artisans, designs of, 191(&fig.), 199(&fig. 19), 200(&figs.)
Pueblo culture: Hispanic artisans and, 188–90, 191(fig.), 192(fig.), 199(&figs.), 200(&figs.), 201; Spanish colonial style, 198–99
Putnam, Benjamin, 174, 180, 182(n7)
Putnam, John, 174, 180, 182(n7)
Putnam, John (elder), 174
Putnam, Miriam, 173–74, 182(n7)
Putnam, Nathaniel, 174
Putnam, Stephen, 173
Putnam cupboard, 178(fig.)
Putnam family, 180

Quakers: influences on Newport colonial style, 23; Philadelphia and, 213; Salem, 174–78, 183(n9), 183(n10), 183(n15); social/trade networks, 1, 3, 13, 29(n13)
Queen Anne style, 33, 46
*Quest of the Colonial, The* (Shackleton and Shackleton), on colonial style, 33

R. and W. Wilson, 209
Rabel, Daniel, 67
Randolph, Benjamin: cabinet shop of, 156, 160; furniture of, 45, 153–54, 167(n4)
Rappahannock River Basin, influences of, 14
Raymond, Nathaniel, 173, 180, 182(n6)
Raymond, Rebecca (Conant), 173, 180, 182(n6)
Raymond, William, 183(n17)
Raymond family, 180, 183(n17)
Reams, Englehart, 96(n20)
*Recueil des Decorations Interieures* (Percier and Fontaine), 121, 134(n51)
Redwood, Abraham, 10, 19
"Replicas from Collectors' Antiques" (Potthast Brothers, Inc.), 45, 56(n5)
*Repository of Arts, Literature, Commerce, Manufactures, Fashions, and Politics* (Ackermann), 112
Reproductions, by Potthast Bros., Inc., 33–34, 36–38, 48–49
"Reproductions That Are An Investment" (Potthast Bros. Inc.), 45(&fig.)

Restorations: Earnest F. Hagen, 32; Hispanic artisans, 193; Potthast Bros., Inc., 36, 37(fig. 10)
Revolutionary War, 165
Reynolds, James, carving of, 160–61, 167(n9)
Rhode Island, 1, 2, 176. *See also under specific cities*
Rhodes, Samuel, 160
Ridgely, Charles Carnan, 75, 109–10, 110, 113
Ringgold, Thomas, 167(n5), 167(n6)
Ringgold parlor, 156, 158(fig. 13), 159, 167(n6)
Robert and J. Adam style, 33
Robineau, Adelaide Alsop, 211
Robineau, Samuel, 211
Robinson, John, 109
Rococo revival style: John Henry Belter, 209; Crawford collection and, 209–10; M. L. Greenwood and Company, 209
Rococo style: Bankson and Lawson, 76; Benjamin Randolph, 153, 156; Philadelphia, 167(n6)
Rogers, Henry (Mrs.), 42
Roman motifs, 119, 209
Roney, William, 107, 130(n15), 130(n17), 133(n45); furniture of, 133(n45)
Rookwood Pottery (Cincinnati), 211
Roux, Alexander, 209
Rushton & Beachcroft, 161

Salem, Mass.: British influences on, 169–81; Quakers in, 174–78, 183(n9), 183(n10), 183(n15); seventeenth-century British style, 169–81; taxes and, 180
Salem school, 169
Salmon, William, 22–23
Sandy Spring, Md., 82
San Felipe pueblo, 199
Santa Cruz, N. Mex., 197
Santa Fe, N. Mex., 197
Saunders, Richard, on Philadelphia painters, 213
Savannah, Ga., exports and, 104, 105
Scott, John L., 107, 130(n17)
Scottish cabinetmakers, 60
Scroggs, Robert, 110
Sculley, Vincent J., on Christopher Townsend, 4
Sears Roebuck, 52

*Secretaires à abattant*, Bankson and Lawson, 61, 62(fig.), 78, 80, 90(&fig. 49), 94(n5), 97(n28)
Seddon, George, 70, 95(n12)
Seddon, George, II, 95(n12)
Seddon, George, III, 95(n12)
Seddon, Thomas, 95(n12)
Seddon Sons and Shackleton, 70, 71, 80
Sefton, William, 129(n13)
Serpentine style, 60(fig.), 61(&fig.), 67(fig. 16), 68, 97(n29)
Seventh Day Baptist Meeting House, 7, 9(figs.), 10(&figs.)
Seymour, John, furniture of, 45
Shackleton, Elizabeth, on colonial style, 33
Shackleton, Robert, on colonial style, 33
Shackleton, Thomas, 95(n12)
Shaw, John, 128(n1), cabinet shop of, 106
Shearer, Thomas, 61
Sheraton, Thomas, 56(n5), 68, 78, 91, 117, 133(n49); on detail in carving, 167(n6)
Sheraton style, 33
Shield-back chair(s), of Bankson and Lawson school, 91, 93(fig. 56), 99(n43)
Shrewsbury Farm, 166
Sideboard(s)/commode(s): Bankson and Lawson, 61, 64(fig. 7), 65(fig. 8), 80–82, 80(figs.), 81(figs.), 82(fig. 35), 97(n29); Edward Priestley, 110, 116(fig. 12), 122(&fig.), 123(figs.), 124, 125(fig. 29), 126, 134(n56), 134(n58); George Seddon, 82; Joseph B. Barry, 121–22, 134(n51); Joseph Krickbaum, 121–22, 134(n51); Potthast Bros., Inc., 35(&fig. 6), 42(&figs.), 46, 49(&fig. 36), 50(&figs.), 51(&figs.), 54, 55, 57(n32), 58(n38); rococo revival style, 210
Side chair(s): Bankson and Lawson school, 91, 92(fig. 53), 93(&figs.); Potthast Bros., Inc., 35(&fig. 6), 39, 40(fig. 16)
Silversmiths, 19
Singleton, Elizabeth (Slater), 98(n37)
Singleton, Esther, 94(n4); on American antique furniture, 33
Singleton, William, 60, 84, 85, 98(n37), 128(n1)
Slater, Hannah (James), 84
Slater, William, 84
Smibert, John, 213
Smith, George, 121, 122, 134(n51)
Smithsonian Institution, 55

Social/trade networks: Quakers in Newport, 1, 23; Quakers in Salem, 174; Salem, 169, 176
Spanish and Native Americans, 188
Society of Upholsterers, 61
Socioeconomics, 1, 3, 22, 43
Sofa(s): Edward Priestley, 115(&fig. 9), 116(figs.), 117, 134(n56); Potthast Bros., Inc., 42, 43(fig. 26); Sotheby's, 29(n17)
South Carolina, 72(fig.), 74(&fig. 23)
Southwick, Cassandra, 174, 175, 177–78
Southwick, Daniel, 177
Southwick, John, 176, 177
Southwick, Josiah, 176, 179
Southwick, Lawrence, 174, 175, 177–78
Southwick, Mary (Trask), 177
Southwick, Ruth (Symonds), 179
Southwick, Sarah (Tidd), 176
Southwick family, 183(n10)
Spanish colonial style: in New Mexico, 185–202; and Spain, 189, 203(n7)
Specialization: Baltimore chairs, 104, 128(n4); Baltimore neoclassical furniture, 62–63, 70, 75; Newport colonial style legs, 16–17(&fig. 30); Priestley and Minskey chair frames, 105
St. George, Robert, on Spanish colonial-style moldings, 198
Stamper-Blackwell parlor, 96(n25), 156, 157(fig. 10), 158(fig. 12), 159, 167(n6)
Stelle, Isaac, 10
Stewart, Henry, 129(n13)
Stewart, William, 129(n13)
Stewart House. *See* Peggy Stewart House
Stickley. *See* L. & J. G. Stickley
Stickley's Craftsman Workshop, 210
Stone, Arthur J., 210
Straight-front style, 66(fig. 13), 96(n22), 97(n29)
Stratford Hall, 168(n10)
Style. *See* Design(s)
Suter, Charles, 109
Swan, Abraham, 121
Sweeney, Richard, furniture of, 129(n7)
Symonds, James, 169; house/shop of, 179
Symonds, John, 169, 179
Symonds, Samuel, 169
Symonds shops: chests/cabinets, 169–71(&figs.), 172(&fig.), 173(fig.), 174(&fig.), 176(&figs.), 177(figs.), 180, 181(fig.), 182(n6), 182(n7); cupboards, 173–74, 178(fig.), 179(fig.), 180, 182(n7)

Table(s): Baltimore rococo style, 132(n40); colonial revival style, 42(&figs.); Potthast Bros., Inc., 46, 53, 54(fig. 45). *See also under specific style*
Talbot County, Md., 101
Tambour bookcases, of Bankson and Lawson, 77
Tambour desk(s): Bankson and Lawson, 63(fig.), 77; John Seymour, 45
Taney, Roger Brook, 110
Telephone stand(s), of Potthast Bros., 46
Thomas, Joseph J., 109
Thomlinson, John, 2
Thompson, Hugh, 71, 85, 110
Thompson, Samuel, 109
Thompson, William, clock movements and, 85(&fig. 40), 98(n40)
*Three Centuries of Furniture in Color* (Molesworth and Kenworthy-Brown), 217
Tiffany and Company: eclecticism style, 210; Japanese motifs and, 211
Tiffany Studios, 42, 43
Tilghman, Richard, 70, 166
Tinges, Charles, 98(n40)
Townsend, Catherine (mother), 3
Townsend, Christopher, 3, 4, 29(n13); furniture of, 10–12(&fig.), 15(fig. 28), 16–17, 21(fig. 36), 22, 24–25(&figs.), 28, 30(n20), 30(n21); house/shop of, 3(&fig.), 4(fig.); influences on, 13
Townsend, Edmund (son of Christopher), 23; furniture attributed to, 26(&fig. 45); furniture of, 25(&fig. 41)
Townsend, Edward, 22, 23, 30(n19)
Townsend, Job, Jr., 22, 30(n19); furniture of, 30(n21)
Townsend, Job, Sr.: furniture of, 3, 10, 12(&fig. 21), 19, 20(fig.), 22, 24–25(&figs.); influences on, 13
Townsend, Job (son of Christopher), 23
Townsend, John (son of Christopher), 23; furniture of, 17, 26(&fig. 44), 28
Townsend, John (uncle), 3
Townsend, Jonathan (son of John), furniture of, 28
Townsend, Joseph, 118(fig. 15), 133(n44); house of, 118
Townsend, Mary (Almy) (great-aunt), 3
Townsend, Patience (Easton) (wife of Christopher), 3
Townsend, Rebecca (aunt), 3
Townsend, Rebecca (Casey) (wife of Job), 3

Townsend, Richard (son of Joseph), 118; influence on Edward Priestley, 133(n44)
Townsend, Solomon, Jr. (brother), 22
Townsend, Solomon, Sr. (father), 3
Townsend, Thomas (great-uncle), 3
Townsend, Thomas (son of Christopher), 23
Towson, Thomas, 121
Trade, 1, 2–3, 59, 60. *See also* exports; imports
Trask, Hannah (Osborne), 171, 172
Trask, Henry, 178
Trask, John, 171
Trask, Mary (Southwick), 178
Trask, William Blake, 171
Trask, William (elder), 177
Trask, William (elder/patriarch), 178, 180
Trask family, 174; genealogy chart, 175(fig.)
Trent, Robert F.: on Boston joiners, 181; on Symonds shop, 169
Trinity Church (Newport), 7, 8(figs.), 10
Troy (New York), and rococo revival style, 209
Tuck, Washington G., 109, 128(n1)
Tulip poplar, 10–11(fig. 20), 96(n23)
Turner, John, 183(n15)
Turner, Mary (Kitchin), 183(n15)

Ulrich, Laurel Thatcher, on New England women, 173
*United Society of Journey Cabinet & Chair Makers of the City of Baltimore, The,* 133(n49)
University City, Mo., 211
Upholsterers: Armistead Green, 107; John L. Scott, 107; John Webster, 161, 164; Plunkett Fleeson, 161–62(&figs.), 168(n10), 168(n11)

Van Briggle, Grueby, and Newcomb, 210
Vargas, Don Diego de, 189
Vase-back chair(s): Bankson and Lawson, 92; Bankson and Lawson school, 92
Venture cargo, 28
Vigtel, Gudmund, on Crawford collection, 207
Virginia, 80; influences on Newport colonial style, 14

*Virginia Carroll Crawford Collection, American Decorative Arts, 1825–1917, The* (Hanks and Peirce), 207
Von La Roche, Sophie, 70

Wady, James, 25
Walker, Thomas C., 131(n33)
Walker family, 134(n55)
Walnut, 14(fig. 26)
Wansey, Henry, 71
Ward, Richard, 1
Ward, Samuel, 10, 12
Ward furniture: dressing table, 12(fig. 21), 16; high chest(s), 10–11(&fig.), 10(fig. 28), 15(fig. 28), 16
Wardrobe(s): Bankson and Lawson, 73; history of, 95(n15)
Warehouses: Baltimore Carpet, Furniture, and Looking Glass Warehouse, 102, 129(n12); Bankson and Lawson, 72–73; John Howe, 129(n12); William Camp, 129(n12)
Warhol, Andy, 124
Washington, George, 50–51, 89(&fig. 48)
Washington Monument, 127
*Weaving A World: Textiles and the Navajo Way of Seeing*, 201
Webster, John, and upholsterers, 161, 162, 164
West, Benjamin, 213
West Indies, 1, 59
Wilbur, C., 35
Wilkinson, Robert, 75
Williams, Otho Holland, 75
Williams, William, 213
Willing, Ann, 70
Wilson. *See* R. and W. Wilson
Wilson, Woodrow, 44
Winterthur Museum, 25, 45, 156, 168(n10)
Wolfe, Elsie, 34; on reproductions, 33–34
Wollaston, John, 213
Wood, types of: mahogany, 10–11(fig. 20), 26(&figs.), 49(&fig. 36), 68, 75, 94(n9), 96(n23), 105; pine, 203(n10); tulip poplar, 10–11(fig. 20), 96(n23); yellow pine, 14(&fig. 26)
Woodhouse, Samuel W., on Cadwalader chairs, 153
Wooton Desk Manufacturing Company (Indianapolis), 211
*World Furniture* (Hayward), 217

*Worldly Goods: The Arts of Early Pennsylvania, 1680–1758* (Lindsey) (rvw), 212–16
Wright, Frank Lloyd, 210
Writing desk(s), of Edward Priestley, 117–18(&figs.)
Writing table(s): Bankson and Lawson, 61, 63(fig.), 64(fig. 6), 77; Potthast Bros., Inc., 45
Wye Heights, 119, 133(n45)
Wye House, 101, 119(&fig. 7), 130(n17), 131(n26), 132(n38), 133(n45)


Yellow pine, 14(&fig. 26)
Younker, Francis: cabinet shop of, 107; furniture of, 104, 107, 129(n7)